D0078025

The Enlightenment Bible

The Enlightenment Bible

TRANSLATION, SCHOLARSHIP, CULTURE

Jonathan Sheehan

PRINCETON UNIVERSITY PRESS
PRINCETON AND OXFORD

Published by Princeton University Press,
41 William Street, Princeton, New Jersey 08540

In the United Kingdom: Princeton University Press,
3 Market Place, Woodstock, Oxfordshire OX20 1SY

Library of Congress Cataloging-in-Publication Data

Sheehan, Jonathan, 1969–
The Enlightenment Bible : translation, scholarship, culture / Jonathan Sheehan.
p. cm.
Includes bibliographical references and index.
ISBN 0-691-11887-6 (cloth : alk. paper)
1. Bible—History—18th century. 2. Enlightenment. I. Title.

BS447.S54 2005
220'.09'033—dc22 2004048328

British Library Cataloging-in-Publication Data is available

This book has been composed in Adobe Caslon

Printed on acid-free paper. ∞

pup.princeton.edu

Printed in the United States of America
3 5 7 9 10 8 6 4 2

ISBN-13: 978-0-691-13069-9 (pbk.)
ISBN-10: 0-691-13069-8 (pbk.)

This book is dedicated to the Grootaers, the Saldañas, and the Sheehans, three families of thinkers.

CONTENTS

PREFACE: FORGING THE CULTURAL BIBLE

We would not be able to accept the formulas of "secularization" as so much a matter of course if we did not find ourselves still within the horizon of the operation of this process.
—Hans Blumenberg, *The Legitimacy of the Modern Age*

Prophets of modernity count the hours until religion's death. They should not hold their breath. Modern society will never lack for religion, not because humans are essentially superstitious or because, in their frailty, they crave supernatural comfort, but because the process of religion's disappearance is itself integral to the self-definition of modernity. For modern society, secularization always is and always must be incomplete. Even as religion seems to vanish from politics and public culture, it never ceases to define the project of modernity, whether negatively, in specters of intolerance and hatred, or positively, in ethics of social justice and equality. Religion is always receding and returning and its repeated tidal flow is essential to the self-image of modernity, which can no more dispense with religion than embrace it.

There are few clearer witnesses to this process than the Bible. If indeed modernity were secular, this provincial and archaic artifact should long ago have been discarded. Instead, its prescriptive content is rejected, even as it has become one of the sturdiest pillars of Western "culture." At the same moment that the Bible is mourned (or celebrated) as a victim of secularism, it is also recuperated as an essential element of that transcendent moral, literary, and historical heritage that supposedly holds together Western society. And this has happened across the intellectual and political spectrum. In virtually every academic study of the Bible, you will find claims that the Bible was "the most powerful cultural influence of its time," that the Bible is "one of the main sources of European culture," or more dramatically, "is the primary and major source of European culture."[1] Look at any textbook on Western civilization and you will discover the same blanket declarations that "we are cultural heirs to a biblical tradition," that

[1] Benson Bobrick, *Wide As the Waters: The Story of the English Bible and the Revolution It Inspired* (New York, 2001), 12; Steven Marx, *Shakespeare and the Bible* (Oxford, 2000), 3; John Riches, *The Bible: A Very Short Introduction* (Oxford, 2000), 99.

the Bible is a "great monument to civilization," that Old Testament theology was "the most important contribution made by the ancient Jewish people to Western civilization."[2] More locally, contemporary American society is saturated with this language. On the conservative side, advocates of the public display of the Ten Commandments speak, for example, of their centrality in creating "Western Civilization and the Common Law of the United States," not their preeminent religious virtues.[3] Others declare the impossibility of "understand[ing] Western culture without reading the Bible" or affirm that the "cultural importance of the Bible is a fact that no one denies" because the "Bible is a central book in our culture."[4] More secular institutions follow suit: the *Teaching Company*, for example, offers a course on The Bible and Western Culture; the nonpartisan Association for Supervision and Curriculum Development declares that the number one goal of teaching religion and the Bible in the schools should be "*Enculturation* . . . to develop an understanding of the ways in which the heritage and traditions of the past influence the present directions and values of society"; and nearly every Great Books program—from St. Johns University to Columbia and the University of Chicago—takes the Bible to be an integral core of the "cultural heritage of the West."[5]

In this light, the sentiments of such an excellent scholar as Robert Alter—that the Bible "seizes the imagination of the modern writer because of his acute consciousness of it as . . . one of the primary possibilities of representing the human condition and . . . historical experience for all the eras of Western culture"—seem quite unremarkable.[6] But they should seem remarkable. The Bible has not always been understood, read, appreciated, and venerated as a piece of Western "culture." Instead, for millennia, the Bible was venerated by Christians and Jews for its revealed theological truths. Culture had no bearing on the Bible if for no other reason than that this ideal of the Bible and this ideal of culture were invented at a particular time, in a particular place, and for particular reasons. Indeed, as the book will show, the "cultural" Bible and this ideal of culture as "heritage" were both invented at the same time and as mutually supporting elements in the moral, spiritual, and educational architecture of what came to be called the West. Even if this heritage ideal has been buried under the welter of connotations that culture has in modern scholarship, the Bible is widely accepted as culture without observing how and why the cultural Bible was forged in the first place.

[2] Lawrence Cunningham and John Reich, *Culture and Values: A Survey of the Western Humanities* (New York, 1982), 1:59–60, 79; John L. Beatty, ed., *Heritage of Western Civilization* (Englewood Cliffs, NJ, 1982), 1:24.

[3] *Stone vs. Graham*, 449 U.S. 39, 41 (1980).

[4] Constitution Party web-declaration, www.constitutionparty.com/the_bible_and_schools.htm; E. D. Hirsch, Jr. et al., *The Dictionary of Cultural Literacy* (Boston, 1988), 1–2.

[5] "Religion in the Curriculum," *Journal of the American Academy of Religion* 55 (Fall 1987): 584; Mortimer J. Adler and Seymour Cain, *Religion and Theology* (Chicago, 1961), xiv.

[6] Robert Alter, *Canon and Creativity: Modern Writing and the Authority of Scripture* (New Haven, 2000), 17–18.

This revolution in the Bible played out on the stage of Europe's Enlightenment. As such, it opens a window onto the story of secularization, whose central drama has traditionally been assigned to eighteenth-century Europe. From the crisis of the European mind, eloquently charted by Paul Hazard, to the French Civil Constitution of the Clergy in 1790, Enlightenment secularization has had an apparently clear-cut plot. For recent historians, Roger Chartier among them, the story is simple: more books, more readers, and more reading bred more skepticism toward king and God alike. But if Chartier and the social historians of ideas have crafted a provocative argument, it is only a negative one. The argument accounts only for the disappearance of authority and cannot comprehend its reconstitution. These terrestrial chickens and spiritual eggs, to paraphrase Boyd Hilton, do little therefore to provide a positive account for how and why specific books are invested with new auras of legitimacy.[7] But the Enlightenment was, this book argues, precisely the moment when the authority of the Bible was reconstituted as a piece of the heritage of the West. This reconstitution was first conjured up by a host of scholars and literati who together forged a model of biblical authority that could endure in a post-theological era. Let me be perfectly clear: I do not mean to suggest that ordinary people in Europe either rushed to embrace this cultural Bible or suddenly found themselves dispossessed of their traditional Bible. Rather, Enlightenment scholars first made available a version of biblical authority that could and would compete with the grinding effects of skepticism. The story of the forging of the cultural Bible—the story that the *Enlightenment Bible* tells—offers thus a different vision of secularization, one that focuses less on the disappearance of religion than on its transformation and reconstruction.

A few words about the title and scope of this book are necessary. This book does not pretend to treat all of those elements that historians have traditionally associated with Enlightenment. In essence, the Enlightenment does not mean, in this book, "Europe during the period circa 1685 to 1800." It is not tied to an essentially philosophical platform, nor does it dwell principally in the ranks of what Jonathan Israel has recently called the "radical Enlightenment," that cabal of philosophers and libertines who haunted many of Europe's devout.[8] Instead Enlightenment here denotes more generally the new constellation of practices and institutions—including scholarship and scholarly techniques, translations, book reviews, salons, academies, new communication tools, and new or revived

[7] Boyd Hilton, *Age of Atonement: The Influence of Evangelicalism on Social and Economic Thought, 1795–1865* (Oxford, 1988), ix.

[8] Jonathan Israel, *The Radical Enlightenment: Philosophy and the Making of Modernity, 1650–1750* (Oxford, 2001).

techniques of data organization and storage—that the eighteenth century used to address a the host of religious, historical, and philosophical questions inherited from the Renaissance, the Reformation, and the Scientific Revolution. These practices and institutions were not value neutral. As Martin Gierl has pointed out in his excellent analysis of the "new communication systems" of the eighteenth century, for example, the very possibility of juxtaposing a spectrum of theological positions within one publication changed the manner in which theological controversy could be waged.[9] But if such institutions and practices make certain kinds of arguments possible, and rob others of their structural efficacy, they do not *force* the Enlightenment to represent what it often has represented, namely a philosophically powered assault on religion. Nor do they force the Enlightenment to enact a merely destructive process of secularization. Instead, they open up the Enlightenment to possibilities of religious reconstruction and recuperation.

It is only in this context that, for me, the idea of an "Enlightenment Bible"—as a positive notion—makes any sense. Philosophical attacks on the authority of Scripture were, of course, key parts of the effort in the eighteenth century to wrestle with religion. This book does not focus on these attacks, not just because they are treated well elsewhere, but also because the Enlightenment Bible was not built by attacks. Instead, it was built by a sustained and serious engagement with the place of the Bible in the modern world. It was produced, this book argues, by a complex set of practices whose most sophisticated instruments were *scholarship*—philological, literary, and historical—and *translation*. Nowhere were the tools more well used; nowhere was scholarship so dedicated; nowhere were biblical translations so common; nowhere was the effort to rebuild the Bible so desperate as in Germany and England, Europe's dominant Protestant countries in the eighteenth century. This should not be a surprise. The Enlightenment Bible was a Protestant creation precisely because the Bible was so fundamental to the entire project of the Reformation as it developed in the sixteenth century and beyond. If, for Peter Gay, the central feature of the Enlightenment was its "essential hostility" to religion; if "eighteenth-century secularism" was for him just another name for an Enlightenment that exposed religion to the withering power of philosophy, this was, in part at least, because his analysis focused so exclusively on France and its *philosophes*.[10] Catholic France—*philosophes* or not—had little interest in rehabilitating the biblical text. But in Germany and England, the Bible was the object of continual and restless inquiry. If the answer to the question "Why should I read the Bible?" was, before

[9] Martin Gierl, *Pietismus und Aufklärung: Theologische Polemik und die Kommunikationsreform der Wissenschaft am Ende des 17. Jahrhunderts* (Göttingen, 1997), 415. On the general topic of Enlightenment and religion, see my "Enlightenment, Religion, and the Enigma of Secularization," *American Historical Review* 108 (October 2003): 1061–80.

[10] Peter Gay, *The Enlightenment: An Interpretation*, vol. 1, *The Rise of Modern Paganism* (New York, 1966), 322–23.

1700, overwhelmingly "because it reveals the means to your salvation," by the middle of the eighteenth century, Protestant answers began to proliferate, jostle, and compete with the standard one. In a sense, the Enlightenment Bible *was* this series of alternative answers.

These answers were produced by scholarship and, above all, by translation. On the surface, this may seem peculiar, since plenty of other textual icons—the American Constitution, or the Magna Carta—have undergone significant changes without altering their textual appearance at all. But the nature of the Bible was, in the early modern Protestant world, intimately tied to translation. From the outset, Protestants praised translation as the cornerstone of their religious revolution. Access to the vernacular Bible was the standard under which Reformers marched in their war against Roman Catholic ownership of Christianity. But reformers also, as the opening chapter shows, worried about translation and its effects on the Word of God. They worried that religious radicals might appropriate the Bible for their own uses and were eager to keep the authority of Scripture firmly under control. As a result, they hugged their own preferred Bibles close to their chests, cherishing them as symbols of their respective confessional identities. In Germany and later in England, Protestants developed the vernacular Bibles that symbolized their confessional commitments and their distinction from the authority of Rome.[11]

In the sixteenth century, in short, translations were tools for consolidating biblical authority and wresting it from opponents. In the eighteenth century, in a similar fashion, scholarly Protestants in England and Germany returned to the biblical text in order to recuperate its authority. But in strong contrast to their Reformation predecessors, they did so not in order to create a single Bible, but rather to build a Bible whose authority was distributed across a variety of disciplinary domains. Moving beyond the King James and Luther Bibles—whose strict confessional identification and embrace by the orthodox ensured their implacable sameness—scholars and literati dedicated themselves to the production of new translations that collectively reshaped the authority of Scripture. The Enlightenment Bible was, by nature, never singular, always plural.

Finally, then, the story of the Enlightenment Bible was a braided one, with conspicuous asymmetries. For most of the period, it was Germany that provided the most productive laboratory for the Enlightenment Bible. It was in Germany that the most sustained efforts were dedicated—in scholarship and through translation—to reforging the authority of Scripture along new lines. It was in Germany that the philological sciences teamed up most effectively and explicitly with the zealous efforts of religious reformers to keep the Bible fresh and relevant to the modern age. And it was in Germany that the most diverse and

[11] Paul Gutjahr, *An American Bible: A History of the Good Book in the United States, 1777–1880* (Stanford, 1999); Peter Johannes Thuesen, *In Discordance with the Scriptures: American Protestant Battles over Translating the Bible* (Oxford, 1999); David Norton, *History of the English Bible As Literature* (Cambridge, 2000).

sophisticated expressions of the Enlightenment Bible were developed. But if Germany was the laboratory, England and English scholars were the crucial technical consultants. Consistently throughout the period, Germans engaged in a productive and essential scholarly exchange with their English neighbors, taking inspiration from English abilities to keep religion alive and vital in the period. English tools were installed and put to new purposes through the century. Only toward the end of the century—and really only in the nineteenth century—was the flow of exchange reversed. If the English gave the Germans the tools to build the Enlightenment Bible, the German philological, historical, and educational juggernaut exported the cultural Bible back to English scholars and literati as the eighteenth century faded from view. This shape to the story lends it a certain complexity, but also allows us to see how the very foundations of biblical authority were renovated. Whereas, for long centuries, the Bible had been a self-legitimating text—it was authoritative because, in affirming itself as God's Word, it affirmed its own authority—now biblical authority was reassigned to the world of human beings. No longer tied to God's Word, the Enlightenment Bible became authoritative by virtue of its connection and relevance to human morality, aesthetics, and history. Instead of theology, culture would be the new rock atop which the legitimacy of the Bible was built.

In this moment, the Bible was made into a piece of "heritage." In turn, this transformation of the Bible became a key element of nineteenth-century *Bildungskultur*, the culture of education that helped shape European nations and institutions for two hundred years. The shift from a biblical to a neohumanist paradigm was profound, however, and required a total realignment of values away from Hebraic norms and toward classical or nationally normative ones. This realignment involved the transposition of scholarly tools developed in Old Testament criticism and translation into a new, classical environment, a transposition predicated on the dissolution of *sacra philologia* as a distinct philological method. It also involved a transposition in values away from a Judeo-Christian framework toward one where Jews were increasingly excluded from the religious patrimony of the Western nations. When the Christian outlook that had made the Hebrews, if not the Jews, a people worthy of closest scrutiny gave way, German and later English scholars decided that the Hebrews simply could not provide the model of universal humanity that would regulate the new ideology of culture. As a result, they were discarded in favor of their upstart cousins, the Greeks and Romans, and their supposedly more ancient relatives, the Aryans and the Indo-Europeans. The Bible was, after all, the heritage of the *West*.

This book has been supported by the generosity of a number of institutions. In its early phases, the Center for German and European Studies, the Mabel Mcleod Lewis Foundation, and the Doreen B. Townsend Center for the

Humanities at Berkeley provided money, time, and forums for discussion and development. The Deutscher Akademischer Austauschdienst and the Andrew Mellon Foundation both supported research at different times in Germany, where I found happy homes in the Universitätsbibliothek at the University of Tübingen and the Bibelsammlung at the Württembergische Landesbibliothek in Stuttgart. Tübingen's Evangelische Stiftsbibliothek was a wonderful resource as well, made all the more pleasurable by the thoughts of treading in the footsteps of Hegel, Hölderlin, and Strauss. Later a Charlotte Newcombe fellowship from the Woodrow Wilson Foundation gave me the time to complete what was then a dissertation. As the project grew in scope in the next years, the Williams Andrews Clark Library, the Center for Seventeenth- and Eighteenth-Century Studies, and the Humanities Consortium at UCLA offered amazing opportunities for discussion, research, and writing. Their respective directors—Peter Hanns Reill and Vincent Pecora—were very kind and supportive. Finally, two institutions made the long process of revision possible: the Center for the Study of Religion at Princeton University and the Arts and Humanities Initiative at Indiana University, which together gave me the time to keep my nose pressed firmly to the grindstone.

More than institutions, however, friends, colleagues, and readers have made this project not only possible but even pleasurable. For the past seven years, Kate Seidl has always been my first reader: her sharp eye kept my writing honest and her perceptive ear detected the better arguments even before I knew what they were. It has been a privilege to share this work with her. I have also been lucky to have two exemplary mentors: before his death in 1995, Amos Funkenstein launched the book—his great generosity and intelligence were inspirations for a generation of students at Berkeley. And ever since, Carla Hesse has pushed my work in new directions with unfailing care and insight. I am deeply indebted to them and to the creative readers I found in Thomas Laqueur, Thomas Brady, and Hayden White. Anthony Grafton took a California refugee under his wing and gave him the gift of an always incisive and generous criticism. Susannah Heschel helped me to put this material into dialogue with the foreign world of the nineteenth century and to see more clearly the historical intersections of Jewish and Christian traditions. Hans Aarsleff, Ann Blair, Robert Darnton, Dallas Denery, Daniel Gross, Jonathan Israel, Suzanne Marchand, Isaac Miller, Martin Mulsow, Marcie Norton, Peter Reill, Daniel Rosenberg, Esther Schor, and Randolph Starn, among others, all either read or commented on parts of this work as it developed, and their contributions were invaluable. Stan Holwitz and his reader together inspired enough choler to see me through the immense labor of revision. At Indiana University, I have been showered with the riches of excellent colleagues. Constance Furey read the entire manuscript and offered many important suggestions. Fritz Breithaupt, Michel Chaouli, Konstantin Dierks, Sarah Knott, and the eighteenth-century studies reading group read and commented on different parts of this project, and their advice has been most useful. *Primus inter pares* was Dror Wahrman, whose patient attention and fertile mind helped to push the book into its present shape. He has been a great friend and interlocutor. Finally, Alice and Jacob have continually served to remind me (and reminding was often necessary) of the pleasures of reading and writing.

ABBREVIATIONS

CHB P. R. Ackroyd, G.W.H. Lampe, and S. L. Greenslade, eds. *Cambridge History of the Bible.* 3 volumes. Cambridge: Cambridge University Press, 1963–1970.

PL J. -P. Migne, ed. *Patrologiae cursus, completus, sive biblioteca universalis, integra, uniformis, commoda, oeconomica, omnium SS. Patrum, doctorum scriptorumque eccelesiasticorum qui ab aevo apostolico ad usque Innocentii III tempora floruerunt . . . Series Latina.* 221 volumes. Paris: Migne, 1844–91.

WA Martin Luther. *Kritische Gesamtausgabe.* 81 volumes. Weimar: H. Böhlaus, 1883.

WABi Martin Luther. *Kritische Gesamtausgabe. Die deutsche Bibel.* 12 volumes. Weimar: H. Böhlaus, 1883.

WABr Martin Luther. *Kritische Gesamtausgabe. Briefwechsel.* 18 volumes. Weimar: H. Böhlaus, 1883.

WATr Martin Luther. *Kritische Gesamtausgabe. Tischreden.* 6 volumes. Weimar: H. Böhlaus, 1883.

The Enlightenment Bible

Chapter One

THE VERNACULAR BIBLE: REFORMATION AND BAROQUE

All scripture is inspired by God and profitable for teaching, for reproof, for correction, and for training in righteousness.
—2 Tim. 3.16

The Enlightenment Bible grew out of the soil of the Protestant Reformation, whose insistence on first principles—*sola gratia, sola fides, sola scriptura*—put the Bible at the center of the enormous struggles that beset sixteenth-century Christendom. The Reformation made the Protestant Bible the engine of political, religious, and imaginative life, an engine defended and cherished well into the nineteenth century. Even more than *gratia* and *fides*, the Bible powered the very project of Reformation. Whatever the theological controversies that arose around predestination, the value of works, or the priesthood of believers, beneath all these, the Bible lurked, as a force of chaos for many Catholics, a force of righteousness for Protestants. Firmly equated with the Word of God and given seemingly infinite autonomy, the Bible provided a theoretical armature to movements that included violent iconoclasts like Thomas Müntzer, the Lutherans in Wittenberg, and the radical peasants in the forests of southern and central Germany. Within two decades after 1517, biblical authority was the battle cry of a host of new religious movements that together promised to alter forever the complexion of European society. Anabaptism, Calvinism, Spiritualism, Zwinglianism: the list swells with reform movements that claimed as their theological, political, and social inspiration the words of the biblical text. To say "scripture alone" was to deny the efficacy and relevance of the Roman Church to divine matters. To say "scripture alone" was to invest reform and reformers with the very authority of God, before which no human institution—church or state—might stand. To say "scripture alone" was, in short, to set up a tribunal before which unbelievers would be judged. In the new religious order emerging in sixteenth-century Europe, only scripture would, in the words of St. Paul, be needed for teaching, reproof, correction, and training.

But at the precise moment that the Bible shouldered such enormous responsibilities, its authority began to quiver under the load. Even in St. Paul, sixteenth-century readers might have sensed the strains. "All scripture is inspired by God and profitable for teaching," Paul wrote in his letter to Timothy.

But did he? For many readers of the new vernacular and scholarly Bibles that populated the period, he did not. Rather he said something somewhat different: "All scripture *inspired by God* is profitable for teaching." Indeed, this second reading would have been the more familiar, since it was taken from the Latin tradition and put into many of Europe's sixteenth-century vernacular Bibles. In Elias Hutter's 1599 Nuremberg polyglot Bible, the Italian, French, and Greek versions embraced the first version, while Spanish, German, and Latin repeated the latter.[1] William Tyndale's 1524 English translation of the New Testament followed the Latin version, but the Geneva and later the King James Bibles followed the Greek. The difference was minor—the presence or absence of the Greek word και ("and")—but the passage meant something quite different in Erasmus's 1516 Greek New Testament than it did in Luther's 1522 German one. What was, in the Greek Bible, a comfortingly secure blanket proclamation of biblical inspiration was, in the German, a distinctly less reassuring profession that only some Scriptures were in fact given by God's hand.[2] If only the truly canonical texts of the Bible were authentic and legitimate, separating the wheat from the chaff became an urgent task. And it was a task made even more urgent when even the fiercest affirmations of scriptural authority, like the words of Paul, turned out to be troublingly ambiguous.

This Greek και was only a token of a problem that had plagued proponents of scriptural authority since the very earliest times. For in the Scriptures, two inescapable yet contradictory qualities were joined. On the one hand, scripture contains, for Jews and Christians alike, the authentic Word of God. From creation, to the giving of the Law, to the prophecies of the Messiah and the last days, the Bible has long supplied the Judeo-Christian world with the knowledge of God. Without it, God would be unknown, his ways a mystery, his laws enigmatic. On the other hand, however, this divine story has been, for millennia, rolled onto sticks, written on papyrus, transcribed onto skin, and enclosed between covers. The Scriptures are a collection of books. They are human artifacts whose integrity has long depended on fallible, forgetful people. In the hands of scribes, new heterodox books might creep into the scriptural canon and new heterodox readings might creep into the text itself. Both profoundly divine and profoundly human, Scripture has usually joined these two qualities in relatively seamless harmony.

Indeed, when the text of the Bible was unremarkable and uncontroversial, as it was for long centuries in the Latin West, the gap between divine and human was nearly invisible. The old joke about the King James Bible—"if it was good enough for Jesus Christ, it's good enough for me!"—works only because the English Bible has become such an ordinary part of religious life as to be virtually

[1] [Elias Hutter], *Novum Testamentum Dni. Nri. Iesu Christi* (Nuremberg, 1599).

[2] Erasmus notes the addition of the conjunction in his annotation to 2 Tim. 3.16 (*Novum Instrumentum* [Basil, 1516]); see also Elias Hutter, ed., *Novum Testamentum* (Nuremberg, 1599).

indistinguishable from the original versions. There was, for medieval Christians (and for many modern ones as well) essentially no reason to suppose that the text of *their* Bible was anything but identical with the Bible itself. But occasionally, the text and canon of the Bible suddenly seems more than ordinary to the faithful. It becomes strange, a document whose qualities need to be investigated and understood. And in these moments, the gap between the Bible's divine content and its human form leaps into view.

Historically, this has been the moment that new translations have appeared. On the one hand, new translations have shined a bright light into that gap between heaven and earth. By calling attention both to the books they produce and to the differences that might lurk between the original and newest versions, scriptural translations have historically forced into the open a set of awkward questions: What happens to the Word of God when it is manipulated by human art? What role can the translation play in transmitting the holiest of knowledge to the unlearned? How can this derivative product be invested with enough power to guarantee its own survival and transmission? On the other hand, however, Christian translations of the Bible have also hidden this gap, building bridges between God's word and human tongues so that they might once more seem unified. Already in the New Testament, Christ metaphorically "translates" the Bible away from the Jews. When he taught the crowds "as one who had authority, and not as their scribes," for example, he proclaimed his independence of the *old* Bible yet grounded his authority on the promise of a new one: "I have not come to abolish [the law and the prophets] but to fulfill them" (Matt. 7.29, 5.17). Christ promised to bridge the gap between a Pharasaic Bible and its divine source. In his own way, Paul too made Christianity into a religion of translation, transferring the Law from Jewish owners to Gentile upstarts. "Mere possession . . . of the Law will not justify any Jew," as Daniel Boyarin put it, and Paul's mission was to transform a too human Bible into a divinely universal text, "a matter of the heart, spiritual, not literal" (Rom. 3.29).[3] In general, the ancient Christian doctrines of *translatio imperii* and *translatio religionis* wrested empire and religions from the pagans and Jews and translated them into "the larger compass of Christian culture," in Rita Copeland's words.[4] In the specific case of the Bible, these moments of translation highlighted its (improper) human form but then quickly overcame it, a bridging of heaven and earth that happened repeatedly in the history of Christianity: in the earliest days, in reform movements like Lollardy, and again, most relevantly, during the Reformation.

For all of the major sixteenth-century reformers—Lutherans, Calvinists, and Anglicans—vernacular translation was the cornerstone of their creeds. "Translations are commanded by God, as Ordinance and constitution of

[3] Daniel Boyarin, *A Radical Jew: Paul and the Politics of Identity* (Berkeley, 1994), 94.

[4] Rita Copeland, *Rhetoric, Hermeneutics, and Translation in the Middle Ages* (Cambridge, 1991), 103.

Heaven itself," for only through vernacular translation could the Catholic Bible be desanctified and revealed as a contingent text used to serve particular human interests.[5] Translating afresh would release the Bible from the grip of the Catholic Church and, at the same time, allow reformers and their "universal priesthood of believers" to take possession of the Bible and make it once more the divine foundation of their own religious institutions.[6] If Protestant vernacular translation bridged the gap, once again, between heaven and earth, it *also* revealed the very human side of the biblical text that the doctrine of *sola scriptura* could never admit. In contrast to a Bible sanctified by long usage and by the external authority of the Church, Protestant vernacular Bibles were clearly the product of human labor and art. Catholic derision of Luther as the "Pope of the Protestants" got its sting from this very point: as a mere human, what could he really have to do with the divinity of the Bible?[7]

And so, speaking most broadly, the history of the vernacular Protestant Bible had two distinct phases before 1700. First, there was the explosion of translations across Protestant Europe. Over the course of the sixteenth century, every major confession and every major language would come to have at least one translation at its disposal. Roughly bracketed by the two most influential translations of the period—the Luther Bible (1522) and the King James Bible (1611)—this period saw a proliferation of vernacular Bibles. This big bang was followed by a big crunch, however, when the project of biblical translation ground to a halt and a canon of vernacular Bibles was set into stone in the seventeenth century. First, the vernacular Bible was made legitimate and authentic; and then it was fixed into a canon that hid those worrisome human aspects of the Bible. With the big crunch came consequences: texts were fixed, liturgies solidified, catechisms hardened into rigid forms. But most importantly for this book, with the big crunch came a sharp separation between vernacular translation and the chief source of its authority in the sixteenth century: biblical scholarship. This separation was fundamental to the seventeenth-century Bible. And its overcoming was the necessary prelude to the invention of the Enlightenment Bible.

The Authority of the Protestant Vernacular Bible: Germany and England

In the third century B.C.E., on the island of Pharos near Alexandria, a monumental and mythical translation was made. The myth is composed of two

[5] Richard Capel, *Capel's Remains* (London, 1658), 50.

[6] Jaroslav Pelikan, *The Reformation of the Bible/The Bible of the Reformation* (New Haven, 1996), 47.

[7] Jaroslav Pelikan, *Reformation of Church and Dogma (1300–1700)* (Chicago, 1984), 332.

slightly different stories. In the first, told by Aristeas, the Egyptian King Ptolemy Philadelphus was so impressed by the holiness of the Jewish books that he asked Eleazer the High Priest to send six elders from each Jewish tribe, men "skilled in the law and able to translate." Together these scholars gathered on the island and produced a version of the Bible that so impressed the elders of Israel that they ordered that "it should remain in its present form and that no revision of any sort take place." The translation was preserved forever in the royal library, "imperishable and unchanged." In the second story, told by Philo of Alexandria, Pharos was not a place of calm scholarly exchange, but one of divine rapture. The seventy translators gathered and "sitting . . . in seclusion with none present save the elements of nature . . . they became as it were possessed, and, under inspiration, wrote, not each several scribe something different, but the same word for word, as though dictated by an invisible prompter." The inspired scholars, the "prophets and priests of the mysteries," bequeathed to the world a divine yet vernacular translation, one that had every claim on authenticity and authority. As Judaism passed into the Greek world, its adherents were free to embrace a Bible utterly transparent to the wishes and words of God.[8]

In different ways, both stories reassured that nothing would be lost in translation, not an "iota, not a dot," as Matthew had it (5.18). In one story, this guarantee was assured by scholarship; in the other by inspiration. Both stories, however, were taken up by church fathers like Irenaeus, Clement of Alexandria, Tertullian, and Augustine, who together forged a myth of the Septuagint durable enough to shape the Protestant vernacular Bible. Even though reformers like Martin Luther did not think much of the Septuagint or its translators—the latter were "inexperienced and ignorant" and the former "foolish and awkward"—nevertheless the models of translation that these stories offered were irresistible.[9] For the translations that proliferated in the sixteenth century, the Septuagint offered a tantalizing gift, that of authority. Vernacular translation was justified and legitimized by the Septuagint mythology, which promised, in effect, that the divine could infuse a derivative translation, that the vernacular, common tongue could build a ladder to God, and that the holiness of his Word need not be shrouded by an esoteric language. Protestant translators, even if they did not embrace the Septuagint themselves, still revered its methods.

In 1530, for example, German presses invested Luther with the same halo of inspiration that surrounded the Septuagint translators and later the Apostles. Philo's praise of the "prophets" of translation was echoed in a New Testament frontispiece that shaped Luther into the very Apostle Matthew himself (fig. 1). Germany's own apostle—the "thirteenth apostle" as he was later known—sat in

[8] *Aristeas to Philocrates*, ed. and trans. Moses Hadas (New York, 1951), 115 (translation altered after original), 221, 223; Philo, *De vita Mosis* in *Philo*, trans. F. H. Colson (Cambridge, MA, 1959), 6:467–69.

[9] Martin Luther, *WATr*, 1:1040.

Figure 1. Luther the incarnation of Matthew, from his 1530 *New Testament*. Courtesy of the Herzog August Bibliothek, Wolfenbüttel, Bibel S. 792.

his place of labor.[10] Quills, pens, and books adorned the desk. But the image was dominated by the double representation of Luther's prophetic office. The Holy Spirit shone its light upon the pages of Luther's book, and Matthew's familiar angel looked on in pleasure. Luther the translator was robed in the garb of divinity and his work assured of its direct and transparent access to God himself. This supernatural halo was attractive to German reformers for obvious reasons: in these early days, after all, the Reformation needed all the authority it could get. Indeed, when the first edition of Luther's translation appeared in September 1522, the Reformation as such was barely conceivable and Luther himself was immensely vulnerable. Only sixteen months earlier he had been condemned by Charles V in Worms, retreating ignominiously to the Wartburg castle where, over the course of some ten weeks, he quickly translated Erasmus's 1519 Greek New Testament into vernacular German, that his audience might "seize and taste the pure Word of God itself."[11] Access to this pure Word of God was, in turn, conditioned on the rebirth that Luther experienced in reading Paul, in which the "gate of Paradise" opened and the meanings of Scripture were opened up to him.[12] Because "nobody can understand God or God's word unless he gets it immediately from the Holy Spirit," translation became, for Luther, a theological and prophetic activity.[13] *Sacrae scripturae comes indissolubilis Spiritus Sanctus*—"the Holy Spirit is the indissoluble companion of the Scriptures"—expressed a similar thought, that proper understanding of the Bible can come only to "one redeemed by Christ."[14] Proper biblical translation demanded, in effect, divine presence.

And yet, in general, the robes of inspiration sat rather uneasily on Protestant reformers. Certainly Luther never declared himself a prophet, and for good reason. Not least he was confronted by, on the one hand, the specter of violent Anabaptists who stressed their personal experience of Christ's presence and, on the other, Catholics who accused him of usurping the rightful authority of the apostolic church. To the right were those who pointedly asked Lutherans, "How do you know that your confession is pious and catholic? Because it pleases you? And because Luther said that your doctrine is divine?"[15] To the left were those who declared that "God writes the real holy scripture with his living finger, not with ink": only *they* rightly heard the "living speech of God" that dwells within the elect.[16] Asserting his own prophetic role would not only have exposed Luther to the Catholic charge of hubris, but it would also have cast him directly into the

[10] Spener, *Theologische Bedencken* (Halle, 1712), 1:275.

[11] WA 10.1.1:728. For Luther's translation at the Wartburg, see Martin Brecht, *Martin Luther* (Minneapolis, 1985), 2:46.

[12] Werner Schwarz, *Principles and Problems of Bible Translation* (London, 1955), 168.

[13] WA, 7:546; see Schwarz's discussion of this (ibid., 171).

[14] Luther, WATr, 5:5904; Heinrich Bornkamm, *Luther and the Old Testament*, trans. Eric W. and Ruth C. Gritsch (Philadelphia, 1969), 120.

[15] Bartholomaeus Arnoldus de Usingen, *Responsio contra apologiam Philippi Melanchthonis* [ca. 1532], ed Primoz Simonitus (Würzburg, 1978), 413.

[16] Thomas Müntzer, "Prague Manifesto" (longer version) in *The Collected Works of Thomas Müntzer*, ed. Peter Matheson (Edinburg, 1988), 365.

spiritualist camp that he reviled so consistently throughout his life. For Luther, "false human holiness and fanaticism" was a threat to his reforms and to the princes charged with implementing them.[17]

And so the prophet Luther was a figure overshadowed by that of the scholar Luther, the Philo story playing second fiddle to the Aristeas. Visually speaking, Luther became a belated St. Jerome, as in this 1530 frontispiece to the *Letter on Translation* (fig. 2), a coarse reproduction of Albrecht Dürer's beautiful 1514 engraving of the patron saint of translators (fig. 3). In Dürer's original, Jerome sits in his study, lion and lamb at his feet, books scattered on nearby bookshelves, observed by Christ on his crucifix and the skull on the windowsill. Jerome is at peace, hard at work producing the translation of the Bible that would serve the Latin Church for a millennium. The Luther image differs only slightly. The lamb is missing, the books are without clasps, the crucifix is gone, and an aggressive epigraph gives the image its polemic edge. Most striking, however, is the absence of the halo, which sits atop Jerome's balding head as a guarantee of the presence of God's voice behind the translation. Luther the scholar, in contrast, is alone, comforted only by his pen and books.

This vision of Luther's scholarly office was absolutely crucial in fashioning the authority of the Protestant vernacular Bible. If inspiration was an idol of the rabble, scholarship—in particular, scholarship on the Greek and Hebrew original texts—was the property of the learned and the sober. It was this, ultimately, that lent the Luther Bible much of its gigantic authority—like medieval translators before him, and Lollards in particular, Luther authorized his vernacular version by linking it with the "originary authority that cannot be overtaken," the Word of God itself. Unlike his medieval antecedents, however, he accomplished this not through "exegetical service to an authoritative text," but through scholarship.[18] Even the Catholic scholar Richard Simon acknowledged that the quest for a "version of Scripture . . . more consonant with the originals" was Luther's great innovation. Unlike inspiration, this innovation was only slowly achieved, whatever the stories of Luther's New Testament. Nor was it the labor of one man alone. Like the scholars on Pharos, Luther assembled a court of scholarly assistants, in particular for the translation of the Old Testament, whose challenges he "could not face without [their] presence . . . and assistance."[19] Among his team were Johann Bugenhagen, Matthäus Aurogallus, and, most importantly, Philip Melanchthon, who donated his knowledge of Greek and Hebrew to his less linguistically gifted friend, spending untold hours helping Luther revise and translate both the Old and New Testament.[20]

[17] Luther, *Vorrede auff die Propheten*, in *Biblia, das ist die gantze Heilige Schrifft Deudsch auffs new zugericht* (1545; rpt. Munich, 1972), 2:1160.

[18] Copeland, *Rhetoric, Hermeneutics, and Translation*, 225, 222.

[19] Luther, WABr, 2:423.

[20] Johann Mathesius (1504–1565) reports that Luther also relied on Justus Jonas, Caspar Cruciger, George Rörer, Berhard Ziegler, and Johann Forster (*Historien von des ehrwürdigen in GOTT seligen thewren Manns Gottes D. Martin Luthers* [Leipzig, 1621], 154b).

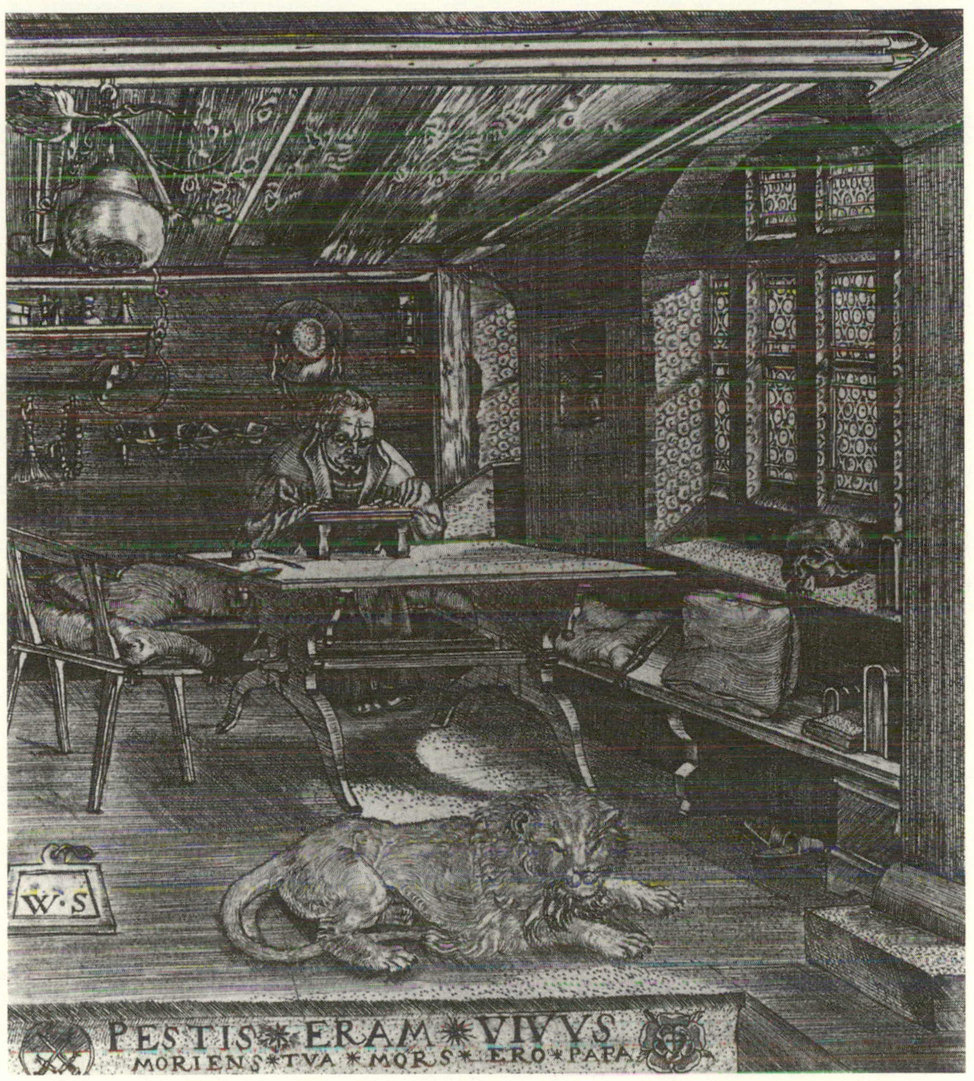

Figure 2. Luther the incarnation of St. Jerome, from a 1530 frontispiece to the *Letter on Translation*. The W. J. Collins Collection, Sterling and Francine Clark Art Institute, Williamstown, Massachusetts.

Figure 3. Albrecht Dürer, *St. Jerome in His Study*, 1514. Sterling and Francine Clark Art Institute, Williamstown, Massachusetts.

This local court was augmented, of course, by the wider world of fifteenth- and sixteenth-century philologians who devoted their labors to scriptural texts and translations. Erasmus was essential to Luther's success, for example, as were the Dutch humanist's controversial Latin translations and annotations of the New Testament. These annotations were, in turn, closely modeled on Italian humanist Lorenzo Valla's *Collatio Novi Testamenti*, reprinted by Erasmus in 1505. From Erasmus and Valla, the circle of biblical scholarship spread widely over the course of the sixteenth century. Careful editorial work; research on manuscripts; text collations: all of these were part of a collective enterprise that produced such magisterial works as the 1520 Complutensian Polyglot, Robert Stephanus's famous Greek editions of the New Testament (1546, 1549, 1550), and Theodore Beza's nine Greek versions toward the end of the century. And hand in hand with this scholarship was a project of translation, an effort to put this biblical philology into practice. Already in the fifteenth century, Valla had declared that Scripture is "nothing more than the best translation," and his methods of translation—whether in the *Collatio* or in the more influential *Elegantiae linguae latinae*—were always scholarly in nature. The Spanish editors of the Complutensian edition saw their project as a "return to the origins of scripture" in order that the "mouth of God" might be most closely mimicked in translation. And for Erasmus, the project of philological purification was never separated from the effort to produce a translation *fidelius, dilucidius, elegantius.* "Without knowing the shape of the letters, no one can read what is written": for these scholars, the chain that linked letters to words to meaning required circulation between brute philology and subtle translation.[21]

When Luther took up his pen to replace the Vulgate—a translation so long used in the Christian Church as to be indistinguishable from the Bible itself—he already had at hand, then, extraordinarily powerful tools for stamping his text with authenticity. "In proportion as we value the gospel," he wrote, "let us zealously hold to the [Greek and Hebrew] languages."[22] He and his coterie of translators did just that, most notably in the case of Job, where they apparently spent four days translating just three lines.[23] Now, there is no doubt that Luther was deeply distrustful of scholarship for its own sake. But his suspicions of people like Jerome and Erasmus—"follower[s] of Cicero and not of Christ"—did not undermine a fundamentally scholarly approach.[24] Even his insistence that the Bible be written for "the mother in the house, the children in the street, the

[21] Nancy Struever, *Theory As Practice: Ethical Inquiry in the Renaissance* (Chicago, 1992), 124; *Vetus testamentum multiplici lingua nu[n]c primo impressum* (Alcalá, 1514–17), +iii^{r}. Erasmus in Erica Rummel, *Erasmus' Annotations on the New Testament: From Philologist to Theologian* (Toronto, 1986), 89. In general, see Jerry Bentley, *Humanists and Holy Writ: New Testament Scholarship in the Renaissance* (Princeton, 1983).

[22] Pelikan, *Reformation of the Bible*, 50.

[23] Martin Luther, "Sendbrief vom Dolmetchen," in WA, 30.2, 636.

[24] Schwarz, *Principles and Problems*, 202.

common man in the market," did not.[25] For Luther, like all of the philological scholars of the period, research on original texts preceded idiomatic translation. When Luther argued that in Ps. 68 "the mountain of God is a *Basan* mountain, or a mountain of fat," should be translated as a "fruitful mountain"—lest the German reader imagine a mountain "smeared with lard or dripping with fat"—he wanted to ensure a good German text but one grounded in the historical usage of the Hebrew language.[26] And this research was the key to the authority of Luther's vernacular text, forging the link between it and the original Word of God. Authenticity, transparency, legitimacy: all of these were granted through the medium of scholarship.

The German desire to ensure the authority of their vernacular Bible was mirrored in England. The English Reformation's first translator, William Tyndale, framed his mission in broadly generous terms. His was only one possible translation, he wrote in 1534, and should "any man find fault" with it, "it shall be lawful to translate it themselves." More poetically, his Bible was "born before its time, even as a thing begun rather than finished." But such generosity threatened to expand the Bible into a kaleidoscope of interpretations, as Tyndale clearly saw: "if it were lawful . . . to every man to play Bo-peep with the translations that are before him, and to put out the words of the text at his pleasure and to put in everywhere his meaning . . . that were the next way to establish all heresies."[27] The vernacular Bible must be able, John Foxe later wrote, to prove "the process, order, and meaning of the text; for else . . . these enemies of the truth would quench it again, either with apparent readings of sophistry . . . or else juggling with the text."[28] The "medicine of Scripture" was only powerful insofar as it was pure and authoritative.[29]

Purity and authority might, in a familiar way, derive from scholarship, which would provide the "one simple literal sense whose light the owls can not abide"[30] Or it might, as John Foxe had it, have been "stirred up of God" himself.[31] In either case, early English reformers, like their German counterparts, yearned for a Bible capable of legitimating itself. But as William Tyndale found out first hand, the vernacular Bible in England was dependent on another source of authority—one with no less a connection to the Septuagint tradition—namely, the power of a King. Where Luther's works could not find authenticity in princely power (because princely power was so fundamentally contested in the Holy Roman Empire), the history of the English vernacular Bible was

[25] Luther, "Sendbrief vom Dolmetschen, 30.2:637.

[26] WA, 38:12. Even the "Sendbrief," the strongest affirmation of "free" translation, held itself to the standard of historical Hebrew and Greek usage—see WA, 30.2:639.

[27] William Tyndale, *The New Testament* (1534; rpt., Cambridge, 1938), 3, 612, 16.

[28] John Foxe, *Acts and Monuments*, ed. Stephen Cattley (London, 1838), 5:118.

[29] William Tyndale, *Five Books of Moses* (1530; rpt., Carbondale, Il, 1967), 7.

[30] Ibid., 3.

[31] Foxe, *Acts*, 5:119.

inseparable from the history of the Crown. This became particularly clear after Henry VIII's 1534 Act of Supremacy, when the church was formally wedded to the monarchy. Although German translations were egg on the face of Charles V, still they posed little direct threat in the highly decentralized political environment of the Holy Roman Empire. Unsanctioned English translations were, in contrast, political dynamite. If the Bible stood *apart* from the king, the Bible stood *against* the king. Whatever his intemperate faults in dealing with the Protestants, Thomas More was surely correct to see the connection between Tyndale's translation and potential sedition. Tyndale's "false translation" moves "people to their own undoing to be disobedient and rebellious to their sovereigns, in affirming that they be not nor [*sic*] cannot be bound by any law made by men," More chided. In encouraging the people to cling to their Bibles, he argued, Tyndale set them in a collision course with their king.[32] And in a way, Tyndale knew this. His last words, as Foxe reports them—"Lord! open the King of England's eyes!"—called for the King to submit to the will of God and to the message of reform.[33]

Indeed, the king was the linchpin, just as he had been at Pharos. The Septuagint was, after all, created at the whim of a king who put it "in [his] library along with other books" that it might remain forever unchanged.[34] In England, the king was less decisive, but nonetheless he played a key role in producing the authority of the vernacular Bible. As early as 1534, talk was in the air of a sanctioned translation, one that would quash the "public wrangling over the Catholic faith," and in 1535, one appeared from the pen of Miles Coverdale.[35] Although Coverdale's Bible was largely a reprint of Tyndale's, the dedication to Henry surrounded the Bible with such a comfortable air of princely power that it no longer posed a challenge to the laws of the realm. As Coverdale put it, this Bible granted "kings and princes" the very authority of God. By releasing Scripture into the "mother tongue," kings were free to "reclaim . . . their due authority, which [the pope] falsely has usurped so many years" and to rule the people now unchallenged. "As there is nothing above God," he declared, "so is there no man above the king in his realm."[36]

While the progress of Protestantism in England stuttered through the sixteenth century, the English Bible remained in flux. The Geneva Bible, executed by the Marian exiles between 1557 and 1560, was begun without the sanction of a king. Scholarship—and especially the scholarly environment of Geneva,

[32] Thomas More, *Confutation of Tyndale's Answer* in *The Complete Works of St. Thomas More* (New Haven, 1973), 8.1:33.

[33] Foxe, *Acts*, 5:127.

[34] Aristeas, *Letter*, 115.

[35] S. L. Greenslade, "English Versions of the Bible, 1525–1611," in *CHB*, 3:147.

[36] Miles Coverdale, dedicatory epistle to *The Bible: That Is the Holy Scripture of the Olde and New Testament* (1535; rpt., Kent, 1975), 34.

"the store of heavenly learning and judgment"—was its foundation, and the scores of annotations that dotted its pages encouraged, as David Norton has noted, the "close study rather than continuous reading" of the biblical text.[37] Through "learning and godliness," the editors of this Bible gathered "brief annotations on the hard places" in order to clarify obscure words and difficult passages, so that, in the end, they might "set forth the purity of the word and right sense of the holy Ghost." Nor was the content of the notes exclusively theological, as the maps of the Holy Land and images of the Hebrew artifacts surely testified. With the ascent of Elizabeth, however, the Bible was once again safely ensconced in the bosom of the monarchy. Just as God inspired the ancient builders of the Temple, the Geneva translators declared, so too would "he endow your grace . . . with a principal Spirit, that you may . . . command things necessary for this most holy Temple," especially the Word of God in vernacular form.[38]

Between 1560 and 1611, the Geneva Bible dominated the English market.[39] By the early seventeenth century, however, it had begun to be seen as "destructive of the person and power of Kings."[40] Underlying the royal demand for a new Bible was a particular fury about the Geneva text's scholarly annotations, annotations that, as Archbishop William Laud complained, were "used to ill purposes" and were, in the words of James, "very partial, untrue, seditious."[41] James's translators did not, of course, reject scholarship *tout court*. Indeed, from the initial call in 1604—when John Reynolds asked the king to sanction a new translation more "answerable to the truth of the Original"—scholarship was essential to the King James Bible (KJB).[42] As a project of academic labor, there were few that could compare with this Bible, built on the labors of fifty-four translators divided into six companies each charged with separate portions of the Bible. But scholarship by *itself* did not play the legitimating role it had with the Geneva Bible. Instead, the text drew its power from the proclamation of the king, who sanctioned it and gave it life.

During the sixteenth century, then, the Protestant Bible across Europe was under pressure, unstable, and changeable. As the fundamental theological and political bedrock of the Protestant faiths, the Bible had to be extracted from its Catholic superstructure. The tools of extraction were common ones: first of all, scholarship; second, princely power; and third, most unusually, inspiration. Scholarship and inspiration provided internal legitimation of the biblical text,

[37] *CHB*, 3:156; David Norton, *Bible As Literature*, 81. On the Geneva Bible notes, see also Christopher Hill, *The English Bible and the Seventeenth-Century Revolution* (London, 1993), 56ff.

[38] *The Bible and Holy Scriptures Contayned in the Olde and Newe Testament* (1560; rpt. Madison, WI., 1969), iii^{r-v}, ii^{v}.

[39] Lloyd E. Berry, introduction to ibid., 14.

[40] Hill, *English Bible*, 58.

[41] Norton, *Bible As Literature*, 92; Hill, *English Bible*, 64.

[42] *CHB*, 3:164.

guaranteeing the living connection between the contemporary vernacular Bible and the apostolic church that Protestants so venerated. Political power provided external legitimation of the biblical text, guaranteeing the living connection between Bibles and the authority vested in kings since Paul himself proclaimed the divine origins of princes (Rom. 13). All of them, however, contrived to set the Bible free, as Protestants saw it, from the shackles of the church, enabling it to function as the wellspring of their own faiths. The amount of intellectual energy invested in this Bible can be seen in the number of translations produced: in Germany, Luther's Bible was printed in new editions and versions for over twenty-five years, with significant revisions in 1534, 1535, 1536, 1539, 1541, 1545, and 1546, for a total of some 430 printings in his lifetime.[43] In Switzerland, the Zürich Bible was born in 1524, reprinted extensively throughout the century, and supplemented by the German Reformed Piscator translation in 1601. In England, major English revisions or new translations were issued in 1535, 1537, 1539, 1560, and 1571. The Dutch established their own authoritative text in 1618 with the States Bible. And the French 1535 Geneva Bible was continually revised until 1588.[44] The big question is, then, Why did it all stop? For if the sixteenth century staged the greatest proliferation of Bibles in the previous history of the church, the seventeenth century was a period of incredible stagnation. Across Protestant Europe, most strikingly in Germany and England, the seventeenth century saw few if any new translations. After 1611, no new translations in England. After 1545, no new Lutheran translations. After 1601, no new Reformed German translations. In the seventeenth century, the impulse to write new vernacular translations essentially died. Why?

The Seventeenth-Century Vernacular Canon

Perhaps the answer is a simple one: the old translations were working fine. Why work so hard to replace a perfectly good thing, one might ask. But in truth, scholars repeatedly suggested revision over the course of the century; they called for new translations and condemned the old ones. Of course, for Catholics like Thomas Ward, the King James Bible was by nature "corrupt and false," because it used the originals—"corrupted and poyson'd . . . with [the] false and abominable *Doctrines*" of Arians and other ancient heretics—to veer

[43] On Luther's editions, see Hans Volz, "Luthers deutsche Bibelübersetzung," in the *Anhang* to: *D. Martin Luther: Die gantze Heilige Schrifft* (Frankfurt, 1972), 41–113. For a chronology of publications and revisions, see Heimo Reinitzer, *Biblia deutsch: Luthers Bibelübersetzung und ihre Tradition* (Wolfenbüttel, 1983), 114–27.

[44] On the English Bible chronology, see F. F. Bruce, *The English Bible: A History of Translations* (New York, 1961). On English Bible versions, see Gerald Hammond, *The Making of the English Bible* (New York, 1983).

away from Latin Vulgate.[45] But even mainstream Protestants, who had little interest in Catholic hesitations, acknowledged that as the "two Testaments are the two paps of the Church," their translation should be ever revised: "No Translation is absolutely perfect, but it may and ought more and more to be perfected."[46] From the more rigorist Protestant line came more rigorist criticisms of the mainstream Bibles, especially the King James. Thus Robert Gell loudly called in 1659 for the "vindicat[ion] of the holy Scripture from false translation, and mis-interpretation." An "exact and perfect *translation* of the holy Bible" is paramount, he believed, for the truths of the current translation were often "rejected, and cast into the *Margent*" or, in smaller editions, discarded entirely.[47] The argument for quality looks flimsy in the face of such discontent.

Protestant translation ended not just because its results were good, then, but because they were useful. They were useful at stopping the process of translation itself, stopping a process very hard to end once begun. Already in the early sixteenth century, Luther saw the perils of unfettered translation, predicting that his version would be "thrown under the bench" or buried in a deluge of second-rate efforts.[48] "Anabaptists overthrow all translations," wrote another critic concerned that, once the bond between church and Bible was severed, anyone might style themselves a translator.[49] This threatened textual abandon cast a shadow across the vernacular Bible, not only menacing the translations created in the heat of Reformation zeal, but also the divine aura of the Bible itself. The principle of *sola scriptura* only functions if we know what the *scriptura* actually says: if there is no consensus about the *scriptura*, the principle has little weight. More translations meant, in short, more disagreement about God's real language. Reformers of later generations thus looked back on their originary Bibles less as gifts "in the language of the day, [of] the most imperishable monuments of the earliest centuries," as Leopold von Ranke wrote some three hundred years later, but instead as a powerful religious canon, heavy artillery in the fight against Catholicism.[50] And so a Bible like Luther's was forged into an authoritative text, a text "accepted as normative for the religious life of a community," a text on which were conferred awesome powers of moral, political, and religious regulation. Just as the Judeo-Christian canons were both "closed" with the "withdrawal of prophetic revelation" in the ancient world, so too was the vernacular canon closed as the sixteenth century drew to its end.[51]

[45] Thomas Ward, *The Errata of the Protestant Bible, or, the Truth of their English Translations examin'd* (London, 1688), a1^{v}, c2^{r}.

[46] Edward Leigh, *Critica Sacra*, 4th ed. (London, 1662), a2^{r}.

[47] Robert Gell, *An Essay Toward the Amendment of the Last English Translation of the Bible* (London, 1659), c3^{r}, b3^{r}.

[48] Luther, WATr, 5:469.

[49] Capel, *Capel's Remains*, 29.

[50] Leopold von Ranke, *Deutsche Geschichte im Zeitalter der Reformation* (Leipzig, 1933), 2:49.

[51] G. W. Anderson, "Canonical and Non-Canonical," in *CHB*, 1:117, 127.

The great success and irony of the sixteenth century, then, is that it invented the tools of biblical decanonization at the same time as it instituted a new vernacular biblical canon. Indeed, translation was crucial to both, not just threatening the normative canon, but also reconstituting it by conferring authority onto the original texts.[52] Canonized translations offered reformers a good answer to questions raised by Catholics perplexed by Protestant bibliolatry. By consolidating the tradition in a single text, reformers retroactively invested their Bibles with the attributes of tradition. This new stability implied that the canon was in fact closed, that the original text was original, archetypal, and complete in itself. "In the matter of religion, all novelty should not only be rejected but also detested": this might seem an odd sentiment for a preface to a sixteenth-century Protestant Bible, but it was not.[53] Protestant translations were not innovations, in the minds of their creators, but rather reconstitutions of an original text.

Protestants stood in a venerable tradition in this respect, since translators have done the same thing throughout the history of the Bible. The first real definition of the Old Testament canon is found in the apocryphal book Sirach, in a prologue written around 130 B.C.E. not by the work's ostensible author, Jesus Sirach, but rather by its translator (from Hebrew into Greek). The clearest demarcation of the corpus of "the law, and the prophets, and the other books of our fathers" that became the Old Testament canon came, in other words, not from within the Hebrew tradition, but rather from outside, from the Egyptian Jews "living abroad" who needed to be "prepared in character to live according to the law" (prologue).[54] Aristeas, for his part, wanted the Septuagint to resolve issues of textual conflict within the Old Testament canon by establishing a finally authoritative version. In the face of the variant texts of the Hebrew Bible that competed in the second century B.C.E., the Septuagint tried to produce an authoritative version, tried to end the enormous difficulties, as Aristeas saw it, posed by those Hebrew laws "committed to writing somewhat carelessly."[55] Translations were—already in the earliest periods—a tool to establish retroactively the authority of the very tradition from which they derived.[56]

[52] This function can have a strongly political valence; see Tejaswini Niranjana, *Siting Translation: History, Post-Structuralism, and the Colonial Context* (Berkeley, 1992).

[53] Calvin's preface to *La Bible, qui est toute la saincte escriture du vieil & du Nouveau Testament* (Geneva, 1588), ii^r.

[54] See P. Kahle, "Problems of the Septuagint" in Jellicoe, ed., *Studies in the Septuagint*, 74; Roger Beckwith, "Formation of the Hebrew Bible," in *Mikra: Text, Translation, Reading, and Interpretation of the Hebrew Bible in Ancient Judaism and Early Christianity*, ed. Martin Jan Mulder (Philadelphia, 1988), 51–52.

[55] D. W. Gooding, "Aristeas and Septuagint Origins: A Review of Recent Studies," in Jellicoe, ed., *Studies in the Septuagint*, 370ff.; Aristeas, *Letter*, 111.

[56] Hence Jerome's simultaneous interest in translation and the canon; Jerome, "Praefatio," *PL*, 28:600–601. See also E. Earle Ellis, "The Old Testament Canon in the Early Church," in *Mikra*, 675ff.

The Reformation was no different. Sixteenth-century translations made the past relevant to the present in order to give it the force of tradition. It was this dialectical relationship with the past that made the history of the biblical canon so intriguing to the reformers. Indeed, one of first pieces of Protestant biblical scholarship was Andreas Karlstadt's 1520 investigation of the canon, which remarked that since "new German bibles are going to be printed," the faithful had better know which ones were divine and which not. Translation helped to make this distinction clear to the reading public in a mechanical fashion. Reformers, Karlstadt thought, should either exclude apocryphal books from the translations altogether, or else mark them clearly as nonauthoritative.[57] Like Karlstadt, Luther focused his attention on the nature of the biblical canon. Not only did he define the books that would count as canonical—the Greek and Hebrew original Scriptures—but he also very actively determined the limits of this canon. He excluded the Latin Bible, of course, but he also rejected some apocryphal books in his Bible translation—1 and 2 Esds., for example, were no better than the tales of "Aesop or even more common books"—and even actively challenged the usual canon of biblical books.[58] In particular, Luther singled out James, Jude, the letter to the Hebrews, and Revelations as outside the inspired canon: Paul did not write Hebrews; Revelations was particularly subject to "stupid" and fantastic interpretations because of its odd idiom; and James was plainly not the work of an apostle.[59] He then physically marked their dubious status by demoting them to the end of his new vernacular Bible. Reformed translation was, in short, both scalpel, used to cut away large hunks of the medieval past, and soldering iron, used to weld the present to the apostolic period in a new configuration called authoritative tradition.

The sixteenth-century vernacular Bible represented, in other words, both a successful break with tradition *and* a successful consolidation of a new tradition. The canon was briefly opened, and then decisively closed. In Germany, Lutherans invested Luther's Bible with the same divine attributes that they gave to Luther himself. Grammarian Johann Clajus's praise of Luther's Bible as the direct product of divine inspiration—"the Holy Spirit, who spoke pure Hebrew through Moses and the other prophets, pure Greek through the Apostles, also spoke German through its chosen instrument, Martin Luther"—was directly paralleled by the worshipful attitude of preacher Matthias Hoe von Hoenegg, who named Luther the "holy wonder worker," the "doctor of all doctors, in the secular arts as well as Scripture," a "*physicus, metaphysicus, astronomus, mathematicus*," a holy man and scholar.[60] In the same vein, popular broadsheets called him

[57] Andreas Karlstadt, *Welche bucher Biblisch seint* (Wittenberg, 1520), Aii^r, Bii^r. See also Hans-Joachim Kraus, *Geschichte der historisch-kritischen Erforschung des Alten Testaments* (Neukirchen, 1969).

[58] Luther, WABi, 12:291.

[59] See the respective prefaces to Hebrews, James, and Revelations, WABi, 7:345, 385ff, 407ff.

[60] Johann Clajus, *Grammatica germanicae linguae* [1578], in *Die deutsche Grammatik des Johannes Clajus*, ed. Friedrich Weidling (Strassburg, 1894), 4. Matthias Hoe von Hoenegg, quoted in Reinitzer, *Biblia deutsch*, 35–36.

the "natural son of the beloved Apostle Paul," a hyperbolic praise mirrored in the comment of sixteenth-century preacher Johann Draconites that "when he read Luther's German Bible, he did not know whether Moses or Luther were more learned."[61] Luther's German, for enthusiasts like Draconites, was properly apostolic, just as authoritative as the most sacred texts in the Christian tradition. When Johann Friedrich Mayer proved in his *Apocalyptic Luther* that Luther was "the Angel flying in the Heavens carrying the Eternal Gospel" (Rev. 14.6–7), we have to assume that the text Luther carried was his own Bible translation.[62]

In England, there was no thirteenth apostle to carry the weight of a canonical text. And still the vernacular Bible was largely sacrosanct. Even those interested in vernacular revisions were convinced of the need for a stable textual center: Puritans, for example, wanted to preserve a canonical text against the anti-biblical ravings of the Quakers and various splinter groups and stressed the need to prevent "other Scriptures, or another gospel" from replacing the canonical one.[63] The committee gathered during the Commonwealth to revise the KJB called it "the best of any translation in the world."[64] Others were equally unrestrained. William Kilburne, in a polemic against the monopoly on Bible printing held by Henry Hill and John Field, called the KJB "the national and common Evidence of our Religion . . . an *Elysian flower* of Supremacie."[65] More cagey but just as confident in the KJB was Bishop Edward Wettenhall, who believed that "our Translations have, or may have, all the Senses the present Original can bear, and besides them, any which the Antient Versions or Glosses can probably affix to the Originals."[66] Despite his interest in revisions, there is little doubt that when the scholar Edward Leigh wrote that "translation openeth the window, to let in the light; breaketh the shell, that we may eat the Kernel; putteth aside the Curtain, that we may look into the most Holy place," he was thinking of the KJB.[67] "Our Bible is the Word of God," declared one Puritan divine emphatically. And after 1644, no more new editions of the Geneva Bible were published, at home or abroad, effectively making the KJB into the English Word of God. The translation project that had begun a century earlier had, for the time being, ground to a halt.

[61] For broadsheets, see John Roger Paas, *The German Political Broadsheet, 1600–1700* (Wiesbaden, 1986), vol. 2, plates 273–77. Draconites quoted in Gustav Georg Zeltner, *De novis bibliorum versionibus Germanicis non temere vulgandis C. E. Triller: & H. J. Reitzii, rationes potissimum sub examen vocans* (Altdorf, 1707), 25.

[62] Johann Friedrich Mayer, *Lutherus apocalypticus* (Leipzig, 1677), 57; for an earlier version of this story, see Johann Bugenhagen, *Eine Christliche Predigt uber der leich . . . des Ehrwirdigen D. Martini Luthers* (Wittenberg, 1546).

[63] For Puritan anti-radicalism, see Peter Lake, *Moderate Puritans and the Elizabethan Church* (Cambridge, 1982). Jessey quoted in Norton, *Bible As Literature*, 98.

[64] Norton, *Bible As Literature*, 97.

[65] William Kilburne, *Dangerous errors in several late-printed Bibles* (Finsbury, 1659), 15.

[66] Edward Wettenhall, *Scripture authentick and faith certain* (London, 1686), 32.

[67] Leigh, *Critica sacra*, A3[v].

Scholarship and the End of Translation

This new immobility in the Protestant Bible was enabled by a strict separation of scholarship from the vernacular Bible. As we saw, scholarship on the Bible in the sixteenth century was intimately entwined with the project of building a new vernacular text. Not only were scholars themselves involved with every phase of these translation projects, but scholarship—philological scholarship in particular—in a more abstract sense was also a key part of the authentication apparatus that gave the new translations legitimate title to the Word of God. But in the seventeenth century, the heyday of antiquarian biblical scholarship, translation became a sideshow. Biblical scholars conducted their work largely if not entirely on the original texts, published their results in a scholared Latin, and expended much energy in producing scores of concordances, dictionaries, and commentaries. But one thing they did not do was translate the Bible again.

Instead, seventeenth-century biblical scholarship cut itself off from the vernacular Bible. In Germany, where philological scholarship was largely moribund during the period, the "strongly doctrinaire side" of Lutheranism took over.[68] Lutheran scholars appointed themselves representatives of a new orthodoxy, the so-called Lutheran scholasticism, which declared the canonical and authentic Scriptures the center of their dogmatic systems. Johann Gerhard, the prince of the scholastics, opened his widely read and imitated *Loci theologici* (1610–1621) with such a declaration: "we believe in the canonical Scriptures because they are canonical Scriptures, that is, because they were given by God and ordained immediately by the inspiration of the Holy Spirit; we do not believe in them because the Church has sanctioned them."[69] Only Scripture, not the church, or its authority, or its tradition, was necessary for salvation. To make this polemical point systematic, scholastics rigorously defined the nature of the biblical canon. What were relatively minor questions for the early reformers—the question, for example, of the Hebrew vowel points and their inspiration—assumed "doctrinal status" for Protestant orthodoxy as it developed a dogmatic scholarship largely hostile to historical and textual investigations.[70] At the same time, orthodox theologians, beginning with the hardline Matthias Flacius Illyricus and his 1567 *Clavis Sacrae Scripturae*, began to develop a new science of biblical hermeneutics with the so-called *analogia fidei*, or analogy of faith, as its central principle.[71] The *analogia fidei*, and post-Reformation biblical interpretation more generally, had

[68] Ernst Troelsch, *Vernunft und Offenbarung bei Johann Gerhard und Melanchthon* (Göttingen, 1891), 27.

[69] Johann Gerhard, *Loci theologici* ([Geneva], 1639), 11.

[70] Richard A. Muller, *After Calvin: Studies in the Development of a Theological Tradition* (Oxford, 2003), 151.

[71] On the development of hermeneutics, see Werner Alexander, *Hermeneutica Generalis: Zur Konzeption und Entwicklung der allgemeinen Verstehenslehre im 17. und 18. Jahrhundert* (Stuttgart, 1993) and Peter Szondi, *Introduction to Literary Hermeneutics* (Cambridge, 1995).

a historical and scholarly component—Flacius Illyricus was himself a historian of some note—yet took the "unity of Scripture" as its fundamental assumption.[72] Biblical passages were ultimately explicable only with reference to a priori dogmatic principles—textual problems demanded not historical but doctrinal solutions. When *hermeneutica* became a neo-Latin topic of analysis in the early seventeenth century, its principal pioneer was Johann Conrad Dannhauer, a Protestant orthodox theologian who determined that since "all ways of knowing are parts of logic" and "interpretation is a way of knowing," hence "interpretation is a part of logic."[73] The "logic" of the Bible was—to the mind of Lutheran orthodoxy—its doctrine, which in turn was rooted solely in the original languages of the biblical texts. One important consequence of this neo-scholastic theological tradition, then, was the exclusion of translation from the domain of serious scholarship. "Only the Hebrew text for the Old Testament, and Greek for the New, are authentic," declared Gerhard, since only the "prophets in the Old Testament and the evangelists and apostles in the New Testament" were truly "God's amanuenses."[74] Translations were thus useful but needed, as theologian Johann Quenstedt said, "hypothetically," not "absolutely."[75] Because authentic doctrine resided only in the canonical, original language books, translations were fundamentally unnecessary for dogmatic theology.

Cut loose from scholarship, and from the mainstream of theological investigation, the vernacular text became a popular Bible, sanctioned principally in the domains of practical theology, preaching, confessing, and so on. As a "treasure of the church," the Luther Bible contained everything necessary for salvation and provided a text in which "even the simplest, indeed even children from childhood on can hear clearly the voice of their God."[76] When Abraham Calov said that "no nation can hear God speak so true in their Bible as we Germans," he meant quite literally *hear*, in sermons, teachings, and conversation. *Study* of the Bible on the other hand was to be conducted in "good Latin texts, in observations and scholia," and confined to the original language versions.[77]

[72] Kathy Eden, *Hermeneutics and the Rhetorical Tradition: Chapters in the Ancient Legacy and Its Humanist Receeption* (New Haven, 1997), 97–98. See also Wilhelm Dilthey, *Hermeneutics and the Study of History* in *Selected Works*, ed. Rudolf A. Makkreel and Frithjof Rodi (Princeton, 1985), 4:35ff. On Flacius's historicism, see Gregory Lyons, "The Art of History in Reformation Germany," (Ph. D. diss., Princeton University, 2003).

[73] Alexander, *Hermenutica generalis*, 53. See also H. E. Hasso Jaeger, "Studien zur Frühgeschichte der Hermeneutik," *Archiv für Begriffsgeschichte* 18.1 (1974): 35–84.

[74] Gerhard, *Loci*, 36; Robert Preus, *The Inspiration of Scripture: A Study in the Theology of the Seventeenth-Century Lutheran Dogmaticians* (London, 1955), 54. See also Preus, *The Theology of Post-Reformation Lutheranism: A Study of Theological Prolegomena* (St. Louis, 1970).

[75] Johann Quenstedt, *Theologia didactico-polemica* (Leipzig, 1702), 227.

[76] Johann Friedrich Mayer, preface to Martin Luther, *Biblia, das ist/die gantze Heilige Schrifft Alten und Neuen Testament* (Ratzeburg, 1690),)(5v.

[77] Abraham Calov, *Kurtzer Entwuff Etlicher Ursachen/daß die Neue Helmstädtische Biebel/Derer Abdruck angefangen/nicht zu publicieren* (Altdorf, 1710), §XVII, e1v.

What was true in Germany held for England as well, where Anglicans and Puritans alike pursued the paths of scholarship without touching the vernacular versions. Bishop Wettenhall was no less patronizing to the unlearned than Calov: "I say still: *Keep to your English Translation,* good people: *keep to what you are.* Your *English Bibles* to you, are the *surest word of Prophecy and Gospel too,* that you can meet with. . . . Accurate even to the envy of other Nations."[78] Like the Germans, the English too were trapped between the "superstitious Romanists" and the "fiery Novellists," as the scholar Brian Walton had it.[79] But unlike the Germans, English (and indeed Dutch) scholars did not pursue their researches under the hegemony of dogmatics. Instead, they were foremost in investigating the lands, peoples, and customs of the ancient Jews, and were intrepid in their explorations of Near Eastern languages and cultures. Scholars like Hugo Grotius, Gerhard Vossius, Samuel Bochart, Edward Stillingfleet, John Selden, and many others pushed biblical scholarship to new dimensions in northern Europe, and in doing so, helped to transform it into one of the most vibrant areas of research in the seventeenth century. New chairs in oriental literature were founded in English universities; scholars collected and documented manuscripts and published their findings in Latin translation. New textual monuments—from the enormous London Polyglot to the late-century compilation of biblical scholarship, the *Critici sacri*—were built. And new areas of research were delimited, among them sacred botany, sacred zoology, and sacred numismatics.[80]

But despite the enormous effort expended in antiquarian biblical scholarship, the vernacular Bible remained in stasis. In the first instance, the annotations that had accompanied the Geneva Bible were removed in 1611, purging it of an irritatingly antimonarchical rhetoric but also displacing scholarship entirely from the text of the vernacular Bible.[81] The new KJB very consciously had no annotations, not in order to make the Bible cheaper but in order to make it less controversial. During the Commonwealth, the Geneva Bible was left unannotated. Although Parliament did recommend a new set of scholarly notes based on the "candor and ingenuity"of the Dutch annotations to the States Bible, these notes were never attached to the text. Instead, they were published separately, a virtual allegory for the relations between scholarship and translation during the period.[82] Notes were available to those who cared, but scholarship was no longer intrinsic to the translation project.

[78] Wettenhall, *Scripture Authentick*, 53.

[79] Walton quoted in Peter Miller, "The 'Antiquarianization' of Biblical Scholarship and the London Polyglot Bible (1653–57)," *Journal of the History of Ideas* 62 (July 2001): 471.

[80] For an introduction to biblical antiquarianism, see *Archiv für Religionsgeschichte* 3 (2001); also Deborah Shuger, *The Renaissance Bible: Scholarship, Sacrifice, and Subjectivity* (Berkeley, 1994); D. C. Allen, *The Legend of Noah* (Urbana, IL, 1949), and Arnold Williams, *The Common Expositor* (Chapel Hill, NC, 1948).

[81] On the Geneva Bible as a radical text, see Hill, *English Bible*, 64–65.

[82] Theodore Haak, *The Dutch Annotations Upon the Whole Bible* (London, 1657), b2^r. These notes were commissioned by a group of divines from the Westminster Assembly.

Beyond the stasis of the vernacular, furthermore, even the text of the *original* Bible was largely static during this period, in spite of the prodigious efforts of biblical scholars to re-create the world of the ancient Jews and Christians. Antiquarian scholarship had the potential both to erode and to buttress the authority of Scripture and, at various times, served both functions. At a time when the authority of the Bible was challenged by radical philosophers, libertines, English revolutionaries, Quakers, and Jews, this scholarship provided new, historically nuanced foundations for biblical customs and practices, even as it applied to the Bible the same techniques of analysis brought to all texts and thus began to dispel some of the sacred aura surrounding the biblical manuscripts.[83] The polyglot Bibles that this scholarship produced were aimed at recreating the "reading . . . generally received into the Church of Christ" in the early years of Christianity but at the same time were very effective at revealing the errors that marred the face of Scripture.[84] But whatever the insights it shed on the nature and history of the Bible, all of this antiquarian scholarship was of no use in reconstructing the original Hebrew and Greek manuscripts of the Old and New Testaments. In particular, the New Testament entered into a virtual textual coma during the period. Whereas the Old Testament was subject to the critical scrutiny of researchers—some, indeed, wished to discard the Hebrew versions altogether in favor of the Septuagint or the Samaritan Bible—the New Testament was to slumber alone.[85] Confessional reasons were probably behind this absence of research among Protestants. While Catholics "fearlessly engaged in the detailed study of the biblical texts" (without ever actually producing new editions!), Protestants were afraid that such researches might show the unclarity of the text and erode its ability to provide authentic theological truths.[86] Whatever the cause, however, the stasis of the seventeenth-century vernacular Bible mirrored the stasis of the Greek New Testament. The new stability was given textual form by the librarian at Leiden University, Daniel Heinsius, whose 1633 edition of the New Testament assured its readers that *textum ergo habes, nunc ab omnibus receptum* (thus you have the text accepted now by all) and became the so-called *textus receptus* of the New Testament.[87] This Greek text was reprinted innumerable times in centuries to come and its authority became proportional to

[83] For this argument, see Martin Mulsow, "John Seldens *De Diis Syris*: Idolatriekritik und vergleichende Religionsgeschichte im 17. Jahrhundert," *Archiv für Religionsgeschichte* 3 (2001); Peter N. Miller, "Taking Paganism Seriously: Anthropology and Antiquarianism in Early Seventeenth-Century Histories of Religion," *Archiv für Religionsgeschichte* 3 (2001); Richard Popkin, *The History of Scepticism: From Savonarola to Bayle* (Oxford, 2003), esp. 219–38.

[84] Walton quoted in Miller, "London Polyglot," 474.

[85] On Vossius and the Septuagint, see J.C.H. Lebram, "Ein Streit um die hebräische Bibel und die Septuaginta," in Th. H. Scheurleer and G.H.M. Meyjes, eds., *Leiden University in the Seventeenth Century: An Exchange of Learning* (Leiden, 1975), 21ff. For Morin on the Samaratin Bible, see *Exercitationes Biblicae, de Hebrai Graecique Textus Sinceritate* (Paris, 1669).

[86] Jacques Le Brun, "Das Entstehen der historischen Kritik im Bereich der religiösen Wissenschaften im 17. Jahrhundert," *Trierer Theologische Zeitschrift* 89 (April–June 1980): 106.

[87] Heinsius quoted in H. J. de Jonge, "The Study of the New Testament," in *Leiden University*, 90.

the breadth of its dissemination.[88] After its publication, new editions of the Greek New Testament—which had enjoyed such an efflorescence in the hands of Erasmus, Robert Stephanus, and Theodore Beza—virtually disappeared until the middle of the eighteenth century.

In Protestant Europe, in other words, the seventeenth century was marked by two great moments of religious textual stabilization. On the one hand, the canon of vernacular Bibles was established, a canon that in large part still shapes the modern English, German, Dutch, and American experiences of the Bible. On the other hand, the canon of original language New Testaments was established. Although it is possible that these two events were merely coincidentally contemporaneous, it seems unlikely. For the sixteenth-century iconoclastic efforts to renew the theological foundations of Christianity prompted both the vernacular translation project and the explosion of New Testament textual scholarship. But as the violent consequences of religious difference made themselves felt both on the continent and in England, and as Protestantism emerged as an institutionalized set of churches threatened just as much by internal division as by external pressure, the need for consolidated and stabilized Bibles became pressing. The destructive religious wars that in the German case left nearly a third of its population dead, pushed clerics, theologians, and politicians from all confessions to forgo the potential chaos that new translations and new theologies offered. In England, the Revolution might have, and nearly did, inspire the newly ascendent Puritans to seek alternatives to a Bible clearly tainted by the touch of royal power and compromise. But in the end, the history of the seventeenth-century Bible followed that of seventeenth-century politics: *cuius regio, eius religio* was matched by the tacit acceptance of *cuius religio, eius scriptura.*[89] Stable Protestant theologies and stable Protestant theocracies needed stable vernacular Bibles.

Given the urge to keep chaos at bay, it is not surprising that the vernacular Bibles produced by Luther and the King James translators retained their place in the sun of the new century. And once the theological imperative to translate was gone, the interest in the actual text of the Bible—the urge to produce better original versions through manuscript research—waned as well, either because these texts represented a kind of religious dynamite better left untouched or because these texts were simply seen as stable fixtures around which an entirely new form of biblical scholarship—historical, antiquarian, scientific—could take place. As a result, as the end of the seventeenth century approached, the Bible seemed a

[88] Bruce Metzger, *The Text of the New Testament: Its Transmission, Corruption and Restoration*, 2nd. ed. (Oxford, 1968), 106.

[89] On confessionalization, see Heinz Schilling, "Confessionalization in the Empire: Religious and Societal Change in Germany between 1555 and 1620," in *Religion, Political Culture, and the Emergence of Early Modern Society* (Leiden, 1992) and "Confessional Europe," in *Handbook of European History, 1400–1600: Volume II: Visions, Programs and Outcomes*, ed. Thomas A. Brady, Jr., Heiko Oberman, and James Tracy (Leiden, 1995).

fairly familiar and established entity. The vernacular texts that shaped the Protestant reforms had become ingrained in popular religious life. They were sufficient enough in the minds of most, scholarly and unlearned alike, to teach the faithful the ways of God, transparent enough that the theological teachings of the Protestant churches would shine clearly. Scholarship was comfortably busy with biblical histories and chronologies; the texts of the Old and New Testament seemed unchanging and unchangeable. The Bible was alive, its significance guaranteed by Protestants who put the Word of God at the heart of their theological systems. The Protestant Bible was at peace. But not for long.

PART I
The Birth of the Enlightenment Bible

AROUND THE YEAR 1700 Protestants in England and Germany discovered that their canonical texts had become or were threatening to become, as one observer sadly wrote, "*strange, awkward, and new.*"[1] The Bible as it had shaped Protestantism, as familiar as family, began to take on darker tones: it was obsolete, it was imperiled, it was deficient, it was insufficient as it stood to confirm the authenticity of the Protestant religions. Whether in the hands of iconoclastic Catholics like the Oratorian scholar Richard Simon; radical philosophers like Baruch Spinoza, Thomas Hobbes, or Pierre Bayle; mainstream critics like Jean le Clerc; or religious radicals like Johann Heinrich Reitz, the foundations of the traditional biblical text became shaky and uncertain.[2] The Bible hungered for a new stability—in England and Germany, scholars and the devout felt this hunger. And so, in answer to this need, the walls erected around the Bible during the great age of confessional strife were breached. No longer was biblical scholarship kept away from either the vernacular or original texts of the Bible. Instead it was asked to rescue the Bible, to make it whole and erase the traces of unfamiliarity that had spread across its face.

At this moment, the Enlightenment Bible was born. The reins on scholarship were relaxed that it might invent a new Bible for a postconfessional Europe. If this new Bible looked similar to earlier antecedents, inside it was a different beast. For although the Bible had always served a variety of functions—liturgical, literary, artistic, scientific—above all, the *theological* function of the Bible guaranteed its place at the very center of European religion and letters. Theological authority infused the Bible with life. Theology was the blood in the veins of Early Modern religious wars. It was the motor driving the vast researches into

[1] Middleton, *Some Farther Remarks, Paragraph by Paragraph, upon the Proposals Lately Published . . . by Richard Bentley* in *Miscellaneous Works of Conyers Middleton* (London, 1752), 435.

[2] On the "radical Enlightenment," see Margaret Jacob, *The Radical Enlightenment: Pantheists, Freemasons, and Republicans* (London, 1981), Martin Mulsow, *Moderne aus dem Untergrund: Radikale Frühaufklärung in Deutschland, 1680–1720* (Hamburg, 2002), and Israel, *Radical Enlightenment.* On Spinoza and the Bible specifically, see J. Samuel Preus, *Spinoza and the Irrelevance of Biblical Authority* (Cambridge, 2001).

biblical antiquities in the sixteenth and seventeenth centuries. But over the course of the new century, the Enlightenment Bible was to move beyond theology. It was to move beyond the doctrinal nuances that had shed rivers of blood in the Early Modern period. Its functions would be ramified and dispersed through the practices of scholarship and translation in Protestant Europe. The result was a Bible whose meaning, significance, and function ensured its vitality in a postconfessional, and post-theological age. The invention of this Bible was a complex and dependent process. First, it depended on the religious landscape of eighteenth-century Protestant Europe, when the religiously devout enthusiastically introduced a far-reaching set of religious transformations that we have come to know as Pietism. And second, it depended on the scholarly landscape of eighteenth-century Protestant Europe, where the Bible was attacked and defended with the tools of historical and textual criticism.

In the early eighteenth century, no place saw such a momentous scholarly drama as England, where the Bible was the stage for a bitter feud about the nature of revealed religion. More specifically, the feud was over the New Testament and its relationship to true Christianity. Miracles, resurrection, the trinity: all of these New Testament doctrinal points were at stake. But the battles sparked by those called radicals, deists, atheists, freethinkers, or libertines, were only about doctrine in incidental ways. The root issue was the possibility of theology itself. Theological disputation, the very notion of theological truth, is only sensible if the fundamental rules for adjudicating truth are shared. In Christianity, from the earliest days until the Enlightenment, these rules were always fixed in the Bible. All Christian theology until this point, whether Protestant, Catholic, Orthodox, or Unitarian, presupposed an authoritative Bible and a stable biblical canon. As the scholar Richard Bentley put it: "if the Deists think to oblige us to give a natural account of those mysteries, without the authority of Scripture, for that we must beg their excuse. . . . we must not submit that our adversaries shall confine us to improper topics and impossible ways of proof."[3] Without the Bible, Bentley tells us, theology itself was bankrupt—just the point of the English deists and their lurking continental brothers in free-thinking. And so in England, scholars like him incisively turned their scholarship, for the first time in many years, onto the text of the New Testament in an effort to confirm or, better, to *prove* the authenticity and stability of the Christian Bible. Theirs was a holding action, an attempt to prevent harm, rather than to reimagine what the Bible is or ought to be. In a sense, then, these textual scholars developed increasingly sophisticated methods just to show what, three generations earlier, everyone had already known. This was not an exercise in pedantic futility, however. For, on the one hand, these English scholars broke through the wall that had kept the text of the New Testament in frozen storage

[3] Richard Bentley, "Of Revelation and the Messiahs: A Sermon" (1696) in *The Works of Richard Bentley*, ed. Alexander Dyce (London, 1838), 3:225.

for 150 years, revealing its complexity to the eyes of Protestants willing to see. And, on the other hand, it was in these early decades of the eighteenth century that English scholars created a set of instruments, a methodological toolbox that would be taken up in Europe's other great Protestant country, Germany, and used to create the conditions under which the Enlightenment Bible would flourish.

That Germans were able to do this was no testament to any native skill, but rather a function of their dense entanglement with the religious movement known as Pietism. For if England was truly a postconfessional nation after 1688—if England was in no danger of becoming either Presbyterian or Catholic, and if its church was entering into a period of unprecedented stability—Germany most definitely was not. Indeed, Germany scarcely deserved the noun "nation" in the late seventeenth century. It was instead a thicket of some 250 small countries, territories, principalities, and cities, loosely affiliated through the messy structure of the Holy Roman Empire. And religion was just as unevenly dispersed across this landscape as politics. The Catholic south, the Protestant north, the Catholic Bavarians, the Lutheran Saxons: these were only the largest trends splitting German religious life right down to the municipal level. In place of English tolerance, the Germans had geographical boundaries, inside of which religions flourished and perished through the exigencies of the princes, who, since 1555, had exercised theoretical sovereignty over the religious preferences of their subjects.[4] This sovereignty, though curbed in 1648, still made state boundaries into both barriers to religious diversity and opportunities for the same. Given the right prince, heterodoxy could flourish largely untouched by imperial law. The same boundaries that kept religious undesirables out also prevented the full enforcement of religious conformity.

It was into this distributed and uncentered world that Pietism seeped in the late seventeenth century. Germany proved fertile ground for it, particularly her Lutherans, who had long chafed under the strictures of scholastic theology and liturgical rigidity. Religious reformers, enthusiasts, philadelphians, separatists came to inhabit the intellectual and cultural landscape of the period. And with them, they brought a deep conviction that the German Bible was in need of a thorough rehabilitation. Luther's translation, canonized now for over 150 years, came to represent a stale and antiquated Protestantism, one that fetishized doctrinal rigor and disregarded the personally transformative potential that Christ offered. And so at century's start and steadily for the next fifty years, the devout focused their attention on the Bible, seeking to produce an ecumenical German Bible unstained by devotion to party and doctrine. The task of Bible translation was undertaken with the highest of expectations: nothing less than a renewal of Protestantism, a second Reformation, was at stake. And to reach these lofty goals, Pietist translators breached the second venerable wall established in the

[4] See Rudolph Vierhaus, *Germany in the Age of Absolutism*, trans. Jonathan Knudsen (Cambridge, 1988), 61ff.

age of confessions, that between the vernacular Bible and the disciplines of biblical scholarship: it was scholarship that underwrote their efforts to reform the vernacular Bible, and it was scholarship that gave the product its claim to authenticity.

The Enlightenment Bible began, in other words, in an entirely different place in Germany than in England. This initial difference—which stemmed from the immensely different historical experiences each country underwent in the seventeenth century—determined the differential history that this book explores. For in Germany, the Bible was pushed outside its safely fortified territory not by frightened defenders of a text against the importunities of atheists, deists, and Catholics, but rather by confident aggressors in a religious confrontation between the insurgent Pietist movement and the powerfully established Lutheran orthodoxy. The Enlightenment Bible was delivered, in Germany, by those committed to transforming, not preserving, the *textus receptus*. It was delivered, in other words, by those who happily wed the vernacular Bible to the media of scholarship and translation, those who wanted more than anything to present the world with a Bible renewed by these media and strong enough to survive in a post-theological age. And this initial difference of position allowed the Enlightenment Bible to thrive in Germany, thrive to such an extent that the enormous outflow of intellectual energy from England to Germany in the early eighteenth century was, by century's end, completely reversed, as Germany became the center of a vibrant biblical scholarship the envy of Protestant nations across Europe.

Chapter Two

SCHOLARSHIP, THE NEW TESTAMENT, AND THE ENGLISH DEFENSE OF THE BIBLE

In the winter of 1710, the English Parliament impeached Henry Sacheverell for his "wicked, malicious and seditious intention to undermine and subvert her Majesty's government and the Protestant succession." The cause was a fiery sermon, preached at St. Paul's Cathedral on Guy Fawkes Day, proclaiming the church in danger. "Her holy communion . . . rent and divided by factious and schismatical imposters; her pure doctrine . . . corrupted and defiled; her primitive worship and discipline profaned and abused . . . her altars and sacraments prostituted to hypocrites, Deists, Socinians and atheists." Nor were these last the only villains in this tragic play: dissenters, nonconformists, "false brethren," Catholics, constitutional innovators, and Whigs all had a role in dragging the Church of England to the very edge of the abyss. And finally, Sacheverell pointed the finger at the queen herself: the Church was "betrayed and run down" by her tolerance and protection for the forces of irreligion.[1] In the weeks to come, the Sacheverell case would upset the entire political landscape of early eighteenth-century England, unleashing stormy battles between liberal Whigs and orthodox Tories, the Low and High Church. The "first age of Party" epitomized in the Sacheverell case entwined political and religious affiliations in dense networks, pitting conservative against moderate in ferocious conflict.[2] And yet, no matter how ardently these parties disliked each other, all were equally convinced of the tremendous threat to the Church posed by those "Deists, Socinians and atheists" that Sacheverell so stingingly condemned.

Although every age tends to see itself midway down the slippery slope to hell, the late seventeenth century seemed a particularly dismal moment for religion in England, as Blair Worden has noted, because of "the challenge posed by what was variously called epicureanism, Socinianism, deism, atheism."[3] High churchmen like Francis Atterbury of course deplored a church infected by the

[1] Geoffrey Holmes, *The Trial of Doctor Sacheverell* (London, 1973), 280, 64–65, 60.

[2] Ibid., "The Electorate and the National Will in the First Age of Party," in *Politics, Religion, and Society in England, 1679–1742* (London, 1986); on the shift to a politics of "national interest," see Steve Pincus, "From holy cause to economic interest: the study of population and the invention of the state," *A Nation Transformed: England after the Reformation*, ed. Stephen Pincus and Alan Houston (Cambridge, 2001).

[3] Blair Worden, "The question of secularization," in ibid., 27.

"Spirit of downright Libertinism and Prophaneness," infected by "Atheism, Deism, Heresy, and every pernicious and destructive Error."[4] But even moderate Whigs like the classical and biblical scholar Richard Bentley were convinced of the threat posed by antagonists who brought "objections . . . from the Old Testament, which they did not believe, against the New one, which they were engaged by all methods to oppose."[5] In controversial literature, writers described the "Complaint of Good Men, that *Atheism* and *Infidelity* grow mightily among us, which is indeed a very melancholly Consideration, but I am afraid is but too true."[6] After the 1660 restoration, complained Sir Richard Blackmore, men began to "sow the seeds of Prophaneness and Impiety, which sprung up apace, and flourish'd."[7] "The number of *Deists* is said to be daily increasing," wrote Ephraim Chambers in 1728.[8] Looking back from midcentury, after the immediate crisis had passed, the Irish scholar John Leland noted the peculiar intensity of the period: "Never in any country where Christianity is professed, were there such repeated attempts to subvert [the] divine authority [of revealed religion], carried on sometimes under various disguise, and at other times without any disguise at all."[9]

This ostensibly extreme threat to Christianity—the "crisis of the European mind" as Paul Hazard put it, or the end of "theology's age-old hegemony," in Jonathan Israel's words—is one of the most overdetermined moments in the history of European man, and interpretations of it are in no short supply.[10] Whether from isolated philosophers, clandestine networks of freethinkers, or organized cabals of atheists, Christianity at the turn of the eighteenth century was, for many, a religion in danger.[11] In few places, however, was this crisis felt so strongly as in England, where deism, Socinianism, and free thought were together perceived, from the late seventeenth century until the 1740s, as the central religious

[4] [Francis Atterbury], "Representation of the State of Religion among Us, with Regard to the Late Excessive Growth of Infidelity, Heresy, and Prophaneness," in *The Political State of Great Britain, Volume I for the Year 1711*, 2nd. ed. (London, 1718), 330, 331. On Atterbury's plot against George I, see Linda Colley, *In Defiance of Oligarchy: The Tory Party, 1714–1760* (Cambridge, 1982), 198ff.

[5] Bentley, "Of Revelation and the Messiahs," 3:222.

[6] Richard Willis, *Reflexions upon a Pamphelet Intituled, An Account of the Growth of Deism in England* (London, 1696), 1.

[7] Sir Richard Blackmore, *Creation: A Philosophical Poem*, 3rd. ed. (London, 1715), xxvi–xxvii.

[8] Ephraim Chambers, *Cyclopaedia: or, an Universal Dictionary of Arts and Sciences*, 5th ed. (London, 1741), s.v. "Deist."

[9] John Leland, *A View of the Principal Deistical Writers that have Appeared in England in the last and present Century* (London, 1754), iii.

[10] Paul Hazard, *The European Mind (1680–1715)* (London, 1953); Israel, *Radical Enlightenment*, 4.

[11] For a short overview of biblical critics, see Bernard Schwartzbach, "Les adversiares de la Bible," in *Le siècle des Lumières et la Bible*, ed. Yvon Belavel and Dominique Bourel (Paris, 1986), 139–66; see also Jacob, *Radical Enlightenment*; Alan Kors, *Atheism in France, 1650–1729: The Orthodox Sources of Disbelief* (Princeton, 1990); David Wootton, "New Histories of Atheism," in *Atheism from the Reformation to the Enlightenment*, ed. Michael Hunter and David Wootton (Oxford, 1992).

bogeymen of the period. This religious climate—of extreme defensiveness about the very possibility of Christianity—shaped the entire English treatment of the Bible in the early eighteenth century, a time almost barren of new Bible translations in England but, simultaneously, a time rich in biblical scholarship and research in the manuscripts of Scripture. In the early eighteenth century, the greatest scholars of the age turned their critical talents to the manuscripts of the New Testament, in the hopes of producing, once and for all, a book—as Richard Bentley wrote in 1716—"which . . . shall have a testimony of certainty above *all other books whatever*."[12] These English scholars opened a doorway between biblical scholarship and the text of the New Testament. Yet this had no apparent effect on the vernacular Bible. Although perhaps the age had simply become "thoroughly accustomed" to the KJB, it is curious that during this great efflorescence of biblical scholarship, virtually nobody thought it worthwhile to rewrite English religious patrimony, virtually no one wanted new Bibles more consonant with the religious sentiments of the day.[13] But these simultaneous developments—great scholarly advance, vernacular stagnation—were intimately linked. In the end, it was the enormous religious anxiety generated by the specter of deism that both powered English scholarly efforts and thwarted the development of an English Enlightenment Bible.

Translation, Scholarship, and the Threat to the New Testament

If English Bible translations were few and far between before 1750, one that *did* appear offers us a vital, if oblique, clue to the economy of religion and scholarship in the period and the seeming paradox of serious scholarship and stagnant translation. A vital clue because its author was William Whiston, a man who became the very symbol of the "Libertinism and Prophaneness" reviled by the new Tory Parliament in the wake of the Sacheverell affair.[14] And an oblique clue because Whiston's 1745 "primitive" New Testament was only the last gasp of a career made notorious by a host of translations, not of the canonical Scriptures, but rather of those parts of the New Testament that the Church had long regarded as apocryphal. First set before the public in 1710, these apocryphal translations shine a bright light into the world of English biblical scholarship and onto the obstacles blocking changes in the English vernacular Bible. And they show most clearly the threat that an unfettered historical scholarship could pose to the sanctity of the New Testament and the discipline of theology.

[12] Richard Bentley, letter to Archbishop Wake, 15 April 1716, in *Works*, 3:477 (my italics).

[13] Norton, *Bible As Literature*, 210.

[14] Eamon Duffy, "'Whiston's Affair': The trials of a Primitive Christian, 1709–1714," *Journal of Ecclesiastical History* 27 (April 1976): 137.

Whiston is not the first person who would come to mind as a Bible translator. Known as a scientist, he succeeded Newton as the Lucasian professor of mathematics at Cambridge in 1701, lectured on pneumatics and hydrostatics, and was well known for his physico-theological polemics with Thomas Burnet over the origins of the earth.[15] In 1708, however, Whiston made a fateful discovery. He discovered the *Apostolic Constitutions*—a fourth-century collection of church law and liturgy attributed to the apostles but deemed apocryphal in the Latin West—and underwent a virtual religious conversion. For Whiston found in these documents the traces of a 1,400-year-old conspiracy against the purity of the Christian faith, a conspiracy begun by the fourth-century bishop of Alexandria, the "ignorant Athanasius," the evil genius behind a feat of textual corruption that left "scarce any one of the Original Books of our Religion" untouched.[16] Like those of Jean Hardouin, the French scholar who revealed (he thought) nearly the entire classical and patristic corpus of texts as one gigantic textual fraud, Whiston's discoveries were paranoid, ridiculous, and ingenious.[17] It was Athanasius and his ilk who used the 325 CE Council of Nicaea to propagate the Trinitarian understanding of Christ against the Arians; it was Athanasius who spent his long life tirelessly attacking the idea that Christ was subordinate to God; and it was Athanasius and his followers who systematically began "Abridging, Corrupting, and Interpolating the Original Books of our Religion," replacing the "Original Words of the Sacred Pen-men" with their own theological convictions.[18] Just as the Jews "corrupted their *Hebrew* and *Greek* Copies of the Old Testament . . . out of Opposition to *Christianity*," Whiston wrote, so too did the Athanasians impose upon Christianity a corrupt vision of Jesus Christ, one perpetuated during the long "Slavery of the Antichristian See of Rome."[19]

But now all would change, for Whiston had discovered the "Original most sacred Laws, Doctrines, and Rules of the Gospel, derived by the Apostles from our blessed Saviour, and by him originally from the supreme God the Father himself." His gift to the Church was a series of translations of these original Gospels, begun in 1711, translations that went through many editions and versions in the first decades of the century. These translations, Whiston believed, contained the original laws of the Christian Church, a comprehensive set of prescriptions covering both minute questions of behavior (adornment, bathing, dinner prayers) and fundamental points of church doctrine (the relationship between Jewish and Christian law, the ecclesiastical structure of Christian

[15] For biography, see James E. Force, *William Whiston: Honest Newtonian* (Cambridge, 1985).

[16] William Whiston, *Primitive Christianity reviv'd* (London, 1712), 1:31., 1:15.

[17] On Hardouin, see Anthony Grafton, "Jean Hardouin: The Antiquary As Pariah," in *Bring Out Your Dead: The Past As Revelation* (Cambridge, MA, 2001), 181–207.

[18] Whiston, *Primitive Christianity*, 1:29, 30.

[19] William Whiston, *Memoirs of the Letters and Writings* (London, 1749), 1:306; Whiston, *Primitive Christianity*, 3:1.

communities, the nature of Christ, and so on). In the "first place" even over the "four Gospels," these laws emanated directly from Christ and were committed to writing "no later" than the year 68 and "clearly some time earlier than the Destruction of *Jerusalem*, AD 70."[20] In these laws, Whiston found everything he needed to reconstruct the holy grail of Protestants since the early days of the Reformation, the very beliefs and rituals authorized by Christ, the essence of "primitive Christianity." The *Constitutions* structured Whiston's Society for Promoting Primitive Christianity, a society surpassing the new Society for Promoting Christian Knowledge (1698) because founded solely on the "Christian Discipline, Worship, and Government . . . originally Enjoin'd and Receiv'd in the first Ages of the Gospel."[21] And they confirmed the doctrinal corruption of modern Christian churches, showing that the doctrine of the Trinity was the product of third-century minds addled by heresy. Before then, not even "any of the wildest Hereticks came to this degree of Absurdity and Contradiction, *viz.* to own that the Father, the Son, and the Holy Spirit were *distinct Beings*, or *Persons*; and were every one . . . *God*; and yet, that after all, they were but *one God.*" Trinitarianism was the spawn of fanatics, the *Constitutions* declared: "Fly before [such heretics], lest ye perish with them in their Impieties." And so when at last Whiston published his 1745 New Testament, he purged it of the unholy Trinity and restored "the plain Doctrine" of the original.[22] Unlike others (including such luminaries as Isaac Newton and Samuel Clarke) who doubted the Trinity in the early eighteenth century, then, Whiston never buried his anti-Trinitarian stances but instead loudly and clearly announced his convictions in the most public forums.[23]

Yet Whiston's apocryphal translations put issues on the table far more pressing than the Trinity. Even Whiston's great opponent, Francis Atterbury, however constipated by his own orthodoxy, saw this clearly. Whiston, to his mind, jeopardized the entire "*Mosaick* Account of the Creation," denied the "Authority of the present Canon of Scripture," and built a scheme by which "the Credibility of the Traditional Facts related in Scripture, must every Age decrease."[24] As Atterbury saw, the central problem was not the theological heterodoxy of Whiston's work. Rather his translations challenged the very possibility of a Christian

[20] Ibid., 3:36, 3:97.

[21] Whiston, "A Proposal for Erecting Societies for Promoting Primitive Christianity," in *Primitive Christianity*, 4:211. This society met from 1715–17 at Whiston's house; among the invitees were Clark and later Bishop of Bangor, Benjamin Hoadly, but "none of them ever came" (William Whiston, *Historical Memoirs of the Life of Dr. Samuel Clarke* [London, 1730], 86). On the SPCK, see Craig Rose, "The Origins and Ideals of the SPCK, 1699–1716," in *The Church of England*, ed. John Walsh et al. (Cambridge, 1993), 172–90.

[22] Whiston, *Primitive Christianity*, 4:21, 3:354–55; Whiston, *Memoirs*, 1:178. In his New Testament, for example, Whiston simply eliminated 1 John 5.7 (see *Mr. Whiston's Primitive New Testament* [Stamford and London, 1745]).

[23] [Atterbury], "Representation," 331, 333.

[24] Ibid., 333.

theology at all, by putting the very canon of Scripture into danger. If there is no standard for judging the truths of theological claims, after all, then the very discipline of theology becomes irrelevant.

How could an apocryphal translation do this? The answer lay in the uses to which biblical apocrypha were put in the period. In general, apocrypha were (and are) a peculiar hybrid, excluded from the canon of the Bible and yet accorded great respect by divines.[25] Throughout the Early Modern period, though, apocrypha—New Testament apocrypha in particular—served a number of purposes. In England, the *Apostolic Constitutions*, or the more generally accepted *Apostolic Canons*, were part of the Church's polemic arsenal against Catholics and religious dissenters alike. In the effort to prove, as one contemporary book title had it, "the novelty of popery opposed to the antiquity of true Christianity," these texts supposedly showed "how exactly our Church does . . . resemble the Primitive."[26] Popular writers like William Cave described in lavish detail this early history of the church, where readers could discover a "*Piety* active and zealous . . . afflicted *innocence* triumphant . . . a *patience* unconquerable . . . a *charity* truly *Catholick* . . . the most excellent *genius* and spirit of the Gospel breathing in the hearts and lives of these good old Christians."[27] The early Christian Church and its writings represented everything that contemporary England was not: piety instead of infidelity, innocence instead of corruption, charity instead of greed. The frontispiece to Cave's *Antiquitates Apostolicae* (1676) offered a visual shorthand for this time of beatific grace (fig. 4), a time dominated by the the grand trunk of the "Church Catholick," growing from the strength of Christ himself and his immediate companions, the Apostles. Though time and growth might thin the branches of faith, the right solution, Cave's image declared, was neither to root branches in new soil nor even to return to Christ himself, as some religious radicals might aspire to do. Instead only the apostolic lineage—the strong trunk of the church—can sustain, unify, and nourish a people in Christ's own holiness. And the apocrypha were used precisely to connect the Church of England to this lineage and thus to combat both appeals to direct divine illumination and to Catholic Church authority. These polemic functions fed scholarly interest in the texts, and by the seventeenth century, prominent English and Dutch scholars—James Ussher and Isaac Vossius in particular—were producing critical editions of them.

[25] See Bruce Metzger, *The Canon of the New Testament: Its Origin, Development, and Significance* (Oxford, 1987), 242.

[26] Peter du Moulin, *The Novelty of Popery Opposed to the Antiquity of True Christianity* (London, 1662); Sykes, *Wake*, 67.

[27] William Cave, *Primitive Christianity: Or, the Religion of the Ancient Christians* (London, 1673), a2v. On Cave, see Eamon Duffy, "Primitive Christianity Revived: Religious Renewal in Augustan England," in Derek Baker, ed., *Renaissance and Renewal in Christian History* (Oxford, 1977), 287–300.

Figure 4. The tree of Christianity, from William Cave, *Antiquitates Apostolicae*, 1676. Courtesy of the Newberry Library, Chicago.

By the later seventeenth century, the interest in apocryphal texts spiked. Beginning in 1698, John Ernst Grabe began to publish his *Spicilegium SS. Patrum ut et haereticorum, saeculi post Christum natum I. II. & III.* This assembly of apocryphal texts was quickly dwarfed by the 1703 *Codex Apocryphus Novi Testamenti*, a vast collection of New Testament apocrypha presented by the Jena scholar Johann Fabricius in Greek and Latin.[28] In this period too, the apocrypha were first translated into English, most notably by William Wake, the future archbishop of Canterbury. In 1693, he translated a collection of apocrypha by the so-called Apostolic Fathers—the Epistles of Clement, the Epistles of Barnabas, and the Ignatian Epistles—that stayed in print throughout

[28] Johann Alber Fabricius, *Codex Apocryphus Novi Testamenti* (Hamburg, 1703–1719).

the eighteenth century.[29] For Wake and many others, such texts "had the character of authoritative works, only just excluded from the formal canon of scripture."[30]

This spike in interest was not the product of anti-Catholic polemics. Instead, it was propelled by the battles between apologetic scholars and those called "deists" or "atheists" over the nature of the New Testament canon. Beyond theological questions—the nature of God, the sinfulness of man, the resurrection of Christ—the fundamental issue in this conflict was, scholars were convinced, the "strange eagerness so many have shewn to subvert the credit and authority of the gospel."[31] And those condemned as libertines did indeed have little truck with the authority of Scripture. Abroad, Spinoza's *Theologico-Political Treatise* (1670) was notorious for its acid criticism of the Bible. Closer to home, the pathetic Thomas Aikenhead disdained "the History of the Impostor Christ" and was hanged for this blasphemy in 1697; Anthony Collins smirked that priests themselves made "the Canon of Scripture uncertain"; and when Matthew Tindal proclaimed that "our Religion must . . . from the beginning of the world to the end, always be the same, always alike plain & perspicuous," he implicitly chucked Scripture into the dustbin.[32] The "rejection of revealed Scripture is *the* characteristic element of deism," writes James Force, and whether the deist movement was phantasmatic or real, there is no doubt that churchmen of all stripes—High, Low, dissenters—believed this to be the key to understanding the deist threat.[33] "We look upon" the books of the New Testament "as Divine and strictly binding to Obedience," wrote John Richardson in 1700: "because they were either wrote or confirm'd by the Apostles of our Saviour, and we believe that they were so wrote or confirm'd by them, not upon the Testimonies of one or two Fathers only, but of the whole Primitive Church."[34] But the deists, as the scholar Edward Stillingfleet put it, "hunt up and and down the *Scriptures* for every thing that seems a difficulty . . . and then by heaping all these together . . . make the *Scriptures* seem a confused heap of indigested stuff."[35]

[29] William Wake, *Genuine Epistles of the Apostolical Fathers* (London, 1693). On Wake and the seventeenth-century study of these letters, see Norman Sykes, *William Wake: Archbishop of Canterbury, 1657–1737* (Cambridge, 1957), 1:63ff. Generally, see Jean-Louis Quantin, "The Fathers in Seventeenth-Century Anglican Theology," in *The Reception of the Church Fathers in the West from the Carolingians to the Maurists*, ed. Irena Backus (Leiden, 1997), 987–1008.

[30] Sykes, *Wake*, 67.

[31] Leland, *Deistical Writers*, 458.

[32] Michael Hunter, "'Aikenhead the Atheist': The Context and Consequences of Articulate Irreligion in the Late Seventeenth Century," in *Atheism*, 225; Anthony Collins, *A Discourse of Free-Thinking, Occasioned by the Rise and Growth of a Sect call'd Free-Thinkers* (London, 1713), 85; Matthew Tindal, *Christianity as Old as the Creation*, 2nd. ed. (London, 1731), 17.

[33] James Force, introduction to William Stephens, *An Account of the Growth of Deism in England*, Augustan Reprint no. 261 (Los Angeles, 1990), iv.

[34] John Richardson, *The Canon of the New Testament Vindicated* (London, 1700), 31.

[35] Edward Stillingfleet, *A Letter to a Deist, in Answer to several Objections against the Truth and Authority of the Scriptures* (London, 1677), 9.

Apocryphal literature and church antiquities generally could be used to combat this. As late as the 1720s, the non-juror Thomas Brett noticed the "general inclination in Divines of the Church of England to inquire into Antiquities of the Christian Church, more than I am persuaded has been at any time since the Reformation."[36] In part, this was part of a wider turn to antiquarian materials characteristic of the period. The new edition of William Camden's *Brittania* (1695), to give one example of many, compiled numismatics, geography, maps, and local history in a rich antiquarian stew much appreciated by a learned class that was turning collecting into a respectable sport for the well-heeled.[37] But church antiquities were particularly treasured across the religious spectrum, from Whigs like John Mill—who wondered "what could be more useful and profitable to the Church than pure and corrected editions of the Holy Fathers"—to the moderate churchman Joseph Bingham, whose *Origines ecclesiasticae* presented what he called a "complete collection of the Antiquities of the Church."[38] Scholars at the turn of the century were apparently following the advice of the non-juror Henry Dodwell, that to combat the "*Irreligion* and *Atheism* which has lately so over-run" England, the most profitable tool was "*Philological* Learning." Dodwell's belief in the "necessity of studying the Fathers of the first and purest Centuries," coupled with his own "*Catalogue* of the Christian Authors and Writings," was typical of the period.[39] For him and many others, apocryphal literature provided key insight into the nature of the earliest churches and, in turn, helped to define and protect the established New Testament canon against importunate attack. By defining the apocrypha, scholars hoped, in other words, to confirm the status of the New Testament as a genuine foundation for Christianity, "to distinguish the Canonical Books of the *New Testament*, from the Apocryphal or Doubtful Books," as Louis Du Pin had it.[40]

But the apocrypha did not *just* serve apologetic functions. Indeed, these writings rang with anxiety because apocrypha were also a weapon *against* the scriptural canon. And here, precisely, is where William Whiston came in. For when Whiston translated the *Apostolic Constitutions*, he was not interested in defending the purity of the New Testament. Nor were his interests merely antiquarian. Instead, his translations of the apocryphal texts were supposed to

[36] Justin Champion, introduction to John Toland, *Nazarenus* (Oxford, 1999), 39.

[37] See Joseph Levine, *The Battle of the Books: History and Literature in the Augustan Age* (Ithaca, 1991).

[38] Quantin, "Reception," 995; Joseph Bingham, *Works* (Oxford, 1855), 1:xxxix. On Grabe, see Günther Thomann, "John Ernst Grabe (1666–1711): Lutheran Syncretist and Anglican Patristic Scholar," in *Journal of Ecclesiastical History* 43 (July 1992): 414–427.

[39] Henry Dodwell, *Two Letters of Advice* 3rd ed. (London, 1691), B2^r, 153, 105. See also Joseph Levine, *Dr. Woodward's Shield: History, Science, and Satire in Augustan England* (Berkeley, 1977), chap. 11.

[40] Louis Du Pin, *A Compleat History of the Canon and Writers of the Books of the Old and New Testament* (London, 1699–1700), 2:16.

replace the canonical Gospels altogether. Whiston insinuated himself, in other words, into the heart of Anglican apologetic scholarship and applied its methods to wholly different ends. In this way, consciously or not, Whiston affiliated his project with the more sinister investigations of New Testament apocrypha conducted by that student of the Leiden scholar Frederick Spanheim, the itinerant deist John Toland.

Historical Scholarship: A Weapon against the Bible?

Apocrypha featured most controversially in Toland's 1699 *Amyntor: Or, a Defence of Milton's Life*, where he happily took them up as cudgels against those "many suppositious pieces [written] under the name of Christ, his Apostles, and other great Persons."[41] With an ironic glint in his eye, Toland followed Henry Dodwell's advice and assembled a lengthy catalogue of books he described alternately as "spurious," "forg'd," and "invented by Heathens and Jews," a catalogue including works venerated among Protestants, like the Epistle of Barnabas and the Epistles of Ignatius. Indeed, of those works attributed to the apostolic writers, Toland happily remarked, "it is the easiest Task in the World (next to that of shewing the Ignorance and Superstition of the Writers) to prove them all Spurious, and fraudulently impos'd on the Credulous."[42]

Although annoying, this list was not terribly frightening in itself. More frightening were Toland's arguments. If indeed some apocryphal texts were genuine products of the apostolic period, he disingenuously asked, "why do they not receive 'em into the Canon of Scriptures . . . ?"[43] If one answered (with Samuel Clarke and others) that apocrypha were excluded on the authority of the church fathers, then Toland had an ace up his sleeve. Since "there is not one single Book in the New Testament which was not refus'd by som of the Ancients as unjustly father'd upon the Apostles, and really forg'd by their Adversaries," why shouldn't the same standard be used to prune radically the New Testament itself?[44] Already in 1689, Richard Simon had insisted that the innumerable "false Gospels, false Acts, false Apocalypses" were difficult to distinguish from the "Originals" of the Bible already lost in apostolic times and so it was only a short step to argue for a basic confusion between the false and the true.[45] This was an outrageous claim

[41] Robert Sullivan, *John Toland and the Deist Controversy: A Study in Adaptions* (Cambridge, 1982), 135. Justin Champion's *Republican Learning: John Toland and the Crisis of Christian Culture, 1696–1722* (Manchester, 2003) regrettably came to my attention too late for me to discuss it here, but largely confirms my findings below.

[42] John Toland, *Amyntor: Or, a Defence of Milton's Life* (London, 1699), 42–43, 38–39.

[43] Ibid., 48.

[44] [Samuel Clarke], *Some Reflections on That Part of a Book Called* Amyntor, *or the Defence of* Milton's *Life* (London, 1699), 36; Toland, *Amyntor*, 56.

[45] Richard Simon, *A Critical History of the Text of the New Testament* (London, 1689), 21, 31.

and provoked furious response from across the religious spectrum. Liberal Anglican Clarke insisted that "the Belief of the Genuineness of these Books . . . does [not] in the least . . . *make the number of Canonical Books Uncertain or Precarious*."[46] The Unitarian Stephen Nye contended "the Books . . . that are lost, or rejected, were not *so* certainly Genuin, to *all* the Churches; as these that are preserved, and made parts of the Canon."[47] And the non-juror John Richardson firmly denied that "those Spurious and our Canonical Books ought to go together."[48]

But Toland was uninterested in such criticism. Instead his only response was an even more destructive inquiry into the apocrypha, his most "relentlessly textual engagement" with scripture, the 1719 *Nazarenus*.[49] Here Toland purported to have found a manuscript of a "NEW GOSPEL . . . never before publicly made known among Christians."[50] This gospel, the Gospel of Barnabas, was "as old as the time of the apostles."[51] It recorded, Toland reported, the core beliefs of the most ancient Christians of all, the Nazarenes, ancient Jewish followers of Christ who rejected the teachings of Paul as impious innovations. In the competition between various "original plan[s] of Christianity," Toland's would—had it been admitted by a judge—taken first prize. The Nazarenes, or Ebionites as he also called them, "observed the original precepts of Jesus, while . . . preserving all that was of value in Judaism."[52] The very first Christians on earth, they stood closest to the original fount of knowledge, Christ himself.

Like Whiston, then, Toland made the biblical apocrypha into a tool for transforming the biblical canon. Both men were dangerous less for their particular arguments, however, than for their methods. In the case of Toland, this method was a parodic form of the historical-critical biblical scholarship practiced in the seventeenth century. He began his work with the discovery of a manuscript. He offered a supposedly careful philological comparison of this manuscript with "the numerous *Gospels, Acts, Epistles*, and *Revelations* . . . handed about in the primitive Church." Like such venerable predecessors as Hugo Grotius and Gerhard Vossius, Toland calmly discussed the historical attributes of his text, which like all "very ancient books," spoke "the language, . . . express[ed] the traditions, and . . . allude[d] to the customs" of its time.[53] Mimicking "a cultural discourse that held at its heart notions of sacred authenticity

[46] Clarke, *Some Reflections*, 9.

[47] Stephen Nye, *An Historical Account and Defence of the Canon of the New Testament* (London, 1700), 31.

[48] Richardson, *Canon Vindicated*, 2.

[49] Champion, introduction to *Nazarenus*, 13.

[50] Toland, *Nazarenus*, 115.

[51] David Sox, *The Gospel of Barnabas* (London, 1984), 49ff. Toland, *Nazarenus*, 145.

[52] Toland, *Nazarenus*, 170. Peter Harrison, *"Religion" and the Religions in the English Enlightenment* (Cambridge, 1990), 165.

[53] Toland, *Nazarenus*, 136, 148. In *Amyntor*, he happily affiliated himself with Henry Dodwell, excerpting long passages from Dodwell's Latin work on Irenaeus (Toland, *Amyntor*, 69).

and originality," Toland accompanied his translations with historical exegesis, just as one would find in any antiquarian treatment of the Bible in the period.[54] No "impudent and shameless" partisan attacks, he argued, should sully reasoned and philological scholarly discourse.[55] Conducted soberly and with accurate historical research, he vowed that his efforts would help divines "to prove the authenticness, divinity, and perfection of the *Canon of Scripture*."[56]

William Whiston would not have appreciated being affiliated with Toland. The sympathies between their projects were nonetheless indisputable, especially when seen not on the plane of authorial intentions, but on that of methodological consequences. Like Toland, Whiston applied all the techniques of historical criticism to the New Testament. Both men treated the apocrypha as standards "to distinguish history from fable, or truth from error, as to the beginnings and original monuments of Christianity" and as monuments themselves to the nature of real Christian practice.[57] And in both, apocryphal texts were not put in the service of apologetics, but rather used to reinvent (or, if you prefer, erode) the Bible and Christianity. In their hands, New Testament apocrypha demonically threatened to undermine and even replace the biblical canon altogether. Whiston's self-assurance that he was merely discovering a neutral historical fact—the repression of the *Apostolic Constitutions* during the reign of Athanasius of Alexandria—was truly naive in this light. Contemporaries too understood the two men's work as symptoms of a conspiracy against the authenticity of the Gospels and, by extension, the church itself. And this was a conspiracy rooted not so much in their intentions—most could see that Whiston was a truly pious man while Toland was not—as in their methods, methods that colonized an older form of Christian apologetics for new ends and displayed the findings across virtually every Early Modern print media. As Francis Atterbury put it:

> They have republish'd, and collected into Volumes, Pieces written long ago on the side of Infidelity. . . . They have . . . charg'd the authentick Articles of this Church, and the *English* Editions of the Bible, with pious Frauds and Forgery. . . . They have, with Ostentation, enumerated the several spurious Treatises forg'd in the earliest Ages of the Church; which they represent as Times of great Fraud and Imposture, on the one hand; of great Ignorance and Credulity, on the other; and they have left this Reflection to be apply'd by their Readers, to the Books of the new Testament.[58]

If an extremist, still Atterbury saw clearly the threat that an unfettered historical criticism posed to the authority of the biblical texts. He also saw clearly the

[54] Champion, introduction to *Nazarenus*, 66.
[55] Toland, *Amyntor*, 13; Toland, *Nazarenus*, 183.
[56] Ibid., *Nazarenus*, 136.
[57] Ibid., 184.
[58] [Atterbury], "Representation," 335–37.

threat that the strategic use of media—collections, re-publications, and, not least, translations—could pose to this same authoritative tradition. The Swiss Jean Ostervald was not alone, in other words, when he made books the "most general" and "most remarkable" cause of the corruption of Christianity.[59] Despite his own fantasy of "burn[ing] and destroy[ing]" most of the world's books, Whiston was not a victim of, but a contributor to the textual and scholarly economy shaping the Bible at the beginning of the eighteenth century.[60] In this sense, Atterbury was surely right to tie him to "Atheism, Deism, [and] Heresy." Whiston may not have liked the epithets, but in the end, it was not his feelings, but his scholarly practices—the strategic use of historical evidences, his barrages of printed polemic, the public forum of translation—that made them so apt.

Textual Scholarship and the Refusal to Translate

And so early eighteenth-century English scholars faced a dilemma. For the first time, the tools traditionally used to explore the nature of religion were wielded by those with less comforting aims. As John Locke mused in 1685, scholars were faced with a difficult choice: if they considered "everything in holy writ . . . as equally inspired by God," they were powerless to cope with the profusion of apocryphal materials that seemed to undermine the Bible entirely. But if they admitted that "certain parts are to be considered as purely human writings, then where in the Scriptures will there be found the certainty of divine authority?"[61] Clutching the doctrine of scriptural inspiration too fiercely prevented any substantial encounter with the human aspects of the Bible. But admitting the humanity of the Bible too lightly invited the wholesale dismissal of biblical authority. English scholarship on the New Testament worked, in large part, under the shadow of this double bind. To get out from the bind, scholars on the New Testament had to come up with different approaches to the sacred text. And it was these approaches and their uses that enabled them to create a wholly innovative form of textual scholarship—effectively opening the text of the New Testament to serious scholarship for the first time in decades—and yet prevented them from putting this scholarship into the public, vernacular domain.

We should not underestimate the difficulty this bind presented to scholars, for on both sides of it lurked frightening figures, real or fantastic. Whiston and

[59] J. F. Ostervald, "A Treatise concerning the Causes of the present Corruption of Christians, and the Remedies thereof" in Richard Watson, *A Collection of Theological Tracts* (Cambridge, 1785), 6:286.

[60] Whiston, *Memoirs*, 1:248.

[61] John Locke, *Correspondence* (Oxford, 1976–1989), 2:748–49. See Justin Champion, "Pere Richard Simon and English Biblical Criticism, 1680–1700," in *Everything Connects: In Conference with Richard Popkin*, ed. James Force and David Katz (Leiden, 1999), 39.

Toland would be counted among them, the latter for his insidious efforts to erode the scriptural canon, the former for his forthright efforts to supplement it with the apocryphal documents he saw as the essential cornerstones to true Christianity. But these two fans of apocrypha were hardly the only frightening figures around. Spinoza was one bugbear—his insistence that the Bible speaks "in a merely human fashion" brought the sacred books down from their holy pedestal—and Richard Simon was another:

> There is no one, Jew or Christian, who does not recognize that these Scriptures were the pure language of God . . . but since men were the guardians of the sacred books, indeed of all other books too, and since the first originals have been lost, it is in all ways impossible that there have not been many changes, as much because of the length of time as by the negligence of copyists.[62]

Paralleling Simon was the scholar and gentleman Anthony Collins, a man "always interested" in the Bible, if for libertine reasons. Because "the most ancient Christian Churches and Priests receiv'd several *Gospels* and *Books of Scripture* . . . that we reject as *Apocryphal*," Collins happily noted, scriptural texts can have "a very different degree of Authority" depending on time and place. The apocrypha, in short, testified to the power that human beings exert over the Word of God. But just as intriguing to Collins as the apocrypha were the variant readings that existed in biblical texts, most problematically in the New Testament. Variant readings—the small differences between manuscripts that have accumulated over the centuries of the Bible's transmission—proved, in Collins's mind, the inability of Christians to determine exactly what the Bible said. And for his starring example of this he turned to the monumental editorial work of the Oxford scholar John Mill, who "publish'd a Book containing all the various Readings of the *New Testament* he has been able to meet with; and they amount . . . to *above* 30000."[63]

This number, 30,000, loomed large in the minds of many who looked at Mill's project. John Toland too praised the "30000 variations, which some of our Divines have discover'ed in a few copies of the New Testament."[64] And the number itself seems to have been discovered in a polemic against Mill by the cleric Daniel Whitby, who was quick to point out how easily these variants could be turned into a weapon against the integrity of the New Testament:

> [Jean] Morinus argued for a depravation of the Greek Text (which would render its authority insecure) from the variety of readings that he found in

[62] Preus, *Spinoza*, 174; Richard Simon, *Histoire Critique du Vieux Testament* (Rotterdam, 1685), 1. On Simon, see Patrick J. Lambe, "Biblical Criticism and Censorship in Ancien Régime France: The Case of Richard Simon," *Harvard Theological Review* 78 (1985): 149–77.

[63] Toland, *Nazarenus*, 130. James O'Higgins, S.J., *Anthony Collins: The Man and His Works* (The Hague, 1970), 31, 54–55, 88.

[64] Toland, *Nazarenus*, 140.

> the Greek Testament of R. Stephens; what triumphs then will the Papists have over the same text [the New Testament] when they see the variations quadrupled by Mill after sweating for thirty years at the work.[65]

Whitby's reference to papists was in part a reference to the priest Richard Simon: How, Whitby asked, can we imagine that God would "demand that the Christians should under gravest penalty order their life" according to a corrupt standard?[66] Catholics, presumably, would like nothing better than to undermine this standard, to show its radical *in*sufficiency in guaranteeing man's salvation. In their hands, 30,000 variants were so many nails in the coffin of Protestantism.

But Whitby was, as James Monk has observed, a "laborious but ill-judging divine," and he never grasped the real nature of Mill's project.[67] Begun in the late 1670s as an expansion of John Fell's 1675 Greek text, Mill's work was, almost literally, a lifetime achievement, completed a mere two weeks before he perished in his bed in 1707. In it, Mill presented readers with a Greek version derived directly from Robert Estienne's sixteenth-century text, the basis of the *textus receptus*. But more significantly Mill underwrote this text with a host of variant readings compiled, he wrote, "from more than 100 MSS. codices," both Greek and Latin, as well as lections found in the early church fathers.[68] Mill's goal was not to rewrite the Greek text. Rather, he wanted to restore "the authentic letter of our Lord's Testament, and the genuine reading of the sacred volumes which He himself gave to the Church through his inspired Apostles" by collecting all the errors time had introduced into the text.[69] These errors did not have to be significant. Indeed, the more insignificant the variant, the more they would confirm the essential doctrinal stability of the Greek text and confirm the ability of the Bible to save men's souls without having to "solve all [its] difficulties."[70] Such a collection, insofar as it helped both to restore the primitive authenticity and purity of Scripture and to confirm the essential coherence of the *textus receptus*, would have the happy result of "destroy[ing] the opportunity for atheists and other enemies of our religion to sneer" at the scriptural canon.[71]

Mill did not worry nearly as much about papists, in other words, as he did about those ready to jettison the Bible altogether. Cleaning up 30,000 variants was a means of sanitizing the New Testament, rendering it impervious to the accusations of the anti-biblical party. It would accomplish, on a textual level, what the discourse on the canonicity of Scripture sought to accomplish on a

[65] Daniel Whitby, *Examen Variantium Lectionum Joannis Millii in Novum Testamentum* (London, 1710), iii. See also Adam Fox, *John Mill and Richard Bentley: A Study of the Textual Criticism of the New Testament, 1675–1729* (Oxford, 1954), 106.

[66] Fox, *Mill and Bentley*, 106.

[67] James H. Monk, *The Life of Richard Bentley* (London, 1833), 1:348.

[68] Fox, *Mill and Bentley*, 54.

[69] Mill, *Prolegomena* to *Novum Testamentum cum lectionibus variantibus* (Oxford, 1707), 154.

[70] Stillingfleet, *Objections*, 5.

[71] Mill, *Prolegomena*, 154.

doctrinal level: namely, it would sort the wheat from the chaff. The investigation of the biblical canon was supposed to assure Christians of the stability of the Bible by discriminating between the genuine and spurious *book*. The investigation of the biblical text was supposed to assure Christians of the stability of the Bible by discriminating between the genuine and spurious *reading*. It proposed that just as the weakness of humanity might be the cause, so might the labor of humanity be the solution to textual corruption.

In this micrological process of textual cleansing, the 30,000 variants were just the beginning. Indeed, as England's foremost classical scholar, Richard Bentley, put it, the number of variants will only go up: as "more copies yet are collated, the sum will still mount higher."[72] Bentley was, as Simon Jarvis has noted, "the foremost representative of the new minute philology: a philology which took a historicist approach . . . to classical Greek and Latin texts." There were excellent antecedents for Bentley's scholarship, of course, but nonetheless he stood at the cusp of a general transformation in English letters as they moved from "a disinterested and gentlemanly humanism" to an "increasingly specialized and even professionalized philology."[73] The well-known conflicts between ancients and moderns, between Bentley and writers like William Temple and William Wotton over the Epistles of Phalaris, were bred from this transformation, which pushed scholars away from the ethics of appreciation and toward the ethics of criticism. When Temple commented that "Criticks . . . trouble themselves and the World with vain Niceties and captious Cavils, about Words and Syllables" he objected to the focus on minute textual details, the micrological labor over manuscripts and editions, that distinguished this "Race of Scholars" from those of generations before.[74]

In 1716, Bentley turned to the Greek New Testament, eager to show that the Bible would not be "made more *precarious*" by the number of its variants, but "more certain and authentic."[75] In a letter to Archbishop of Canterbury William Wake, Bentley lamented the "alarm . . . made of late years with the vast heap of various lections found in the MSS. of the Greek Testament." John Mill was on his mind in this letter. So were the reactions to Mill's project, both those that praised and those that mourned his vast collection of variants. Bentley felt supremely confident that he could turn these alarming reactions to the good. Study of the MSS. had convinced him that:

> I am able (what some thought impossible) to give an edition of the Gr. Test. exactly as it was in the best examples at the time of the Council of Nice.

[72] Richard Bentley, *Remarks upon a late Discourse of Free Thinking* in *Works*, 3:349.

[73] Simon Jarvis, *Scholars and Gentlemen: Shakespearian Textual Criticism and Representations of Scholarly Labour, 1725–1765* (Oxford, 1995), 21.

[74] William Temple, "Some Thoughts upon Reviewing the Essay of Ancient and Modern Learning," in *Works* (London, 1720), 1:299.

[75] Bentley, *Remarks*, 352.

> So that there shall not be 20 words, nor even particles' difference . . . so that that book, which, by the present management, is thought the most uncertain, shall have a testimony of certainty above all other books whatever.

If Collins insisted on the corruption of the text, Bentley most cogently argued for its possible liberation from taint. Variant readings did not indicate corruption; nor did they make the text unstable. For "surely those *various readings* existed before in several exemplars; Dr. Mill . . . only exhibited them to our view." If religion was "true before," then it cannot be less so now for having these variants in plain view. "Depend on't, no truth, no matter of fact fairly laid out, can ever subvert true religion, Bentley insisted."[76] Or, as he put it elsewhere, "let the *fact* prove as it will, the *doctrine* is unshaken."[77] Bentley's goal was to set these facts in the clearest light possible, given the darkness that time had spread across the text of scripture.

Bentley and Mill together represented a shift in English biblical scholarship, as specialized philology and microscopic textual analysis began to dominate the field and scholars turned back to the *text* of the Bible after a long hiatus. As Kristine Haugen has nicely put it:

> In the years around 1700, English scholars made a radical change in the way in which they studied the ancient Mediterranean world. In the seventeenth century, the form that dominated English scholarly publishing was the massive synthetic treatise on the comparative history of ancient cultures. . . . In the eighteenth-century, this kind of writing essentially vanished from scholarly circles, to be replaced by the minutely focused genre of the textual edition.[78]

Pace Arnaldo Momigliano, the move in the English eighteenth century was not away from "the emendation of texts," but toward a more disciplined and scientific practice of emendation.[79] The "rise of the relative autonomy of scholarship" in early eighteenth-century England was tied to this methodological shift.[80] But the question remains: *Why* did biblical scholarship make the micrological shift circa 1710? What purpose did it serve?

I would suggest that it served the same apologetic purpose sought by the literature defending the canon of the New Testament, namely, that it served to neutralize any threat that historical scholarship by the likes of Spinoza and

[76] Letter of 15 April 1716 in Bentley, *Works*, 3:477, 348, 349.

[77] Letter of 1 January 1717, in ibid., 3:485.

[78] Kristine Haugen, "Transformation in the Trinity Doctrine in English Scholarship: From the History of Beliefs to the History of Texts," *Archiv für Religionsgeschichte* 3 (2001): 149. For more detail, see also her "Richard Bentley: Scholarship and Criticism in Eighteenth-Century England," (Ph.D. diss., Princeton University, 2001).

[79] Arnaldo Momigliano, "Ancient History and the Antiquarian," in *Studies in Historiography* (New York, 1985), 1.

[80] Jarvis, *Scholars*, 8.

Simon, John Toland and Anthony Collins might pose to the sacred authority of the Bible. In part, we might see this as Hans Frei has, namely that "the struggle between Deists and orthodox defenders had moved to the arena of fact claims."[81] But only in part, for as we have seen, the struggle was not between "deists" and the "orthodox" but rather between "deists" (or their spectres) and just about every one else. Haugen has it better when she frames it more ecumenically: "scholars," in general, "needed . . . a new set of methods if they were to distinguish their own practices definitively from those of the intellectually unwashed."[82] Only meticulous philological scholarship could serve as an adequate defender of the biblical text against its challengers.

Points of theological doctrine were not the main issue here: the resurrection, the trinity, and so on were only side notes in a struggle in which the Bible itself was at stake. Because "the real text of the sacred writers does not now (since the originals have been so long lost) lie in any single MS. or edition, but is dispersed in them all," it was the job of the philologian to resurrect this text.[83] John Mill's massive collection effort was only the first step in the resurrection process, since collection only guaranteed that "readings . . . are put upon *equal credit*," meaning that even "the most recent, most vile and contemptible of all" might still keep their sacred aura." So if the phoenix of the Bible was to emerge out of the ashes of scribal error, the critic—read Bentley here—must first collect, but then *restore* this lost text, giving back to Christianity the precious jewel held at the beginning of the fourth century. As Bentley himself put it, the text he would produce would be "consecrate[d] . . . as a . . . *magna charta*, to the whole Christian church; to last when all the ancient MSS here quoted may be lost and extinguished."[84]

Now we may have our doubts whether Bentley's criticism was "so luminous and convincing . . . [that] no friend of religion has [since] been heard to decry the critical study of the inspired writings."[85] But certainly the ease with which he demolished both Collins and Whitby, and the scope of his New Testament project, made him very popular among the cadres of scholars anxious to avoid falling into either of the two traps that Locke so ably identified in 1685. Among his most avid fans was the dean of Worcester, Francis Hare, who sung praises of the Olympian Bentley for the world to hear. Bentley was the "perfect Master in the learned Languages, and in all Antiquity." He "vindicated *Christianity* itself from the most plausible and specious Oppositions of its Enemies." He taught Christians to seek "the *true* Text" and to give up their "vain defense" of the "*printed* one," which "instead of preserving the Authority of the Sacred Books . . . [has] given a handle to Libertine Spirits." For Hare, Bentley offered a new set of

[81] Hans Frei, *The Eclipse of Biblical Narrative: A Study in Eighteenth- and Nineteenth-Century Hermeneutics* (New Haven, 1974), 67.

[82] Haugen, "Trinity Doctrine," 151.

[83] Bentley, *Remarks*, 353.

[84] Ibid., "Proposals," in *Works*, 3:525, 489.

[85] Monk, *Life of Bentley*, 1:348.

techniques for dealing with the uncertainties of the Bible, the techniques of criticism, exacting and measured, which shows how "every Particle and Syllable . . . contribute their Share to the Exactness and Perfection of the whole."[86] Even Bentley's opponents saw these techniques as his main innovation. The crotchety librarian Conyers Middleton, Bentley's longtime opponent in the internecine squabbles of Cambridge University, was annoyed at Bentley's "*critical Niceties*" and outraged at an arrogance that would presume that "his Edition must needs last, when all the *antient Manuscripts* are not only *lost*, but . . . *extinguished* too."[87]

Middleton shows us more than pique. He shows us that the battle about scholarly ethics had profound consequences for the wider study of the Bible. Are all of these variant readings to the Bible, asked Middleton, not just "*curious* and *nice* Observations"? Are they "Discoveries of any *real Service to Christianity*"? Or useful more to the "*Learned*, than the *Christian* Reader"? These questions might have been disingenuous but they did get to the essence of this battle.[88] *Cui bono*? Who exactly is supposed to benefit from specialist scholarship? If specialist scholarship did *no* service to Christianity at large and benefited only the learned reader; if it only acted as a barrier to a more public Christian knowledge, then perhaps it was not the model for biblical scholarship. But Bentley and Hare were seemingly blind to this question. Bentley honestly thought that his edition of the Greek Testament *would* benefit Christianity as a whole. Hare's hyperexaltation of the critic—" 'tis a Work worthy of so great a Genius, 'tis a Master-piece, even among your Works, no body could have writ it but your self. . . . you have here outdone your self "—certainly took for granted the overwhelming cultural importance of this project.[89] As one correspondent wrote in 1717, "the souls of millions of mankind" depended on his new text.[90] Such sentiments had an odd ring to them, however, given the actual texts these scholars produced. John Mill's gigantic Greek New Testament, perhaps the last great work of Latin scholarship in England, was daunting even to the learned. Bentley's critical annotations were focused at a level of microscopic rigor formidable to the uninitiated. Neither of them deigned to put this work in the vernacular domain, nor was there any plan to do so. Scholarship on the New Testament was, in other words, to stay rigorously distinct from the public Bible as consumed in more ordinary churches and households. Perhaps, Middleton commented, "a correct and just Translation" of the standard edition would suffice for the ordinary "*Purposes of Religion*."[91] Given their practices, Mill and Bentley would have had to agree.

[86] Francis Hare, *The Clergyman's Thanks to Phileleutherus* (London, [1713]), 27, 31, 37–38, 43.

[87] Conyers Middleton, *Remarks, Paragraph by Paragraph, upon the Proposals lately published . . . by Richard Bentley* in *Miscellaneous Works*, 334, 335.

[88] Middleton, *Further Remarks*, 367.

[89] Hare, *Clergyman's Thanks*, 34.

[90] John Shaw to Richard Bentley, 29 March 1717, in *The Correspondence of Richard Bentley* (London, 1842), 2:532

[91] Middleton, *Further Remarks*, 368.

It was therefore no accident that this new professionalized scholarship produced no new vernacular translations. The great service their work was supposed to perform was pitched to the philologian and his newfound scholarly precision. The main job of English biblical scholarship of the early eighteenth century, in other words, was the defensive preservation of the Bible against external attack. Unfamiliarity with the biblical text was not the main problem on its critical horizon. Rather, an arrogant overfamiliarity with the text was its bugbear, the overfamiliarity represented by people like Collins and Toland. Scholarship, new editions, philological minutiae: all of them worked to set up protective barriers around the text of the New Testament, in order that it might be safeguarded against those who would seek its utter demise.

Stagnation and Scholarship

In the context of such a defensive reaction, the stagnation of Bible translation in the first half of the century is more understandable. If the interest in the Bible was there, the will to translate was largely absent among the scholars qualified to do so. Scholars were simply too busy trying to preserve the authority of the Bible as it had already existed in centuries past and had little energy for the project of renovating this authority. More strongly put, their energies were precisely directed *away* from the perilous translations generated by the likes of Toland and Whiston. Instead they specialized, taking talents for meticulous editing developed in classical scholarship and applying them—in the most narrow ways—to the text of the New Testament. And this turn to specialized philology accomplished some of the goals that Francis Atterbury set in his prosecution of Whiston. If the king did not in the end actually curtail the "present excessive and scandalous Liberty of Printing wicked Books at Home," Bentley and the early eighteenth-century philologians at least locked the sacred books away from public consumption, surrounding the text of the Bible with a web of specialized techniques and languages.[92]

If such a defensive posture helps us to understand why English biblical scholars used philological specialization to break through the wall that had separated the New Testament from serious scholarship since the early Reformation, it also sheds light on the control that the King James Bible retained over the vernacular biblical idiom even (or perhaps especially) among the cognoscenti. Anthony Johnson's 1730 exclamation—"Happy! thrice happy! hath our *English* Nation been, since God hath given it learned Translators, to express in our Mother Tongue the Heavenly Mysteries of his holy Word"—was not alone in the period.[93]

[92] Atterbury, "Representation," 344.

[93] Anthony Johnson, *An Historical Account of the several English Translations of the Bible* [1730] in Watson, ed., *Theological Tracts*, 3:100.

John Locke too reflected how "St. *Paul's* Epistles, as they stand translated in our English Bibles, are now by long and constant Use become a part of the English Language."[94] Jonathan Swift described the Bible and prayer book as "a kind of standard for language, especially to the common people."[95] And the *Edinburgh Review* later praised it as "perhaps the best executed, and most unexceptionable work of the kind, that ever appeared in the world. It has, in fact, for about 150 years past, been the standard by which the ideas affixed to words, have been determined."[96] This establishment of the King James Bible as a model literary text—one enshrined by its appreciation by the "common people"—stood in perfect harmony with the efforts of biblical scholars to keep their findings within the safety of scholarly languages and complicated practices.

Even the one place where the vernacular Bible thrived in this period testified to an inner urge to keep new translations off the table. These were the poetic confections produced by writers ranging from the dissenter Isaac Watts to Alexander Pope, from Edward Young and John Husbands to Joseph Addison. A lighter version of the seventeenth-century "Protestant poetics" described by Barbara Lewalski was at work here, as the metaphysical poetry of John Donne and George Herbert was accommodated to the sensibilities of the Augustan age.[97] Watts, for example, distinguished himself with a series of paraphrastic religious poems—the *Horae Lyricae* (1706)—aimed at "elevat[ing] us to the most delightful and divine sensations" by reinvigorating the poetry and singing of the Psalms. These poems were to clarify the Christian essence of psalmody, lifting the "veil of Moses . . . thrown over our hearts" to reveal a living and breathing faith.[98] By all accounts, Watts was successful at doing this: his hymns, poems, and later *Psalms of David, Imitated in the Language of the New Testament* (1719), were all immensely successful in the eighteenth century. These last were no ordinary literal translations, since such would "darken our religion, by running back again to judaism." Instead Watts purged the psalms of their Jewish trappings and revealed what he took to be their Christian essence. For the opening of Ps. 22, what Watts entitled "The Sufferings and Death of Christ," he replaced the familiar "My God, my God, why hast thou forsaken me?" with this:

> Why has my God my soul forsook,
> Nor will a smile afford?
> (Thus David once in anguish spoke,
> and thus our dying Lord.)[99]

[94] Locke, *A Paraphrase and Notes on the Epistles of St. Paul* (Oxford, 1987), 1:107.

[95] Norton, *Bible As Literature*, 211.

[96] *Edinburgh Magazine*, 2 (1758): 127.

[97] Barbara Kiefer Lewalski, *Protestant Poetics and the Seventeenth-Century Religious Lyric* (Princeton, 1979).

[98] Isaac Watts, *Horae Lyricae* in *Works of Isaac Watts* (London, 1810), 4:253.

[99] Watts, *Psalms*, in *Works*, 4:115, 142.

Admittedly it may be easier to remember a metrical, rhyming psalm, but the results had little resemblance to the Bible. Nor was it easy to imagine Christ moaning such words in his dying passion. But Watts was not alone in his paraphrastic impulse. In a somewhat less devotional mode, Joseph Addison too provided poetic biblical paraphrase for public consumption. His rendition of Ps. 23.2 ("He leads me beside still waters; he restores my soul") was not untypical for the Augustan sensibilities of the day, though it undoubtedly strikes the modern reader as comically odd:

When in the sultry Glebe I faint,
Or on the thirsty Mountain pant;
to fertile Vales and dewy Meads,
My weary wand'ring Steps he leads;
where peaceful Rivers soft and slow,
Amid the verdant Landskip flow.[100]

For Addison, the Psalmist reinforced the need for "religious Meditation," for recalling and exalting what Edward Young later called his "Night Thoughts," those "deep Impressions . . . apt to vanish as soon as the Day breaks."[101] The fascination with the "Language from Heaven" would continue throughout the period and have a variety of effects on the biblical text (see chapter 6), but its popularity across the devotional spectrum testifies to a certain cultural comfort with the genre, one characterized by, as Murray Roston has it, "artificiality and repetition."[102] I would suggest that the pleasure taken in artificiality indicated a certain discomfort with the literal text of the Bible itself, a discomfort that stemmed in part from a fear lest the Bible become, as Conyers Middleton put it, "*strange, awkward, and new to us*."[103] "Lay aside the humour of criticism," wrote Watts in 1706, for criticism threatens to crush the pleasure of the biblical text.[104] It is difficult to know if Watts had people like Toland or like Bentley in his mind, but in either case, he was certainly far more comfortable with an "artificial" Bible than he was with its concrete letters. Biblical poetry in this early century can justly be read, then, as an effort to keep the literal vernacular Bible in the wings.

And the one significant effort to bring it front and center—Daniel Mace's 1729 Greek-English New Testament—illuminates finally the protective instincts governing English scholars as they confronted the Bible. His Greek and English parallel texts, the former "corrected from the Authority of the most

[100] [Joseph Addison], no. 441, 26 July 1712, *The Spectator*, ed. Donald F. Bond (Oxford, 1965), 4:51.

[101] [Addison], *Spectator*, 23 August 1712, 4:143.

[102] John Husbands, preface to *A Miscellany of Poems by several Hands* (Oxford, 1731), b2^{v}; Murray Roston, *Prophet and Poet: The Bible and the Growth of Romanticism* (London, 1965), 33.

[103] Middleton, *Further Remarks*, 435.

[104] Watts, *Horae*, 255.

Authentic Manuscripts," show a man reluctant to translate without a great deal of scholarly weaponry in reserve.[105] Like Bentley and Mill, Mace confronted the demon of "Infidelity so loudly and so justly complained of," but like them he could not imagine a Bible separated from the strong defense of scholarship. Modern scholars had "studiously declin'd" to translate the Bible again, Mace complained, and yet his text showed clearly why: it was a book whose translation was fully subservient to the scholarship. Scholarly advance and vernacular stagnation were, in other words, part of the same forces shaping the English Bible.[106] Scholars studiously declined to translate the Bible precisely because their interests were not in religious renovation, but in religious preservation, not in redefining their religious patrimony, but in protecting it.

It was only late in the century—deism effectively dead, and religion once more on the march with the revivals of Hutchinsonianism and, more importantly, Methodism—that the English project of Bible translation began to pick up steam, as the objectives of Biblical scholarship shifted slowly away from protection and toward renewal. "Biblical criticism can be said to have become almost respectable in England" in the 1750s, in David Katz's words, but before it either represented a dangerous form of historical scholarship or was engaged in a rearguard defense of the Bible per se.[107] Even this midcentury expansion was sluggish: only in the 1780s did a host of translations begin to pepper the English religious landscape. This is a story we will tell later on, but it will be one shaped by these earliest encounters between scholars and their imagined enemies. The strong separation between scholarly and vernacular texts and the defensive posture of biblical scholars toward their religious traditions that so dominated the early eighteenth century prevented England from developing a productive and positive relationship between scholarship and the Bible. Reimagining the nature of the Bible through the use of scholarship would be reserved for Germany, where the positive power of religious ardor was channeled into reforming the vernacular Bible.

[105] [Daniel Mace], *The New Testament in Greek and English* (London, 1729), title page. On Mace, see Jarvis, *Scholars and Gentlemen*, 38, and H. McLachlan, "An Almost Forgotten Pioneer in New Testament Criticism," *The Hibbert Journal* 37 (1938–39): 617–25.

[106] [Mace], *New Testament*, v, iv.

[107] David Katz, "Isaac Vossius and the English Biblical Critics, 1670–1689," in *Scepticism and Irreligion in the Seventeenth and Eighteenth Centuries*, ed. Richard Popkin and Arjo Vanderjagt (New York, 1993), 171. Generally, on English Bibles in the eighteenth century, see Scott Mandelbrote, "The English Bible and Its Readers in the Eighteenth Century," in *Books and Their Readers in the Eighteenth Century: New Essays*, ed. Isabel Rivers (London: Continuum, 2001). My thanks to Professor Mandelbrote for calling my attention to this essay.

Chapter Three

RELIGION, THE NEW TESTAMENT, AND THE GERMAN REINVENTION OF THE BIBLE

In 1710 the leading mouthpiece of Germany's Lutheran orthodoxy, Valentin Ernst Löscher's *Unschuldige Nachrichten von Alten und Neuen Theologischen Sachen*, reported the publication of John Mill's Greek New Testament. Enthusiasm was the order of the day for this "beautiful and praiseworthy work" and its author's "uncommon industry." Mill's careful notes had produced, Löscher exclaimed, a truly "kingly work," a "well-ordered thesaurus" for the critical study of the New Testament. They answered Löscher's hopes, eight years prior, that "more Greek MSS might be sent from the Orient" and that the existing manuscripts be "collated with more diligence" in order to "preserve the honor and purity of the holy originals."[1] Given the ruckus raised by Mill's 30,000 variants in England—the homeland of philological criticism at the turn of the eighteenth century—the embrace of philological scholarship by an orthodox Lutheran seems a bit surprising. Löscher and other hard-line German theologians, whether in Wittenberg or Leipzig, were neither able philologians, nor especially interested in philology, and, to a man, they were impatient with great seventeenth-century critics like Hugo Grotius. But they were unflappable in the face of what seemed in England a potentially disastrous threat to the stability of the biblical text. When Christian Reineccius published a selection of Mill's notes as part of his *Biblia quadrilinguia Novi Testamenti* (1713), Löscher again was ebullient in his praises of what was, to Löscher, a truly wonderful work of polyglot scholarship.[2] Not even the English anxiety about the biblical canon ruffled Löscher's feathers. When he reviewed William Whiston's iconoclastic *Essay on the Epistles of St. Ignatius*, he very moderately called for "a scholar with . . . talent" to investigate the epistles more thoroughly. And John Richardson's *Canon of the New Testament Vindicated*—a text we might expect to appeal to a biblical conservative—received only fainthearted praise.[3]

If we knew nothing about Löscher and the other orthodox theologians of the period, we might attribute such mildness to temperament. But Löscher was a fearsome opponent, a fierce, effective, and tireless combatant in the religious

[1] [Valentin Ernst Löscher], *Unschuldige Nachrichten der alten und neuen theologischen Sachen* 10 (1710): 21, 23, 26, 27; 2 (1702): 716.

[2] [Löscher], *Unschuldige Nachrichten* 13 (1713): 948.

[3] [Löscher], *Unschuldige Nachrichten* 4 (1704): 701, 665.

polemics that echoed throughout the end of the seventeenth and well into the eighteenth century. Why such blithe acceptance of what seemed to the English orthodoxy lethal threats to religion itself? Löscher's review of Richardson affords an interesting clue. Richardson's ire, if we remember from chapter 2, was directed at John Toland, the deist whose *Amyntor* sparked such a flood of apologetic writings among the English faithful. But strangely enough, Löscher either overlooked these polemics, or else was wholly unconcerned by them, concentrating instead on Richardson's amiable conflict with the French historian Jacques Basnage. Whether he misunderstood the real anxieties driving the piece, or ignored them, in either case, clearly he did not share them. Deism was simply not a source of significant anxiety for Löscher. Although certainly critical of those he called "Socinians," Löscher's bile only really began to flow when he gazed on those advocates of "enthusiasm" and "fanaticism," the so-called Pietists who, since 1675, had successfully orchestrated a religious renewal in Protestant Germany of such breadth that they happily called it their "second Reformation."[4] Löscher painstakingly and gleefully reprinted the anti-Pietist edicts promulgated across the Holy Roman Empire circa 1710—in Hanover, Prussia, Braunschweig, Schleswig-Holstein, Nuremberg, and Denmark, among other places. Every volume of the *Unschuldige Nachrichten* had an index heading on "*opere anti-fanatico*" that detailed the latest aberrations of eccentric German zealots like Johann Petersen, Gottfried Arnold, and Johann Dippel. And it was for these zealots that Löscher and his orthodox supporters reserved their unbridled hatred.

Unlike England, then, Germany in the early eighteenth century was not obsessed with deism. Instead, it was still trying to process the religious conflicts that had so devastated the Holy Roman Empire in the seventeenth century. What came to be known as Pietism—initially an insult, later embraced as a badge of honor—was a product of these conflicts.[5] It grew out of the reform movements in German Lutheranism that sprang up in the early decades of the seventeenth century when reformers tried to encourage people "to study and learn . . . the living practice of the sacred divine Word."[6] During the immense upheavals of the Thirty Years War—endless violence, economic stagnation, religious uncertainty—these reform movements were an ever-present parallel to the orthodox theology that dominated Germany's universities. Johann Valentin Andreae's potent and strange combination of Lutheran chiliasm, utopian dreaming, and Rosicrucianism was one spiritual response to the violence and disruption of the first fifty years following 1600. But he was not alone. The signature

[4] Martin Schmidt, "Spener und Luther," in *Der Pietismus als theologische Erscheinung: Gesammelte Studien zur Geschichte des Pietismus, Band II*, ed. Kurt Aland (Göttingen, 1984), 156.

[5] For some general works on Pietism, see F. Ernst Stoeffler, *German Pietism During the Eighteenth Century* (Leiden, 1973); Richard Gawthrop, *Pietism and the Making of Eighteenth-Century Prussia* (Cambridge, 1993); Martin Brecht, ed., *Geschichte des Pietismus*, 2 vols. (Göttingen, 1993).

[6] Martin Brecht, "Das Aufkommen der neuen Frömmigkeitsbewegung in Deutschland," in *Geschichte des Pietismus*, 1:134.

book of this reform movement, Johann Arndt's *Vier Bücher von wahren Christenthums*, was printed in over one hundred editions over the course of the seventeenth and early eighteenth centuries.[7] Jakob Böhme, Joachim Betke, Christian Hoburg, and many others also channeled the psychic disruptions of their age into a mystical devotion to Christ, devotion that was exemplary for German Pietism when it blossomed around 1675.[8]

Fear of this invigorated and growing religious movement plagued orthodox Lutherans of the day. Already by 1700, Pietism had become quasi-institutionalized under the leadership of clerics Philip Jakob Spener and August Hermann Francke, most notably in the town of Halle, where the elector of Brandenburg and later king of Prussia Frederick I established a university in 1694 that would train generations of Pietist theologians and scholars. Public support of the Pietists by the Reformed (Calvinist) Hohenzollerns—who were anxious to ward off religious conflict with their Lutheran subjects—and endless labor by the Pietists themselves transformed Halle into *the* premiere research institution in early eighteenth-century Germany. With its orphanages, primary schools, and printing presses, Halle became the center of a pedagogical revolution that made its clerics the dominant contenders for positions in eighteenth-century schools and parishes, as well as in the burgeoning Prussian army.[9] Not only were Pietists successful in the political arena, they also managed to inspire a raft of parallel spiritualist movements. By the end of the eighteenth century, entire territories in the Holy Roman Empire—like that of Sayn-Wittengenstein-Berleburg—had become enclaves of philadelphians, millennialists, and religious separatists.[10] Orthodox university theologians across Germany vigorously opposed all of these changes: the resulting eruption of polemic literature completely jammed the literary airwaves from 1690 until at least 1715.[11] Given this vitriolic environment—where the fate of Lutheranism itself seemed in the balance—it may be less surprising that, for Löscher, John Mill's scholarly innovations seemed like small potatoes in the face of clear and present danger.

Bible scholarship and Bible translation in Germany, in other words, took its leave from a peculiar and particular religious context. Unlike England, where

[7] Werner Koepp, in his *Johann Arndt: Eine Untersuchung über die Mystik im Luthertum* (Aalen, 1973), documents over one hundred editions in all languages (see pp. 302–304), likely a gross underestimate (see Johann Wallmann, *Philipp Jakob Spener und die Anfänge des Pietismus* [Tübingen, 1970], 14 n. 49).

[8] See Brecht, "Frömmigkeitsbewegung," 151ff. and "Die deutschen Spiritualismus des 17. Jahrhunderts," in *Geschichte des Pietismus*, 1:205ff.

[9] On Pietist pedagogy, see James Van Horn Melton, *Absolutism and the eighteenth-Century Origins of Compulsory schooling in Prussia and Austria* (Cambridge, 1988), 30ff. and Anthony La Vopa, *Grace, Talent, and Merit: Poor Students, Clerical Careers, and Professional Ideology in Eighteenth-Century Germany* (Cambridge, 1988), 137ff.

[10] On the geography of "radical Pietism," see Hans Schneider, "Der radikale Pietismus im 18. Jahrhundert," in *Geschichte des Pietismus*, 2:107–97.

[11] On the immense materials produced, see Gierl, *Pietismus und Aufklärung*, 108ff.

the contest was framed as one between the pious and the despoilers of religion *tout court*, in Germany, the fire of confessional conflict—over doctrine, liturgy, theology and so on—still burned hot. The same zeal that made the Reformation such a productive period for biblical translation in Germany, in other words, still drove the early eighteenth-century invention of what would become the Enlightenment Bible. This zeal welded together the Pietist subjective religion of love and rebirth and the pragmatic textual techniques that were finding their early articulation across Protestant Europe. It also gave impetus to the translation project so vigorously pursued by the Pietist, and particularly the radical Pietist, movement. With religion in hand, translators moved beyond the English effort to hold the line against the forces of impiety and began to imagine a *new* Bible. This Bible, they hoped, would break free of the chains of dogmatic orthodoxy. It would, they hoped, soar freely into a post-theological future, beyond the confines of doctrine and dogma that had so shackled the spirit of Lutheranism. But the very process of forging this new Bible had unintended consequences. The fire of religious reform would, in the end, set the stage for the Enlightenment Bible.

Subjective Religion and Scholarly Practices

In 1710 a curious volume was published in the north German town of Wandesbeck. Entitled *Biblia pentapla*, the book offered the reader five competing New Testaments: Luther's 1545 version; Caspar Ulenberg's 1630 Catholic version; Johann Piscator's 1602 Reformed version; the 1636 Dutch States translation; and the "new translation" of Johann Heinrich Reitz, an itinerant radical Pietist and religious separatist.[12] Given Reitz's beliefs, it is little surprise that Valentin Löscher singled him out as the source of "indifferentism, fanaticism, and naturalism" that infected the *Biblia pentapla* and the entire Pietist movement.[13] Interestingly, though, Löscher's fury was not especially stirred by Reitz's idiosyncratic translation of the Greek, a translation that made the Bible into a sourcebook of Pietist faith. Instead, his ire focused on a footnote in this text, namely Reitz's footnote to 1 John 5.7, the famous Johannine Comma that had plagued scholars from Erasmus on.[14] Reitz's note was a simple one: it said

[12] The entire Bible is entitled: *Biblia pentapla: das ist die Bücher der heiligen Schrift des Alten und Neuen Testaments nach fünf-facher deutscher Verdolmetschung* (Wandesbeck, 1710–1712). The New Testament was published in 1710, and the 1711–12 Old Testament, remarkably, included the Jewish-Yiddish translation of Josel Witzenberger. See, generally, Hans-Jürgen Schrader, "Die *Biblia Pentapla* und ihr Programm einer 'herrlichen Harmonie Göttlichen Wortes,'" in *Zwiesprache: Beiträge zur Theorie und Geschichte des Übersetzens*, ed. Ulrich Stadler (Stuttgart, 1996), esp. 205–209.

[13] [Löscher], *Unschuldige Nachrichten* 10 (1710): 33.

[14] On the Johannine comma, see Metzger, *Text of the New Testament*, 101f.; Bentley, *Humanists and Holy Writ*, 152–53.

only that the verse had been left out of Luther's 1523 edition and "was also missing in many old Greek exemplars, in some Latin, in the Syrian, Arabic and Moorish translations."[15] But Löscher's reaction was swift. "Oh, how good it would have been, if some of these dangerous glosses had been left out," he exclaimed. "How does this note . . . serve the layman except to create a confused conscience?"[16]

Löscher's response was telling. Given his reaction to Reineccius, he had no principled objection to polyglots; given the reaction to Mill, no principled objection to textual scholarship either. But he did have a principled objection to *Reitz's* scholarship, and the key problem centered on the layman: Reitz's work made available to everyone the fruits of scholarly labor, the erudite Latin fruits that had, in the tradition of Lutheran orthodoxy, been reserved solely for the tables of the learned. Scholarship in the vernacular, by contrast, threatened to confuse the common reader. It threatened to show openly what scholars had known since the days of Erasmus: namely, that the Bible was not a text whose language could be precisely determined. Instead, it was a text whose formation depended on the ingenuity of human beings, whether in preventing inevitable corruptions or in rehabilitating texts already corrupted as they passed from generation to generation.

In general, German Pietism is rarely associated with scholarship. At least since the early eighteenth century, critics and historians of Pietism have tended to look to Pietism for its affective qualities, for its stress on the subjective experience of redemption and Christ's love. For someone like Löscher, the visions of Christina Bader in 1699 were exemplary, Bader who: "claimed that an angel spoke to her . . . heard a voice calling as loud as the most strident song in church, speaking constantly of woe and God's anger . . . smelled an incessant sulfurous stink of fire and death as a sign of God's rage . . . prophesied of loud sorrows for the land of Württemburg."[17] And when, a year later, in April 1700, the news broke of the extraordinary religious devotions in Berleburg—where, over the course of three weeks, two "witnesses of Christ," Carl Anton Püntiner and Ernst Christoph Hochmann von Hochenau, led an uncommon piece of religious theater in which the actors became the biblical high priests (Moses, Aaron, Eliezer, Elias, Zacharias, and others) and fell into ecstatic trances, tearful fits of prayer, and delirium up to thrice daily—this would have confirmed Löscher's sense that Pietism was typified not by scholarship but by enthusiastic devotion and the subjective embrace of Christ.[18] And it was not only the orthodox that reacted to Pietists in this way. Already by 1736, a certain cultural picture of the Pietist was ripe for caricature by writers like Luise Gottsched, whose *Die Pietistery im Fischbein-Rocke* mocked an

[15] Johann Heinrich Reitz, note to 1 John 5.7 in *Biblia pentapla*.

[16] [Löscher], *Unschuldige Nachrichten* 10 (1710): 616–17.

[17] [Löscher], *Unschuldige Nachrichten* 2 (1702): 416–17.

[18] See Heinz Renkewitz, *Hochmann von Hochenau (1670–1721): Quellenstudien zur Geschichte des Pietismus* (Witten, 1969), 118–22.

overly enthusiastic mother. Having fallen into a religious faint, she needs only her daughter shouting in her ear "Arnold! Petersen! Lange! Gichtel! Francke! Tauler! Grace! Rebirth! The inner spark!" to rouse her.[19] And for the most part, modern scholars have relied on this cultural picture as well. The "general . . . significance of Pietism" is, as Carl Hinrichs put it thirty years ago, usually ascribed to its "turn from an objective dogmatic-ecclesiastical belief to individual religiosity and subjective piety."[20] For Gerhard Kaiser, "the Pietist withdraws into his experience of piety."[21] Or, more recently, Pietists embraced the "passive and receptive self of the believer"and longed for its complete "union with God's will."[22]

For modern scholars of this period, this subjective side to Pietism is precisely what is modern about it. As Hinrichs has it, Pietism prepared the way for "the modern concept of the individual" and was a "precursor and precondition for the German movement, its poetry, philosophy, and in part historicism."[23] The more objective developments within Pietism—the economic theory that structured the Halle community, for example, the concrete organization of time for students, the inculcation of ideals of obedience into German citizens—have not been overlooked in the quest to connect the first and second halves of the eighteenth century. But in the domain of cultural production, the subjective strains of the Pietist ethos have remained dominant. And so, Pietism is traditionally connected with the development of the intellectual dispositions that came to characterize later German philosophy: individualistic, inward looking, at times otherworldly, disinclined to political activism.

Rather than align dispositions, this chapter aligns intellectual and more particularly scholarly *practices*. Rather than looking just at what Pietists *thought* about religion, in other words, I want to look at what they *did* with the documents that for millennia have given Christianity its solid textual core. Certainly a strong emphasis on the individual experience of God's presence *seems* antithetical to a scholarly and objective treatment of Christianity's texts. But this antithesis was, in the case of Pietism, a false one. From the very beginning, the institutionalization of Pietist teaching within the walls of higher learning was a physical confirmation of an objective impulse within the movement. Universities, as Halle's leading light, August Hermann Francke, said, should be "the true garden and orchard-school of God, through which all is built, improved, and made fruitful."[24] What made Halle into "the leading, the most modern German university" of its day was its concrete scholarly bona

[19] Luise Gottsched, *Die Pietisterey im Fischbein-Rocke* (Stuttgart, 1968), 38.

[20] Carl Hinrichs, *Preußentum und Pietismus* (Göttingen, 1971), 1.

[21] Gerhard Kaiser, *Pietismus und Patriotismus im literarischen Deutschland: Ein Beitrag zum Problem der Säkularisation* (Frankfurt a.M., 1973), 7.

[22] Gawthrop, *Pietism*, 142.

[23] Hinrichs, *Preussentum und Pietismus*, 1.

[24] Francke, "Der Grosse Aufsatz" (1704) in Otto Podczeck, ed., *Abhandlungen der sächsiche Akademie der Wissenschaften zu Leipzig. Philologisch-historische Klasse* 53.3 (Berlin, 1962), 77.

fides.[25] Francke personally ensured that philology would stand at the top of the scholarly ladder. His *Collegium Orientale theologicum,* founded in 1702 and headed by the biblical scholar Johann Heinrich Michaelis, was the pinnacle of the Halle system. It was dedicated to the "words of scripture . . . in the vernacular languages, at first in the originals, and later in the versions" and languages taught included Hebrew but also "Chaldeian, Syrian, Samaritan, Arabic, Ethiopian, [and] Rabbinical [Hebrew]." For the more advanced students, Turkish, Persian, and Chinese were to be taught, as well as more familiar languages such as modern Greek, Polish, Italian, and Russian.[26] The very first project of the collegium was the compilation of a version of the Hebrew Old Testament (1720).[27]

Even for those unqualified for the *Collegium orientale*—the some 40 percent of the total student population that went through the theological faculty—philology was a necessary part of their training.[28] It was not that scholarship for its own sake was worthwhile. Like many others in the period, Francke criticized scholarship ungoverned by the love of God: "It is better only to know a little, humbly and with modest insight, than it is to possess the treasures of scholarship in idle self-complacency."[29] Or, more directly put, if "[the theologian] does not use the holy Word of God to become a true Christian, then, even if he becomes . . . a master of Scripture, it will be of no real use to him."[30] The command to read the text was always paralleled by the injunction to "read and observe the heart." And yet philology was never absent from Francke's theological program: a student must, he affirmed, become a "textual theologian" to be any theologian at all.[31]

Broadly speaking, Francke was part of a larger effort within Pietism to move beyond the dogmatic theology so precious to seventeenth-century Lutherans and, in consequence, to turn the fruits of pious scholarly labor over to the layman to savor. For this we could look to Gottfried Arnold, whose 1699 *Unpartheyische Ketzer- und Kirchengeschichte* combined an iconoclastic *ad fontes* sensibility, a paradoxical insistence on the necessity of heresy, and a thoroughly

[25] Wolfgang Martens, "Hallescher Pietismus und Gelehrsamkeit oder vom 'allzu grossen Misstrauen in die Wissenschaften,'" in *Res Publica Litteraria: Die Institutionen der Gelehrsamkeit in der frühen Neuzeit* (Wiesbaden, 1987), 508.

[26] Otto Podczeck, "Die Arbeit am Alten Testament in Halle zur Zeit des Pietismus: Das Collegium Orientale theologicum A. H. Franckes," in *Wissenschaftliche Zeitschrift der Martin-Luther-Universität Halle-Wittenberg* 7 (August 1958): 1060.

[27] Johann Heinrich Michaelis, *Biblia Hebraica ex aliquot Manuscripta* (Halle, 1720); see Karl Heinrich Rengstorf, "Johann Heinrich Michaelis und seine 'Biblia Hebraica' von 1720," in Norbert Hinske, ed., *Zentren der Aufklärung I: Halle. Aufklärung und Pietismus* (Heidelberg, 1989), 15–70.

[28] La Vopa has 41.8 percent matriculating in theology in the decade 1721–1730 (*Grace*, 145).

[29] Thomas à Kempis, *Imitatio Christi*, quoted in Martens, "Hallescher Pietismus," 498. See also Martens, *Literatur und Frömmigkeit in der Zeit der frühen Aufklärung* (Tübingen, 1989), 50–76.

[30] Francke, "Idea studiosi theologiae," (1712) in *Werke in Auswahl*, Erhard Peschke, ed. (Berlin, 1969), 174.

[31] Kurt Aland, "Bibel und Bibeltext bey August Hermann Francke und Johann Albrecht Bengel," in *Pietismus und Bibel*, ed. Kurt Aland (Witten, 1970), 89.

affective notion of God's relationship to man.[32] Or we could look at the strange commentary on the Song of Songs by the millennialist and philadelphian Johann Petersen, who compared ten different versions (in four languages) of Songs 6.7–9 in order to show that "in all of the translations the meaning of the Holy Spirit is found."[33] More telling was the example of otherworldly Philip Jakob Spener—Francke's teacher and spearhead of the Pietist movement until his death in 1705—who actively reread the heritage of the Reformation as one of scholarly advance. The Luther Bible was an "incomparable treasure" of the church, but Luther was himself merely a man.[34] His amazing "erudition and scholarship" and his "study of the holy languages, Greek and Hebrew" guaranteed his translation's accuracy but, at the same time, subjected it to correction should scholarship advance to new insights.[35] No Bible, Spener firmly insisted, was so perfect that "some expressions might not be rendered better, clearer, more accurately, and more in consonance with the original text."[36]

Francke took these words literally, making a name for himself in 1695 with his *Observationes biblicae*, a monthly publication that went through the Luther Bible with a fine scholarly comb, picking out various lousy readings, misinterpretations, and mistranslations. In May 1695—after a barrage of criticism from orthodox theologians—Francke defended his enterprise with a simple question: "Did Luther, in his German version of Scripture, produce in each and every case the correct literal reading of the original . . . ?" The simple answer was "no," but even the *question* shifted the terms of the debate. Instead of asking "*is it allowable*?" one should, he said, ask an entirely objective and factual question: "is it translated correctly . . . or not?"[37] In this shift, Francke put the Luther Bible in the hands of a simple but powerful tool, that of philological analysis. As he put it in his more radical piece, the 1712 "Kurtzes Project": "all scholared Germans who understand the original languages . . . correctly, must acknowledge and confess, that in the [Luther] version, there are still here and there many incorrect and unclear translations."[38] Already Francke assumed that scholarship and translation would be parts of the same enterprise, namely, making the fruits of biblical scholarship—the most accurate vernacular version possible—available to all German readers. And Francke's printing presses at the Halle—a key part of the institutionalization of Pietism—were supposed to

[32] Erich Seeberg, *Gottfried Arnold: Die Wissenschaft und die Mystik seiner Zeit* (Darmstadt, 1964), 227ff.

[33] Johann Petersen, *Vollständige Erklärung des Hohen Lieds Salomonis* (Büdingen, 1728), 168.

[34] Spener, *Theologische Bedencken*, 954.

[35] Spener, introduction to Christoph Seidel, *Lutherus redivivus* (Halle, 1697), a2r.

[36] Spener, *Theologische Bedencken*, part 1, 275; *Lutherus redivivus*, br.

[37] Francke, *Observationes biblicae* (May 1695) in *Werke in Auswahl*, 263, 266.

[38] Francke, "Kurtzes Proiect unpartheischer privat-Gedanken von einer Emendation der Teutschen Bibel," in August Nebe, ed., "Neue Quellen zu August Hermann Francke," *Beiträge zur Förderung christlicher Theologie* 31 (Gütersloh, 1927), 27. There is some dispute about the authorship of this article; see Beate Köster, *Die Lutherbibel im frühen Pietismus* (Bielefeld, 1984), 161–66.

become the publishing organ of this new philological enterprise: texts in "German, Latin, and Greek" as well as Hebrew, Syrian, Ethiopian, and Slavonian were expected, as was a "universal-historical work" that was to compete with the "critical and historical works" so beloved in England and Holland.[39]

In reality, Halle's great success was not with critical work, but with the mass publication of the Bible in such huge numbers that, as the director of the Halle press Heinrich Elers bragged, "not even the poor could say that they could procure no Bible because of the high cost."[40] And the numbers seem to confirm Eler's boast: between 1711 and 1719, the Halle presses churned out 100,000 New Testaments and 80,000 complete Bibles and, within a hundred years, over a million New Testaments and nearly 2 million complete Bibles, a staggering amount for the eighteenth century.[41] These were almost exclusively unrevised Luther Bibles and so, in many ways, the Halle Pietists were—for all their criticism of Luther's text—the greatest developers of its enormous market share. Business sense—and Halle was, if nothing else, an engine of pious profit—probably governed these decisions in large part. Whatever the reason, the real task of developing a scholarly translation was *not* shouldered by the institutionalized Pietism in Halle. Instead it fell on the backs of those more marginal Pietist figures, shadowy members of the radical Pietist underground that existed in a network of sympathetic towns and territories across the Holy Roman Empire. And it was this radical Pietist network that over the course of the next thirty years would produce more new Bible translations than ever seen during the sixteenth and seventeenth centuries.[42]

Johann Otto Glüsing—the editor and compiler of the *Biblia pentapla*—was at the center of this network. Editor of Jakob Böhme's works and the founder of the ascetic "Angelbrothers" society, Glüsing was a key part of a group of separatists and spiritualists who gathered in Altona (a hotbed for Spinozists, Mennonites, radical Pietists, and Jews) in the early years of the eighteenth century.[43] The *Biblia pentapla* represented, for Glüsing, an entirely new direction for the German Bible. As Hans-Jürgen Schrader has recognized, it "opened the door to confessional tolerance and ecumenical ideas."[44] Because, in Glüsing's words, "different German translators . . . have different dialects," the *Biblia pentapla* would provide all Germans with access to all the translations. In this way, the Lutheran, the Catholic, and the Calvinist reader could each "view and

[39] Heinrich Elers in Francke, "Grosse Aufsatz," 148, 152.

[40] Ibid., 151.

[41] Kurt Aland, "Pietismus und die Bibel," 36.

[42] For a general overview of Pietist translations, see Beate Köster, "'Mit tiefem Respekt, mit Furcht und Zittern': Bibelübersetzungen im Pietismus," *Pietismus und Neuzeit* 24 (1998): 95–115.

[43] Schrader, "Biblia pentapla," 208. See also Stefan Winkle, *Die heimlichen Spinozisten in Altona und der Spinozastreit* (Hamburg, 1988). On Gichtel, see Gertraud Zaepernick, "Johann Georg Gichtel und seiner Nachfolger Briefwechsel mit den Hallischen Pietisten, besonders mit A. M. Francke," *Pietismus und Neuzeit* 8 (1982): 74–118.

[44] Schrader, "Biblia Pentapla," 205.

examine whatever column or translation he chooses" but should their text seem unclear, he could "compare [his version] with the other translations, to see if these speak more clearly."[45] The side-by-side placement of representative biblical texts was to serve, then, both as an ecumenical bridge between readers, giving them a common language of religion, and as a means to unify a Bible divided by centuries of confessional strife.

But ecumenism was only one interesting aspect of the *Biblia pentapla*. Certainly it was peculiar that Glüsing framed the issue of religious difference in terms of dialect, as if the political, institutional, and theological divisions that had, a short fifty years prior, killed off some one third of the German population, depended on varieties of pronunciation. More significantly, the *Biblia pentapla* was simply remarkable in its confidence that no obstacle to the written Word was too great. "[E]ven the simplest reader will not be altogether unaware," proclaimed Glüsing, a radical theosophist and philadelphian, "that the Evangelists and Apostles wrote in the eastern language most familiar at that time. . . . Nowadays that same Holy Spirit of Jesus Christ speaks still to all nations . . . such that the Holy Spirit and its light in our souls might be called the real original text, and languages only the expression and illustration of that text." Linguistic difference, in this scheme, evaporated in the face of the "real original text" of the New Testament impressed into the believers' hearts by the Holy Spirit. Although "the writings of the Evangelists and the Apostles in Greek are called the original text," the *real* original text lay within the Evangelists themselves. Translations are only weak, then, "owing to the weakness of the translators." "No one with unwashed hands," Glüsing cried, no one "without the baptism of the holy spirit . . . should allow themselves to practice that so important office of the translator and scribe of divine secrets!" With the right translator, though, the *Biblia pentapla* could conceivably become the perfect translation, one that would, as Glüsing put it, "serve as a perfect replacement of the Greek original text."[46] In effect, then, the *Biblia pentapla* was to provide an exact substitute for the original text. It would provide its readers with a transparent view of God's Word, one unobstructed by human ignorance. If Pietists generally sought to demolish "the entire theological doctrinal system," they did this not just by emphasizing the "emotionally productive elements" of Christianity, but also by making a post-theological Bible, one in which the faithful reader would find God's message to man in its starkest clarity.[47]

The *Biblia pentapla* offered *two* ways to make this post-theological Bible. As such, it stood at the crossroads of the two objective methods that radical Pietism used to transform Christianity's sacred texts. On the one hand, the *Biblia pentapla*—like the venerable scholarly tradition of the polyglot Bible—used

[45] [Johann Otto Glüsing], *Das Neue Testament*,)()(^{v}.

[46] Glüsing,)()(^{v}.

[47] Kaiser, *Pietismus und Patriotismus*, 7–8.

techniques of accumulation to weave a web fine enough to capture God's Word. As such, it was linked with the formal conventions of biblical scholarship as it developed in the sixteenth and seventeenth centuries (though unlike the Complutensian or Walton's English Polyglot, the *Biblia pentapla* was, to my knowledge, the first attempt to put this scholarly practice entirely into the vernacular domain). On the other hand, the *Biblia pentapla* offered a passage to God opened by a single translator—Johann Heinrich Reitz—who, with washed hands and baptized by the Holy Spirit, presented humanity with the exact essence of His Word. Reitz's translation guaranteed this access through its fidelity to the original manuscripts. It was a formal effort to re-create in their perfection the original manuscripts of the Bible, and more specifically the New Testament, by an obsessive insistence on literal translation. I will call these two different methods scholarly and linguistic objectivism. Both methods were key to the radical Pietist project to replace theology—long monopolized by orthodoxy—with a text whose meaning was perfectly reproduced for the reader. The history of the post-theological Bible and, indeed, the Enlightenment Bible more generally must therefore start here, at the far fringes of the radical religious underground inhabiting the early eighteenth century.

Linguistic Objectivism: The Quest for a Perfectly Literal Translation

The year 1703 was a bad one for orthodox guardians of the Luther Bible. "I can easily imagine that it will not please everyone," Caspar Triller laconically commented, and indeed his 1703 New Testament translation pleased almost no one.[48] The criticisms ran the gamut of theological invective: Thomas Ittig assured his readers that for the "Arian" Triller, "the saving teaching of the satisfaction of Christ and forgiveness of sin thus acquired . . . is a thorn in his eye"; the translation was banned in Lüneberg; Johann Fecht described Triller as "a corrector who was obscure, idle, and injurious to Luther and others"; and Georg Zeltner compared Triller to Penelope "unweaving . . . the web" of Luther's good work.[49] And 1703's second irritant—the New Testament of Johann Heinrich Reitz, featured translator of Glüsing's *Biblia Pentapla*—fared no better. Orthodox theologians accused the new translator of a swarm of more or less mortal heresies. Indifferentism, naturalism, fanaticism, Socinianism, Arianism, Nestorianism, acephalism, crypto-calvinism: the list went on. The

[48] Caspar Ernst Triller, "Vorrede," to *Eine mit dem Grund-Text genauen übereintreffende Ubersetzunge* [sic] *des Neuen Testaments* (Amsterdam [?], 1703), unpaginated.

[49] Thomas Ittig, preface to *Biblia, Das ist: Die gantze Heilige Schrifft Altes und Neues Testaments verteutscht durch D.Martin Luthern* (Leipzig, 1708), 15; Michael Lilienthal, *Biblisch-Exegetische Bibliothek* (Königsberg, 1739), 104; Fecht paraphrased in Jacob Friedrich Reimmann, *Catalogus Bibliothecae Theologicae, Systemato-Criticus* (Hildesheim, 1731), 319; Zeltner, *de novis bibliorum*, 62.

invective was fierce, but the threat was apparently real. For Triller and Reitz represented the nightmare of orthodoxy: the latter once a follower of Pietists Theodor Untereyck and Philip Spener, now a confirmed spiritualist; the former an ostensible Socinian but one whose translation made him, in the eyes of Valentin Löscher, a "hyper-Pietist" like Gottfried Arnold or Johann Petersen.[50] And if Triller's work fell onto largely deaf ears, Reitz's was received with applause, at least in some circles, and went through at least four editions by 1738, much to the dismay of the Leipzig book commission.[51]

Reading the 1703 translations would test the patience of any reasonable reader, especially any reader sitting far from the eighteenth century. For this reason, perhaps, scholars have paid them little heed, preferring the magisterial genius of Luther's literary opus to these apparently shabby and low imitations. And yet, literary quality was not at all the issue for these translators. Rather it was pointedly irrelevant to the translation project of radical Pietism, and so treating these texts from this perspective too quickly accedes to the views of their critics. Take, for example, the various versions of the Lord's Prayer, the most common prayer in Christianity, and the only one directly given by Jesus to his apostles. First, the well-known:

> Our Father who art in heaven, hallowed be thy name. Thy kingdom come. Thy will be done, on earth as it is in heaven. Give us this day our daily bread; And forgive us our debts, as we also have forgiven our debtors; And lead us not into temptation, but deliver us from evil.[52]

Here is Triller's version:

> Our Father who (you are) in the Heavens / let your name be holy / let your kingdom come / let your will be done as in heaven, so too on earth.

[50] Valentin Ernst Löscher, *The Complete Timotheus Verinus, Part Two*, trans. Robert J. Koester (1718; Milwaukee, 1998), 29. On Reitz, see Johann Goeters, "Der reformierte Pietismus in Deutschland 1650–1690," *Geschichte des Pietismus*, 1:241ff; see also his article "Der reformierte Pietismus in Bremen und am Niederrhein im 18. Jahrhundert," *Geschichte des Pietismus*, 2:372–427. Also see Rudolf Mohr, "Ein zu Unrecht vergessener Pietist: Johann Heinrich Reitz (1655–1720)," in *Monatshefte für evangelische Kirchengeschichte des Rheinlandes* 22 (1973): 46–109 and Agatha Kobuch, *Zensur und Aufklärung in Kursachsen: Ideologische Strömungen und politische Meinungen zur Zeit der sächsisch-polnischen Union (1697–1763)* (Weimar, 1988), 110–11. For a complete list of sources on Reitz, see Hans-Jürgen Schrader, *Literaturproduktion und Büchermarkt des radikalen Pietismus* (Göttingen, 1989), 570–78.

[51] On the reaction to the translation by Johannes Olearius, see Kobuch, *Zensur und Aufklärung*, 111.

[52] Luther's version: "Unser Vater in dem Himel. Dein Name werde geheiliget. Dein Reich kome. Dein Wille geschehe / auff Erden / wie im Himel. Unser teglich Brot gib uns heute. Und vergib uns unser Schulde / wie wir unsern Schüldigern vergeben. Und füre uns nicht in Versuchung. Sondern erlöse uns von dem Ubel. Denn dein ist das Reich / und die Krafft / und die Herrligkeit in Ewigkeit. Amen." All citations from the Luther Bible will come from: *Biblia: Das ist: Die gantze Heilige Schrifft/Deudsch/Auffs new zugericht*, ed. Hans Volz (1545; rpt. Munich, 1974). All English quotations are from the Revised Standard Edition (RSV).

> Give now us the bread essential for us (the bread that serves our essence) (επιουσιον) / and forgive us our debts / just as we forgive our debtors / and do not bring us into (do not give us up to) a temptation / rather redeem us from evil / for yours is the kingdom and the power / and the majesty in eternity. Amen.[53]

Even obscured by its 150-year-old orthography, Luther's version would still have been far more familiar than Triller's outlandish one. The differences were striking. In contrast to Luther's nine distinct sentences, Triller used only two, loading these with garlands of relative clauses. To make matters worse, Triller not only included the Greek επιουσιον ("for the coming day"), but also inserted three different parentheticals, which together destroyed the spoken rhythm of the passage. Ironically, then, Triller effectively silenced the most common prayer in the Christian tradition.

If Triller's translation of the Lord's Prayer replaced oral devotions with silent reading and reflection, these same qualities also shaped Reitz's work. Here is his Lord's Prayer:

> Our Father who (you are) in the Heavens / holy be your name / your kingdom come / your will be done as in heaven / so too on the earth. Our Bread that belongs to essence† / give us now. And forgive our debts / just as we also forgive our debtors. And do not bring us into temptation / rather save us from malice / since yours is the kingdom / and the power and majesty / in eternities. Amen.
>
> †is superessential[54]

Although Reitz gestured to oral usage—breaking up the prayer into four sentences, repeating some of Luther's familiar phrases—he too built a text designed principally to be read, opting for scholarly detail and, most striking of all, fidelity in translation over literary flow. This zeal to produce an absolutely literal translation was to become the governing impulse of much of the radical Pietist Bible project.

[53] The German reads: Unser Vater / der (**du bist**) in den Himmeln / dein Nahme werde geheiliget / dein Königreich sey. gekommen / dein Wille geschehe wie im Himmel auch auf der Erde. Unser (επιουσιον) zu wesentliche (**das zu unsern Wesen dienliche**)Brodt gib uns heute / und erlasse uns unsere Schulden / wie auch wir erlassen unsern Schuldigern / und bringe uns nicht hinein [*sic*] **übergib uns nicht**) in eine Versuchung / sondern erlöse uns von dem Bösen / denn dein ist das Königreich und die Macht / und die Herrligkeit in die Ewigkeiten Amen.

[54] The German reads: Unser Vater / der (du bist) in den Himmeln / geheiliget werde dein Name. Dein Königreich komme / dein Will geschehe wie im Himmel / also auch auf Erden. Unser Brod das † zum Wesen gehört / gib uns heut. u. erlass uns unsere schulden / gleich wie wir auch erlassen unsern schuldnern. U. bringe uns nicht in die Versuchung hinein / sondern errette uns von dem Argen / dan dein ist das Königreich/u. die Kraft u. die Herrlichkeit / in die Ewigkeiten / Amen. †überwesentlich ist

This desire had a long history. It can be traced back even before the New Testament was written, to the accounts of the fabled Greek translation of the Pentateuch. Philo of Alexandria's story of the seventy translators who, inspired by God, produce independent yet identical translations of the Torah, was prototypical for the inspirational model of biblical translation, one which retained the exact substance of the original transposed into a new language. In a sense, then, the inspired translation would be absolutely literal: every letter of the original would be perfectly reproduced in the new version. There would be no discrepancy between the two texts. And so when Jerome declared that in Holy Scripture "even the order of the words is a mystery," he was hearkening back to the sense that, in the case of the Bible, the inspired and the literal translation should coincide.[55] This literal-inspirational tradition was thus always an option for the biblical translator. But few seized on it with as much enthusiasm and vehemence as the early eighteenth-century Pietists. If Reitz was too modest to imagine that an "entirely perfect translation" might flow from his own pen, still he insisted that all good translations keep "the same expressions and words that the Holy Spirit used, and . . . as far as possible, translate word for word."[56] His mentor in matters literal was the "illuminated teacher Robert Gell," whose 1659 *Essays toward the Amendment of the last English-Translation of the Bible* had insisted that translators "preserve the *Letter of the Scripture intire* [*sic*]; how inconvenient, yea, how absurd soever it seem to our carnal reason." Only extreme literalism guaranteed access to "the Original tongues" and preserved the "*holy Spirit of God.*"[57] Reitz seized on Gell (whose work was published in Berleburg in 1723) and declared his intention to write an absolutely literal Bible, one whose very letters would reveal the Holy Spirit in its naked clarity.[58]

But literal translations posed some serious problems. On the one hand, they lacked what Triller called "elegant German." "If you really want to express the original," he insisted, "you cannot enter into [the realm] of elegant German very much."[59] So when he translated the first clause of the Lord's Prayer as "who (you are) in the Heavens (*Himmeln*)"—a thoroughly un-German usage, as the theologian Georg Zeltner pointed out—he was translating τοιζ ουρανοιζ, "in the heavens."[60] Keeping the original in its exact state demanded *incorrect* German usage: grace of expression was sacrificed on the altar of literal truth. On the

[55] Jerome, *Epistle LVII*, in Philip Schaff and Henry Wace, eds., *A Select Library of Nicene and Post-Nicene Fathers of the Christian Church*, 2nd series (Grand Rapids, MI, 1954), 6:113.

[56] Glüsing, *Biblia Pentapla*,)()(^{v}; Reitz, "Vorrede,")(3^{v}.

[57] Gell, *Essay toward Amendment*, a2^{r}, c3^{r}.

[58] On German usage of English devotional materials, see Edgar C. Mackenzie, "British Devotional Literature and the Rise of German Pietism" (Ph.D. diss., University of St. Andrews, 1984). On Gell and Pietism, see Brecht, "Die Berleburger Bibel: Hinweise zu ihrem Verständnis," *Pietismus und Neuzeit*, 8 (1982): 177.

[59] Triller, "Vorrede," unpaginated.

[60] Zeltner, *de novis bibliorum*, 73.

other hand, these clumsy translations represented a distinct theological position on the *claritas scripturae*, the clarity of Scripture. We preserve the Word of God in its entirety, Robert Gell earlier claimed:

> Because . . . even the most *literal text* . . . may, beside the *letter*, have also a *spiritual meaning*. And therefore when we meet with such seeming *unfruitful Scripture*, which affords not much matter in the *letter*, we may then judge, that, according to the *manifold wisdom of God*, there is a ground of some *more notable meaning* of the *Spirit*; as where *rich Mines* are, there the *surfaces of the earth* yields not much fruit.[61]

Where Lutherans traditionally emphasized scriptural clarity—for if Scripture was unclear, how could it serve as the foundation of a true faith?—it was the *obscurity* of biblical passages, produced by their subterranean significance, that piqued Gell's interest. Just where the text seemed most obscure, was where the greatest depths of content lay buried. The strictest kind of literalism, therefore, revealed these zones of significant obscurity without glossing them over in the name of sense. In this manner, Gell joined at the hip a strictly objective idea of the biblical text and that spiritual subjectivism so long associated with Pietism.

This combination of subjective aims and objective methods epitomized the radical Pietist treatments of the Bible in the early eighteenth century. All of them tried to put objective techniques into the service of a subjective and affective theology. "What we read, let us read so that . . . the words of David and the other holy men are made living in us," was Johann Petersen's description of this enterprise.[62] In Reitz's words, the inelegant German was a necessary feature of his translation: "God's words are always hard for natural men, who neither can grasp them nor can confine their reason to the school and simplicity of Christ." His theology, in other words, had literary ramifications. Unlike Luther, who sought to replace the Vulgate with a German text whose language would sound familiar to its readers, Reitz's goal was unfamiliarity. A completely legible Bible, one that mirrored absolutely God's words, would convey the peculiarity of the text.[63] At the outermost fringes of literalism, the inspired translator accessed the purest spiritualism.

This subversive program explains why the critics of these new translations obsessed about clumsy diction. "There is no good German in this translation,"[64] one grumbled; the translation was "not only unintelligible, but also obscure";[65] because "the sense of the original words is not translated into understandable German," the Bible itself would seem to be "an absurd book in the original

[61] Gell, *Essay toward Amendment*, A3[r-v].

[62] Johann Petersen, *Die Psalmen Davids* (Frankfurt, 1721),)()(3[r];

[63] Reitz, "Vorrede,")(4[r], (3[v].

[64] Lilienthal, *Biblisch-Exegetische Bibliothek*, 103–104.

[65] Johann Franciscus Buddeus, *Isagoge*, 1369.

version."[66] Theologian Georg Zeltner flung in Reitz's face the words of August Hermann Francke—the Bible "must be given to the Germans . . . such that their language does not seem foreign or incomprehensible."[67] "Who would not prefer to read the good, German, clear New Testament of Luther, rather than getting used to this New Testament, translated by Reitz with affected incomprehensibility?" asked Thomas Ittig in the preface to his 1708 Luther Bible.[68] This language of aesthetic distaste masked two pressing anxieties. First, theologians feared lest the Bible be made ridiculous, "rude and repellant" in the words of Jerome.[69] If the Bible sounds alien, if it becomes, in the words of Conyers Middleton, "*strange, awkward, and new*," then how could the common reader venerate it?[70] The ordinary reader would not, after all, perceive the the Greek text hiding behind the odd German diction. Instead the German would stand like a shroud over the meaning of the originals. Second, theologians feared lest this universal Bible unravel the entire enterprise of theology, which, if taken as a language of interpretation of God's Word, would have no further raison d'etre in the face of a perfectly clear Bible. After long owning the tools of interpretation, now orthodox theologians were facing the prospect of their final demotion.

In a paradoxical sense, then, the literal translators of radical Pietism tried to expose what biblical scholars had kept safely ensconced behind the walls of erudition. Like the Pietists, scholars had long known that the original texts were at times baffling and mysterious. Like the Pietists, scholars had long contended that objective (philological, historical) strategies could open a window onto the scriptures as they existed in antiquity. And like the Pietists too scholars had long used their objective strategies as a weapon against theological and dogmatic rigidity. But if these strategies were long kept away from the vernacular Bible, the Pietist translations—however inferior in their scholarly quality—launched them onto a very public stage. Hardly accomplished scholars themselves, still they made full use of scholarly tools: parenthetical elements, footnotes, alternative readings, and so on. Scholarship was never its own end: Reitz rejected the "dictionaries and philology" of "school-scholared critics" while Triller wanted only to correct the "dangerous errors" for the sake of the "salvation of souls."[71] But the tools of scholarship did serve their quest for an absolutely literal and wholly universal text. Triller's parentheticals both provided various alternative translations of the Greek and indicated where German was adding to the original materials. Reitz extended his notes to include some variant textual traditions. For 2 Pet. 1.19, for example, where the text reads: "And we have the firmer prophetic word," the note

[66] [Valentin Löscher], *Unschuldige Nachrichten* 3 (1703): 579, 581.

[67] Zeltner, *de novis bibliorum*, 71, 73.

[68] Thomas Ittig, "Vorrede,"):():():():(2.

[69] Jerome, *Epistle XXII, to Eustochium*, in *Nicene and Post-Nicene Fathers*, 6:35.

[70] Middleton, *Further Remarks*, 435.

[71] Reitz, Vorrede,)(3^{v}; Triller, "Vorrede," unpaginated.

read: "thus we have something firmer than the prophetic word." The latter possibility, smacking of fanaticism, was roundly condemned by Zeltner, Löscher, and others. Its significance, however, stemmed not so much from its theological provocation, but from the desire to encompass in the vernacular all of the possible variants in the original. Scholarship was yoked to the program of literal translation: together these would allow their work, in the words of Glüsing, to "serve as a perfect replacement of the Greek original text."[72] As such, these translations—ostensibly the very last German translations—would cut short the practice of theology. Anyone who could read the Bible would, after all, already have access to the Logos of God.

But of course, these were not the last translations. Instead, the literalist project was carried out to its bitter end by the radical Pietist translators who followed on the heels of Reitz and Triller. Indeed, the zeal for the perfect text reached its apotheosis and collapsed in two New Testaments published nearly simultaneously in the early 1730s. The more comprehensible was the product of the perverse mind of Johann Kayser, a follower of Jakob Böhme and an acquaintance of the alchemical enthusiast Friedrich Oetinger.[73] The flavor of his 1735 translation was hardly subtle, as in this passage from Romans (13.1–2):

> Any soul or man should be subject to the "ordained" authorities, which are raised up "over others, and over these have authority": because there is no "legitimate" authority, except from God; "that he instituted these either owing to his love or to his anger." But the legitimate authorities are ordained by God "for the good": "that one should be subject to them." Thus that whoever resists "this selfsame" authority, "and does not wish to be subjected," he resists "and struggles against" the decree of God: those however who resist "them," will incur "their" judgment; "and will be damned to the punishment for disobedience both by the authority and by God."[74]

Just as a comparison, the standard English version reads:

> Let every person be subject to the governing authorities. For there is no authority except from God, and those that exist have been instituted by God. Therefore he who resists the authorities resists what God has appointed, and those who resist will incur judgment.

[72] [Glüsing], *Das Neue Testament*,)()(v.

[73] One "Johannes Kaiser Serheimensis" entered Tübingen in 1697 (see *Die Matrikeln der Universität Tübingen Band 2 1600–1710*, ed. Albert Bürk und Wilhelm Wille [Tübingen, 1953], 442). On Kayser, see Max Goebel, "Geschichte der wahren Inspirations-Gemeinden, von 1688 bis 1854," *Zeitschrift für die historische Theologie* (1855): 355 and Albrecht Ritschl, *Geschichte des Pietismus* (Bonn, 1884), 2:365.

[74] Timotheus Philadelphus [Johann Kayser], *Das Neue Testament nach dem Buchstaben und buchstäblichen Verstand des Grund-Textes übersetzt* (1735).

Punctuated by repeated interpolations, Kayser's text afforded a translation and commentary in one package, here softening the real challenge of Paul's attitude toward authority, namely that it is always ordained by God. Kayser's apparently minor additions—that one is subject only to the ordained authority, that only *legitimate* authority stemmed from God—transformed Paul's conservatism into a religious radicalism.[75] As a critic of church authority, Kayser's subversions were understandable. As a reformer of the Bible, they were quite telling. For his interpolations were not precisely commentary, in the traditional sense. Indeed, by refusing to make a substantive distinction between commentary and translation, Kayser effectively merged the two. At times, in fact, the quotation marks used to signal commentary mysteriously disappeared, as above where the word "legitimate" was first marked as commentary, then integrated into the text without mark. The result was a seamless whole in which commentary—the traditional province of theology—fused with biblical idiom.

In Kayser's hands, then, Scripture was given the appearance of a self-interpreting text. You do not need a separate language of theology to understand the Bible, Kayser implicitly claimed, since his interwoven text already offered the universe of possible scriptural meanings. All commentaries, all interpretations, even the Greek original version, were replaced by a new, all-embracing biblical idiom. Moreover, through this idiom, Kayser strove to "awaken" the reader to the real "word of God." "The meaning of the spirit is . . . the true original text," Kayser insisted, since the "reborn layman understands the original text of the holy Scriptures better . . . than the most experienced master of worldly knowledge and language."[76] Once again, then, an objective textual technique or practice—that of interleaved translation—was yoked to spiritual subjectivism, and the effect was a Babel-like confusion, in which the most familiar text of all suddenly appeared alarmingly foreign.

These alienating effects paled in comparison, however, to those of Johann Jakob Junckherrott. Indeed, Junckherrott's 1732 translation brought the entire literalist paradigm of translation to its spectacular end. While Junckherrott was an obscure fellow, his Bible was the product of the Offenbach separatist milieu and embraced the literalist project with a zeal that practically leaped off the page.[77] Here is the same passage from Paul we saw above:

> All souls to essences *there* outside holding themselves *there* above should arrange themselves *there* underneath since *there* is no *there* outside essence not thus from God *there* the being *there* outside essences are arranged

[75] Interestingly, this passage was also given a similarly subversive meaning by Catholic reactionaries in eighteenth-century France: see Dale Van Kley, *The Religious Origins of the French Revolution: From Calvin to the Civil Constitution of the Clergy* (New Haven, 1996), 231.

[76] Kayser, *Das Neue Testament*,)(1^{v}, (3^{v}-)(4^{r}.

[77] For a mini-biography, see Friedrich Andrea Hallbauer, *Animadversiones theologicae in licentiam, novas easque germanicas Sacri Codicis versiones codendi* (Jena, 1741), 84–85.

> beneath the being of God. Thus whoever places themselves against it, places themselves against both the ordering itself of the *there* outside essence [and] *there* against the order of God *there* for it *there* through it, [and] *there* against themselves a judgment will be taken *therein*.
>
> [Alle seele weesenheiten da aushin habenden sich da drüberhin soll ordnen sich da unterhin dann nicht ist eine weesenheit da aushin so nicht von Gottes da die aber seyende da weesenheiten da aushin unter des Gottes seyende geordnet worden da sind da. Also beydes der ordnende sich der weesenheit da aushin da zugegenhin der des Gottes ordnung da fürhin da durchhin sich hat gestellt da zugegenhin die aber stellende sich da zugegenhin ihnen selbsten ein urtheil werden nehmen dahin].[78]

Rendering such a passage into English is obviously no easy task. At times, in fact, the German is utterly incomprehensible. But Junckherrott's refusal to acquiesce to the standards of orthography, punctuation, and syntax was crucial for the exact German replication of the Greek text. Translating Greek participles with German ones, Junckherrott strove to retain root meanings even where sense was thereby destroyed. The first clause, for example, translated the adjectival participle υπερεξουσαιζ (governing) as a full participial phrase, rather than (as Luther and everyone else had it) a simple adjective. He kept gerunds in their substantive form, rather than converting them to relative clauses, and gave precedence to etymological roots over actual meaning. Alongside his overbearing literalism, in addition, was his rhythmic interpolation of elements foreign to the Greek text, in particular huge quantities of the adverb *da*, "there." Such additions might seem antithetical to the absolutely literal translation, but only if one forgets that, as Junckherrott reminded us, Scripture has "two meanings, one is literal, and is suited to death, and the other is the meaning of the spirit, which is living." Anyone who "wants to make the dead letter living must . . . remove its particular context."[79] The adverbs enlivened the dead letter, gave the text a pulse. The fact that they were not actually present in the original text was not important if indeed, as Junckherrott believed, they served to animate the *real* original text, the "meaning of the spirit."

With Junckherrott the paradoxes of the literalism program blossomed into full flower. His New Testament was almost entirely incomprehensible. By making the single word the most fundamental unit of meaning, he successfully dissolved the meaning of its clauses, sentences, and verses. He obliterated German idiom in the name of resurrecting the living letter of the Greek, just as, at the same time, he destroyed the Greek text as a vehicle for meaningful communication. In the same breath as he rejected the dead letter, he fetishized the Greek word—the meaning of Scripture became wholly formal, bound to the

[78] Johann Jakob Junckherrott, *Das Neue Testament des HERRER Unser JESU Christi* (Offenbach, 1732), 452.

[79] Ibid., †a2.

arbitrary conventions of orthography and grammar. Given such destructive effects, it is no wonder that the conservative theologian Johann Goeze would call this "the only book in the world to which the proverb 'there is no book so bad . . . in which something good cannot be found' does not apply."[80] Beyond its eccentricities, however, this translation clearly marked the extremes that the literalist project—powered by religious conviction—would go to create a biblical text liberated of external control. Making the dead letter alive through formal means was a paradoxical program, but one with the highest goal: creating a Bible free from theology.

Scholarly Objectivism: The Biblical Encyclopedia

The same goal energized the greatest and most significant literary production of radical Pietism, the Berleburger Bible (1726–40). In place of literal translation, this latter monument embraced the other method of producing a universally legible text, the use of scholarly compilation. In contrast with the *Biblia pentapla*'s archive of German New Testaments, the Berleburger Bible was a veritable encyclopedia of biblical interpretation, whose contents ranged from allegorical spiritualism and numerology, to travel writings and anthropology. For the first time, too, these materials were presented entirely in the vernacular. The scholarship thus played a role consonant with the translation itself and was woven into the very practice of Bible translation. This combination of elements makes the Berleburger Bible a crucial link in the story of the Enlightenment Bible. The ties it established between enthusiastic theology and scholarly inquiry begin to clarify how the Enlightenment Bible was born.

The Berleburger Bible was a unique text. Most obviously, it was the first full translation of the entire German Bible since 1601 and it moved decisively away from the New Testament obsessions of the other Pietists.[81] Indeed, the bulk of its materials was dedicated to the Old Testament, which, by its very nature, brimmed with historical, anthropological, theological, and linguistic information, materials that lent themselves to the scholarly practices the Berleburger translators embraced. As a consequence, the Berleburger Bible was a simply massive text. Instead of the slim quartos and octavos of Reitz and Triller, it spanned eight folio volumes, topped over 8,000 pages, and took some sixteen years to complete. Such a monumental text could not be published on the fly. It needed money, a dedicated publisher, and the support of a benevolent prince, all of which it found in Berleburg, a magnet for religious separatists in

[80] Goeze quoted in Köster, "Bibelübersetzungen," 102.

[81] The exception to this was Heinrich Horche's *Mystische und Profetische Bibel* (Marburg, 1712), a Bible that I have excluded from my discussion because it is a commentary on the Luther Bible. On it, see Norbert Fehringer, "Philadelphia und Babel: Der hessische Pietist Heinrich Horche und das, Ideal des wahren Christentums" (Ph.D. diss., Universität Marburg/Lahn, 1971), 196–211.

the early eighteenth century and one of the centers of religious heterodoxy in the early eighteenth century. Like many of of his brethren, the director of this new translation, Johann Friedrich Haug, gravitated to this community of religious radicals, creating there—with the essential help of his family's printing shop—a fertile environment for separatist and philadelphian heresies.[82]

If you only read the preface, you might think that the Berleburger Bible was simply the latest incarnation of the older Pietist translations. Like earlier radicals, Haug stressed that the "Holy Scriptures should have not a double or triple meaning, rather a single meaning." The various strategies of interpretation—literal, spiritual, prophetic—together revealed not different levels of meaning, but "only one divine meaning," which embraced and comprehended within itself all apparent variety. All differences would be resolved within one text, just "as a man, though he consists of body, soul, and spirit, is and remains not three men, but only one." The goal of the work, then, was to reveal this meaning, "not to introduce new teachings, but to extol the old and new message of love." Such a revelation was particularly necessary "in these final days, when the light dims and door of secrets opens," when "we believe no longer in this or that witness . . . but are ourselves convinced" of the truths of God.[83] In its philosophy and its awkward German, the Berleburger Bible thus looked much like the ordinary fare of radical Pietism.

But open the text further, and these superficial resemblances evaporate. Packed onto each page of the Berleburger Bible were reams of commentary, printed in two columns of tiny font, atop which floated a thin layer of biblical text. The commentary pulsed with theological, historical, genealogical, chronological, allegorical, and numerological details gathered together apparently at random. Citations sprawled all over the early modern intellectual map: from the ancients to the moderns, from Thucydides, Herodotus, Plato, Josephus, and Origen to Johann Reuchlin, Athanasius Kirchner, Hugo Grotius, Brian Walton, and Isaac Vossius.[84] Spanning genres, references included geographical information, philological and historical commentary, philosophical musings, numerological data, and more straightforwardly mystical writings. What was true of Johann David Michaelis's 1769 translation—that the translation itself "must be seen as the side show [and] the notes in contrast as the

[82] See Martin Hofmann, "Theologie und Exegese der Berleburger Bibel (1726–1742)," *Beiträge zur Förderung christlicher Theologie* 39 (1937). See also Josef Urlinger, "Die geistes- und sprachgeschichtliche Bedeutung der Berleberger Bibel: Ein Beitrag zur Wirkungsgeschichte des Quietismus in Deutschland" (Ph.D. diss., Universität Saarland, 1969); Brecht, "Die Berleburger Bibel"; Kobuch, *Zensur und Aufklärung*, 112–14; and Hans-Jürgen Schrader, "Pietistisches Publizieren unter Heterodoxieverdacht: Der Zensurfall 'Berleburger Bibel,'" in Herbert Göpfert and Erdmann Weyrauch, eds., *"Unmoralisch an sich"*. . . *Zensur im 18. und 19. Jahrhundert* (Wiesbaden, 1988), 61–80.

[83] [Haug], *Die Heilige Schrift Altes und Neues Testaments/nach dem Grund-Text aufs neue übersehen und übersetzet* (Berlenberg, 1726),)(3^{v}, (4^{r}.

[84] For a fuller list, see Urlinger, "Berleburger Bibel," 50–75.

immensely rich centerpiece"—was, if anything, more applicable to the Berleburger Bible.[85]

The Berleburger Bible, therefore, stepped boldly onto the path of scholarship. Its goal was to produce the perfect translation solely by means of accumulation, by arranging all the information any reader might need to make sense of the Bible, and subsuming it within an ostensibly unifying spiritualist commentary. More than anything, this new monumental Bible resembled that signpost of ostensible modernity, Pierre Bayle's *Dictionnaire historique et critique*, rendered in spiritualized prose. Apparently the resemblance between the Berleburgers and this hero of Enlightenment skepticism was not lost on the editor of the *Auserlesene Theologische Bibliothek*, who linked them explicitly, albeit ironically. His attack on the Berleburger Bible was couched in the language of Bayle, specifically the article "Aaron," which castigated "a certain Bible translation, which he called a cunning and plagiarized (*obreptice & subreptice*) Version . . . recalling in the meantime that the simple and ignorant would be able to protect themselves less than the intelligent and knowledgeable." Like Bayle's "certain translation," the editor argued, the Berleburger Bible was not "a work for all people, in all classes," largely because of the glosses.[86] Using Bayle to criticize the Berleburger Bible was a rhetorically amusing strategy. Bayle, after all, was one of the chief bogeymen of the orthodox, both in France and abroad. A Huguenot who spent much of his life in the Netherlands, Bayle found his works, including the 1697 *Dictionnaire* and the 1686 *Commentaire philosophique*, banned across Catholic Europe and found himself saddled with a reputation as a coddler of atheists. Though contemporary scholars disagree whether Bayle himself leaned toward the atheism he comforted, nonetheless, as Jonathan Israel has recently argued, he certainly *looked* like a dangerous freethinker to the religiously orthodox (and even radical) of the day.[87] So the association of Bayle and Berleburg was one replete with sarcastic and critical intent.

But if sarcastic, still the two works did share remarkable similarities, especially in their formal modes of presentation. Take, for example, the innocuous verse of Leviticus: "In this year of jubilee each of you shall return to his property" (25.13). Haug underwrote it with a comprehensive explication, using cabalistic numerology, mystic theology, and chronology to unfold its subtle secrets, and reading it as a hint of "the great restoration of all rational creatures" to come at the end of the seventh jubilee (fig. 5).[88] The explanation of the system

[85] Johann Eichhorn, "Johann David Michaelis: Einige Bemerkungen über seine litterarischen Character," *Allgemeine Bibliothek der biblischen Literatur* 3(1791): 886. See also Dieter Gutzen, "Bemerkungen zur Bibelübersetzung des Johann David Michaelis," *Was Dolmetschen fur Kunst und Erbeit sey: Beiträge zur Geschichte der deutschen Bibelübersetzung*, ed. Heimo Reinizter (Hamburg, 1982), 76.

[86] [Johann Christoph Colerus, ed.], *Auserlesene Theologische Bibliothek* (Leipzig, 1727), number 22:917.

[87] Israel, *Radical Enlightenment*, 339–40; for a vision of Bayle as a fideist, see Elizabeth Labrousse, *Pierre Bayle*, 2 vols. (The Hague, 1963–4).

[88] [Haug], *Heilige Schrift*, 1:544.

544 **Das III. Buch Moseh.** **Cap. XXV.**

13. In diesem Jubel-Jahr sollt ihr ein ieder zu seiner Haabe wieder kommen.

14. Wann

Wie nun hierinnen das Jubel-Jahr und Sabbath- oder Erlaß-Jahr einander gleich waren/ also waren sie hinwiederum in andern Dingen unterschieden. Denn im Jubel-Jahr kam ein ieglicher wieder zu seiner Haabe und zu dem Seinigen/ welches im Erlaß-Jahr nicht geschahe.

Hier aber möchten wir wol ausrufen: O welch eine Tiefe der Weißheit und Erkenntniß GOttes! Denn die Geheimnisse sind sehr gros/ welche hierunter verborgen liegen/ die GOtt der HErr in dieser letzten Zeit/ da die 6 grosen Werck-Tage zu Ende lauffen/ denen Kindern der Weißheit mit Macht eröffnen/ und/ gleichwie er im 6ten Jahr seinen Segen doppelt gegeben/ also auch in dieser 6ten grosen Zeit den Reichthum seiner Erkenntniß mit vielem Segen ausstürtzen wird/ so daß viele über die Geheimnisse der Schrifft kommen/ und grosen Verstand darinnen finden sollen. Aus welcher reichen Erkenntniß man dann eben auch soviel zurückschliessen kan/ daß demnach die letzte Zeiten vorhanden seyen. Dann GOtt verringert sich nicht in Eröffnung seiner Wunder/ sondern kommt damit immer herrlicher und herrlicher hervor: da hergegen der Feind seine Wercke gros anfängt/ womit es doch zuletzt auf ein Lami ausgehet.

Zuvorderst ist denn in diesem Jahr den Glaubigen diß grose Geheimniß vorgestellt worden/ wie es nun viele erleuchtete Seelen in unseren Zeiten also einsehen/ daß hiermit auf die grose Wiederbringung aller vernünfftigen Geschöpffe gesehen werde/ daß dieselbe nach dem Verlauff von sieben Ewigkeiten/ deren Währung GOtt allein bekannt ist/ und in deren ieder eine Ruhe sich offenbahren wird vor Seelen/ die in der Mühseligkeit und Elend gesteckt haben/ sich alsdann gantz allgemein erstrecken werde; daß dann mit Nachdruck GOtt wird alles in allen seyn/ 1. Cor. 15/28. und also ein ieder wieder zur Besitzung GOttes/ als seines Ursprungs/ kommen wird: womit er dann auch wieder zu seiner väterlichen Haabe der ewigen Glückseligkeit im Himmel und zur Freyheit der Kinder GOttes gelangen wird; wann er erst mit dem verlohrnen Sohn die Träbern mit den Säuen/ den unreinen Geistern/ wird in der Hölle in den Pein-Ewigkeiten geschmäckt haben. Luc. 15/16.

Es ist auch bedencklich/ daß das erste Jubel-Jahr nach diesem Gesetz ungefähr in das 2500ste Jahr von Erschaffung der Welt eingefallen: da dann schon 50 Jubel-Jahre waren vorbey-gegangen: welches zeiget/ wie die Jahre bey GOtt gar eigentlich werden abgemessen seyn/ da alles zu seiner Zeit geschehen wird; wie dann auch diese grose allgemeine Versöhnung/ als das Ende und Beschluß aller der Wercke GOttes/ alsdann geschehen wird/ wann mit Nachdruck wird erfüllt werden/ daß Christus geworden die Versöhnung für der gantzen Welt Sünden. 1. Joh. 2/2. Daher dann auch dieses Jubel-Jahr auf den grosen Versöhnungs-Tag ausposaunet wurde und zugleich seinen Anfang nahm. Und

Warum wird das für unglaublich bey vielen gerechnet/ was hier so geheimnißreich enthalten/ und von einigen erleuchteten und fleissigen Schrifft-Forschern so glaubwürdig entdecket worden? Daß nämlich in dieser heiligen Sieben-Zahl nach dem tiefen Sinn und der Multiplication oder fortgängigen Vermehrung die Zeiten der Ewigkeiten und die gantze Währung bis zur gäntzlichen Wiederbringung der gantzen Schöpffung verborgen liege.

Es ist ja unstreitig/ daß das Gesetz geistlich ist; oder soll zum wenigsten unstreitig seyn/ wie auch Paulus glaubte: Röm. 7/14. und daß folglich auch unter allen dessen vorbildlichen Dingen grose Geheimnisse verborgen liegen.

So sind es nun auch gute und heilige unverwerffliche Gedancken/ welche gantz gewiß mit der Glaubens-Aehnlichkeit gar wol übereinkommen/ wann einige dafürhalten/ daß in der Ewigkeit/ die gewisse abgetheilte und bestimmte Währungen in sich begreifft/ der völlige Reinigungs-Circkel der gantzen Creatur vorgebildet/ und einem grosen Sabbath-Jahr von 7mal 7000 Jahren/ die also 49000 Jahre ausmachen/ gleichen werde/ bis auf das grose Jubel-Jahr/ das 50000ste/ da ein ieder wieder zu seiner Haab und Erbtheil kommen solle.

Wie aber diese Zeiten und Jahre zu rechnen/ das begehrt man sich nicht herauszunehmen zu determiniren/ sondern will hier nur mit verhoffender Genehmhaltung des billigen Lesers/ und Bitte um diese Billigkeit in der Aufnahme/ die da alles zur Prüfung vor sich kommen läßt/ ob sie gleich nur das Gute zu behalten schuldig ist/ die Gedancken eines geheimen Philosophi(a) die man selber auch im übrigen an seinem Orte stehen lässet/ hiervon noch über diesen Text beyfügen/ nach dessen Erklärung diese Sieben-Zahl und Ewigkeiten-Währung bis aufs Jubel-Jahr in sich hält fünff Millionen siebenhundert vier und sechzig tausend achthundert und ein Jahr/ nach hierbey folgender Rechnung;

7
7
1 ————
49
7
2 ————
343
7
3 ————
2401
7
4 ————
16807
7
5 ————
117649
7
6 ————
823543
7
————
5764801

” da nämlich nach fünffzigmal-hunderttausend/ als dem grosen Hall- und Jubel-Jahr/ und wiederum siebenhundert tausend Jahren*/ nach und nach alle menschliche Creaturen/ so in der Verdammniß gelegen/ wiederum zu ihrer Haabe und ihrem ewigen Erbe gelangen werden. In den übrigen vier und sechzig tausend und achthundert Jahren aber die gefallenen Engel. In dem letzten Einen Jahr aber wird (nach der Einsicht dieses Autoris) der gefallene Sohn der Morgenröthe (der Lucifer)/ als der Ursprung alles Verderbens/ in der allerletzten und grausamsten Qual und gäntzlichen Verlassenheit von allen verdammten Menschen und bösen Geistern/ gantz blos und allein stehen/ und das Leiden und die Qual der gantzen Creatur in gantz-unermeßlichem Grimm und unergründlicher Marter ausstehen müssen/ und recht fühlen/ was es sey/ von der Quelle des Lichts und Lebens abgeschieden und gantz allein zu seyn: bis er endlich seine Bosheit und Fall erkenne/ und nach der niemals-aufhörenden göttlichen Barmhertzigkeit in JEsu Christo dürste/ und also auch wiederum zu Gnaden/ zu seiner Haab und Erbe/ zu seiner ersten Herrschafft/ Licht und Herrlichkeit/ gelange; und also vollendet werden die bestimmten Geheimnisse dieser Haushaltung/ da GOtt alles in allem/ der Teufel aber nicht mehr seyn/ noch der Tod und die Hölle gefunden werden/ sondern in dieser wundervollen Umkehrung alles wiederum vollkömmlich gereinigt/ und auf dem Ruhe-Punct/ das ist/ in GOtt/ immer und ohn einziges Aufhören/ alle Freude und Seligkeit geniessen und dero theilhafftig bleiben wird. Denn

” Daß dergleichen grose Zeiten der bestimmten Qual seyn müssen/ gibt der heilige Text anderswo genugsam zu erkennen/ da in demselben sooft gefunden wird von Ewigkeit in die Ewigkeiten/ oder von den Zeiten in die Zeiten/ das ist/ in einer unbegreifflichen Folge. Da aus der öfftern Wiederholung dieser erschröcklichen Worte genugsam zu schliessen/ daß dem also seyn müsse.

” Weil aber diese Zeiten nicht anderst als in den Zahlen begreifflich und auszusprechen sind; die Zeichen aber/ so da wirken den Unterscheid Tages und Nacht/ auch aller Jahre und Zeiten/ alsdenn nicht mehr seyn werden/ so können wir auch durch diese unsere vergängliche Zeiten keinen rechten Begriff dieser bestimmten Zeiten und Ewigkeiten haben.

v. 14.

(a) Aut. Operis Mago-Cabbalist. & Theosoph. Cap. 6. P. 1.

* ” Niemand irre sich hiebey/ als ob man just solche irdische Jahre und Zeiten verstünde/ wie wir ietzo haben. Man muß sich aber eines begreifflichen Wortes bedienen/ weil man nicht finden kan/ wo nach Zerstörung unserer sichtbaren vergänglichen Welt in dem neuen Jerusalem ein anderes/ um die Währung der Verdammniß zu bestimmen/ seye.

Figure 5. Lev. 25.13 from the Berleburger Bible, 1726. Courtesy of the Bethany Theological Seminary.

of jubilees was confused, however. It was not, for instance, clear how to calculate the date of the great jubilee. First, it seemed possible that there was one jubilee every 50 years (per Lev. 25.8–12), meaning the great jubilee was long gone. Alternatively, one might reckon the great jubilee came only after "a great Sabbath Year of seven times 7000 years, which makes 49000," in which case the great jubilee might last 8,000 years or 1,000 years, depending on whether it coincided with the seventh jubilee, or began only after it was finished. Finally one could, per one "secret philosopher," calculate the Sabbath Year exponentially. This put the great jubilee some 132,256 years in the future (figuring, as Haug did, the world to be about 5,000 years old), but lasting a good long time: at minimum 823,543 years, but ranging to a maximum of 5,764,801 years. All of these were dubious, however, since "these dates are only comprehensible and expressible in the numbers, and the signs, which cause the difference between night and day, and between years and ages, will at that point no longer exist; thus we cannot in these, our fleeting times, have any correct concept of these determined ages and eternities." We might at this point sympathize with the *Fortgesetzte Sammlung*, which picked this commentary as a prime example of what was obfuscatory, "erroneous, and misleading in the Berleburger Bible."[89] What the commentary might mean was, after all, nearly impenetrable. Generally speaking, the muddled point seemed to be that despite the multiple datings of the final jubilee, in the final analysis numerology was meaningless. And such doubling and dizzying effects of the annotations were common in the Berleburger Bible. Indeed the very form of the annotations promoted these vertiginous results, where everything was clear enough at the outset but quickly spun out of control. Annotations doubled up on the page, sometimes supporting but often contradicting one another, and the result was a continuous subterranean dialogue filled with inexplicable argumentative turns and reverses.

Such effects dramatically marked the commentary to Exod. 32.15, when Moses comes down from the mountain carrying two tablets inscribed with the Ten Commandments (fig. 6). Three different layers of notes worked in this text: parallel references (to Exod. 31.18, 34.29), commentary, and notes to the commentary. The commentary concentrated on the inscription of the commandments on the tablets. On the one hand, perhaps "the two tables were like two pages of a book, which one holds together, and moves from one across to the other when reading." Or, it is possible "that the Law was doubly inscribed, such that when Moses held the tables in his hand . . . he had the complete Ten Commandments in front of himself on each side, and the people standing opposing him on the other side could thus read them completely." Assuming the first to be true, as Haug tentatively did, how were the commandments distributed on the tablets? Some authorities (including Philo and Josephus), Haug tells us, thought there must be five on each tablet. Others, like St. Augustine,

[89] *Fortgesetzte Sammlung* (1727) 6:1175.

Cap. XXXII. Das II. Buch Moseh. 403

14. Da gereuete es den HErrn; wegen des Uebels / das er geredet hatte seinem Volck zu thun.
15. Und Moseh wandte sich und stieg
von dem Berge hinab / mit den zwo Tafeln (a) des Zeugnisses in seiner Hand.
Die Tafeln waren auf ihren beyden Seiten geschrieben: auf dieß- und auf jen-
seits waren sie geschrieben. (a) c. 31/18. 34/29.
16. Und die Tafeln die waren ein
Werck GOttes / und die Schrifft das
war GOttes Schrifft / so in die Tafeln
gegraben war. c. 24/12. 2. Cor. 3/7.
17. Und Josua hörete das Geschrey
des Volcks / da sie jauchzeten / und er
sprach zu Moseh: Es ist ein Geschrey
eines Streits in dem Lager.
18. Er aber sprach: Es ist nicht ein
Geschrey wie man beym Sieg ruft / noch
ein Geschrey wie man bey der Niederla-
ge ruft. Ich höre ein Geschrey eines
Singens um einander.
19. Und es geschah / als er nahe zum Lager kam / und das Kalb und die Reigen
sahe; da entbrannte der Zorn Moseh /
und warf die Tafeln aus seinen Händen /
und zerbrach sie unten an dem Berge.
20. Und er nahm das Kalb das sie
gemacht hatten / und verbrannts in dem
Feuer / und zermahlte es / bis daß es zu
Pulver wurde / und sträute es aufs
Wasser / und gabs den Kindern Israel
zu trincken. 21. Und

v. 14. Aber ach was ist das nicht für eine Güte GOttes / auf das einzige Wort eines seiner Knechte die gerechte Rache aufzuhalten! wann er nemlich vernichtiget ist / nichts eigenes besitzet / und in allen Dingen die Ehre GOttes allein zum Zweck hat. Und

Wir sehen zugleich hierin / wie alle Verheissungen und Dräuungen Bedingungs-weise geschehen / daß der Mensch durch jene nicht sicher werde / und bey diesen auch nicht verzweifele / sondern sich aufs Flehen begebe / welches ein Groses / auch für andere / vermag / wann es ernstlich ist. Jac. 5/16. &c. Und die Menschen sollten erkennen / was sie an einem sonderbaren Freund GOttes vor einen grosen Schatz und Beschützer unter sich hätten; daß sie solche doch in Ehren halten mögten. Siehe 5. Mos. 9/12. &c. 4. Mos. 14/11. &c.

v. 15. Es werden hier die Tafeln beschrieben / daß sie auf ihren beyden Seiten geschrieben gewesen: welches man so begreiffen kan / daß die zwey Tafeln wie zwey Blätter eines Buchs gewesen / die man zusammenlegt / und von einer Seite zur andern übergehet wann man lieset / welches die Bedeutung des Worts Seite hier ausdrucken mag; und daß also auf der einen Seite oder Blat die ersten vier Gebote von der Liebe GOttes / und auf dem andern die sechs übrigen Gebote von der Liebe des Nächsten / beschrieben gewesen. Und ist es wahrscheinlich / daß sie so künstlich mögen zusammengefüget gewesen seyn / daß man solche zwey Tafeln hat zusammenlegen / und also auf- und zumachen können / als 2 Blätter in folio, daß es also 4 Seiten gewesen wären.

Doch will anderen wahrscheinlicher vorkommen / daß das Gesetz doppelt eingegraben gewesen / also daß / wann Moseh die Tafeln in der Hand hielte / ehe sie in die Lade des Bundes verwahrlich beygeleget worden / er die 10 Gebote auf einer Seite vollkömmlich vor sich gehabt / und das Volck so gegen ihm stund dieselben auf der andern Seite auch gantz habe lesen können.

Wenn aber die Tafeln in- und auswendig beschrieben gewesen / so mögte doch die erstere Meynung vorzuziehen seyn.

Indessen ist sich dabey nicht so sehr aufzuhalten / als vielmehr auf das zu sehen / was zu bemercken gegeben werde in den

Beyden Seiten) Nämlich die Liebe soll doppelt seyn gegen GOtt und gegen den Nächsten; und nach beyden Theilen / Leib und Seele / bewiesen und ausgeübt werden.

Wie die 10 Gebote darauf eingetheilt gewesen / darüber ist sonst auch viel Fragens und Disputirens unter den Gelehrten und verschiedenen Religions-Verwandten. Philo (a), Josephus (b), und R. Jud. Leo (c), wollen / daß auf ieglicher Tafel 5 Gebote gewesen. Andere setzen wahrscheinlicher 4 auf eine / und 6 auf die andere; weil die ersteren in mehr Worten die letzteren aber kürtzer verfaßt sind. Doch noch andere geben der ersten auch nur 3 / der anderen aber 7 / und berufen sich auf die hebräischen Accente / welche selbst solche Eintheilung anhandzugeben schienen. Wie dann auch so alles in eine Zahl der Vollkommenheit gefaßt ist: 10 / 3 und 7. Die erste Tafel hat auch so ihre Absicht auf die H. Drey-Einigkeit: also daß das erste insonderheit auf den Vater / das ander auf den Sohn / das dritte auf den H. Geist / zielet (d). In eben solcher Ordnung kan auch das 4te aus dem ersten / das 5te aus dem andern / das 6te aus dem 3ten / hergeleitet werden. Wiederum hat das 7de mit dem ersten und vierten / das 8te mit dem andern und fünfften / das 9te aber mit dem 3ten und 6ten / ihre genaue Verwandschafft. Das 10de endlich ist ein solch Gebot / in welches ein iegliches der übrigen hinein- und welches in alle übrige wieder zuruckfliesset. Also:

1 -- 2 -- 3
4 -- 5 -- 6
7 -- 8 -- 9
10

Hingegen führen die so sie in 4 und 6 eintheilen auch ihre Gründe an / und haben nichtweniger verschiedene Patres, als z. E. Athanasium (e), Chrysostomum (f), Ambrosium (g), vor sich.

Allein / ist es denn auch der Müh werth / daß man darüber streitet? Liesse man nur Christum durch seinen Geist den Gehorsam wircken / welchen das Gesetz fordert / und im Glauben von uns erhalten kan; so mögte man im übrigen die Abtheilung machen wie man wollte. Hingegen mag man 3 zur ersten / und 7 zur andern / oder 4 zur ersten und 6 zur andern / zählen; wenn man nicht im Leben damit übereinstimmt / so ist alles eitel und nichts.

v. 16. In die Tafeln gegraben) Mit schwartzen Assyrischen Buchstaben / sagen die Hebräer; welches andere von der heutigen Hebräischen Schrifft auslegen.

Es ist aber vielmehr darauf zu sehen / daß diese erste Tafeln und deren Beschreibung gar eigentlich GOttes anfängliches Ebenbild im Menschen vorstellen / welches ja freylich ein Werck GOttes und auch GOttes Schrifft war.

v. 19. Da Moseh das Kalb erblicket / hat er aus gerechtem Eifer für GOttes Ehre / und auch ohne Zweiffel aus göttlichem Trieb / die Tafeln vor ihren Augen zur Erden geworffen und zerbrochen. 5. Mos. 9/17.

Die Zerbrechung der Tafeln bildet den Fall des Menschen und die Zerstörung des göttlichen Ebenbilds ab.

v. 20. Verbrannts -- zermahlte es zu Pulver) Daraus wird geschlossen / daß er ein guter Chymicus müsse gewesen seyn.

Gabs den Kindern Israel zu trincken) Die Hebräer halten davor / daß diß Wasser eben die Wirckung gehabt / daß den Schuldigen die Hüffte geschwunden / und der Bauch geschwollen / wie das bittere Wasser. (a)

(a) *Wagens.* not. 6. ad Mischn. Sot. c. 3. sect. 4. *Bochart.* hieroz. part. 1. l. 2. c. 34.

Eee 2 v. 21.

(a) Lib. de Decal. p. 579. (b) Antiq. l. 3. c. 6. (c) de templo l. 3. c. 1. §. 4. (d) vid. Augustin. quæst. in V. T. l. 2. Tom. 4. & in Libr. de decem chordis c. 5. 6. Tom. 9. (e) Synops. S. ad Exod. (f) Tract. in c. 25. Matth. hom. 51. (g) in c. 6. ad Ephes.

Figure 6. Exod. 32.15 from the Berleburger Bible, 1726. Courtesy of the Bethany Theological Seminary.

thought the distribution ought to be three and seven, in which "the first table has its purpose in the Holy Trinity . . . [and] in such an order the fourth could be derived from the first, the fifth from the second, the sixth from the third . . . [and thus] the seventh has a genuine relation to the first and third, the eighth with the second and fifth, the ninth with the third and sixth." The tenth would then provide a capstone to the whole process. Still other authorities, like Athanasius, Chrysostom, and Ambrosius, determined the pattern to be four and six. But after laying out this welter of different ideas, Haug brusquely dismissed them all: "one can count three on the first and seven on the second, or four on the first and six on the second: if one doesn't thereby harmonize with life, everything is vain and nothing."[90]

After threading your way through the page of argument, only to wind up at this facile truism, it is tempting to say, along with the editor of the *Fortgesetzte Sammlung*, that "I wish that this commentary was as orderly, understandable, and inoffensive as it is wide-ranging."[91] Indeed, eighteenth-century theologians were confused about how to respond to this monumental collage. "Negative" might sum up the reactions, which called for its prohibition, demanded its "poison and imbecility" be revealed, lamented that it "often departs without any reason from Luther's version," that it appeared "very affected and in many places . . . very ungerman," and labeled its authors libertines, Donatists, and Müntzerites.[92] Modern scholars have been similarly unsure how to reconcile the scholarly apparatus with the spiritualist aspirations of the work. But, as we have seen, this combination of subjective religion and objective textual practices was not unusual in this period. It would be shortsighted, for example, to argue that the scholarship "seems like a foreign presence in the overall context."[93] Nor is it helpful to dismiss the "variety and richness" of the Berleburger Bible in favor of its "consistent work of [theological] interpretation": this is only to write off its enormous work of scholarship and so to sacrifice the very qualities that made it unique.[94]

Instead, for a revealing description of the book, we might look to Ernst Cassirer:

> there is no hierarchy of concepts, no deductive derivation of one concept, but rather a simple aggregation of materials, each of which is as significant as any other and shares with it an equal claim to complete and exhaustive treatment. . . . he never follows a definite plan assigning limits to the various types of material and distinguishing the important from the unimportant, the relevant from the irrelevant.[95]

[90] [Haug], *Heilige Schrift*, 1:403.

[91] *Fortgesetzte Sammlung* (1727) 6:1166.

[92] *Fortgesetzte Sammlung* (1727) 6:1176; *Fortgesetzte Sammlung* (1736): 6:701, 702.

[93] Hofmann, "Theologie der Berleburger Bibel," 200.

[94] Brecht, "Die Berleburger Bibel," 199.

[95] Ernst Cassirer, *The Philosophy of the Enlightenment* (Boston, 1951), 202.

Cassirer was not describing the Berleburger Bible, of course, but Bayle's *Dictionnaire*. The article "Aaron"—used as the stick to beat the Berleburgers—and its convoluted discussion of the Golden Calf fit Cassirer's bill perfectly. Some, Bayle wrote, "believe that Aaron did not make an entire calf, but only a head." Others said that the "powder of the Golden Calf" was placed on the beards of worshipers as a "special mark." This second, apparently irrelevant issue occasioned a ramble through sixteenth-century Bible translations, seventeenth-century criticisms of them, and oblique jabs at scholarship, which—like the Golden Calf—shows how the educated "can keep themselves from snares, while the ignorant cannot." Even this ostensibly clear point disintegrated, finally, in Bayle's conclusion that the gilded beards were mere "rabbinic" fantasy, showing how even the learned were quite incapable of avoiding delusion.[96]

If Bayle's dictionary was "the Bible of the eighteenth century," it had much in common with the Bible of the radical Pietists, especially insofar as both fetishized formal techniques of presentation.[97] In both, the accumulation of detail had an apparently spontaneous and accidental character. It was not governed by any apparent overarching theme, or directed to any apparent single point. Thus the account in "Aaron" moved quickly from this translation to a discussion of the combustibility of the Golden Calf, the artistic ability of Aaron, and so on. Bayle's dictionary worked through a series of asides, which separately made sense, but taken together never combined into a single message: it was, in Oscar Kenshur's words, a "skeptical journey" whose essence is "precisely that one never arrives."[98] The Berleburger Bible embarked on a similar journey, one that looped through "Hebrew and rabbinic literature . . . the cabalism . . . travel descriptions . . . geographic, scientific, and chronological investigations, [and] lexica," wandering through fields of information in a distributed, unhierarchical manner.[99]

What was the effect of such disorder? In the first instance, it led almost inevitably to accusations of plagiarism, accusations that both Haug and Bayle confronted with remarkably similar language. In his 1726 Pentateuch preface, for example, Haug insisted that:

> since I gladly confess that I have taken much from other instructive and spiritual theologians of all stripes and religions, and sought only to take the kernel from them . . . [thus] I did not always stick precisely to their words, even less did I plagiarize or steal their scholarly position. . . . In this manner service will be provided to many, that they will find here collected what otherwise is scattered here and there in many books.[100]

[96] Pierre Bayle, *Dictionnaire Historique et Critique*, 3rd ed. (Rotterdam, 1720), s.v. "Aaron."

[97] Ruth Whelan, *The Anatomy of Superstition: A Study of the Historical Theory and Practice of Pierre Bayle* (Oxford, 1989), 10. On Berleburg and Bayle, see my "Enigma of Secularization," 1077–80.

[98] Oscar Kenshur, "Pierre Bayle and the Structures of Doubt," *Eighteenth-Century Studies* 21 (Spring 1988): 300.

[99] Hofmann, "Theologie der Berleburger Bibel," 200.

[100] [Haug], preface to *Die Heilige Schrift* (1726),)(4r.

Bayle deployed a similarly bibliographical defense:

> I considered that a work like this one should serve in place of a library. . . . Many, who love the sciences, do not have the means of acquiring books; others do not have the leisure of consulting the fiftieth part of the volumes they've bought. . . . I put this together so that they might see at the same time the historical facts, and the proofs of these facts, along with an assortment of discussions and circumstances.[101]

In both cases, then, here was an explicit admission that the issue was less one of theological or philosophical unity, than one of formal, almost bibliographical unity. The idea was, for both quasi-encyclopedists, to collect what was scattered, to assemble it in one place, to place it before the readers, and, in doing so, to make whole what was lost. Just as Bayle's *Dictionnaire*, or the later French *Encyclopédie*, was arranged only by the arbitrary letters of the alphabet rather than by type or scheme, the Berleburger Bible contained essential incoherencies between levels of interpretation (spiritual, physical, literal) that were given systematic form only by the arbitrary arrangement of information within the broad structure of the biblical books.[102] The linguistic unity sought by earlier Pietist translators was, in other words, replaced by the formalistic practice of gathering and collecting in one place all the relevant data—spiritual, moral, historical, geographical—that could be brought to bear on a particular passage. These constellations of information were then unified, formalistically, by the order of passages and books laid out in the text of the Bible, with the ultimate goal of "reproducing the true divine service in spirit."[103]

Such a comprehensive project was not a job for an author as much as an editor. In many ways, Bayle was one of the last author-compilers to produce such an ostensibly comprehensive work. After him, the work of synthesizing and unifying an ever-increasing corpus of knowledge was taken over by teams of editors, engaged in projects that far outlasted their oversight. The *Encyclopédie* was, of course, the great example of such a project, but one can speak of others as well: the *Curieuses und Reales Natur-, Kunst-, Berg-, Gewerck-, und Handlungs-Lexicon* begun by Johann Hübner and finished by Georg Zincken; the sixty-four-volume *Grosses vollständiges Universal-Lexicon* begun by Johann Zedler and finished by Carl Ludovici; and the *Allgemeinen Gelehrten Lexicon* begun around 1700 by Johann Mencke and continued by Christian Jocher, then Johann Dunkel, then Johann Adelung, then Heinrich Rotermund, then Johann Meusel, and finally, as late as 1969, Karl Hennicke. And, last, the Berleburger Bible, whose publication was engineered by Johann Haug, but supplemented as well by at least two to five other authors, including Ludwig Christoph Scheffer

[101] Bayle, *Dictionnaire*, 1:b[r–v].

[102] On the Bible as encyclopedia, see my "From Philology to Fossils: The Biblical Encyclopedia in Early Modern Europe," *Journal of the History of Ideas* 64 (January 2003): 41–60.

[103] [Haug], *Heilige Schrifft*, 6:)(2[r].

and the notoriously heterodox Johann Christoph Edelmann.[104] To my knowledge, this was the only Bible in the eighteenth century to go this route, to rely on multiple contributors working on multiple entries. For this reason, the Berleburger Bible showed no trace of that assertion so characteristic of early separatist translations: that the translator needed to be baptized into his unique task by the Holy Spirit. Here there was no unique translator, but several of them working on different projects. In this new, encyclopedic presentation, what was needed was not a master organizer, but a master framework, an organizational principle that could break up and distribute the vast amounts of information available to the modern reader. The Berleburgers found this framework in the Bible.

For this reason, the most polemic and critical feature of this new encyclopedic project was the notes and the entries, not the translation itself. It was not merely plagiarism that bothered their critics, Bayle's and Haug's disingenous protestations to the contrary, but rather the never innocent process of collection. Such was clear to Haug by 1737, when he began to counter the attacks of his critics on the annotations:

> It is indeed an easy thing to pick out the most prestigious of the hundreds of exegetes and bible commentators, and to record them one after the other with their books, chapters, paragraphs, and pages, and to say: the treasured Schmidt, the famous Lightfoot, the scholarly Frischmuth, the industrious Rambach, the inspired Luther, &c has this or the other opinion; I, on the other hand, have this one. Does the reader, whom one writes to please, then know which *sensus literalis*, which literal meaning is the correct one?

The job of the editor was not just to collect, but rather to put this collection in the service of a mission, in this case, building a spiritualist Bible. Motivated collection, Haug claimed, allowed the Berleburger Bible to be more than "merely a new translation" and instead to present a host of "poisonous and, to the old [unredeemed] man, truly deadly annotations."[105] The Berleburger Bible was to be not just a collection of opinions, but also a spiritual arsenal for battle against men untouched by the new covenant. The chief weapons in this arsenal were the paratext, the annotations, and the footnotes.

In the end, then, it was not the stress on the "personal experience of the Biblical text," nor the love of the *sensus mysticus* that made the Berleburger Bible such a monument in Bible translation.[106] What made the Berleburger Bible so important was its integration of the separatist ideology of a universally legible

[104] On the participants in this project, see Brecht, "Die Berleburger Bibel," 179.

[105] [Haug], preface to *Die Heilige Schrift* (1737),)(2^{v}-)(3^{v}.

[106] Dieter Gutzen, "Poesie der Bibel: Beobachtungen zu ihrer Entdeckung und ihrer Intepretation im 18 Jahrhundert," (Ph. D. diss., Universität Bonn, 1972), 43.

Bible into a vernacular encyclopedic format. There is no question, after all, that the Berleburger translators were firmly planted in heterodox religious soil. Like translators from Reitz to Junckherrott, they quested after "the true and best original text of the spirit," saw their Bible as "not so much for the scholarly and those with lust for knowledge, but for the simple . . . souls" and disdained confessional difference in favor of a universal biblical text.[107] All of the criteria for a religiously charged biblical universalism were there.

But the means of achieving such universality were radically different. No longer content with linguistic universalism, Haug and his team moved to a scholarly universalism, one that sought to hold together the centrifugal forces of confessionalized theology by means of scholarly apparatus. The question was not whether the Berleburger Bible was "influenced" by Enlightenment philosophy. Rather, it reconstituted its object of study, the Bible, through the media of Enlightenment. These media did not imply philosophical positions, nor were they developed to further philosophical aims. Instead, they were developed as techniques of collection, presentation, and organization that proved remarkably adaptable to a variety of different philosophical, religious, and scholarly aims. At the same time, they were not neutral with regard to their message. Bayle was not more of an Enlightenment figure than Haug, but he was a much cannier human being, one who saw more clearly the kinds of arguments that could be sustained within the media. It is certainly true, for example, that the use of dense annotations and conflicting notes made Haug's theological interest in the organic unity of the biblical message extraordinarily difficult to sustain. But if contradictory, Haug's project made the implicit point that scholarly data *had* to be considered even in the day-to-day vernacular Bible.

This was a profound change from the seventeenth century, a century characterized by the sharp separation of the vernacular Bible and erudite scholarship. For orthodox Lutherans like Valentin Löscher, this border between the ordinary Bible and scholarship was crucial to maintain, for it was by enforcing the border that the discipline of theology itself was kept healthy: "when talking about . . . the usual Bibles, critical *cura* does not obtain: rather, it is here that *theology* happens."[108] Theology itself, as practiced in the 150 years since the Reformation, depended on this division between vernacular knowledge and learned discourse: it was this separation after all that kept theology in the hands of the trained. It is no surprise then that seventeenth-century theologians were reluctant to give scholarship free access to the vernacular, nor a surprise that the Pietist attack on dogmatic theology should include a scholarly revision of the vernacular Bible. This new Bible, shorn of all theology and freely available to interpretation by all, offered an exhilarating yet frightening freedom, collapsing the distinction

[107] [Haug], preface (1726),)(2; [Haug], preface (1737),)(2^{v}; Haug cites Gell in a number of places, including the commentary to Lev. 21.20 and in the 1737 preface.

[108] [Löscher], *Unschuldige Nachrichten* 17 (1717): 629.

between scholarly and lay domains. It was this collapse, in the end, that the encyclopedia was designed to effect. Just like a contemporary encyclopedia, those of the eighteenth century were not specifically for scholars, but for general readers who wanted a world of information at their fingertips. In its rafts of quotations, and its myriad annotations to every verse of the Bible, the Berleburger Bible gave such a world to its vernacular readers, who, for the first time, had access to a synthetic overview of largely Latinate scholarship concentrated in one place. This penetration into the vernacular domain was part of the missionary project of this Bible. By including everything and organizing it according to formally unifying principles, Haug seemed to say, we will transcend the particulars of our theological differences, and succeed in producing a nonpartisan, universally rejuvenating text, one deadly to the old man.

Scholarly Translation and the End of Theology

With Haug, then, we can see in fuller outline the legacy that the radical Pietist project would leave to the Enlightenment Bible. On the one hand, consistently and remorselessly, the Pietists attempted to rid the Bible of its theological superstructure, to remove that "wood, hay, and stubble of human inquisitiveness," as Spener put it, that the Lutheran Church had erected around its sacred text.[109] For over a century, German Protestants had seen firsthand the effects of theological rigidity on religious, cultural, and social life. It was no accident that the ecumenism of many Pietists was intended to remove the theological blinders that confessional commitment had put on the Protestant world as a whole. Subjective experience of God's will and love was one method of removing these blinders: if the authority to speak for God were available to all who sought rebirth, then the *discipline* of theology would lose its effect. No longer could theology have an independent authority distinct from the human experience of the divine. Another method of overcoming the authority of theology was biblical translation. For radical Pietists—from Reitz to Haug—translation was a weapon against theology. Through translation, the essential and immanent meaning of the Bible would be revealed to all with ears to hear. Bible translation was the attempt to awaken the reader to the real original text of the Bible, the essential truths inscribed inside the human heart. In this sense, the perfect translation would reach beyond itself. It would liberate the reader from the words on the page, and awaken the spirit of God.

On the other hand, this quest to move beyond theology was pursued with rigorous (if odd) objective techniques. Although in theory perhaps any text might awaken the inner word of God, in practice, the radical Pietists were committed to those specific textual practices they were convinced would lead

[109] Philip Jakob Spener, *Pia desideria*, trans. Theodore G. Tappert (Philadelphia, 1964), 56.

humanity to true piety. Literalism and scholarship had curious multiplying effects, though, ones that would become utterly characteristic of the Enlightenment Bible. Despite all the insistence on the universality of their translations, the radical Pietists restlessly proliferated Bibles, offering new translations again and again and never able to settle finally on a single definitive version. The Bible was, for them, a project rather than an object, a project that was repeatedly undertaken in the first third of the eighteenth century. As their objective techniques were applied, with greater and lesser success, to the biblical text, that wall between the scholarly and the vernacular Bible erected during the great age of canonization crumbled. But with it crumbled as well that monolithic Bible of earlier centuries. By moving the Bible beyond the hegemony of theology, Pietists opened it up to the dispersive media of the Enlightenment. The Enlightenment Bible, as it was elaborated in the second half of the century, would be a ramified and distributed project, never a single canonical text. Translation and scholarship merged to give Germany a universe of possible Bibles, all written in the name of rehabilitating the Bible for modern consumption. And the conditions for this change were first produced, in Germany, by religious zeal.

PART II

The Forms of the Enlightenment Bible

In 1747 an anonymous writer complained about the decline of religion in Germany. The "word 'freethinker' is . . . an entirely new word," the author grumbled, "and our current century discovered it first. God, if only the German language did not have such a word to name such people, just as Hebrew had no word to designate atheists."[1] Among many of the devout in midcentury Germany, the mood was gloomy. In Prussia the young prince Frederick II had assumed the throne in 1740 and showed few of the pious traits that had marked his father. In the same year, the philosopher Christian Wolff marched triumphantly back to the University of Halle, from which the Pietist Johann Lange had driven him some seventeen years earlier for religious heterodoxy. In 1744, by order of the young Frederick, the Royal Academy of Sciences was reconstituted in Berlin. The French *philosophe* Pierre-Louis Moreau de Maupertuis was invited to head it and its charter specifically excluded the investigation of "revealed theology."[2] In academic life, the theological faculty at the new university of Göttingen became, by the 1760s, the dominant force in German religious letters, a faculty deliberately separated from the consistorial governance of the Lutheran church.[3] These and other factors gave those who considered themselves defenders of the faith reason to fear the coming century.

Not everyone was scared, of course. Theological faculties remained vibrant places of research, and religion remained a subject of deepest interest. Some were in fact convinced that they stood on a threshold of a new reformation. The second half of the century, wrote L. T. Spittler enthusiastically in 1782, "will perhaps be recognized as the most brilliant period of Lutheran Church history."[4] But

[1] [Anonymous], *Uhrsachen des Verfalls der Religion und der einreissenden Freydenkerey* (Berlin, 1747), 17.

[2] Adolph Harnack, *Geschichte der königlichen preussischen Akademie der Wissenschaften* (Berlin, 1900), 2:263. On Maupertuis and the academy, see Mary Terrall, *The Man Who Flattened the Earth: Maupertuis and the Sciences in the Enlightenment* (Chicago, 2002).

[3] See Sorkin, *The Berlin Haskalah and German Religious Thought: Orphans of Knowledge* (London, 2000), 24f.

[4] Ibid., 13.

such sentiments were exceptions in the face of the anxiety, widespread not just among the orthodox but also among the scholared classes more broadly, that Germany was beginning to feel from the effects of the same deistic scourge that had plagued England in the early part of the century. Feeling, of course, does not reality make. Caution is particularly important in this case, when the common historical wisdom argues that "like a luminous cloud, the empiricism and rationalism that had shadowed England moved across the English Channel."[5] Such an explanation offers little real explanatory purchase on the transformations in German cultural life in the period. But it is true to say that the fear of rationalism, the fear of skepticism and deism, did indeed embed itself in the theological faculties, among scholars and critics alike. If, as the Orientalist scholar Johann Eichhorn perceptively noted in 1791, "deism forced British theologians to devise defenses" for the Bible through means scholarly, in the second half of the eighteenth century, Germans also found their work shaped by the specters of atheism, shaped by the fear that religion might not survive its conflict with reason.[6]

In this new context, England's successful repulsion of atheism became an important example for Germans anxious about the future of religion. As early as 1697, Andreas Hochstetter praised England in his *Oratio de utilitate peregrinationis anglicanae* for its religious virtues, which should be a model for the young German scholar.[7] By the middle of the century, the model was imported back to Germany. When Georg Wolfgang Panzer translated Samuel Nelson's 1758 *Universal Bible: or every Christian Family's Best Treasure* as the *Antideistische Bibel*, it spoke volumes both about German anxieties and about the solutions they imagined would mitigate them.[8] Indeed, the most massive Bible project of the eighteenth century was a translation of English commentaries on the Bible: Romanus Teller and Jakob Brucker's *Die Heilige Schrift des Alten und Neuen Testaments* (1749–1770). At nineteen volumes of translated English annotations, this monster work included authors as diverse as Simon Patrick, Thomas Stackhouse, Edward Pocock, Isaac Newton, John Selden, and Robert Boyle.[9] Conspicuously absent, unsurprisingly, were the voices of skeptics: this was a work designed for apologetic uses only. As Marijke de Lang has it, "historical and literary criticism of the gospels in Germany emerged . . . as a reaction to the radical criticism of religion of an earlier period."[10] If "Bible criticism . . . essen-

[5] William Baird, *History of New Testament Research: From Deism to Tübingen* (Minneapolis, 1992), 91.

[6] Johann Eichhorn, "Johann David Michaelis," 883.

[7] Andreas Hochstetter, *Oratio de utilitate peregrinationis anglicanae* (Tübingen, 1697).

[8] Samuel Nelson, ed., *Universal Bible: or every Christian Family's Best Treasure* (London, 1758); Georg Wolfgang Panzer, *Antideistische Bibel, das ist die heilige Schrift des alten und neuen Testaments mit Anmerkungen und Erklärungen erläutert* (Erlangen, 1766–78).

[9] Romanus Teller and Jakob Brucker, *Die Heilige Schrift des Alten und Neuen Testaments* (Leipzig, 1749–70).

[10] Marijke H. de Lang, "Literary and Historical Criticism As Apologetics: Biblical Scholarship at the End of the Eighteenth Century," *Nederlands Archief voor Kerkgeschiednis* 72 (1992): 149.

tially went back to the battle against the deists," in Germany, scholars looked not just to the problems but also to the scholarly solutions invented in the fiery decades of England's early 1700s.[11]

Novel uses were given to these English swords, however, because German religious scholarship was always shaped by the subtle ambitions of Pietism. Behind nearly every important scholar in the second half of the eighteenth century lurked, somewhere in the background, the shadow of Pietism. Many were direct products of the university system at Halle, which continued to play a dominant role in theological and scholarly realms through the 1750s. Some were themselves Pietists, driven to scholarship either to combat the religious enthusiasms of their more radical brethren or to battle the dangers of skepticism. And some were lapsed Pietists, turning their energies away from devotion to the inner light, and toward devotion to the biblical text. None, however, were content with the fundamentally defensive posture toward the Bible that characterized England and English scholarship through the 1740s. In keeping the Pietist urge to reform, Germans undertook more than the sterile preservation of the Bible from harm. They began a sustained effort to remake the Bible—vernacular and scholarly—that it might be left, in the end, both safe and meaningful. In this light, it is less surprising that when our 1747 grumbler was pressed for a *solution* to the problem of religious decline, his first call was for a new translation of the Bible, a task that, when completed, would have "infinitely great" effects, keeping doubters quiet and calming the faithful.[12]

In a general sense, that this effort to reform the Bible should come from Protestants made historical and theological sense. In eighteenth-century France, the Bible was a particular concern to neither Catholic apologists nor devotees of the new rationalism. Clericalism and church authority were the hot-button issues there. But Protestantism was, after all, the religion of *sola scriptura*. Buried in its heart, since the early days of the Reformation, was an essential assertion about the nature of the biblical text and its relationship to people. The Puritan divine Richard Capel put it most bluntly in 1658 when he wrote:

> our Bible is the Word of God. . . . the Bible translated is the Word of God. . . . this book, & no other, *is the very Word of God*. . . . nothing can work saving grace in any man to the conversion of his soule, but the very Word of God. . . . this the word translated hath wrought in me, therefore I know by this, that the Scripture translated is the word of God."[13]

Capel's repetitive insistence on the equivalence of the biblical text and the commands of God might indicate some degree of anxiety about this relationship.

[11] Rudolf Smend, *Epochen der Bibelkritik* (Munich, 1991), 14.

[12] [Anonymous], *Uhrsachen des Verfalls*, 48

[13] Capel, *Capel's Remains*, 93, 96–98.

But insistence on this point was fundamental, for the entire project of Protestant theology—not to mention the political authority that it claimed from the Scriptures—depended on this equivalence. In the terms of the reformers, all true theology depended on the Bible. In turn, the authority of the Bible was guaranteed by power of theological proclamation. The Bible—not the church—was "every Christian family's best treasure" because it clearly told how human beings should seek and find their salvation.

The Enlightenment Bible was produced when Germans broke this essential link between theology and the Bible. If German radical Pietists had implicitly challenged the connection between the two in the early part of the century, as the century waned German scholars made the distinction between the Bible and divine speech into an integral part of their religious platform. Although "the *Word of God* is clearly outside of, and above, all critique," wrote the Lutheran theologian Johann Semler, no one knows "how many written books were accepted in [early] Christianity as canonical in their teachings."[14] Although these written books eventually became the biblical canon, they were fundamentally distinct from that entity he called the Word of God. "Holy Scripture and the Word of God must be differentiated," he maintained, and if it made him a "naturalist" to ascribe "the power of Christianity to its truths, and not to . . . this or that book," then so be it.[15] In his late eighteenth-century obituary for Semler, Eichhorn already saw this distinction as the greatest of Semler's insights. What a discovery it was, Eichhorn exclaimed, that the New Testament was only "of local and temporal character, and neither for all times and peoples, nor an indispensable source for Christianity."[16] Gotthold Lessing—one of the few, in Eichhorn's mind, able to puzzle through Semler's hideous prose—put it in his usual pithy way: "at root the difference between the letter and the spirit of the Bible is exactly the same . . . [as that] between the Holy Scriptures and the Word of God."[17] "There was religion before there was a Bible," was another way to put it.[18] Or, as the theologian Johann Tobler wrote in 1771, a crucial distinction, lost on many of the "unlearned," must be made between "God's Word or revelation, and the Bible." The Bible is subject to degradation and corruption, but God's Word remains "eternal, unchanged, like God himself."[19]

If we were to cast this new distinction in political terms, it would be analogous to the divorce between sacrality and the monarchy that characterized Europe on the tail end of absolutism. The political ferment of the eighteenth century that

[14] Gottfried Hornig, *Die Anfänge der historisch-kritischen Theologie: Johann Salomo Semlers Schriftverständnis und seine Stellung zu Luther* (Göttingen, 1961), 88.

[15] Johann Semler, *Abhandlung von freier Untersuchung des Canon* (Halle, 1771), 1:73, 88.

[16] Eichhorn, *Allgemeine Bibliothek*, 5.1 (1793): 75.

[17] Lessing, *Axiomata, wenn deren in dergleichen Dingen gibt* in *Werke und Briefe in zehn Bände*, ed. Wilfried Barner (Frankfurt a.M., 1985), 9:63–4.

[18] Lessing, "Gegensätze des Herausgebers," in *Werke*, 8:312.

[19] Johann Tobler, *Anmerkungen zur Ehre der Bibel, bey Anlass der Michaelis'schen Uebersetzung des Alten Testaments* . . . (Halle, 1771), 4.

responded to this crisis of sacred power produced a variety of answers to an old question, namely "What is the source of state power?" In a similar way—and to return to my introductory points—this divorce effected between God's own tongue and the words on ancient parchment opened up the space for new answers to the old question "What is the ultimate source of biblical authority?" Here, however, the analogy stopped. For if the new politics of the period might be styled "secular"—at least insofar as it was characterized by conscious efforts to distinguish between the state and religion—the same may not be said about the Bible. Instead, in this case, the new answers to the old question were efforts at *recuperation*, efforts to keep the Bible safe and well in a post-theological age. These new answers were given in a host of new Bible translations, all of which, in different ways, yoked the vernacular Bible to the performance of biblical scholarship.

These new answers were, in effect, the Enlightenment Bible. And the crucible of their formation was Germany, which, by the middle of the century, had become the dominant European force in research and investigation of the biblical text. England (and the Netherlands for that matter) had long been left behind, producing after 1750 very little noteworthy scholarship on the Bible. Although English translations, too, grew in the second half of the century, the experimentation with the biblical text that characterized German work was largely absent. Indeed, in Germany, the Bible was endlessly discussed, debated, reformed, and regenerated. If the old answer to the old question "What is the ultimate source of biblical authority?" was "theological truth," the new answers were distributed across a variety of humanistic and historical disciplines. This distribution of the Bible—the fact that the Enlightenment Bible was ineluctably *plural* in character—was a symptom of the media effects of Enlightenment. Just as political discussion in the period was distributed across a variety of new outlets—newspapers, coffee houses, or what have you—so too was Bible distributed across a variety of genres, scholarly practices, and disciplines. It was not an accident that Enlightenment Bible had no single center, that it was not an object as much as a project. If the Bible had always functioned in Christian Europe as an essentially unified text—indeed, its theological importance depended on this unity—the post-theological Enlightenment Bible would build its authority across a diverse set of domains and disciplines. Its authority had no essential center, but instead coalesced around four fundamental nuclei. Philology, pedagogy, poetry, and history: each offered its own answer to the question of biblical authority, answers that were given literary form in the guise of new translations.

The following section offers a set of overlays. Each chapter is a virtual transparency, covering essentially the same temporal ground, but offering a vision of these nuclei and the various logics they imposed on the text of the Bible. By recursive overlay, the full dimensions of the new map of the Bible are revealed. And its geography has two major features, features that had long been merged in the history of Christianity, but to which the Enlightenment Bible would give its own unique topographies: the New and Old Testaments. The divergence of the new and old covenants was a fundamental consequence of the recuperation of the Bible in the eighteenth century. But it was not the only one. For as the Bible was distributed across a disciplinary network—no longer explicable within a single explanatory framework—its meanings would be similarly distributed. Authorities proliferated and diversified, laying the groundwork for the ultimate transformation in the period: the production of a fully cultural Bible, a Bible whose legitimacy and authority was embedded no longer in theology, but in that complex of literature, teaching, scholarship, and history that came to be called culture. As such, then, the translations of this later period, circa 1730s to circa 1770s, made possible the emergence, at the end of the period, of a Bible whose contours still help to shape the contemporary understanding of this most peculiar monument in our literary heritage.

Chapter Four

PHILOLOGY: THE BIBLE FROM TEXT TO DOCUMENT

In his first journal entry for the year 1751, John Wesley described this holy encounter:

> One Sunday morning I was just going to open my Bible when a voice . . . seemed to say very loud, "God, for Christ's sake, hath forgive thee." I started up, took the candle, and searched all about to see if anyone was near, but there was none. I then sat down, with such peace and joy in my soul as cannot be described. . . . Soon after it was repeated . . . still louder, which drove me on my knees to prayer, being overwhelmed with the love of God and, for the time, utterly incapable of doubt or fear.
>
> I now saw the New Testament in a different light than I had ever done before. All the day I was comforted with promises from it. . . . Yet the thought, "May not all this be a delusion?" frequently darted into me. But it as often drove me to prayer, upon which all doubt presently vanished.[1]

In Wesley's story, the Bible played an uneasy part. The Bible revealed God's promises to man. But fully believing these promises was a different matter for chronically doubting humans. Only prayer and the aural confirmation of God's presence could drive off this doubt and reassure the reader that the promises would be kept. Before the Book could be opened without fear, in other words, the voice of God had to speak and carefully guide the nervous reader to confident joy. This combination of devotion to the Bible, and anxiety about its promises, was not unique to Wesley. Indeed, it was already a familiar part of German Pietism, where ecstatic rebirth revealed a real Word of God unseen by ordinary men. This convergence of concerns between two movements separated by language and context was not wholly fortuitous, especially since Wesley had looked to the Moravian Pietists for guidance and inspiration as he helped transform the "holy club" of 1730s Oxford into the energetic movement of religious revival that came to be called Methodism.[2] Wesley's anxiety was the same as that which

[1] John Wesley, *Journal and Diaries*, in *The Works of John Wesley*, eds. W. Reginald Ward and Richard P. Heitzenrater (Nashville, 1991), 20:374.

[2] See Henry D. Rack, *Reasonable Enthusiast: John Wesley and the Rise of Methodism* 2nd ed. (Nashville, 1992), 85ff. For general sympathies among evangelicals, see W. Reginald Ward, *The Protestant Evangelical Awakening* (Cambridge, 1992).

powered the radical Pietist translation project, which tirelessly strove to make objective textual forms reveal God's immediate touch. Nor was Wesley immune to the Pietist desire to combine a theology of sanctification with a deep appreciation of the biblical text. It was after all only four years later that Wesley published his 1755 *Explanatory Notes upon the New Testament*, a revised version of the King James Bible accompanied by copious annotations.

But in this publication, the similarities began and then grinded to a halt. For Wesley's New Testament never had the ambitions of his Pietist brethren. It was never designed to replace the King James Version, or to become a universal ecumenical text. Instead, Wesley wanted to avoid "all curious and critical inquiries, and all use of the learned languages" and presented only edifying commentary, commentary that would be a virtual translation of the *Gnomon Novi Testamenti* of the German Pietist scholar Johann Albrecht Bengel.[3] This intersection of German and English interests—though only one of many in the period—can stand as shorthand for different roles that religion and scholarship played in these two Protestant nations. For Wesley and the other Methodists, biblical scholarship was, in itself, a fruitless enterprise. Countless times in their writings they rejected scholarship as radically insufficient for their project of religious reform. "My soul is sick of this *sublime* divinity!" exclaimed Wesley in 1739, "Let *me* think and speak as a little child! Let *my* religion be plain, artless, and simple!"[4] Wesley might not have gone as far as his companion George Whitefield, who condemned "our common learning, so much cried up, [that] makes men only so many accomplished fools," but nonetheless his interests took him far from the scholarly domain.[5] His religion of experience—in which God's love "must be felt, if it is in the soul, as much as fire upon the body"—set the internal domain of feeling high above philological inquiry.[6] Certainly contemporaries saw this aversion for scholarship and gleefully mocked it, imagining Whitefield's polemics against "your Church-doctors, your dunce-doctors, your book-learned blockheads, your barking dogs, that can bark and can't bite."[7] Although Methodism injected into the English religious scene a devotional vibrancy missing since the English Revolution, never did Methodists make scholarship a cornerstone of their religious rejuvenation. Apologetics aside, then, the idea that Wesley was one of the "great religious scholars of the eighteenth century" is simply absurd.[8] Instead, Wesley and his brethren shunned scholarship as an affirmation of Methodism's independence of the Georgian Church and its controversies, in which scholarship was wielded as

[3] John Wesley, *Explanatory Notes upon the New Testament* (1755, 1954), 7.

[4] Ibid., *Journals*, 20:131.

[5] Horton Davies, *Worship and Theology in England* (Princeton, 1961), 3:179.

[6] Isabel Rivers, *Reason, Grace, and Sentiment: A Study of the Language of Religion and Ethics in England, 1660–1780* (Cambridge, 1991), 1:239.

[7] Davies, *Worship*, 3:181.

[8] Robin Scroggs, "John Wesley As Biblical Scholar," *Journal of Bible and Religion* 28 (1960): 417.

a weapon by the faithful and iconoclastic alike. The Bible guaranteed divine presence in Wesley's theology but was seldom seen in its full complexity. Indeed, the "substance of all the Bible" could be boiled down, he commented, to just two words, "faith and salvation."[9]

The contrast was stark, then, between Wesley and his favorite biblical interpreter, Johann Albrecht Bengel, a man who, while devoutly Pietist, was also one of the great textual scholars of the early eighteenth century. Picking up the reins of philology that had fallen slack in England after the death of Richard Bentley, Bengel attempted to put the New Testament manuscripts into rational order and to codify the most important rules of New Testament textual criticism. Not content to stop there, Bengel instead labored long and, in 1753, posthumously gave to the German-speaking world a translation that would for the first time, as he put it, "carefully express the true Greek original."[10] If the traditionally urgent efforts to revise the Greek New Testament diminished greatly in England as the real threat of deism faded by the 1740s, in Germany scholars like Bengel seized on English and Pietist scholarly models and channeled them in new directions. Where Methodists would continue to insist on the equivalence of God's Word and the Scriptures, German scholars—many of them devout, most of them products of Pietist milieus—would take advantage of the freedom offered by a Bible loosened from its theological foundation.

The philological Bible was one avatar of this freedom. Put in a negative sense, philology was one of the tools that German scholars used to reinvest the Bible with authority and meaning once its essential connection with theology was broken. Put positively, philology was liberated from the problems of theology and allowed to remake the Bible in its own image. The philological and textual-critical tools developed in England by luminaries like John Mill and Richard Bentley were, in Germany, given the liberty wholly to change the biblical text. Scholars like Johann Semler, Johann Griesbach, and Johann David Michaelis were only a few of those who put philology into the service of a new detheologized Bible. At the real beginning of this story, however, sat Bengel, who brought translation and scholarship to new synthesis and who thereby affords us a particularly clear lens on the early development of an Enlightenment Bible. In his work, biblical scholarship and the demands of the vernacular edition converged and together they produced a translation of the New Testament whose principal aims stood outside of theology and whose principal methods were philological. Over the second half of the century, this philological Bible would be elaborated, both within the domain of pure text criticism and within the vernacular editions published in ever increasing numbers as the century waned.

[9] John Wesley, "The Scripture Way of Salvation," in *Works*, 2:156.

[10] Johann Albrecht Bengel, *Das Neue Testament* (Stuttgart, 1753), xi.

The Manuscript Machine: Genealogy

When John Mill's New Testament hit the reading rooms of early eighteenth-century Germany, it made a huge splash. Although scholars across Europe had long known about the variant readings, Mill's work—as we have seen—was the first to reveal the true depths of the problem. At root, this problem was (and still is) the outrageous number of existing manuscripts or witnesses. Although seventeenth-century scholars were unfamiliar with all of the frightening variety of New Testament manuscripts, even in 1650 it was one of the messiest texts known to the scholarly world. As if in denial, scholars ignored this messiness until century's end, when finally John Mill laid down his pen and, we remember, offered his readers a collection of variants approaching the near mythical total of 30,000. In England, we remember too, scholars like Bentley were convinced that this number would only rise, as increasing micrological study of the textual witnesses revealed a panoply of unforeseen differences. Not everyone was as relaxed about the apparent variety of biblical readings, of course. Anthony Collins's delight at what seemed a proof of the weakness of the biblical text was precisely matched by Daniel Whitby's anguish over a new legion of evidence ostensibly corrosive of the authority of the New Testament.

Whitby was hardly scholar enough to dismantle Mill's edifice. Nonetheless, his strategy for dealing with Mill became standard among continental Europeans in the early eighteenth century: he attempted to organize textual criticism into discrete critical canons, rules to make sense of the chaos that apparently engulfed the Bible. In this effort, he picked up where the 1699 *Ars critica* of Dutch Remonstrant Jean Le Clerc had left off. An able biblical scholar and well known for his controversial writings, Le Clerc had long worked to organize biblical scholarship to protect "the fundamental articles" of Christianity, in Martin Klauber's words, against the excesses of both historical and atheistic criticism.[11] At a time when "Libertines . . . make use of their Philosophy and Criticism, to overthrow the most sacred and most solid Doctrines of our Religion," Le Clerc's 1690 *Five Letters Concerning the Inspiration of Scripture* suggested that only a reasoned historical scholarship could ensure that "the Authority of Scripture continues in full force."[12] For scholars like Whitby, this entailed the organization of interpretive rules. Similarly disposed were the Dutch scholar Gerhard of Maastricht and the German theologian—and colleague of Johann Albrecht Bengel—Christoph Matthäus Pfaff.[13] Pfaff's 1709 lament,

[11] Martin Klauber, "Between Protestant Orthodoxy and Rationalism: Fundamental Articles in the Early Career of Jean LeClerc," *Journal of the History of Ideas* 54 (October 1993): 628.

[12] Jean Le Clerc, *Five Letters Concerning the Inspiration of the Holy Scriptures* (n.p., 1690), 125, 114.

[13] Pfaff includes in his *Dissertatio critica de genuinis librorum Novi Testamenti lectionibus* (Amsterdam, 1709) most of the forty-three canons eventually affixed to Gerhard's New Testament (*Novum Testamentum. Post priores Steph. Curcellaei, tum & DD. Oxoniensium labores* [Amsterdam, 1711]).

that Mill had not produced his own canons of criticism, was a clue to the significance of this codifying impulse.[14] After the collection of Mill, Pfaff implied, the problem was how to organize these critical tools in a productive fashion. Once we have gathered all the variant readings, what then? What was the textual, philological, historical, and theological value of these readings? How could they be systematized and understood?

These questions drove Bengel's textual work on the New Testament. As a youth, he had encountered John Fell's New Testament and "was tortured by its terrible variety of readings."[15] But by 1721, such tortures had eased: "If the Holy Scriptures, which have been copied so many times, and have so often passed through the erring hands of men, were without error, that would be a miracle so great that belief in it could no longer be called belief." "Put cheerfully aside this doubt that once tortured me so horribly!" Bengel advised his friend Jeremias Reuss.[16] What prompted this new sanguinity was Bengel's discovery of the powers of criticism. "In the divine word no diligence is too much, unless it be perverse," and the most diligent approach to the Bible was textual and philological criticism.[17] Through criticism, the chaos of Mill's variants could be dispelled. Where Gotthilf August Francke thought it "a waste of time to continue to dwell on criticism of the N. T." because all variant readings had already been collected, Bengel realized that collection was only the first step of philological criticism.[18] We do not investigate the Bible, Bengel wrote, "in order that the number of variant readings might be accumulated without discrimination." After collection, the real work begins. And this is work for a critic—that is, someone capable of choosing between the variants, understanding their origins, exercising judgment. By choosing, the critic can reduce the variants "to a most pleasing minimum . . . so that, from those [variant readings] about which . . . there remains dispute, the more certain might be selected."[19] Once Mill had collected the pieces, in other words, it took a critic to put the puzzle back together, to reveal the order underlying the chaos.

The task of the philological critic was, then, the condensation of the significant from the random. And no one went further than Bengel did in condensing Gerhard of Maastricht's forty-three critical canons. Indeed, just four words, Bengel declared, "should be able to distinguish the true readings from

[14] Fox, *Mill and Bentley*, 91–92.

[15] Johann Albrecht Bengel, *Prodromus Novi Testamenti Graeci recte cauteque adornandi* (Stuttgart, 1725), xvii. On Bengel, see Kurt Aland, "Johann Albrecht Bengel als Textkritiker," *Bericht der Stiftung zur Förderung der neutestamentlichen Textforschung für die Jahre 1985 bis 1987* (Münster, 1988), 9–22.

[16] Letter of 24 February 1721, quoted in Gottfried Mälzer, *Johann Albrecht Bengel: Leben und Werk* (Stuttgart, 1970), 156.

[17] Bengel, *Prodromus*, vi.

[18] J. Ch. Fr. Burk, ed., *Dr. Johann Albrecht Bengel's literarischer Briefwechsel* (Stuttgart, 1836), 76.

[19] Bengel, *Prodromus*, x.

all the false ones."[20] The four words—*proclivi scriptioni praestat ardua* (the harder reading is better than the easy)—would in later years be shaved down to the even leaner *difficilio lectio potior*, a standard canon of present-day textual criticism. The canon put the critic in the shoes of a monk. Imagine this monk, the rule said, cramped from long hours sitting in a cold and dark scriptorium. Suddenly he chances across a confusing passage in his text. He squints and still it makes no sense. It must, he concludes, be a mistake, perhaps a slip of the previous scribe's pen. So, if the monk is circumspect, he then glosses the unclarity in the margin, leaving a note that might, over time, creep into the text itself. If less circumspect, our sore and tired monk changes the passage, clears up (in his mind) the problematic piece of writing, and substitutes for the obscure original a passage better suited to his own theological or grammatical tastes.

Given such monkish proclivities, the wise textual critic assumes that corruption works to simplify, rather than complicate. The harder reading, in short, tends to be the better. This rule was, it should be said, not unknown to the early eighteenth century. Certainly Jean Le Clerc had proposed a similar idea some 25 years earlier and Erasmus some 175 years before that.[21] But unlike Erasmus or Le Clerc, Bengel made the rule into the very keystone of his textual theory, for the rule of the harder reading provided him with an explanation for textual error and a strategy for choosing between the variant readings. After its application, Bengel proclaimed hopefully, "barely a fifth of the variant readings . . . will remain. *Deo gratia.*"[22] If scholars since Quintilian had seen that errors might enter MSS through addition, subtraction, and transmutation, Bengel's principle of the harder reading showed how this happened and how the errors might be emended.[23] It did this by moving the discussion of error from a purely mechanical question to the level of historical psychology. Rather than seeing copyists as imperfect Xerox machines, Bengel imputed a rationale to their practices. Once this rationale is reconstructed, the true text might be resurrected.

Bengel's canon was intuitively simple, but had far-reaching consequences. Not least, it overturned the so-called *sensus clarior*, "the clearer meaning," a rule long emphasized in seventeenth-century biblical criticism and advocated strongly by Mill's critic Daniel Whitby.[24] When Whitby proposed that

[20] Ibid., xii.

[21] Le Clerc's exact formulation was: "Si omnia sint paria, non multum quidem interest quae eligatur; sed si una ex iis obscurior sit, caeterae clariores, tum vero credibile est obscuriorem esse veram, alias glossemata" (*Ars Critica* 6th ed. [Leiden, 1778]), 2:293). Jerry Bentley has shown that Erasmus already understood the principle; see his "Erasmus, Jean Le Clerc, and the Principle of the Harder Reading," *Renaissance Quarterly* 31 (Autumn 1978): 318.

[22] Bengel, *Prodromus*, xii.

[23] See E. J. Kenney, *The Classical Text: Aspects of Editing in the Age of the Printed Book* (Berkeley, 1974), 29.

[24] On the *sensus clarior* and *sensus melior*, see Francois Laplanche, *L'Écriture, le sacré, et l'histoire: Erudit et politiques protestants devant la Bible en France au XVIIe siècle* (Amsterdam, 1986), 211ff.

"the reading that, *caeteris paribus*, establishes the clearer meaning . . . is to be preferred to the others," he was expounding the *sensus clarior*.[25] By contrast, the *lectio difficilior* subordinated ideals of rationality to the exigencies of scribal and historical irrationality. Thus the rationalist proposal—that "the reading that is absurd and that is convicted of absurdity either by what precedes or what follows it, should be rejected"—was discarded. Instead, "often also that reading is really absurd, which does not appear so; that reading not really absurd, which does appear so."[26]

At the same time, the *lectio difficilior* also forced scholars to attend more carefully to the problems of the biblical manuscripts. In what language, for example, was the New Testament actually written? Well, as Bengel realized, "the whole and perpetual spirit of the language employed by the writers of the New Testament was distinctively Hebraizing." God in his wisdom ensured that the Gospels descended "to the level of their immediate auditors and earliest readers," Hellenized Jews who spoke neither a purified Hebrew, nor Attic Greek.[27] Ancient copyists and modern readers alike are thus heirs to the obscurities that this original idiom produced. Reconstructing the New Testament depends, therefore, on reconstructing the logic of these obscurities. And idiom was only one hurdle in this race to reconstruction. Rather, to understand and remedy the accreted errors in the text of the New Testament, the scholar must turn a penetrating gaze not only to idiom, but also to the theological, liturgical, hermeneutical, and grammatical dispositions of scribes who might well "substitute hermeneutic and liturgical *scholia* (held either in their memory or in the margins) . . . [or] formulas or phrases from the books of their churches" for the "native words."[28] Only by understanding the logic of *all* of these factors could scholars guarantee their success. This was a big job, and with centers of scribal learning spread as far apart as Constantinople, Rome, and Britain, it became truly monumental. But Bengel had a tool to help him, indeed his most important tool and most important contribution to biblical criticism, that of genealogy.

The tool of genealogy was produced by the imperative implicit in the principle of the harder reading that manuscripts must be weighed rather than counted. As the Swiss scholar Johann Wettstein—Bengel's opponent in the field of biblical philology—put it, "codices are to be evaluated by their weight, not their number."[29] It was simply untrue that "a great number of

[25] Whitby, *Examen*, ix.

[26] Gerhard of Maastricht, "Canones critici," preface to *Novum Testamentum*, §XXII, 14; Bengel, *Gnomon of the New Testament*, ed. Andrew Fausset, trans. James Bandinel (Edinburgh, 1875), 32.

[27] Johann Albrecht Bengel, *Gnomon Novi Testamenti in quo ex nativa verborum vi, simplicitas, profunditas, concinnitas, salubritas sensuum coelestium indicatur* (Tübingen, 1742), §XIV.

[28] Bengel, "Apparatus Criticus," in *Novum Testamentum Graecum* (Tübingen, 1734), 382.

[29] Johann Wettstein, "Animadversiones et cautiones ad examen Variarum Lectionum N. T. necessariae," in *Libelli in Crisin atque Interpretationem Novi Testamenti*, ed. Johann Salomo Semler (Halle, 1764), 99.

manuscripts, perhaps twenty or more, confirms and proves the received and common reading, so long as it makes sense"[30] More is not better, in other words, in manuscript criticism. Instead *better* is better. Just as more variants do not a better text make, more witnesses do not ensure that the original character of the text is fairly represented. If the job of the true Bible scholar was to "elicit . . . the genuine reading from the variety of readings," then genealogy offered him sure guidance through the overgrown forests of manuscripts and variants.[31]

To clear the path to a pure New Testament, Bengel proposed that all New Testament manuscripts be divided into groups based on shared sets of variant readings. Each group would cluster around a set of variants generally not found in other groups. These groups, Bengel hypothesized, represented separate manuscript traditions "from which the variants have descended." Even if the original codices—the mothers, as it were, of the manuscript traditions—were no longer in existence, they still made themselves felt by stamping their children with distinctive variant readings. "The genesis of varying readings," therefore, Bengel wrote, "can be investigated . . . through major and minor affiliations, through families, tribes and nations of codices . . . and all of this laid before your eyes in a sort of genealogical table . . . in order to convince even the most idiotic of doubters."[32] Such a table might look like figure 7, which shows a closed recension—a lineage of manuscripts—of the existing codices (A, B, C, etc.) and their lost archetypes ([a], [b], [c]). In this figure, [a] is the original, now absent manuscript. Its direct offspring, A, is thus as important a witness as all the rest of the manuscripts (B–E) taken together, since at best these are offspring of the archetype [b]. Even if, therefore, all of these last manuscripts agree on a variant reading, their total weight is still no greater than A taken by itself, since it represents a more direct link to the lost original. "One codex from the first hand is more important than many produced from the rest of the codices." Nor is A necessarily an older manuscript than B–E. There could, for instance, be a number of lost copies between A and [a]. But as long as the line was kept pure, A would still have the closest direct kinship to [a]. Thus, "it appears, that the quality [of a codex] indeed does not always depend on its antiquity."[33] By

[30] Gerhard of Maastricht, "Canones critici," §XII, 13.

[31] Bengel, "Apparatus criticus," 374. The principle of weighing manuscripts had been articulated earlier: Angelo Poliziano wrote in his *Miscellanea* that "the testimonies of the ancients should not so much be counted up, as weighed." Like Bengel, Poliziano wanted "to discriminate, to reduce the number of witnesses that the scholar need take into account," as Anthony Grafton has shown. Interestingly, Poliziano's interests also led him to the genealogical model of manuscript evaluation. See Anthony Grafton, *Joseph Scaliger: A Study in the History of Classical Scholarship* (Oxford, 1983), 1:26. Also see Sebastiano Timpanaro, *Die Entstehung der Lachmannschen Methode* (Hamburg, 1971), 4, and Kenney, *Classical Text*, 10–11.

[32] Bengel, "Apparatus criticus," 380, 387. See Martin West, *Textual Criticism and Editorial Technique* (Stuttgart, 1973), 32ff.

[33] Bengel, "Apparatus criticus," 379, 430.

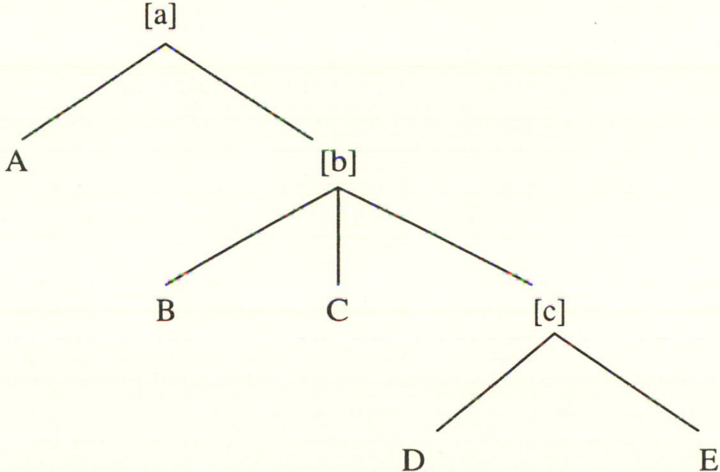

Figure 7. Genealogical Table. Closed recension. MS. in capitals are existing codices and those in brackets are lost archetypes.

comparing the family of manuscripts B–E with the single manuscript A, a scholar might be able to reconstruct the lost original [a].

This explanation is a thoroughly modern one, of course, for genealogy is still *the* dominant strategy for reconstructing lost codices. Bengel himself never drew up one of these tables, and it would take nearly a hundred years before any one else took his cue and did so. He did, however, first discern the outlines of what he (and later scholars) came to call the New Testament "superfamilies": the so-called Asiatic family—stemming from Constantinople, and ultimately from the recension of Lucian of Antioch—and the African, which included in general the Alexandrian Greek codices, and especially Origen's recension.[34] And despite the technical developments still in the wings, his work augured an important change. In the attempt to codify the science of textual recension, Bengel turned his attention from the actual text of the Bible to the manuscripts that secretly underlay it. Seeing that each manuscript had a particular history and seeing that reconstruction of this history might allow a form of indirect access to the lost original biblical texts, Bengel transformed these texts. No longer could they be seen exclusively as carriers of theological truths. Instead, they came to stand for something beyond their own theological, or even literary, content. The texts—and more accurately the manuscripts—became pieces of nonliterary evidence. They became, in short, documents.

[34] Bengel, "Apparatus criticus," 429. On ancient recensions of the Greek New Testament, see Bruce Metzger, "The Lucianic Recension of the Greek Bible," in *Chapters in the History of New Testament Criticism* (Leiden, 1963), 1–41.

The Manuscript Machine: The Documentary Bible

What one might call the "documentary impulse" was already implied in the nascent discipline of paleography, whose birth pains roughly corresponded with the development of New Testament textual criticism. Pride of place in this development is usually given to the French monk Jean Mabillon. Mabillon's famous 1681 *De re diplomatica libri VI* responded to the Jesuit Daniel Papebroch's claim that "almost all of the documents of the Merovingian time . . . [were] not genuine," including the treasured manuscripts of Mabillon's own Maurist order.[35] Mabillon wanted to reestablish the authority of these Latin documents by classifying the hands in which they were written. In the process, he ended up founding the science of paleography, classifying (as it turns out incorrectly) scribal hands into four classes: Gothic, Longobardian, Francogallican or Merovingian, and Saxon. The Maurist Bernard de Montfaucon would follow in Mabillon's footsteps and use the tools developed in his *Palaeographia graeca* (1708) to rebut the idiosyncratic claims of that arch-skeptic Jean Hardouin, who doubted the authenticity of all classical literature (excepting only the Latin works of Cicero and Pliny, Virgil's *Georgics*, Horace's *Satires* and *Letters*, and the Greek texts of Homer and Herodotus).[36] Montfaucon's retort to Hardouin was, in essence, that Greek manuscripts, hands, and letters have a history too complicated for one forger to produce. If all scribes unconsciously reveal their own historical context by the handwriting they adopt, a single forger could never duplicate the variety of unconscious historical signatures that mark the textual record.[37]

This idea of the textual unconscious was key to the documentary impulse. By divorcing the physical features of the manuscript from its literary content, and by using these physical features to historicize the manuscript, both Mabillon and Montfaucon successfully removed the question of literary content from the domain of serious scholarship. In a sense, they operated within that wider shift from "gentlemanly humanism" to a "professionalized philology" that we have already seen in English letters in the early part of the eighteenth century.[38] For those on the modern side of the *querelles des anciens et des modernes*, like the Maurist brothers, scholarship should not be distracted by the idle pleasures of aesthetic judgment. Nor should it be moved by the particular arguments made in the texts it analyzed. Rather, it should invent nonliterary techniques (of which paleography was one) for evaluating documents. "In [modern] editions of older books, errors and doubtful readings, very often occur, which are not found in the older exemplars," Montfaucon pointed out,

[35] See Ludwig Traube, "Geschichte und Grundlagen der Paläographie und Handschriftenkunde," *Vorlesungen und Abhandlungen* (Munich, 1909), 1:19. Also see Blandine Barret-Kriegel, *Jean Mabillon* (Paris, 1988).

[36] Traube, "Paläographie," 1:31.

[37] On Montfaucon, see Traube, "Paläographie," 1:35–42.

[38] Jarvis, *Scholars and Gentlemen*, 21.

and so "it is useful to discern their ages, so that whatever does not exist in the older exemplars, will be deemed to be introduced into the more recent exemplars."[39] A simple point, perhaps, but behind it lay a whole mechanism for distinguishing between types of parchment, various inks, scribal hands, and punctation that took no account of the literary merits of the work it evaluated. This was, all in all, a mechanism for transforming works of literature into the nonliterary evidence that Arnaldo Momigliano some fifty years ago saw as the great tool of the Age of Antiquaries.[40]

In the case of New Testament criticism, this conversion of texts into documents would take place under the gentle touch of Bengel.[41] On the one hand, he invented a machinery for cataloguing and ranking manuscripts, irrespective of their provenance. In assessing a manuscript, the trustworthiness of the scribe, the beauty of the scripts, and the richness of the materials were all essentially irrelevant. Indeed, in itself, any one manuscript was nearly worthless. Only when manuscripts were set into a constellation of other manuscripts, compared and grouped, could the textual scholar hope to move toward those now lost, but original superfamilies. Agreement between sources was only important, in this logic, when it spanned across the widest variety of textual traditions available. Readings present only within one tradition (no matter how many manuscripts are in that tradition) are far less interesting, then, than those present in a variety of traditions separated in time and space. "What truly counts," Bengel exclaimed, "is the *diversity* of witnesses that are separated least from the source, from the first writer, and that are separated farthest from one another."[42] Bengel's manuscript machine, in other words, had little time for individual examples, and even less for connoisseurship. Instead, it was designed to process and organize large quantities of textual information.

On the other hand, his manuscript machine also transformed the status of error in the New Testament codices. Since the seventeenth century, error was a plague on the biblical house. Richard Simon's 1678 *Critical History of the Old Testament*, we remember, began with an excursus on error: since "the first originals have been lost," the Bible has seen numberless "changes, as much because of the length of time as by the negligence of copyists." In his *Critical History of the Versions of the New Testament*, Simon returned to this theme, insisting that both the Greek and Latin versions of the New Testament had, in ancient times, seen "alterations . . . so great, that *Origen's* Art of Critic could not entirely remedy them." This "Confusion in the Books of the New Testament" was

[39] Montfaucon, *Palaeographia Graeca* (Paris, 1708), ii.

[40] Arnaldo Momigliano, "Ancient History and the Antiquarian." Wettstein too took up the Bible as a document, most vividly in his introduction to the *Prolegomena*, which he begins by describing the physical materials and colors of codices (*Novum Testamentum Graecum editionis receptae cum lectionibus variantibus* [Amsterdam, 1751], 1).

[41] Bengel wrote to Montfaucon in January of 1724 asking about manuscripts for an edition of Chrysostom's *De sacerdotio* and was clearly familiar with his work (Burk, ed., *Bengels Briefwechsel*, 85).

[42] Bengel, "Apparatus criticus," 429.

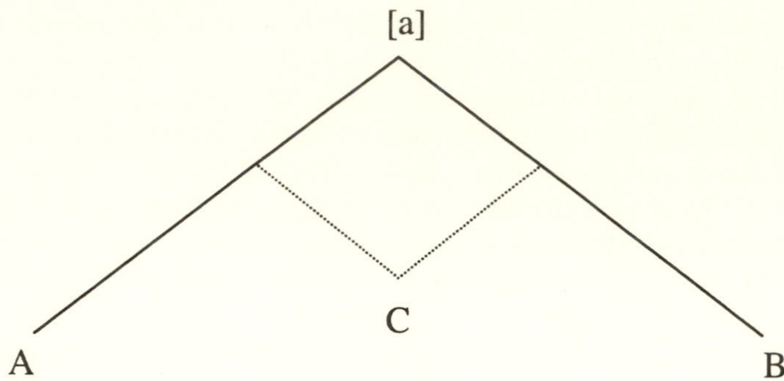

Figure 8. Genealogical Table. Open recension. The MS C is formed by combination of A and B (indicated here by dotted lines).

largely irreversible for the modern critic owing to the antiquity and ubiquity of the errors. Protestants who made Scripture alone the basis of their creeds did so at their peril, therefore, since the "innumerable faults" found in even the most beautiful manuscripts put the entire biblical text into question.[43]

Where previous generations of Protestant scholars would have quailed (and did) at the thought of these errors, Bengel embraced them with both arms. They were, in fact, the key to solving the most difficult problem in manuscript criticism, that which arose when scribes consulted more than one text when copying their new version. When, as Bengel put it, "from the somewhat eclectic efforts of the scribes, [new] codices are generated from other diverse codices," contamination can occur between the families. If this happens, the closed recension figure no longer applies. Instead, an open recension results (fig. 8). In this case, the textual tradition gets so tangled that determination of the archetype becomes a difficult and intricate practice. Even in this complicated case, though, "any nation or family should retain distinct signs of their origins."[44] These signs were the errors introduced during the copying process, the only clues researchers had to the history of the manuscripts.

Imagine, for example, that an editor has the three manuscripts pictured in figure 8, manuscripts that share many similar readings, but differ also in other places. Assuming that C is produced by combining A and B, the following situation results: A and C will sometimes agree in error against B, B and C will sometimes agree in error against A, but A and B will almost never agree in error against C. In this version of the open recension, C can effectively be eliminated as an independent witness. Although Bengel did not describe this open recension

[43] Simon, *Histoire critique*, 1; *Versions of the New Testament*, 20, 53, 73.

[44] Bengel, "Apparatus criticus," 388.

so clearly, his manuscript machine presumed that that error and its transmission was the key to unlocking the relationships between manuscripts. In it, error became a positive aspect of the biblical text, an asset to the textual critic. "The consensus of two codices," he declared, "of which one is old, one is new, one is emended, one is full of errors, offers help firmer than two twin manuscripts both old and good." The most fruitful error was not so much the giant omissions and transpositions, but the "subtle difference" that "the scribe . . . easily overlooked and neglected." By escaping the scribe's editorial eye, these differences preserved the familial affiliations between manuscripts. It was these very differences, "the more minute variations," that "Mill himself . . . neglected or omitted from the codices he recended."[45] Indeed, like Bentley before him, Bengel saw that "Mill's method can [not] be accused of 'micrology,' since still greater accuracy is desirable."[46] Bengel's own micrological method forced him to work out the subtlest details of manuscripts in order to capture their tenuous affiliations and generate a genealogy of the manuscript tradition. In this method, errors functioned less as parts of a text than as nonliterary evidence for and against genealogical relationships. Not only were they necessary, they were welcome: as evidence of scribal interventions into the text, they made the history of a manuscript legible.

Only to the critic for whom Bible was a document, one whose theological content was essentially bracketed or set aside, could error have this function. In this sense, this transformation of error into evidence hearkened to the incipient separation—fully articulated by Johann Semler some years later—between the pure Word of God and the Scriptures corrupted by the hands of men. With this separation too we can speak of a detheologization of biblical scholarship, where scholarship is neither governed by, nor a threat to theological truths. Even though Bengel repeatedly affirmed in his works that the "word of the living God" was equivalent to the Holy Scriptures, still his manuscript machine implied the opposite.[47] It implied that the theological message of the biblical texts was in no way relevant to the kind of scholarship done on the biblical documents. The question of error represented this change at its most dramatic. For Bengel, unlike generations of Protestant scholars, theologians, and apologists, the issue of biblical error was fundamentally irrelevant to the truth of Christianity. More errors did not entail greater uncertainty about the Bible. Nor were they evidence for the depravity of God's Word. If textual error was among the key weapons that Catholics, deists, and skeptics applied to biblical authority, here Bengel appropriated the weapon while neutralizing its theological charge. In his hands, the question of error became solely a text-critical one. Errors were *evidence*, evidence for the various histories of manuscripts whose reconstruction paved the road to an uncorrupted Scripture.

[45] Ibid., 431–32.

[46] Bengel, *Prodromus*, vi.

[47] Ibid., *Gnomon Novi Testamenti*, §I.

Criticism, Philology, and the Vernacular Bible

Philology substituting for theology: we might expect this from a devotee of secularism. But Bengel was hardly secular. Instead, as one of the leading Pietists in the south German state of Württemberg, he walked the *via media* between the enthusiastic devotions of the religious radicals and the stern hand of Lutheran church orthodoxy.[48] A fan of eschatology and of the Book of Daniel, Bengel combined millennial expectations with sober scholarship. Although his prediction that the world would end on 18 June 1836 was fortunately incorrect, he was hardly someone to dismiss theology and theological speculation *tout court*.[49] Instead, like almost all scholars of his generation and the ones to come, he was deeply concerned about the fate of religion, theology, and the Bible in the modern era. His synthesis of scholarship and Bible study was typical for these generations, who were fundamentally devoted to keeping the Bible relevant and meaningful to modern readers. For Bengel, such meaning could be found in criticism.

It is no accident that Bengel coined the phrase *apparatus criticus*, for example, nor that Bengel demanded that criticism must "animate and moderate" religion and piety.[50] The critic must approach the Bible, in the words of the eclectic German philosopher Christian Thomasius, knowing that "a drop of judgment is much better than a pound of memory."[51] Or, in the later words of Viscount Bolingbroke, "criticism separates the ore from the dross, and extracts from various authors a . . . true history."[52] In textual terms, a drop of critical analysis and historical judgment was better by far in Bengel's view than a pound of unanalyzed and uncategorized variant readings. This convergence of scholarship and criticism was not unusual in the eighteenth century, which, as the "critical age," renewed the etymological meaning of the Greek word κρινω (to distinguish, judge, or decide) and reinvested the term with a powerfully positive force.[53] Jonathan Swift's cutting image of an incestuous "*Criticism*" flanked by "*Ignorance*, her Father and Husband . . . [and] *Pride* her Mother" was a volley in a bookish battle he was destined to lose.[54] For the critic became the emblem of

[48] For general analysis of south German Pietists, see Martin Brecht, "Der Württembergische Pietismus," *Geschichte des Pietismus, Band II*, 230–37, and Hartmut Lehmann, *Pietismus und weltliche Ordnung in Württemberg vom 17. bis zum 20. Jahrhundert* (Stuttgart, 1969), 40–51.

[49] For his predictions see his *Ordo temporum* (Stuttgart, 1741).

[50] Bengel, "Epilogue," *Novum Testamentum Graecum*, 870.

[51] Christian Thomasius, *Gedanken oder Monatsgespräche über allerhand neue Bücher* (Halle, 1688), 2:614.

[52] Lord Bolingbroke, *Letters on the Study and Use of History*, in *Works* (London, 1844), 2:217

[53] In general, see Reinhart Koselleck, *Critique and Crisis: Enlightenment and the Pathogenesis of Modern Society* (Cambridge, MA, 1988).

[54] Jonathan Swift, "The Battle of the Books" [1710], in *A Tale of a Tub with Other Early Works, 1696–1707*, ed. Herbert Davis (Oxford, 1957), 153.

the age, a symbol of the triumph of judgment over memory. Translated into the terms of biblical scholarship, collection made way for the critical evaluation of various readings. Richard Bentley's famous dictum, that "*nobis et ratio et res ipsa centum codicibus potiores sunt*," was perhaps an extreme example of the new critical spirit, but it was a spirit that extended far and wide in the eighteenth century.[55] Bengel was no exception, and although he would never give up a manuscript in favor of a disembodied *ratio*, his manuscript machine demanded textual inspection so detailed it approached paranoia. "Where there is no . . . suspicion, no critical method can be introduced," as the theologian Friedrich Schleiermacher later said, and Bengel's critical micrology demanded an unprecedented suspicion about the details of the text.[56] Only such suspicious attention promised to uncover affiliations between manuscripts and ultimately to recover the lost apostolic text.

It was an apparent paradox, then, that Bengel never let his suspicious, micrological criticism make it into the text of the Greek New Testament itself. Indeed, Bengel changed almost nothing in his actual edition. He allowed himself to intervene only in the text of Revelations, a text that the *textus receptus* had long injured, owing to Erasmus's precipitous back-translation of various Vulgate passages to augment his single Greek codex of the Apocalypse.[57] With this exception, though, the goal to "accept not one syllable not already accepted" was for the most part met.[58] But this paradox was, in the end, only a superficial one. Indeed, the refusal to intervene (even when intervention seems absolutely imperative) was also wholly typical of eighteenth-century criticism, in which, as Pierre Bayle declared, the "dual role of prosecutor and defender . . . [turned] the critic into a non-partisan authority, into the advocate of reason."[59] In his heart, the ideal scholar had opposing commitments. On the one hand, he was supposed to be on the side of truth and thus remain distant from the sectarian conflicts that plagued seventeenth-century scholarship. On the other, he was supposed to intervene actively in matters critical. In order to retain the neutrality of criticism—the neutrality that guaranteed criticism its insights into truth—Enlightenment critics and scholar-critics separated themselves from the objects of criticism, whether theological, legal, moral, or political. The beloved adjectives "nonpartisan" and "impartial" were coined to name this refusal to "take part." In the religious sphere, this refusal manifested itself in (or

[55] "Both reason and the nature of the case are better for us than a hundred manuscripts;" Bentley quoted in John Edwin Sandys, *A History of Classical Scholarship* (New York, 1967), 2:406.

[56] Friedrich Schleiermacher, *Hermeneutik und Kritik*, ed. Manfred Frank (Frankfurt a. M., 1977), 255.

[57] On back translations, see Bruce Metzger, *Text of the New Testament*, 99–100.

[58] Bengel, *Prodromus*, iii. Eduard Reuss notes a total of 149 differences between Bengel's text and the Elzivirian *textus receptus* (*Bibliotheca Novi Testamenti Graeci* [Braunschweig, 1872], 177–78).

[59] Koselleck, *Critique and Crisis*, 109.

perhaps more accurately was motivated by) the fierce censure of sects and sectarianism that permeated all early Enlightenment scholarly literature. In Germany, Pietists and rationalists alike decried partisanship as anathema to the project of conserving the truth.[60] Even as it proved scholarship's freedom from zealotry, the embrace of impartiality also put certain restrictions on the activity of the scholar. Real-world objects could be discussed, but only from a distance, and actual interference with these objects became, at least for now, a violation of the rules that enabled criticism to function. I am not sure that Paul Hazard meant exactly this when he wrote that "the critic, as such, may not put any gloss or interpretation of his own upon the text," but such would work well to describe the turn-of-the-century birth of criticism.[61] Even clearer was Reinhard Koselleck's comment that "the moral tribunal became political criticism not only by subjecting politics to its stern judgment, but vice versa as well, by separating itself as a tribunal from the political sphere."[62]

Just as the division between morality and politics provided a space for the neutered political criticism that characterized absolutist Europe, so too did the division between text and apparatus provide a space for a contained textual criticism. Bengel's work was a prime example here, where the apparatus held revolutionary implications for the text, but where the division between the two was rigorously maintained. Many critics, Bengel complained, argue that "*because* this reading exists in MSS., in versions, here and there in the fathers, *therefore* we defend it. . . . [but] where the reading pleasing to them is weak, then they say: *although* the reading exists in MSS., in versions, here and there in the fathers, *nevertheless* we do not admit it."[63] Bengel's answer to this dilemma was to let *none* of it into the text, lest he (or any critic) fall under the sway of his own prejudices. In a sense, then, his critical philology functioned only if it confined itself to the margins.

In Bengel's Greek New Testament, he devised an ingenious way of doing this. The edition presented a very clean text underlaid by the variant readings. Each reading was assigned a grade, ranging from α, meaning that the variant given underneath the text is certainly the correct reading, to β, meaning that the variant is more likely than the received reading, all the way to ε, meaning that the variant is certainly incorrect. Rather than put the variants into the text, in other words, he signaled their appropriate place from the sidelines, preserving at the same time both the freedom to criticize *and* an intact text of the Greek New Testament. This marginal criticism precipitated attacks both from orthodox theologians (who accused him of "unnecessarily and without cause chang[ing] . . . the text of the N. T.") and from rationalist scholars (who saw this

[60] See, e.g., Gottfried Arnold, *Unpartheyische Kirchen- und Ketzer-Geschichte* (Frankfurt a. M., 1699); also Gierl, *Pietismus und Aufklärung*, 386–87.

[61] Hazard, *European Mind*, 183.

[62] Koselleck, *Critique and Crisis*, 102.

[63] Bengel, "Apparatus criticus," 424.

strategy as a sop to "evade all scandal and satisfy infirm consciences").[64] But Bengel was less concerned about critics than readers, in whom he wished to induce a certain experience, the experience of choice. Only if readers see all "emendations derived faithfully from manuscripts . . . in the margin" can they sincerely "explore their truth and enjoy their wholesomeness." In this way, "truth and modesty . . . are mated together; until, with the growing wisdom of posterity, the text absorbs the residual marginal crumbs."[65] Probabilistically organized marginalia—in Bengel's scheme—thus had a special moral and epistemological virtue: they put the choice into the hands of the readers, giving them enough information to make an informed decision about the variants. The onus of choice might only be laid on the readers, in other words, if the received text was maintained and the activity of criticism moved to the margins. Viewed more broadly, it was not that "commentary has yielded to criticism," as Foucault wrote, but that criticism took place in and through commentary, took place in the apparatus, on the margins and in the editorial process.[66] And Bengel extended this critical approach when he turned his hand to New Testament translation.

This German New Testament—and its connection to philology and the vernacular Bible—was augured already in April 1724, when Bengel contacted the notorious translator Caspar Triller (see chapter 3), describing how he had "begun to annotate the Greek New Testament . . . not so that variant readings might be accumulated, but in order that the authority of single readings and the credibility of the decisive ones . . . might be tested."[67] Two years later, he was invited by the Berleburger translators either to contribute an original language text or to aid in the translation effort itself.[68] But Bengel's project only really began in 1740, when he published a translation of the Apocalypse along with a commentary. The translation was prefaced with the following caveat: "This translation of Revelations can . . . serve as a trial [*Probe*] for the German translation of the entire New Testament, which I wrote a while ago, but decided not to publish, unless there seems to be a tolerable hope to see more fruit than controversy about it."[69] Bengel's hopes were quickly dashed by an unsympathetic theological old guard whose response was as immediate as it was predictable. "We wish," wrote the editor of one notoriously intolerant journal, "that the author might turn his scholarly efforts to more important concerns, since the German translation of Luther remains everlastingly victorious."[70]

[64] [Johann Hager], *Fortgesetzte Sammlung* (Leipzig, 1738), 160; [Wettstein], *Bibliothèque Raisonnée des Ouvrages des Savans de l'Europe* 13 (July–September 1734): 210.

[65] Bengel, "Notitia Novi Testamenti Graeci recte cauteque adornandi" (1731) in *D. Io. Alberti Bengelii Apparatus Criticus ad Novum Testamentum*, ed. Philip David Burk (Tübingen, 1763), 639.

[66] Michel Foucault, *The Order of Things* (New York, 1970), 80.

[67] Bengel's *Nachlass*, Württembergische Landesbibliothek Stuttgart, cod.hist.fol.1002.40.

[68] The information on the Berlenburg invitation comes from a letter to an unknown, dated 13 March 1731 (Burk, ed., *Bengels Briefwechsel*, 10).

[69] Bengel, *Erklärte Offenbarung Johannis . . . übersetzet* (Stuttgart, 1740), a5^r.

[70] *Frühaufgelesene Früchte der theologischen Sammlung von Alten und Neuen* (Leipzig, 1741), 200.

This reaction apparently delayed the publication of the full translation until 1753, when Bengel was literally on his deathbed.

The emphasis on a pure original was indeed the central thesis of Bengel's translation project. To the modern ear, this sounds as unremarkable as it is irreproachable, but was not so in times past. Even scholars were not fully convinced: the philologian Christoph Heumann, for example, actually berated Bengel for using a revised original text. As for himself, he proudly declared, he followed "the common Greek text" in his 1748 translation.[71] But for Bengel, the corrected original version was absolutely essential for *any* new translation: "a translation must be based on a truly revised original text." This philological commitment distinguished, in Bengel's mind, his version from "others, for example, Reitz, Triller, Junckherrott" who "concerned themselves little about the condition of their Greek exemplars."[72] Where the radical Pietists were happy to seek the original texts inside their hearts, Bengel insisted on the real thing.

The translation itself was composed of text unbroken by chapter-and-verse headings underlaid by a commentary. Here is Bengel's version of the Lord's Prayer:

> Now pray, as follows: Our Father in the Heavens, let thy name be holy, let thy kingdom come, let thy will be done, as in heaven, so too on earth. Give us now our daily bread. And leave aside our debts, just as we leave aside our debtors. And lead us not into temptation, rather save us from evil (*Argen*). [Because thine is the kingdom and the power and the majesty in eternity. Amen.]
>
> **9 what follows**) with little. Everything is here encompassed that concerns God and us. **Thy, Thy, Thy; ours, us, etc.**
>
> **11 daily)** the need of which stretches from the present to the following day.
>
> **12 our debts)** We should not only apologize for our debts of sin altogether, but whoever has in one way or another, in some manner insulted God, should in particular recognize and apologize for such insults, and give honor to Him.
>
> **13 from evil)** The evil one is the devil, the temptor.
>
> **Because—Amen)** There are, in addition to the Latin and Egyptian translations, old Greek exemplars, in which these words do not appear. This is treated more explicitly elsewhere.

Bengel's edition was split between its slightly awkward translation and a comprehensive set of "useful annotations." As this passage makes clear, the annotations ran the gamut of edifying pieties, pedantries (the definition of "daily," for example), and philological comments. These latter were, on the whole, rather

[71] Christoph August Heumann, *Das Neue Testament* (Hannover, 1748), 2:xxii.

[72] Bengel, *Neues Testament*, xiii.

uncommon in the text, in accordance with Bengel's late efforts to move away from scholarship. "I am so fed up with the scholarly world," he wrote in 1749, "that I do even what has to be done (which is still in vain) almost against my will."[73] Despite this disgust with letters, however, Bengel periodically returned to philology and philological explanation in his translation (Matt. 16.18, 19.17, John 14.16, and so on). This note to the bracketed Lord's Prayer doxology was the most significant, principally since Bengel had devoted so many pages to this passage in his Greek New Testament. Undoubtedly in the back of his mind was the fact that the Vulgate omitted this doxology, and only when Luther and other Protestants looked to the Greek manuscripts did the doxology enter the Western church. Though it is usually ascribed, in modern times, to an early transposition of the Greek Orthodox liturgy into the gospel, in Bengel's time the authority of the doxology was hotly disputed.[74] Bengel himself was undecided as to its worth, concluding finally that "concerning the whole matter, let the reader judge."[75]

Such a comment might well serve as the epigraph for Bengel's entire translation project. Whereas the radical separatists looked to generate a pan-confessional, universal text by means either linguistic or scholarly, Bengel self-consciously styled his translation as a variant on a theme, an alternative for the curious reader. "In the oriental and occidental communities, both ancient and modern, many translations into a single language have always been made, tolerated, appreciated, and used": why not in Germany? If a multitude of Bible versions—Coptic or Syriac, English or French—could coexist elsewhere, why the strife that attended German efforts? "I seek to offer, not a better, but a different [New Testament] than Luther's," Bengel avowed, so that readers might judge and choose for themselves an agreeable version. In the array of available translations, Bengel's was a philological version, one concerned to reproduce with perfect fidelity "the true Greek original text."[76] The ultimate goal was "a German text, upon which I might found and build my German interpretation of the New Testament, and not always have to say about the Luther translation: 'In Greek it actually says such and such.' "[77]

Here we can see the first self-conscious embrace of the ramified Enlightenment Bible, a Bible functionally distributed across a variety of different functions and domains. If, for Habermas, the new eighteenth-century art critic differed from the judge because he offered only a "judgment of one private person

[73] Mälzer, *Bengel*, 108.

[74] See Bruce Metzger, *A Textual Commentary on the Greek New Testament* (London, 1971), 16–17. On the eighteenth-century conflict about the doxology, see Johann Adam Osiander, *Schediasma Criticum, quo authentia clausulae orationis dominicae rationibus selectoribus asseritur* . . . (Tübingen, [1737]); also Sigismund Jacob Baumgarten, *Authentiam Doxologiae Matth. VI. Com. XIII* (Halle, 1753).

[75] Bengel, "Apparatus criticus," 467.

[76] Ibid., *Neues Testament*, viii, ix.

[77] Mälzer, *Bengel*, 215.

among all others" and thus could not demand agreement from his hearers, then Bengel's biblical translator distinguished himself from the theological judge because he too foreswore the right to absolute truth.[78] In so doing, Bengel the Pietist offered the earliest version of the Enlightenment Bible, consciously acknowledging that philology could recreate *a* Bible, but not necessarily *the* Bible. Stepping away from the radical Pietist desire for the perfect translation, he set his own version within a wider constellation of translations, at the center of which sat Luther's "preeminent, heroic work." As Bengel saw it, new translations simply could not replace the Luther Bible. Indeed, the proliferation of Bibles only made the need for the preservation of a common standard more urgent, especially in the realm of practice. And so, like the *textus receptus* of the Greek New Testament, Bengel reasoned, "one should, in the Bible printed under [Luther's] name, change nothing and add nothing not from Luther."[79] It was precisely at this time, too, that Luther's Bible itself was subjected to rigorous textual history, its editions, printings, and histories laid out for scholarly discussion. From Johann Melchior Krafft, Christian Reiniccius, and Gustav Zeltner, to Johann Melchior Goeze, Johann Georg Palm, and Johann Panzer, histories of the Luther Bible and its editions became a major scholarly genre over the course of the century.[80] If the Luther Bible had itself become a historical object, fixed in 1545, then according to Bengel's logic, new translations should not seek to replace it. Rather they should serve only to augment it. As such, new versions would function as variant readings on the dominant German language text, as vernacular *variae lectiones* whose worth had to determined by the discerning reader. In particular, by including "a continuing commentary," translators ensured that their works would never be "dangerous for the Luther translation."[81] Even the most edifying, pious annotations thus functioned to mark the new translations as variant readings, simultaneously denaturalizing new translations and preserving an intact Luther Bible.

Bengel's model was, thus, a scholarly and philological one. Not that his translation had all of the philological accoutrements of a critical edition, for at times Bengel seemed to insist that "*not only criticism, but also . . . philology*" should be kept separate from the vernacular text.[82] Rather, Bengel saw translation as a solution to the problem that he had run into in 1742 with *Gnomon*

[78] Jürgen Habermas, *The Structural Transformation of the Public Sphere* (Cambridge, MA, 1989), 41.

[79] Bengel, *Neues Testament*, xii, xi.

[80] See, inter alia, Johann Melchior Krafft, *Prodromus historiae versionis Germanicae Bibliorum* (Hamburg, 1714–16); Christian Reineccius, *Vertheitigung der Teutschen Bibel Lutheri* (Leipzig, 1718); Johann Georg Palm, *Historie der deutschen Bibel-Uebersetzung Martini Lutheri* (Halle, 1772); Johann Melchior Goeze, *Sorgfältige und genaue Vergleichung der Original-Ausgaben der Uebersetzung der Heiligen Schrift* (Hamburg, 1777); Georg Martin Panzer, *Entwurf einer vollständigen Geschichte der deutschen Bibelübersetzung D. Martin Luthers* (Nuremberg, 1791).

[81] Bengel, *Neues Testament*, xii.

[82] My italics. Bengel, preface to the *Novum Testamentum Graecum*, *4^{r-v}.

Novi Testamenti, in which he tried "vexingly to separate the one [domain] from the other," to separate the scholarly from the vernacular, the erudite from the popular.[83] The difficulty of this separation convinced him, in the end, that full German annotations were imperative. The translation was "inseparably bound" to these never-completed annotations, for through it, Bengel hoped to reunify what the *Gnomon* wanted to separate, namely the philological and the exegetical aspects of the Bible.[84] In his translation would be found pious edification, emphasis on the original language text, occasional philological commentary, and, most importantly, a thoroughly scholarly understanding of how new translations should function within the general economy of midcentury Bibles. Thus criticism and philology would be integrated into the vernacular Bible.

In this regard, the similarities, rather than the differences, clearly stand out between Bengel and the German Pietist count Nikolaus von Zinzendorf. A giant figure in the eighteenth century and crucial to the development of English Methodism, Zinzendorf was first educated at Halle, but soon broke from the mainstream Pietists to found a new, utopian religious community in the Saxon town of Herrnhut. This community became the center for an enthusiastic and alternative religious experiment exported as far as South Africa and the Arctic circle. Zinzendorf spent much time, spent much money, and underwent much physical hardship promoting this community. One of his key tools was his pen, which prolifically generated scores of treatises, hymnals, and poems in the name of his new religion of love. This pen produced, in 1739, a new translation of the New Testament.[85]

Like many commentators, Bengel roundly abused Zinzendorf 's New Testament. In his most public condemnation of the Count, the *Abriss der so genannten Brüdergemeine* (1751), Bengel exclaimed that the text was "not the purely apostolic, but the [Herrnhuter] New Testament."[86] In particular, Bengel saw in Zinzendorf 's translation a tendency to soften the harder words of God, such as where Zinzendorf translated "bad people" in place of "sinners" (Matt. 9.10), or "worrysome conditions" for "temptations (Luke 19.9).[87] But it was to *Bengel* that Zinzendorf looked for inspiration, in particular to Bengel's Greek New Testament, which Zinzendorf used to justify his elimination of all of the readings "that are marked . . . with an a or b."[88] And despite the antagonism between

[83] Bengel, *Gnomon Novi Testamenti*, §XXIV.

[84] Mälzer, *Bengel*, 213.

[85] On Zinzendorf, see Erich Beyreuther, *Der junge Zinzendorf* (Marburg am der Lahn, 1957); *Zinzendorf und die Christenheit, 1732–1760* (Marburg am der Lahn, 1961).

[86] Bengel, *Abriss der so genannten Brüdergemeine* (1751), in *Materialien und Dokumente*, ed. Erich Beyreuther, 2nd series (Hildesheim, 1972), 10:202–203.

[87] Bengel, *Abriss*, 182–83.

[88] See "Errinerungen des Hrn. Gr. v. Z. wegen seiner Ersten Probe der Ubersetzung des Neuen Testaments an seine Herren Gegner" (1741), in *Nikolaus Ludwig von Zinzendorf Hauptschriften*, ed. Erich Beyreuther and Gerhard Meyer (Hildesheim, 1963), 6:202–203.

them, both shared a similar ideal of the translation enterprise as one that was supposed to produce an alternative, not an authoritative, New Testament version. Like Bengel—and like many translators right through the nineteenth century—Zinzendorf called his first edition of the New Testament a *Probe*, a test or experiment. His second edition he entitled an "*abermaligen Versuch*," a renewed attempt, or a "*Schul-Exercitium*," a school exercise. All of these he distinguished from the "*textus sacer*," the priestly or authoritative text, which remained the Luther Bible.[89] In the end, the Luther Bible would be supplemented and clarified, not replaced. For both Bengel and Zinzendorf, then, the aim of translation was to provide a reader with choices and to lay the burden of choice on him. More than anything else, it is this agreement between otherwise staunch foes that confirms the power of the new philological Bible as it emerged in the middle of the eighteenth century.

The Philological Answer

When the scholar Johann Eichhorn ruminated on early-century scholarship, it was Bengel who leaped to his mind. Above all others, Eichhorn wrote in 1793, it was Bengel who made criticism into a viable biblical discipline: "He penetrated deep into the inner content of the texts of the manuscripts, the variants in the translations, and the church fathers. Correctly he arranged the witnesses into classes!"[90] The work of Bengel, in Eichhorn's mind, paved the way for the elite textual scholars who would take the critical tools developed by the south German Pietist and put them to new ends. Chief among Eichhorn's elite was Johann Semler, who, like Bengel, was a scholar of the New Testament, one who saw the *lectio difficilior* and the genealogical organization of manuscripts as a crucial step forward in New Testament textual criticism.[91] And, like Bengel too, Semler embraced the principle that the entire message of the Bible could be determined from only a few genuine passages, guaranteeing that, whatever mistakes might have slinked into the Bible over the centuries, the fundamental message remained intact. Indeed, Semler himself looked back to Bengel for the early lineage of this principle. Semler saw clearly what Bengel himself repeatedly denied, that if one argued (as Bengel did) that "from even the most corrupt of exemplars . . . faith, hope, love can grow," or (as Semler did) that "no one needs the whole [Bible]; another passage leads another person to salvation," these were the first steps toward the distinction between the text of the Bible and the Word of God: "So far as we and our own needs are concerned, the whole Christian scheme of salvation can be assembled and employed just

[89] Zinzendorf, "Erinnerung," 16.

[90] Johann Eichhorn, *Allgemeine Bibliothek der biblischen Litteratur* (Leipzig, 1793), 5:49.

[91] Johann Semler, *Apparatus ad liberalem Novi Testamenti interpretationem* (Halle, 1767), 45.

as well, just as correctly and fully, from a single book, from a few small passages of many books, as from all together."[92] The result was a kind of devil's bargain, made perhaps unconsciously by Bengel, but deliberately by Semler. On the one side, theology and human salvation were inoculated to the findings of textual critics. The corruption of the biblical texts could not enfeeble the truths of Christianity. On the other side, though, this very inoculation meant that textual critics were free to dismiss theologians anxious to preserve intact the essential Christian truths. No longer did theology have any bearing on the enterprise of philology. Philology was, in essence, free.

As I argued earlier, this loosening of the essential bond between the Bible and theology destroyed the hierarchy established in seventeenth-century Protestantism and traditionally present in Catholicism, a hierarchy that placed theology atop the Bible. In Catholicism, the authentic interpretations of the Church served to harmonize any discrepancies within the biblical text while, among Lutheran theologians, the beloved "analogy of faith" unified the biblical message by making theological precepts into a governing interpretive scheme. If "all doctrine and interpretation of Scripture in the church, must be . . . guided according to the analogy of faith," then, in essence, theological truths need to be determined *before* the Bible can be understood.[93] But by the middle of the eighteenth century—and it is this that Semler both diagnosed and represented—the hierarchy had broken down. Now the Bible stood proudly alongside theology, which took its truths from some portion of the scriptural text, but left the rest to be dealt with by the application of what Semler called "criticism."[94]

In the fifty years after Bengel's death, this reversal of fortunes would multiply translations, "like creeping insects," across the German Protestant world.[95] In the vernacular domain, translations with philological purposes became common scholarly currency. One does not have to look far to see text criticism at work: nearly every translator after 1750, with some notable exceptions, was anxious to prove that the texts they used were the best available to modern scholarship. By the end of the century, philology assumed pride of place even among German Catholics, for whom Bible translation was essentially unimportant and uninteresting during most of the Enlightenment. Prague's Christoph Fischer, for example, declaimed against the slavish love of both the Vulgate and the "common Greek text," declaring that he would pursue "ancient manuscripts, church teachings, and translations" to determine the correct readings.[96] "All of theology,"

[92] Bengel, *Prodromus*, xvi.; Werner Kümmel, *The New Testament: The History of the Investigation of Its Problems* (New York, 1972), 64.

[93] Preus, *Post-Reformation Lutheranism*, 97.

[94] Gottfied Hornig, *Johann Salomo Semler: Studien zu Leben und Werk des Hallenser Aufklärungstheologen* (Tübingen, 1996), 167.

[95] Anonymous review of George Christian Knapp's Psalms translation, *Allgemeine deutsche Bibliothek* 42.1 (1780): 32.

[96] Christoph Fischer, *Die heilige Schrift des neuen Testaments* (Prag, 1784),)(5^{v}.

wrote the anonymous translator of a 1775 edition of Paul's letters, "is essentially linguistic scholarship."[97] Most telling are the ruminations of the secondary-school pedagogue Friedrich Walther, whose *Probe . . . einer Uebersetzung der kleinen Propheten* (1779) contained an encomium to text criticism as the true fundament of secondary learning. It is absolutely essential that the "child be led as early as possible to a . . . *correct taste* in philology, and to a *fundamental* learning of the original languages." The child must be soaked with "the *best and the healthiest taste in Biblical philology*, with the *best and most fundamental ways of interpreting scripture*, and particularly with the *genius of the original languages*." Only translations filled with "*critical* and *philological* annotations" can serve as the "strongest weapons" against religious disbelief; only such translations can provide the "single true source of religious knowledge" for young readers.[98]

As we will see in chapter 8, this philological Bible would begin to resonate in late-century England. But with few exceptions, the English philological project that had produced such luminaries as Mill and Bentley had, by 1750, gone dormant. Not so in Germany, where the enterprise of philological translation was accompanied by rigorous investigation of the biblical manuscripts. After Bengel's death, responsibility for this task fell to Johann Jakob Griesbach, who became the most significant textual scholar in Enlightenment Germany; Griesbach, who divided the manuscripts of the Bible into three families, distinguished between the synoptic gospels (Matthew, Mark, and Luke) and the Gospel of John, and began systematically "abandon[ing] the Textus Receptus."[99] With Griesbach, the so-called documentary hypothesis—the sense of the Bible as a compilation and collation of texts dramatically exemplified by Jean Astruc in his 1753 *Conjectures sur les memoires originaux dont il paroit Moyse s'est servi pour composer le Livre de la Genèse*—had arrived at the doorstep of the New Testament.[100] The Bible had indeed become a document, and by the 1760s, Germany would become the center of European scholarship on its manuscripts. Nowhere in Europe was so much scholarly energy, so much cultural capital, so many university positions, and so many publishing dollars devoted to the biblical text as in Germany. If, in prior centuries, classical philology had taken pride of place in continental European letters, by 1750, "the page had turned," as Sebastiano Timpanaro had it, and German hands did the turning.[101] When the great nineteenth-century scholar Karl Lachmann condemned "the entire philological criticism of the eighteenth century" as "haphazard and desultory," he unwittingly repudiated the very environment that made the neutral textual

[97] [Anonymous], *Pauli Brief an die Römer aufs neue übersetzt* (Leipzig, 1775), a5^{r}.

[98] Friedrich Walther, *Probe und Ankundigung einer Uebersetzung der kleinen Propheten* (Stendal, 1779), 8, 5–6, 9, 4, 3.

[99] Metzger, *Text of the New Testament*, 121.

[100] On Jean Astruc, see Eamonn O'Doherty, "Conjectures of Jean Astruc, 1753," *Catholic Biblical Quarterly* 15 (July 1953): 300–304.

[101] Timpanaro, *Entstehung der Lachmannschen Methode*, 21.

criticism of the New Testament possible. Only after criticism has cut itself free from theology, after all, can one even ask Lachmann's fundamental question: "what can it matter to a critic, if a reading is important or not?"[102] Together textual criticism and translation helped to make this cut, responding to the threats of enthusiasm and skepticism alike and seeking to "rescue the history of Christian origins" by dedicated efforts to the "scientific, analytical study of the New Testament."[103] Together scholarship and translation, in other words, helped to produce a philological Bible. As a tool for teaching, a subject of scholarly research, and a disseminated document, the authority and authenticity of the Bible were guaranteed—in these domains—by the exercise of philological scholarship.

[102] Karl Lachmann, "Rechenschaft über seine Ausgabe des Neuen Testaments," *Theologische Studien und Kritiken* 3 (1830): 818.

[103] Luigi Salvatorelli, "From Locke to Reitzenstein: The Historical Investigations of the Origins of Christianity," *Harvard Theological Review* 22 (1929): 270.

Chapter Five

PEDAGOGY: THE POLITICS AND MORALS OF THE ENLIGHTENMENT BIBLE

In 1768 the English dissenting minister Edward Harwood suggested that, when Christians pray, they ought to say:

> O Thou great governour and parent of universal nature—who manifest thy glory to the blessed inhabitants of heaven—may all thy rational creatures in all the parts of thy boundless dominion be happy in the knowledge of thy existence and providence, and celebrate thy perfections in a manner most worthy thy nature [*sic*] and perfective of their own![1]

As a version of the Lord's Prayer, Harwood's translation left something to be desired. Over 250 words long—triple the usual number—it transformed the prayer's memorable brevity into a windy eulogium to a rational deity and his ever-improving subjects. A "liberal" translation of the New Testament, Harwood's text "cloathe[d] the genuine ideas and doctrines of the Apostles with that propriety and perspicuity, in which they themselves . . . would have exhibited them had they *now* lived and written in our language." Literal translations were improper, Harwood contended, because the "idioms and structures" of the ancient authors were so "essentially different" from modern ones that any attempt at exact reproduction generated only a "barbarous and unintelligible" version of the Bible.[2] A "wild and ungovernable" writer, the poet John Dryden had insisted some hundred years earlier, "cannot be translated literally": although the "sense of an author . . . is to be sacred and inviolable," paraphrase was essential for overcoming the "narrow compass of [an] Author's words."[3] Since, for Harwood, the ancient Jews were the very epitome of a wild people, only a free version would tempt the person of "liberal education and polite taste," repulsed by Jewish literary barbarisms, to "peruse the sacred volume," much to the ultimate advantage of "truth, liberty, and Christianity." As such,

[1] Edward Harwood, *A Liberal Translation of the New Testament* (London, 1768), 15. This could be compared profitably with Benjamin Franklin's new version of the "Our Father": see Benjamin Franklin, *Writings* (New York, 1987), 638ff.

[2] Harwood, *Liberal Translation*, iii.

[3] John Dryden, *Ovid's Epistles* (London, 1680), a2^{r}, a3^{r-v}. On Dryden and translation, see Judith Sloman, *Dryden: The Poetics of Translation* (Toronto, 1985) and William Frost, *Dryden and the Art of Translation* (New Haven, 1955).

Harwood's translation would afford a great service to the cause of religion, curing the scourges of "deism, infidelity, and skepticism" with a Bible made meaningful for a polite age.[4]

In the same year that Harwood's New Testament appeared in book-sellers' stores, England's literary republic was garlanded by the appearance of Thomas Chubb's *Posthumous Works*. Chubb—one of the last deists in England before its general decline in the 1740s—was hardly a fan of the biblical text as it stood. Like the new theologians in Germany, Chubb was unconvinced that "that collection of *writings*, commonly called the Bible" was identical to "the *very word* of God."[5] The Bible "is a *collection* of Books, wrote at *different*, and, some parts of it, at very *distant* times, by a *variety* of persons, upon *many* subjects; whose authors, as they plainly appear to have had very different *sentiments*, and sometimes, perhaps, to have differed from *themselves*."[6] Between the deist and the dissenter stood a field of affiliations and a striking difference. Both were convinced, for example, that the gospel teachings should be understood morally. Chubb ameliorated the Christian notion of sin, for example (arguing that "sin is a *moral* not a natural evil"), in the same way that Harwood ameliorated the "hunger and thirst for righteousness" that motivates Christian zeal by translating it as the "sacred ardour to attain universal virtue."[7] Both were also convinced that the Bible, written long ago in the far-off Mediterranean, was stained by an idiom unsuitable to convey essential truths to the modern human ear. But where Chubb—and deism more generally—imagined natural religion to be sufficient in itself to "qualif[y] a man for eternal salvation" and thus (in his own mind) consigned the biblical text to the dustheap, Harwood clearly worked with a different set of principles. At the very least, his efforts were recuperative, aimed not at replacing the Bible but at making its truths digestible to the sensitive stomachs of the modern age. And pedagogy was the enzyme to accomplish this. Once the Bible was made pedagogical—suited to moral teachings—it became a very tasty comestible.

The pedagogical push was only half-heartedly an English phenomenon. Until the 1780s Harwood was the sole representative of this genre, and his translation precipitated no large responses, either positive or negative. Not so in Germany, where translators were more consistently tempted to imagine the Bible as an educational handbook, and where such temptation triggered fierce reactions from theologians and politicians alike. While English authorities were unconcerned by translators like Harwood, their German counterparts most certainly were not. Instead, the German creators of the pedagogical Bible incurred some of the

[4] Harwood, *Liberal Translation*, v, viii.

[5] Thomas Chubb, "Remarks on the Scriptures," *Posthumous Works of Thomas Chubb* (London, 1768), 1:8. On Chubb, see Henning Graf Reventlow, *The Authority of the Bible and the Rise of the Modern World* (Philadelphia, 1984), 384ff.

[6] Chubb, "Remarks," 5.

[7] Thomas Chubb, "An Enquiry Concerning Sin," in *A Collection of Tracts on Various Subjects* (London, 1730), 105; Harwood, *Liberal Translation*, 9.

most rigorous punishments the state had to offer. Translators were exiled, imprisoned, and fined, their works confiscated and burned. Over the course of the eighteenth century, this was consistently the most perilous way to renovate the biblical text. Translators in this vein not only ran afoul of the authorities, but also provoked some of the most widespread theological uneasiness of the century. Indeed, it was testament to the great energies invested in remaking the Bible that this genre of Bible translation was perpetuated at all. It would have been easier by far just to *argue* for the pedagogical content of the Bible. Argument was, after all, harmless for the scads of German theologians, critics, and libertines who described the Bible as a corpus of useful moral maxims and were untouched by state authority. The inventors of the pedagogical Bible apparently went beyond the pale of mere argument, however, for they found themselves consistently punished by the hostile guardians of public decency. Translation and politics here touched each other most closely. Why?

For a clue, we might look to Frederick the Great's 1779 letter to his minister Karl von Zedlitz calling for a thorough reform of Prussia's school curricula. Key to this reform was the introduction of the proper teaching of rhetoric and logic. To do this, Frederick wrote, "the good authors must above all be translated into German . . . Xenophanes, Demosthenes, Sallust, Tacitus, Livy, and Cicero."[8] Reading these authors and comparing their Greek and Latin texts to the German translations, Frederick thought, should be a central component of mass education, a means of producing "orderly and reasonable" citizens.[9] Translations were—in Frederick's mind—an instrument of state. Insofar as they might guide citizens into correct societal behavior, they would help ensure civil order. Correct translation of books, especially those that educated young children, was thus of pressing importance to political authorities. It was a historical irony, then, that the outcast theologian and school reformer Karl Friedrich Bahrdt responded to Frederick's call, sending him a translation of Tacitus and proposing that it be part of a series of cheap pocket editions available to all schoolchildren that they might become "familiar with the spirit of the Ancients."[10] Bahrdt was teaching and translating Tacitus because he had been forbidden to teach theology at the University of Halle, where he had fled after incurring the wrath of the imperial authorities in the late 1770s. The source of this wrath was his Bible translation.

The encounter of Frederick and the "notorious Dr. Bahrdt" can serve as a parable about the pedagogical Bible more broadly. The translators who, between 1735 and the 1780s, produced the pedagogical Bible—from Johann Lorenz

[8] Frederick the Great, letter of 5 September 1779, in Otto Bardong, ed., *Friedrich der Grosse* (Darmstadt, 1982), 504. On Frederick's interest in Cicero, see Johan van der Zande, "The Microscope of Experience: Christian Garve's Translation of Cicero's *De Officiis* (1783)," *Journal of the History of the Ideas* 59 (January 1998): 75–94.

[9] Bardong, ed., *Friedrich der Grosse*, 505.

[10] Sten Flygt, *The Notorious Dr. Bahrdt* (Nashville, 1953), 242.

Schmidt to Bahrdt himself—were themselves pedagogues, responsible for primary school education in a variety of different capacities. Their Bibles were written for, and justified by, their need to serve the interests of the young. If Frederick's slogan "argue as much as you will . . . only obey!" was shorthand for the political constraints on German cultural production, then these translations were, in this rubric, disobedient. Indeed, the translations exactly qualified—in Immanuel Kant's answer to the question "What is Enlightenment?"—for state restriction. They did not exemplify the "public use of one's reason," the domain of utter freedom in Kant's vision. Instead, these pedagogical instruments expressly violated the injunction that the clergyman, "as a consequence of his office," must teach even what he does not believe: "As a priest he is not free, nor can he be free, because he carries out the orders of another."[11]

The pedagogical Bible, in other words, laid claim to a proscribed authority. By putting theory into practice, by bringing their reforming visions into the domain of private teaching, by offering themselves as definitive versions, they insisted on their exclusive rights over the authority of the Bible. Not content merely to experiment with the theory of the moral Bible, these versions strongly contended that only the imprimatur of reason and rationality could keep the Bible fresh and applicable to the modern world. The universalism of the Holy Spirit, which drove the radical separatists to their bizarre ends, was matched here by a universalism of moral instruction. Even in the "pedagogical century," then, these Bibles were worms in the apple of tolerance, inviting both social and political sanction.[12] Although relatively few in number, they attracted the attention of legions of commentators. Ultimately it was not merely their rational content that made them so culturally malodorous, but rather their missionary ardor to provide a new and universal standard, in the words of Paul, "for reproof, for correction, and training in righteousness" (2 Tim. 3.16).

Clearing Away the Shit: The Wertheimer Bible and the Politics of Interpretation

If we imagine the Enlightenment Bible as a set of tools for making a new Bible, then the 1735 *The Divine Scriptures from before the Times of Jesus* was the shovel.[13] Heavy and clumsy, this text dug away at the orthodox vision of a Bible

[11] Kant, "What Is Enlightenment?" in *Foundations of the Metaphysics of Morals*, trans. Lewis Beck (Indianapolis, 1959), 92, 88.

[12] On the "pedagogical century," see Helmut König, *Zur Geschichte der Nationalerziehung in Deutschland im letzten Drittel des 18. Jahrhunderts* (Berlin, 1960), 40.

[13] [Johann Lorenz Schmidt], *Die göttlichen Schriften vor den Zeiten des Messie Jesus* (Wertheim, 1735). See also Paul S. Spalding, *Seize the Book, Jail the Author: Johann Lorenz Schmidt and Censorship in Eighteenth-Century Germany* (West Lafayette, IN, 1998); Hermann Ehmer, "Die Wertheimer Bibel: Der Versuch einer rationalistischen Bibelübersetzung," *Jahrbuch der Hessischen*

legitimized by the traditional tools of theology. When it first appeared at the Easter book fair in Frankfurt, however, it raised few hackles. Indeed, a buyer would have been impressed with its quality. Unlike most eighteenth-century German books—notable only for their cheap paper and runny ink—this book was beautifully designed and printed in a huge edition of 1,600 copies. But once our prospective buyer opened it, he found something startling inside. Turning to Gen. 1, he would read that: "All worldly bodies, and our earth too, were created at the beginning by God. Concerning Earth in particular, it was at the start completely desolate: it was surrounded with a dark fog, and water flowed around it, atop which strong wind began to blow."[14] Puzzled, our buyer might check his memory against his Luther Bible, where he would see that: "In the beginning God created the heavens and the earth. The earth was without form and void, and darkness was on the face of the deep; and the Spirit of God was moving over the face of the waters."[15] Our reader would not have to be particularly disputatious to detect the gulf that separated Luther's version from the "free translation" he held in his hand. Translating the Hebrew *ruach* as "wind" was only the most obvious difference, but not an insignificant one, since the word is nearly always rendered πνευμα, *spiritus*, or spirit. Struck perhaps by its unfamiliarity, the buyer might glance down at the note on "wind," where he would find this explanation: "Because the vapors would prefer to thin and rise into the sky at the equator, rather than at the poles, thus the equilibrium of the flowing material would be destroyed. Hence the wind."[16] Whatever the meteorological accuracy of this explanation, it did little to make the text seem ordinary to an average reader. The most familiar passages in the Old Testament—and the most familiar story about the world's creation—were totally changed. God's secure oversight of the first days of the universe was gone. In place of miracle, our buyer would find only the same laws of pressure, flow, and temperature that govern all natural processes. What became known as the Wertheimer Bible made the sublimely incomprehensible creation of the universe into a regular process of natural history.

In doing so, it provoked an unprecedented scandal. "Has there ever been a more vexatious mocker of scripture and the Christian religion?" thundered Johann Georg Walch in 1736, and the answer was a resounding "No."[17] After

---

Kirchengeschichtlichen Vereinigung 43 (1992): 289–312; Kobuch, *Zensur und Aufklärung*, 69ff.; and Wilhem Schmidt-Biggemann, "Mutmassungen über die Vorstellung vom Ende der Erbsünde," in *Die Neubestimmung des Menschen: Wandlungen des anthropologischen Konzepts im 18. Jahrhundert* (München, 1980), 171–92.

[14] Schmidt, *Die göttliche Schriften*, 3.

[15] This is the RSV of course. Luther's text read: "Am Anfang schuff Gott Himel und Erden. Und die Erde war wüst und leer / und es war finster auff der Tiefe / Und der Geist Gottes schwebet auff dem Wasser."

[16] Schmidt, *Die göttliche Schriften*, 5.

[17] Johann Georg Walch, *Historische und Theologische Einleitung in die Religionsstreitikeiten, welche sonderlich auss der Evangelisch-Lutherischen Kirche entstanden* (Jena, 1736), 5:228.

its publication, the news of its heterodoxy quickly spread and by October 1735 it was proclaimed by the Altdorf theological faculty to be "an offensive, scandalous, and dangerous work, because the author has scattered in it many naturalistic, Socinian, and evil principles repudiated . . . by all the religions tolerated in the Holy Roman Empire." The charge against the Wertheimer Bible was led by Joachim Lange—the most powerful figure in Halle Pietism after the death of August Hermann Francke—who screamed that "not only should the continuation [of publication] be halted, but the remaining exemplars should be suppressed, indeed annihilated."[18] Within months, bans on the book poured in from across Germany: nearby Nuremberg led the way, but soon the book was officially sanctioned by officials in Frankfurt, Saxony, Prussia, and finally, on 15 January 1737, by Emperor Charles VI himself in Vienna.[19] By 1739, according to the *Acta Historico-Ecclesiastica*, eleven separate collections of documents, no fewer than ninety-one publications, and thousands of journal and pamphlet pages had appeared, all dedicated to demolishing both the translator and his naturalistic, even atheistic Bible.[20]

Under such intense scrutiny, it did not take long for the hidden scoffer to lose his protective mantle of anonymity. Already by June 1735 it was clear to authorities that the translator was Johann Lorenz Schmidt, the tutor of the sons of widowed Countess Amöna Sophia von Löwenstein-Wertheim-Virneburg. Schmidt was a product of a Pietist intellectual milieu: a student of Johann Franz Buddeus (a moderately Pietist philosopher and theologian at the university of Jena), he corresponded with August Hermann Francke in the years before the latter's death in 1727, was part of a small Pietist conventicle in Schweinfurt, and later, after inquiries into the foreign missions, was offered a job in St. Petersburg by the vice director of the Halle orphanage, Johann Rambach.[21] After some tortured soul-searching about his calling, asking "God that he let me know his gracious pleasure in the matter," he decided instead to move to the court at Wertheim, a position won in no small measure by "his obvious religious devotion" but also by his facility in general humanistic learning, including a good knowledge of Hebrew.[22]

When Schmidt picked up his pen to write what would become his most infamous monument, it was thus with an eye toward religious pedagogy. As he later wrote, "I retain the same attitude I had when I wanted to be employed as a missionary among the pagans."[23] For Schmidt, however, pagans inhabited not

[18] Ehmer, "Wertheimer Bible," 301.

[19] For censorship information, see Spalding, *Seize the Book*, chaps. 5–7.

[20] My count of the volumes and collections reviewed in the *Acta Historico-Ecclesiastica* (Weimar, 1737–39).

[21] Spalding, *Seize the Book*, 16f. On Buddeus, see Mulsow, *Moderne aus dem Untergrund*, 310 n. 4 and 311.

[22] Spalding, *Seize the Book*, 20, 21.

[23] Ibid., 26.

just far-off Russia or India, but dwelt right there in the heart of Christian Europe. Even these pious intentions did little, however, to convince theologians of his integrity: together "all three major religions in Germany," Johann Sinnhold proudly reported, "stood firm against this annoying work."[24] Schmidt's Scripture showed him to be "such a mocker of these writings, and such an enemy of religion, the likes of which has never been seen."[25] "Since the birth of Christ" never has "the sun shone on such an impudent twister of Scripture, indeed a forger of the text."[26] "He judges Christ and the apostles by his own false and deceitful heart," grumbled Johann Fresen.[27] Particularly galling was the timing of Schmidt's translation, which coincided perfectly with the the 200th anniversary celebrations of the Luther Bible.

This furor cannot be ascribed to Schmidt's naturalism alone. Certainly there was, in England and Germany, a venerable tradition of "physico-theology" that offered an explicitly religious reading of nature as well as a naturalist reading of the Bible. Since the 1690s, the English Boyle lectures had employed such venerable commentators as Richard Bentley, Samuel Clarke, and William Derham to show the concinnity of nature and Scripture. Many of these lectures and other related works were translated into German in the 1720s and 1730s, at which point a native tradition of physico-theology took root across the German-speaking lands. Naturalism was the dominant motif, for example, in Friedrich Lesser's pop-science series, which included the 1735 *Lithotheologie* and the 1738 *Insecto-Theologia*, while Johann Scheuchzer's 1731 *Kupfer-Bibel* provided four hefty volumes of naturalist explanation of the Bible. None of these unsettled the devout untowardly. But like the bull that sat on the bumblebee, orthodox theologians leaped and snorted at the sting of Schmidt's translation. Ultimately, the translation stung not because of its naturalism, but because of the pedagogical authority it demanded for itself and for human interpreters generally.

This demand for authority permeated the entire conflict about the Wertheimer Bible. But nothing showed it more clearly than the quarrel about Schmidt's translation of Gen. 3.15, the so-called protoevangelium. In its classic Lutheran incarnation, the protoevangelium read:

> Und Ich will Feindschaft setzen zwischen Dir und dem Weibe / und zwischen deinem Samen und irem samen / der selb sol dir den Kopff zertretten / Und Du wirst In in die Verschen stechen.

[24] Johann Nicolaus Sinnhold, *Historische Nachricht von der bekanten und verruffenen sogenannten Wertheimischen Bibel* (Erfurt, 1737), 37.

[25] Johann Zedler, *Grosses vollstandiges Universal Lexicon aller Wissenschaften und Kunste* (Leipzig, 1748), 55:603.

[26] Sinnhold, *Historische Nachricht*, a2^{v}.

[27] *Samlung derjenigen Schriften welche bey Gelegenheit des wertheimischen Bibelwerks für oder gegen dasselbe zum Vorschein gekommen sind* (Frankfurt and Leipzig, 1738), 256.

(I will put enmity between you and the woman, and between your seed and her seed; he shall bruise your head, and you shall bruise his heel.)

Capitalizing this verse for emphasis, Luther commented in his 1545 marginal note that "this is the first *evangelium* and promise of Christ given to the world / That he should overcome sin, death, and hell, and deliver us from the violence of the snake."[28] Luther's veneration of the verse was not idiosyncratically Protestant. Rather, for all three major Christian confessions—Lutheran, Reformed, and Catholic—Gen. 3.15 was the key that opened the locked mysteries of Scripture. It was the verse that first made the Old Testament legible, as it were, to the Christian reader, "proving" that Christ was no latecomer, but rather present from the very beginning of the world.[29] As such, it was the opening gesture in a typological reading of the Bible, the first move in the venerable Christian strategy of unifying the two Testaments by discovering in the Old prophetic traces of the New.

For a verse so laden with theological baggage, Schmidt's translation was utterly unacceptable: "Thus in the future there will be a steadfast enmity between you and the woman and both your progenies, such that men will step on the head of the snake, and the latter will bite the former on the foot." The note to the passage laconically reported only that "[Men] will tread on your head. That is, the progeny of the woman will do this."[30] Outrageous, said Joachim Lange in his *Philosophical Mocker of Religion*: Schmidt's passage "ridicul[ed] the entire Christian religion, since to him the seed of the woman is in no way Christ, nor is the snake Satan."[31] By making a singular noun usually translated "seed," into the plural "progenies," Schmidt turned the singular "he" into the general category "men." In this translation, Christ was in no way signified in the protoevangelium. Instead, Schmidt's protoevangelium offered only a rationale for the mutual loathing that has long characterized the relations of people and snakes. No longer, in other words, could Gen. 3.15 show *anything* about Christ: the former key to the rest of Scripture was broken.

As angered as they were by this passage, Schmidt's critics saw it as only one skirmish in his scandalous battle to take over the Bible by obscuring "those places which . . . treat the basic teachings of the entire Christian religion."[32] In this battle, there was no more intimidating weapon than Schmidt's interpretive canon that "the first author must be understood on his own terms." At first

[28] Martin Luther, *Biblia*, 1:29.

[29] In patristic thought, the woman is Mary, whose seed, Jesus, will be the Redeemer of the New Testament: see Franz Drewniak, *Die mariologische Deutung von Gen. 3,15 in der Väterzeit* (Breslau, 1934), 14ff., and Dominic Unger, *The First Gospel: Genesis 3:15* (St. Bonaventure, NY, 1954).

[30] Schmidt, *Die göttlichen Schriften*, 16–17.

[31] Joachim Lange, *Der philosophische Religions-Spötter in dem ersten Theile des Wertheimischen Bibel-Wercks entlarvet*, 2nd ed. (Leipzig and Halle, 1736), 8.

[32] Ibid., 6.

glance it appeared a fairly simple notion, demanding only that readers focus their attention solely on the text at hand. "It would be a twisted thing," Schmidt wrote, "if one were to seek concepts from [the first author's] words in later writings, published only much later on."[33] Or, as Gotthold Ephraim Lessing later wrote: "I have always believed that it should be the duty of the critic who takes it upon himself to judge a work, to confine himself to this work alone."[34] But if simple, the canon was also dangerous to the Bible, for it attacked the entire project of Christian commentary, which since antiquity took it for granted that the variety of biblical texts were interpretively unifiable. The practice of typology, for example, depended on the assumption that the New Testament shed light on the Old. When Schmidt demolished the traditional Christological reading of Gen. 3.15, then, it was only a local application of his general principles. Gen. 3.15 not only *did* not refer to Christ, it *could* in no circumstances *ever* be related to Christ. Not even the use of parallel passages (which to this day explain unclear verses by similar ones in other books) was permissible in this scheme. Once this comparative tool was denied to the Christian commentator, in short, no longer could he unify the disparate books of the Bible into a harmonious whole, nor could he read the Bible as the seamless unraveling of God's unified program. Instead, the Bible would become a series of disconnected set pieces, no more related than Chaucer and Joyce, or Shakespeare and Kafka. Just as Baruch Spinoza—whom Schmidt introduced to the German-speaking world in his 1744 translation of the *Ethics*—made the Pentateuch into typographical rather than spiritual fact by denying that it had a single author, Schmidt's interpretive rule mooted the question of authorship, and thus de facto denied that either Moses or the Holy Spirit could in any way conserve the unity of biblical meaning.[35]

In effect, like the Pietists, Schmidt wanted to tear the Bible out of the hands of traditional Christian theology. Orthodox theologians understood the stakes immediately and repetitively condemned Schmidt's canon.[36] But Schmidt budged not one inch, for the canon was the cornerstone of the entire effort to "lay out divine truths in such clarity as the other sciences have . . . achieved."[37] Just as the Bible must be read like any other book, so too must its concepts be understood like those of any other discipline. Following the philosopher Christian

[33] Schmidt, *Die göttlichen Schriften*, 44.

[34] Gotthold Ephraim Lessing, *Briefe, die neueste Literatur betreffend*, in *Werke*, 4:723.

[35] Baruch Spinoza, *Sittenlehre: widerleget von dem beruhmten Weltweisen unserer Zeit Herrn Christian Wolf* (Frankfurt and Leipzig, 1744).

[36] See Johann Sinnhold, *Fortgesetzte Historische Nachricht von der bekannten und verruffenen sogenannten Wertheimischen Bibel* (Erfurt, 1738), 106; Walch, *Historische und Theologische Einleitung in die Religionsstreitigkeiten der Evangelisch-Lutherischen Kirche* (Jena, 1739), 5:1297 and Joachim Lange, *Anmerckungen über die freye Ubersetzung des ersten Theils der Göttlichen Schriften* (Wittenberg, 1735), 14.

[37] [Schmidt], *Die fest gegründete Wahrheit der Vernunft und Religion* . . . [1735], in: *Samlung*, 84.

Figure 9. Image of a stream with the Latin inscription "The taste is the same" on the title page of *Die göttlichen Schriften vor den Zeiten des Messie Jesus* (Jantz Bq #2242) located in the Rare Book, Manuscript, and Special Collections Library, Duke University, Durham, North Carolina.

Wolff—driven from Halle by Joachim Lange in 1723 and tarred by association when the Wertheim tumult overwhelmed the German literary scene—Schmidt wanted to ensure the conformity of divine truth and the human truths of natural philosophy and mathematics. Schmidt's frontispiece (fig. 9) presented a symbolic version of this reconciliation of reason and faith: "Idem sapor," the taste is the same, not because he literally translated the biblical text, but because he reproduced the rational structure that underlay it.

This ultimate vision of the Wertheimer Bible set it firmly within the pedagogical project of the eighteenth century, which consistently sought to transform the teaching of religion that had dominated German schools since the late Reformation. Already Pietism had seen religious pedagogy as sorely needing reform. Its schools, catechisms, and low-cost Bibles were all efforts to ameliorate a system of rigid catechismal indoctrination that had long enjoyed only lackluster success in instilling in students either "true piety" or the "necessary sciences."[38] The Pietist personalization of religion had its pedagogical side as well, especially insofar as it prioritized the transformation of the character and inner life of the

[38] August Hermann Francke, "Ordnung und Lehrart," (1702), in *Pädagogische Schriften*, ed. Hermann Lorenzen (Paderborn, 1957), 93. On Pietist pedagogy, see Richard Gawthrop and Gerald Strauss, "Protestantism and Literacy in Early Modern Germany," *Past and Present* 104 (1984): 31–55.

child over outward forms of discipline. Pietism did not by itself solve the pedagogical challenges of its day, however, and by the 1730s, the sense of a general crisis in religious education was widespread. Even the great encyclopedia of the time, Johann Zedler's *Universal Lexicon*, complained in 1737 that: "As soon as our children know how to repeat the catechism questions quickly, as soon as they have memorized the gospels, the Psalter, and other good proverbs" then all Christian teaching comes to an end.[39]

Schmidt's pedagogical mission fit into this larger picture, but his methods resembled less those of August Hermann Francke than those of John Locke, who, as early as the 1680s, had recognized that mere access to the Bible would not solve the problem of Christian learning. Indeed, in his letter to Edward Clarke later reprinted nearly verbatim in *Some Thoughts Concerning Education* (1690), Locke raised his eyebrows at Christian pedagogy: "What an odd jumble of thoughts must a child have in his head concerning religion, who in his tender years reads all the parts of the Bible indifferently, as the word of God, without any other distinction. I am apt to think, that this, in some men, has been the very reason why they have never had clear and distinct thoughts of it all their life time."[40] For Descartes and Locke, later Christian Wolff and Schmidt, the formation of clear and distinct ideas about God was the cornerstone of any true religious pedagogy. Language was both the barrier and means of creating these clear and distinct ideas. For Locke, words had been corrupted over time, and had to be stripped down to reveal stable underlying ideas. Like "children, [who] being taught words, whilst they have but imperfect notions of things, apply them at random," mankind has always assumed that its words were clear *without* going through the trouble of an actual purification.[41] Locke's *Essay Concerning Human Understanding* was one such attempt at purification. In Germany, the purification effort took a more literal form when Christian Wolff successfully purged the German language of many Latin and French philosophical terms and created a native philosophical terminology whose boundaries were specific and clear.[42]

Where Wolff remained content with philosophical purification, Schmidt took the same impulse straight into the heart of the Bible, hoping to make its conceptual architecture clear to the human eye. We must lay out "the clear concepts" of the Bible and prove "their correctness in an orderly fashion from the entire work."[43] This task demanded Herculean labors, cleansing the Bible of the "imperfections" created by Moses' "base manner of speaking" and turning these imperfections into conceptual gold.[44] More colorfully put: "When shit lies

[39] Zedler, *Universal Lexicon*, s.v. "Kinder-Zucht," 15:616

[40] Locke, *Educational Writings*, ed. James L. Axtell (Cambridge, 1968), 315.

[41] Locke, *An Essay Concerning Human Understanding* (New York, 1959), 2:161

[42] On Wolff's terminology, see Eric A. Blackall, *The Emergence of German As a Literary Language*, 2nd ed. (Ithaca, NY, 1978), 26ff.

[43] Schmidt, *Die göttlichen Schriften*, 22.

[44] Schmidt, *Samlung*, 90, 99.

in the street in front of the houses, it is, in that place, an evil thing. But as soon as someone carries it off to the fields, the same stuff is no longer disreputable and contributes to the fertility of the land."[45] Clearing away the shit might be an appropriate metaphor for Schmidt's task. And the shit, in this case, was the Hebrew idiom, which may have been proper to the ancient Jews but which stood as a barrier between modern man and the truths of the Bible. To sanitize the Bible—to achieve the linguistic purity cherished by Locke and Wolff—one needed a "free" translation, one aimed not at verbal but at conceptual fidelity. Footnotes, even outright pedantry, were also solvents used to reveal the logic underlying the slop. The slightly irritating tone of the "wind" note in Gen. 1 became a triumphant blast later on in the Bible, when Schmidt defined, in notes 272 and 996, such words as "door," "mother," "stick," and "bread." Critics missed the point, though, when they asked "whether such words and things, which are defined in an affected and pedantic way, are not already known to every person and even some children . . . ?"[46] Pinning down the exact meaning of words, no matter how banal, was crucial in defining the exact concepts found in Scripture. The "new pedantry," as Joachim Lange put it, was a deliberate policy in Schmidt's work—through it, Schmidt would create new, pure, and authoritative Bible.[47]

In the end, it was this pedagogical insistence on purity and authority that made Schmidt so problematic. Like any good pedagogical text, this one was presented in the key of apology. Neither content to jettison the biblical text, nor merely to claim that Scripture *could* be intelligible, Schmidt wanted to prove it in concrete form. "Because not everyone is capable of understanding Scripture . . . in each age teachers are called on to teach the others," Schmidt proclaimed, and saw himself as called to teach those who lived in the age of Enlightenment.[48] And he paid the price for this audacity. Although his patrons—the young counts Vollrath and Friedrich—tried to protect him from the blast of bad publicity, neither had reached his majority and so they were subject to the much less tolerant Protestant regency governors of Wertheim. First Schmidt was dismissed from his tutorship in late 1735. Then, over the course of the next two years, his books were banned across the Holy Roman Empire in a show of "rare political consensus," as Paul Spalding has noted.[49] The republic of letters lent Schmidt some support. Christian Wolff lamented the "intrigues" of theologians like Lange; the literary scholar Johann Gottsched complained of the "hypocrisy" of Schmidt's critics, who were looking more for fame than for truth; and the theologian Johann Fröreisen protested that German Protestants were on the verge of creating "another *Catalogum librorum*

[45] Schmidt, *Die göttlichen Schriften*, 40.

[46] Zedler, *Universal Lexicon*, 55:611.

[47] Lange, *Religions-Spötter*, 43.

[48] Schmidt, *Die göttliche Schriften*, 20.

[49] Spalding, *Seize the Book*, 141.

prohibitorum."[50] But once the emperor himself weighed in on the matter, outward public support for Schmidt withered. It fell to the Catholic co-ruler of Wertheim, the Prince Karl Thomas, to "secure [Schmidt's] person and start legal proceedings against him."[51] Schmidt was quickly arrested by twenty soldiers and held in the prince's palace. The process that followed was convoluted in a manner typical of the byzantine workings of Holy Roman Imperial bureaucracy: factions were formed, plots schemed, papers shuffled, delayed, waylaid, and mislaid.[52] Although comic in hindsight, it was a tense year for Schmidt, waiting in prison for the Dickensian system of justice to run its rough course. In the end, though, this course was never finished. In early April 1738 the young counts gave Schmidt twenty florins and advised him to tuck his tail between his legs and flee, which advice Schmidt gratefully took.

Looking back on this episode from the 1780s, the church historian Johann Schlegel was puzzled: "Who would have thought that a Protestant theologian like Lange" would have involved the emperor "in a scholarly battle that should simply have been aired among Protestants . . . ?"[53] Schlegel's puzzlement was genuine, but his description of the battle as "scholarly" was to misread the problem of Schmidt's pedagogical Bible. Schmidt was the lightning rod for so much political electricity precisely because he never convinced his enemies that he was indeed engaged in a "scholarly" or disinterested enterprise. The ecumenical league of intolerance—formed of the confessional factions, Lutherans and Catholics alike, who under normal circumstances were the most bitter of enemies—was held together because Schmidt's Bible was seen as highly interested. In a sense, Schmidt's Bible represented a "fourth species of religion," a creature effectively banned in the 1648 Peace of Westphalia and repeatedly reinvoked as a specter of fear throughout the period.[54] Orthodoxy in all forms thus unified against it. If we were to put it in Kant's terms, the "complete freedom" that should belong to a scholar vanished for Schmidt the moment that he draped his translation with the heavy cloak of pedagogical authority. Even for Kant, the teacher "has no freedom to teach according to his own lights."[55] For the less tolerant theologians of midcentury, Schmidt had essentially rewritten the key tool of religious teaching. As Samuel Hollmann wrote in 1735: "no philosopher will, in the future, try to resolve his doubts in [Abraham] Calov's *Biblia illustratis* [*sic*] or other similar books. Rather he will let himself be instructed by this translation in the meanings that must be ascribed to Scriptural

[50] Wolff, letter dated 8 November 1736, quoted in Gustav Frank, "Die Wertheimer Bibelübersetzung vor dem Reichshofrat in Wien," *Zeitschrift für Kirchengeschichte* 12 (31 October 1891): 289: Gottsched, letter to Schmidt, 10 January 1737, quoted in ibid., 292; Fröreisen in unpaginated preface to Schmidt, *Samlung*.

[51] Imperial rescript, 15 January 1737, quoted in Spalding, *Seize the Book*, 137.

[52] For the details, see ibid., chaps. 7 and 8.

[53] Johann Rudolph Schlegel, *Kirchengeschichte des achtzehnten Jahrhunderts* (Heilbronn, 1788), 2:341.

[54] See *Instrumenta Pacis Westphalicae*, ed. Konrad Müller (Bern, 1966), 47.

[55] Kant, "What Is Enlightenment?" 88.

passages if they are to accord with the most indisputable truths of reason."[56] By fashioning this tool of instruction, Schmidt transgressed all the limitations set on biblical interpretation, opening it up to those unconfirmed in its traditional practices. The negative reaction was vicious but predictable. And similar reactions attended the pedagogical Bible, even as the nature of pedagogy radically shifted in the second half of the century.

The Pedagogical Century

As a token of this shift, we can look to the historical fantasy that Gotthold Ephraim Lessing furnished German literary savants in 1780. His *Education of the Human Race* conjured up an ancient people, the Jews, and their ancient religious "primer," the Old Testament. Bearing the first elements of the education of mankind, these people and this primer embodied the aboriginal relationship of man and God. The revelations of the Old Testament—"education, which affected and still affects the human race"—nurtured mankind in its childhood, gradually leading to knowledge of the true God. But just as children outgrow their first toys and books, after a time a maturing mankind sensed the inadequacy of the Old Testament. At this point, "a better teacher had to come, and rip the exhausted primer from the hands of the child.—Christ came." His primer, the New Testament, would become the textbook for an adolescent humanity groping its way toward full autonomy. Over the centuries of its maturation, this humanity took the New Testament as the "*non plus ultra* of its knowledge" and used it as a scaffold for its own development. In time, though, even this primer wore thin for a humanity finally approaching adulthood. The eighteenth century was on the cusp of this final metamorphosis, ready to give up the New Testament and begin moving toward "the time of a *new eternal Gospel*," the last age of man, the "time of perfection."[57]

Lessing's short tract was a manifesto for the pedagogical century, a century where instruction, education, and the formation of an autonomous mankind were at the collective center of cultural and intellectual production. Standard histories of the period begin with John Locke and his stress on the "cultivation of virtue" as the principal goal of the pedagogue.[58] Despite the Lockean origin, however, pedagogical reform never really took center stage in England until the very end of the century, when the twin forces of the Sunday school movement and utilitarianism made pedagogy a subject of pressing concern.[59] But continental Europe was a different story. In the earlier period, Locke's goal

[56] Hollmann quoted in Frank, "Reichshofrat in Wien," 290.

[57] Lessing, "Die Erziehung des Menschengeschlechts," in *Werke*, 10:99, 75, 88, 91, 92, 96.

[58] On Locke, see James Bowen, *A History of Western Education* (London, 1981), 3:176ff.

[59] On this later phase, see Thomas Laqueur, *Religion and Respectability: Sunday Schools and Working-Class Culture, 1780–1850* (New Haven, 1976); also, Bowen, *Western Education*, 3:286ff.

of fostering virtue—translated for the German public in 1708 and distributed in a variety of forms by eclectic philosophers like Christian Thomasius—resonated with a society already prepared for pedagogical change by Pietist innovations and the wider sentiments for university and primary school reform. This gentle pressure in the first half of the century was completely overtaken by the virtual tidal wave of pedagogical passion, a "mania" for pedagogy, that swept across the continent in the 1760s.[60] By the end of that decade, pedagogy was a key epicenter in German cultural life, drawing enormous attention from religious commentators, social theorists, historians, and political leaders alike. The 1763 Prussian edict establishing compulsory primary schooling might serve to mark the beginning of this era, when reformers sought to replace the aristocratic dedication to self-advantage with a middle-class meritocracy that would sow "the seeds of civic virtue."[61] Although ultimately ineffective, the edict envisioned education as a key tool for unifying an economically and geographically fractured society. For the first time in Europe, primary education became an interest for a state seeking to create an orderly and reasonable society. This institutional change was neatly paralleled by the near simultaneous publication of Jean-Jacques Rousseau's *Émile* (1762), whose enormous success in France and Germany signaled the interest of the literate classes in social and moral reform through education. Following on Rousseau and others, the pedagogical mania of the 1760s shifted away from Locke's stress on ordered, conceptual clarity and toward a more organic process of learning by experience. In Rousseau's scheme, "Locke's great maxim"—that children ought to be taught reason first—only produced stupid children. The first book that Emile would read—his "whole library"—was *Robinson Crusoe*, because it taught the radical self-sufficiency that should precede "all notions of social relations."[62] Practical reformers set this interest in the creation of moral autonomy in children at the center of their efforts to reform the highly disciplined and largely Latinate schooling environments that dominated Europe.[63]

In Germany, pedagogical journals such as the *Philanthropische Archiv* and the *Pädagogische Unterhandlungen* sprang up in the 1770s as ways to spread the gospel of pedagogical reform far and wide. These literary forms had institutional counterparts, in particular the *Philanthropinum* established in 1774 by Johann Basedow in Dessau, which put reform into practice and established a curriculum in which memorization was replaced by living experience.[64] The

[60] Annette Bridgman, introduction to *Education in the 18th* Century, ed. J. D. Browning (New York, 1979), 1.

[61] Johann Georg Hamann quoted in La Vopa, *Grace, Talent, and Merit*, 202. On compulsory schooling, see Melton, *Absolutism*.

[62] Jean-Jacques Rousseau, *Émile, or On Education*, trans. Allan Bloom (New York, 1979), 89, 184, 185.

[63] See Bowen, *Western Education*, 3:192–93.

[64] On Basedow, see Bowen, *Western Education*, 3:198ff.; also Friedrich Paulsen, *Geschichte des gelehrten Unterrichts* (Berlin, 1921), 2:51ff.

Dessau *Philanthropinum* was one of the great sensations of its day, prompting no less a figure than Kant to praise it for its "revolution" in teaching. "The attentive eyes of experts in all countries" were on Dessau, Kant wrote, watching to see how renewed pedagogy transformed children.[65] Basedow built his curriculum to match the Enlightenment scheme for child development: in particular, learning began with practical life, both inside and outside the classroom. Theory came after practice, and the moral development of the individual student preceded social discipline. Punishment was out, play was in.

The Bible would not stand outside of this pedagogical revolution. Already in Germany, "the Bible boom of the eighteenth century" was under way, driven by the "enactment of school ordinances which . . . required Bible reading in the primary schools."[66] And reformers like Basedow put the Bible square in the center of their pedagogical musings. Just as Frederick II complained, in his 1763 *General-Land-Schul-Reglement*, about the number of catechisms that "flood" the land, the catechism also was the "enemy" of religion in Basedow's philanthropinical plans, for it only encouraged the idle recapitulation of words without analysis.[67] At the very moment that Christianity became a religion of recapitulation, it lost its power over skeptics: "why should I believe what stands in the Bible before I recognize . . . the existence of God?"[68] But unlike Frederick II and the Pietists before him—who wanted to solve the problem of catechisms by replacing them with the pure biblical text—Basedow was considerably more skeptical that an unadulterated Bible would ensure good religious education. The Bible was strong stuff for a child, as Locke had indicated much earlier, not least for the variety of incomprehensible tales that overshadowed the central questions of God, man, and salvation. Of all the gristly bits of the Bible, the Old Testament was particularly indigestible, strewn with "passages that are at times obscure and that at times appear to contradict both each other and natural religion," but even the New Testament had its difficulties.[69] Where Locke had recommended preparing "a good History of the Bible for young People to read"—and publishers in Germany and England had responded with children's Bibles condensed for young ears and eyes—for Basedow the answer was not to remake the Bible in the image of the child, but rather to remake the child in the image of the Bible.[70]

[65] Kant, *An das gemeine Wesen* (1777) in Ulrich Hermann, *Aufklärung und Erziehung* (Weinheim, 1993), 107.

[66] Gawthrop and Strauss, "Protestantism and Literacy," 50.

[67] *Friedrich des Grossen Pädagogische Schriften und Äusserungen* (Langensalza, 1885), 126; Paulsen, *Geschichte*, 2:54.

[68] Johann Basedow, *Methodischer Unterricht der Jugend in der Religion und Sittenlehre der Vernunft* (Altona, 1764), xv–xvi.

[69] Basedow, *Methodischer Unterricht in der überzeugenden Erkenntniss der biblischen Religion* (Altona, 1764), 6–7.

[70] Ruth Bottigheimer, *The Bible for Children: From the Age of Gutenberg to the Present* (New Haven, 1996), 44.

Under Basedow's plan, then, correct religious teaching demanded that study of the biblical text come late, only after the development of the child's moral and intellectual faculties. And this for two reasons. First, the Bible cannot command rational assent until rationality itself has been established in the child. Second, the exact content of the Bible cannot be truly established until the child has come to know God through his or her own faculties. Only if the child's religious sensibility has been properly developed before he or she reads the Bible can it be assured that the child will read it correctly. This intuition—that the Bible might actually *damage* correct religious teaching—was embraced by the heir to Basedow's philanthropinism: Joachim Heinrich Campe. Campe—a theologian, director of the Dessau *Philanthropinum* after 1776, and later Jacobin—insisted the Bible in itself could not serve as the first tool in a child's religious teaching. Instead the "essential teachings . . . that lie hidden under dark images and inexplicable expressions" must be revealed to the light before the Bible itself might be properly understood: "this is the only way . . . to stem irreligion and to quiet the doubters." And for Campe, the hero who revealed the essential doctrine, who uncovered the essence of modern religion, was Lessing, the "great prototype" who taught that "a divine plan of education manifested itself in the history" of Christianity.[71] In a swift blow, then, Lessing seemed to revolutionize both theology and pedagogy.

But Lessing diverged in one crucial way from pedagogical and theological reformers of his day. In Lessing's historical fable, proper pedagogy did not redeem the Bible at the end of the day. Like a textbook that has outlived its purpose, in Lessing's fantasy, the Bible was simply too exhausted to contribute to the future education of mankind. This sentiment not only informed Lessing's *Erziehung*, but also his most controversial publication project, the so-called *Fragments from an Unnamed Author*, a set of texts that Lessing—in his position as librarian at Wolfenbüttel—began to have printed in 1774.[72] These *Fragments* offered a thoroughly ideological history of Christianity, one in which Jesus was a Jewish political figure, not a Christian religious one, and in which Jesus' teachings had been fundamentally reconstructed by frustrated apostles who shifted his worldly and specifically Jewish teachings into a supernatural and universally Christian domain. Lessing did not necessarily agree with this story. But he published the *Fragments* both to stir up "the stagnant theology of his time" and, more importantly, to overthrow what he called "bibliolatry," that Protestant affection for the Bible that underlay the Reformation.[73] The *Fragments* provided

[71] Ludwig Fertig, *Campes politische Erzeihung: Eine Einführung in die Pädagogik der Aufklärung* (Darmstadt, 1977), 73–74, 70.

[72] Albert Schweitzer, *The Quest of the Historical Jesus* (New York, 1948), 21ff.; see also Colin Brown, *Jesus in European Protestant Thought, 1778–1860* (Durham, NC: Labyrinth, 1985).

[73] Lessing, "Bibliolatrie," [1779] in *Sämtliche Schriften*, ed. Karl Lachmann (Leipzig, 1886–1924), 16:470ff. Toshimasa Yasukata, *Lessing's Philosophy of Religion and the German Enlightenment: Lessing on Christianity and Reason* (Oxford, 2002), 23.

Lessing an opportunity to distinguish strictly between the Bible and the Word of God:

> In short: the letter is not the spirit; and the Bible is not religion. As a result criticisms of the letter and of the Bible are not also criticism of spirit and of religion. Because the Bible obviously contains more than that which belongs to religion . . . Also, religion existed before there was a Bible. Christianity existed, before the evangelists and apostles wrote.[74]

The *Fragments* showed, for Lessing, that Christianity's dependency on the Bible was perilous. Better to jettison the Bible, and salvage religion, than lose both. Lessing's pedagogy of revelation would thus take mankind away from the Bible and toward a religion independent of any text.

In this view, Lessing was in the minority. Orthodox Protestants, of course, continued to cherish their Bible as a divine book. Pedagogical reformers saw the Bible as the final testing ground for budding reasonable minds. And, finally, even contemporary rationalist theologians, so-called neologians like Wilhelm Teller, Johann Semler, and Johann Jerusalem, were firmly convinced that the Bible was a crucial part of even the most modern theological program. It was this conviction, in part, that underwrote Lessing's unflattering comparison of neology and orthodoxy as "liquid manure . . . compared with impure water."[75] But neologians were adamant that tension between reason and revelation could be resolved if only the Bible were reformed along undogmatic lines. One strategy for such reform was biblical paraphrase: as early as 1747, Johann Jerusalem proposed to paraphrase the New Testament, to expose "the history of the book and the community to which it was addressed" and to offer a Bible unfettered by dogmatic commitments.[76] Later, Johann David Michaelis—in the years before he turned to historical criticism (see chapter 7)—and Johann Semler released their own paraphrases of New Testament material and helped introduce German readers to the English paraphrastic tradition. This latter tradition, ranging from Philip Dodderidge's *Family Expositor* to John Locke's *Paraphrases and Notes on the Epistles of S. Paul*, began to appear in German in the 1740s and then consistently until the 1770s.

All of these paraphrases served pedagogical purposes. In particular, they invested the Bible with the power to reform human morals. In this supposition, they were in good company in the period. Even the *Fragments*, in their own way, insisted that Jesus was a teacher of human morality. "The goal of Jesus' preaching and teaching," its author declared, was aimed at "a change of mind, an unfeigned love of God and neighbor. . . . There are no great mysteries or

[74] Lessing, "Gegensätze," in *Werke*, 8:312.

[75] Yasukata, *Lessing's Philosophy*, 22.

[76] Karl Aner, *Die Theologie der Lessingzeit* (Halle/Saale, 1929), 204. On neology, see Brown, *Jesus*, 8ff.

points of doctrine. . . . There are nothing but moral teachings and the duties of life, which should improve men inwardly and from the whole heart."[77] Lessing must have at least intuited the connection between the radical *Fragments* and the broader pedagogical biblical project. After all, when he was called upon to identify the fragmentist, he protected his friend Hermann Samuel Reimarus from public scrutiny and instead pointed the finger at a figure already familiar in the story of the pedagogical Bible, Johann Lorenz Schmidt.

The pedagogical Bible as it developed in the second half of the century, however, would depart in important ways from the Wertheimer Bible. One direction was already implicit in the paraphrastic projects that sprang up in the 1730s, nearly all of which were composed of materials from the New Testament. Overall, the pedagogical Bible followed this lead, forswearing interest in the Old Testament and instead devoting its energies almost entirely to the New. Where Schmidt felt that the restoration of the Pentateuch was crucial to the recuperation of Christianity—because it laid out the conceptual architecture not just of revelation but of the world itself—in the second half of the century, the Old Testament would have few moral or pedagogical lessons to offer. From Lessing and others, the pedagogical Bible would take Jesus as an exemplary world-historical (rather than particularly Jewish) figure; from Reimarus and others, it would imbue this figure with the moral tone we would expect to see in a piece of Enlightenment pedagogy. Finally, it would embrace the practice of translation as a means of revealing the universal moral applicability of Jesus' ministry. This embrace set the pedagogical Bible in an uneasy tension with the reforms accomplished by Basedow and others. Where the philanthropinists hoped to remake children in the image of the Bible—and thus be prepared to confront all of the ambiguities that a standard translation offered—the pedagogical project was driven by the need to renew the Bible from the ground up. Paraphrase and children's Bibles were simply not enough to make the Scriptures ring true in the modern ear. At some point, every mature reader would want to confront the text of the Bible itself. The pedagogical Bible was designed for this moment, designed to present the reader with a new and authoritative collection of texts containing within them the essence of Christianity. Once again, then—unlike the neologians, Reimarus, or Lessing—translators moved from the public domain of scholarly freedom to the perilously private domain of teaching.

New Testament Pedagogy: Christ the Moral Hero

The publication of the first fully pedagogical New Testament coincided exactly with the pedagogical mania that blazed in Germany's 1760s. Its translator, Christian Tobias Damm—teacher of Greek at a Berlin gymnasium—was, like most of the characters in this story, born into religious heterodoxy. His father

[77] Hermann Samuel Reimarus, *Von dem Zwecke Jesu und seiner Jünger*, 2nd ed. (Berlin, 1784), 16.

was apparently a follower of the separatist Johann Petersen—evidence, one critic wrote, of the "*fremdgläubige Blut*" that "ran through members of the entire family."[78] Because of his beliefs, the family was apparently driven out of their town and took refuge in Halle, under the protection of the Pietist Baron von Canstein. Damm then studied at the university and remained to all outward appearance a fairly traditional Lutheran. But when his New Testament was published anonymously in 1765, this veil of conformity was torn away. Even the brute physical presence of his New Testament was daunting. If, for Schmidt, the notes were the means of presenting a conceptually ordered text, in Damm's text, the 6,370 notes overwhelmed the text altogether.[79] Like Schmidt's, then, Damm's text had the appearance of a scholarly work, even though, as one commentator said, these (often pedantic) notes generally contained "neither criticism nor philology."[80] And like Schmidt's too, Damm's translation was markedly unfaithful to the originals, preferring conceptual simplicity to the Baroque obscurities of the native idiom.

In Damm, the pedagogical Bible was explicitly bound to the moral reform of humanity. To have a sense of this, one need look no further than the Resurrection story told in Matthew:

> At the end of the week, and when the light began to dawn on the first day of the week, Mary Magdalene and the other Mary went to look at the grave. But behold, there occurred a mighty **shaking**: for an angel of the Lord came out of the heavens, came and rolled the stone from the opening, and seized it.[764]
>
> [764]The main event here is the strong blow of an earthquake, by which the great stone was moved from the entry to the grave. And this happened before the women came there. All the rest are ancillary events. If anyone is bothered by the appearances of the angel, he should be content that such ancillary events signify nothing. God does not demand that we believe what is for us inconceivable: he cares about the main issue, our adherence to the simple and reasonable teachings of Jesus.[81]

This clumsy passage was wholly typical of the Damm translation. Why, a curious reader might ask, is the earthquake the main event? To all appearances, after all, the verses were far more concerned with the angel's appearance than with the shaking. Theologically speaking, too, the angel—not the quake—ultimately guaranteed to the two Marys that Jesus had risen. And to say that the resurrection of

[78] [Johann Ulrich], *Ueber den Religionszustand in den preussischen Staaten seit der Regierung Friedrich der Grossen* (Leipzig, 1778), 1:227.

[79] Damm based his translation on Bengel's Greek text, incorporating many of Bengel's variants in his translations of Matt. 20.34, 21.12; 1 Tim. 3.16; 1 John 5.7, and many other verses; see *Das Neuen Testament unsers Herrn Jesu Christi Erster Theil, der die vier Evangelisten in sich enthält* (n.p., 1765), a3[v].

[80] Reviewer for the *Göttingische Anzeigen von Gelehrten Sachen* 1 (24 January 1765): 75.

[81] [Damm], *Neue Testament*, 219.

Jesus was an "ancillary event" was quite the understatement. But these eccentricities were consistent with Damm's effort to rewrite the Bible as a handbook of the "reasonable teachings of Jesus."

The teachings were simple. For Damm, all Christianity derived from the first principle that "Jesus was endowed by God with insight, wisdom, and courage" and appointed to create a "universal and simple religion, one useful to all mankind." The aim of this religion was the "betterment of [man's] moral life."[82] As a teacher, Jesus brought mankind a set of practical and reasonable truths untainted by the mysteries that had long shrouded Christian doctrine.[83] "One must never interpret a word or expression in such a way that it defies general human reason," declared Damm, and "the size and number of mysteries" is no guarantee of the truth of religion.[84] Over Damm's reasonable religion, those cryptographers of the Bible, church theologians, would no longer have the first say. Instead, his pedagogical Bible would lay Christianity open to public examination, revealing "a complete system of religion," including "definitions of Christ . . . mysteries . . . redeemer, Lord and so on" that all might be understood.[85] It was to be the ultimate pedagogical tool for convincing skeptics and orthodox alike as to the continued relevance of Christ's teachings. Ultimately, Damm's translation had the loftiest of goals: the final resolution of all the exegetical and dogmatic anxieties that had plagued Christianity since the very beginnings of the Church.

Given such provocative content—once again, content that moved beyond mere public speech and verged into the private domain of pedagogy—it was a wonder that Damm escaped largely unpunished. As it was, he was lucky to live in Prussia, indeed in Berlin, the center of Germany's freethinking Enlightenment. From very early on, rumors circulated widely that Damm had been deposed from his post and that he had been fined for his translation.[86] These rumors would have been encouraged by the confiscation of his work in Leipzig. But the very credibility of the rumors testified to the dangers that beset the pedagogical Bible. If Damm had lived in Saxony, for example, it is unlikely he would have gotten off so lightly. As it was, though, he was a fortunate man, one who enjoyed the protection of the Marquis d'Argens, the great friend of Frederick II, who, at least according to some sources, intervened for him with the king and provided him the opportunity to publish.[87] Few moralizers of the late century had such noble intervention to assure the safety of their persons and intellectual property. And without it, the pedagogical Bible was a dangerous project indeed.

[82] Damm, *Betrachtungen über die Religion* (n.p., 1773), 78, 74.

[83] Damm, preface to Matthew, *Neuen Testament*, b2^{r}-b3^{v}.

[84] Damm, preface to Luke, *Neuen Testament*, a2^{v}.

[85] *Allgemeine deutsche Bibliothek*, 1.2 (1765): 93.

[86] *Göttingische Anzeigen*, 1:75.

[87] [Ulrich], *Religionszustand*, 231.

Karl Friedrich Bahrdt, for his part, learned of the hazards of the pedagogical Bible first hand. Indeed, his case—much publicized and vilified across the literary world in the late eighteenth century—put the stakes of pedagogy at their clearest. At the root of the conflict was this theologian, vagabond, and scoundrel's 1773 *magnum opus*, the *Latest Revelation of God, Told in Letters and Stories.*[88] These letters and stories offered readers, once more, a thoroughly alien New Testament. Matt. 4.23–24 shows its disorienting effects clearly:

> And joined by [his Apostles, Jesus] traveled through all of Galilee and preached publicly in the synagogue the comforting news of the new religion, into which God invited all of humanity with the promise of eternal life: on doing so, he (in order to acquire the trust of the people) healed all kinds of illnesses and burdens; which in turn spread his name throughout all Syria, so that soon people began to bring all kinds of people afflicted by painful evils, even the ecstatic,(*) the sleepwalkers, the paralytic.
>
> (*)The Jews called "ecstatic" people who, through sickness or passions . . . have been made mad, so that their speech or movements no longer correspond to those common among men. They believed that there was a spirit in them governing their organs. Hence Christ too treated them so, without the Evangelists actually naming the illnesses.

Bahrdt's translation was ostentatiously alien. He was hardly shy of adding his own spin, even his own sentences, to the text at hand. You will, for example, find God's invitation to humanity in no other Bible I know. Nor are Jesus' missionary activities usually given quite such a pragmatic, even ideological, turn. Nor will you commonly find such a bold effort (even if in a footnote) to debunk both the Christian veneration for ecstatic religious experience and its belief in demonic possession. And Bahrdt inserted these teachings directly into the Bible itself.

Bahrdt's strategies were new and even more dangerous than those of Schmidt and Damm. With a few exceptions (and the above passage was one) Bahrdt wholly eschewed even the *appearance* of impartial scholarship that had marked the earlier texts and had set them off at least visually from the familiar Luther Bible. His texts were spare, devoid of all scholarly commentary and barren of annotations—for, as Bahrdt said, who wanted to read "pages of notes"? He made no concession whatsoever to scholarly disinterest, and instead aimed to revamp the very language of the Bible itself. Consistently, he strove to give his text the familiarity already found in ordinary Bibles. He did this by refashioning the Bible into a piece of contemporary German prose. Consider, he wrote, that "the authors of Holy Scripture were unlettered people . . . [and] that the Greek

[88] On Bahrdt, see Flygt, *Notorious Dr. Bahrdt* and the large bibliography compiled by Otto Jacob and Ingrid Majewski, *Karl Friedrich Bahrdt: radikaler deutscher Aufklärer (25.8.1740–23.4.1792): Bibliographie* (Halle, 1992).

in the New Testament was a bastard of a language." Should not then the language be cleaned up, that the text might be comprehensible to modern readers and appealing to modern sensibilities? Even the Luther Bible was besmirched by a prose ill-suited to the modern reader, beset by "oriental syntax and dictionary expressions" that introduce "much mystical, obscure and shadowy lumber into dogmatics." To cleanse these impurities, Bahrdt modernized the Bible's "dreadful oriental dialogue," replacing it with "pure German expressions" reflective of the "content of the Bible, not its form."[89] In the case of the demoniacs, then, modernization demanded rewriting the Jewish superstition of spiritual possession as a form of ordinary madness.[90] Possession might have rung true to the ancient Hebrew ear, but it would not do for the modern German one. By applying this principle across the board, the Bible would not only become amenable to a modern literary sensibility, but also "unusable for orthodoxy."[91]

Critics were unimpressed. Among the literati, Bahrdt and what Johann Herder later called "Bahrdtianism" found little favor, even if most supported his right to publish.[92] His work did attract the attention of the period's foremost man of letters, Johann Wolfgang Goethe, who enjoyed himself immensely at Bahrdt's expense. Goethe's *Prolog zu den neuesten Offenbarungen Gottes* has the dilettante Bahrdt gazing at his translation and exclaiming: "this is how I would talk if I were Christ"! But later the four Apostles and their familiars arrive at his garden party and their crude appearance shocks his delicate sensibilities.

> People would be appalled.
> They are not accustomed to such broad beards
> such long coats and wide pleats
> and your beasts, let me say
> would scare everyone right out the door

exclaims Bahrdt, and sends them on their way.[93] But amusement was only one possible reaction. For others, like Heinrich Köster, the editor of *Die neuesten Religionsbegebenheiten*, Bahrdt's modernization efforts ruined the experience of reading the Bible. A good translation should "retain the ethos of the period

[89] Karl Friedrich Bahrdt, *Die neueste Offenbahrung gottes in Briefen und Erzählungen*, 1st ed. (Riga, 1773),)*(5^{v}.

[90] On this tradition of "enthusiasm-critique" common to the German and English eighteenth centuries, see Hans-Jürgen Schings, *Melancholie und Aufklärung: Melancholiker und ihre Kritiker in Erfahrungsseelenkunde und Literatur des 18. Jahrhunderts* (Stuttgart, 1972).

[91] Bahrdt, *Geschichte seines Lebens, seiner Meinungen, und Schicksale* (Berlin, 1790–91), 2:236.

[92] Johann Herder, letter to Friedrich Klopstock, 5 December 1799, in *Briefe* (Weimar, 1984), 8:106.

[93] Goethe, *Prolog zu den neuesten Offenbarungen Gottes* [1774], in *Sämtliche Werke nach Epochen seines Schaffens*, ed. Karl Richter (Munich, 1985), 1.1:695.

found in the original." Not only can the oriental style "enrich our own language," but Christians have also gotten "so accustomed to the language of Scripture that their own patterns of thought have been shaped by it." Bahrdt, by contrast, made the Bible "flat and powerless" in his quest to "ban all metaphoric, figurative, and sensuous language from religion."[94]

For Köster this was not just an aesthetic problem. Rather, his aesthetic modernism was closely linked to his theological perversions. At the forefront of these was Bahrdt's rendition, in the second edition of the translation (1777), of John 1.1:

> The logos existed already at the beginning of the world. It was with God (but not yet visible to any mortal eye) and God was the logos.*
>
> *I am almost convinced that this reading is false and that it should read: "And there was only God and the logos." Logos means the messenger, the spokesman of God, he who speaks with men in the name of God.[95]

The theological charge in the passage lay principally in the final passage: "And there was only God and the logos." Not only was this an alteration unwarranted by even the "richest collections of variants," said Köster, but it also confirmed that Bahrdt's "entire system" denied the divinity of Christ.[96] When professor Johann Miller was asked by the Imperial Aulic Council to review Bahrdt's translation for its offenses against the three acceptable confessions, he too found Bahrdt's version of John 1.1 difficult to reconcile with any acceptable teaching of the "eternal divinity of our lord and savior, Jesus Christ." And Bahrdt's "ungerman" and "offensive" passage was only one of many "obscene expressions . . . [and] modernizing turns of phrase" that made the translation highly suspect.[97] Modernizing language, in other words, went hand in hand with the modernizing theology of a translation that sought the "humanization of the Bible" at all costs.[98] The reader of the Bible, Bahrdt exclaimed, "thirsts after truth, wants to educate himself " and his translations were to offer this education, providing its reader with a religious system commensurate with human reason.[99]

If those who ignore the past are condemned to repeat it, then Bahrdt's blissful ignorance of the history of the pedagogical Bible had dire consequences. When Bahrdt first published his translation, he was a happily employed professor of

[94] [Heinrich Köster], *Die neuesten Religionsbegebenheiten mit unpartheyischen Anmerkungen für das Jahr 1778* (Giessen, 1779), 63, 61, 66, 63, 69.

[95] Bahrdt, *Die neueste Offenbarung Gottes*, 2nd ed. (Frankenthal, 1777), John 1.1.

[96] [Köster], *Religionsbegebenheiten*, 84–85.

[97] The Göttingen review was republished in full in the *Acta Historico-Ecclesiastica Nostri Temporis* (Weimar, 1779), 1036–73, here 1044–46, 1072.

[98] Aner, *Theologie der Lessingzeit*, 206.

[99] Bahrdt, *Neueste Offenbahrung* (1773),)*(5^{v}.

theology at Giessen, where he had arrived after he was hounded out of the University of Leipzig for his ostensible relations with a prostitute, and out of the University of Erfurt for heretical theological lectures. But in early 1775—warned that a "tempest" was coming and that his translation would be taken up into the Imperial book examination system—Bahrdt resigned his post in Giessen, leaving behind considerable debt, and fled to Switzerland. There he embarked on a new career, this time—not surprisingly given what we know about the pedagogical Bible—as an educational reformer in a newly founded boys school in Switzerland. Indeed, it was philanthropinism's spokesman Johann Basedow himself who, having just successfully founded the *Philanthropinum* in Dessau, had the brilliant idea that Bahrdt ought to direct this experimental school. Like the Dessau school, the new Swiss institution, founded by a group that included such luminaries as Johann Lavater and Johann Bodmer, aimed at a full renewal of pedagogical principles. Although Bahrdt proved an incompetent director, this move to Switzerland was, nonetheless, fateful. It was in Switzerland that Bahrdt published the second edition of his New Testament translation, as a gift and tool for his young charges. Like the first, this was a version designed to rehumanize and remoralize a system of religion buried under the weight of encrusted orthodoxy.[100] And it was this expressly pedagogical second edition that pushed Bahrdt onto the road from itinerant scholar to (eventual) prisoner of conscience.

On 29 March 1779, the Imperial Aulic Council—aided at times by Pope Pius VI himself—pronounced a blanket condemnation on this second edition, banning it and calling, as in Schmidt's case some forty years earlier, for its complete confiscation. Although the Göttingen theological faculty tried to protect Bahrdt, their efforts were in vain, and Bahrdt was "adjured . . . to recant and make plain confession of the divinity of Christ . . . on pain of banishment from the Imperial domains."[101] This recantation came in Bahrdt's provocative 1778 *Confession of Faith* and succeeded only in unifying that league of intolerance that had so effectively opposed Schmidt. This confession, Bahrdt later wrote, "contained nothing but an open explanation that I cannot understand the Trinity and the Divinity of Christ in the way Athanasius explained it. . . ."[102] "I am, as far as my faith is concerned," Bahrdt defiantly declared, "bound by no man's authority, but I have the right to test all things."[103] But in his Bibles and his *Confession*, Bahrdt did more than merely test. In his explicit role as teacher, he also made his own heterodoxy into a pedagogical instrument of reform. In doing so, Bahrdt violated that barrier between public speech and private teaching that

[100] For the Swiss school, see Flygt, *Notorius Dr. Bahrdt*, chap. 13; see also the broader discussion of pedagogical reform in: Manfred Agathen, *Geheimbund und Utopie: Illuminaten, Freimaurer und deutsche Spätaufklärung* (Munich, 1984), chap. 6.

[101] Flygt, *Notorious Dr. Bahrdt*, 194.

[102] Bahrdt, *Geschichte*, 4:71.

[103] Article 10 of the *confessio fidei*, quoted and translated in Flygt, *Notorious Dr. Bahrdt*, 200.

governed the political reactions to the Enlightenment Bible. The orthodox wings of Catholicism and Lutheranism alike reacted fiercely and in concert, forging an alliance against Bahrdt that cast him out of his role as theological instructor. Even that scion of Protestant rationalist theology, Johann Semler, focused his ire on Bahrdt's teaching. For Semler, Bahrdt's confession actually violated the integrity of his office by forcing his convictions on an unwitting public.[104] And this despite the fact that, as one scholar complained in 1779, "Semler believes what Bahrdt does."[105]

In the years after the *Confession*, Bahrt managed to find sanctuary under Frederick the Great and his tolerant minister for ecclesiastical affairs, Karl Freiherr von Zedlitz, teaching (to Semler's disgust) at Halle. But even in Halle, he was prohibited from holding any public lectures on theological topics and forced to teach Greek and Roman classics. Following the death of Frederick the Great, however, life took a downturn for Bahrdt, especially after he found himself in violation of the new King Frederick William's 1788 *Edict on Religion*, an effort to restore religious virtue by, among other things, punishing "clergymen, preachers, [and] schoolteachers" guilty of public religious heterodoxy.[106] Indeed, Bahrdt eventually found himself in prison as a result.

Since what brought him, in the end, to such a pass was a series of translations, we can use Bahrdt to bookend the history of the pedagogical Bible. In the case of Bahrdt, the difficulties and paradoxes of an era of religious apology found their clearest expression. Although the 1773 Bible was designed to give "friends of the most agreeable religion" a translation that "could serve to firm up their faith," Bahrdt's rejection of doctrine, his belief in the pedagogical reform of religion, and his pursuit of a pedagogical Bible all put his work firmly into the private sphere of teaching, crossing the line from speech to practice.[107] Johann Ulrich may have complained in 1780 that Bahrdt's translation should not have been subjected to legal proceedings, because "the jurisdiction of the highest imperial court does not extend to spiritual matters," but just as the Wertheimer Bible consistently overstepped the boundaries of proper disinterested scholarship, so too did Bahrdt's Bibles leave purely "spiritual matters" behind.[108] In short, Bahrdt—like Schmidt and Damm before him—sought to rewrite the German vernacular Bible: he saw his translation not as an experimental version, but as a

[104] On Bahrdt and Semler, see Aner, *Theologie*, 103ff. and Flygt, *Notorious Dr. Bahrdt*, chap. 22. In later years Semler would support the highly repressive *Religionsedikt*, much to the shock of his Enlightenment observers: see Aner, *Theologie*, 107.

[105] Johann Gleim to G. E. Lessing, 22 July 1779, in Lessing, *Sämtliche Schriften*, 21:265.

[106] Bahrdt, *The Edict of Religion: A Comedy* (Lanham, MI, 2000), 38. For an introduction to this immense controversy, see the 118 microfiches assembled by Dirk Kemper: *Missbrauchte Aufklärung? Schriften zum preussischen Religionsedikt vom 9. Juli 1788* (Hildesheim and New York, 1996).

[107] Bahrdt, *Neueste Offenbahrung* (1773),)*(5^v.

[108] [Ulrich], *Ueber den Religionszustand*, 5:495.

new authoritative one, one that could lead the German nation out of the mysticism and obscurity that had characterized both dogmatic theology and the Luther Bible itself. Bahrdt may have *claimed* that he would "never cause Luther's Bible to be discarded and his own put in its place," but his actions spoke louder than words.[109] Indeed, Bahrdt might have been speaking about himself when he wrote of Christ that he "gathered all the scattered parts of rational theology and gave the world a religion that returned to reason its rights and to virtue its worshipers."[110] For these reasons, his translation, like those of Damm and Schmidt, was a highly unstable force in the later eighteenth century. Not many of these translations were produced, and probably for good reason, since the fallout from them was so severe. But even though few in number, the very fact of their production in the face of such ill-fated outcomes testified to the extreme desire to recuperate the Bible and create it afresh in the language and tone of moral pedagogy.

The End of the Pedagogical Bible

In 1783 Joachim Heinrich Campe organized the first *Society for Practical Educators*, with the goal of "professionalizing, systematizing, and departmentalizing pedagogy."[111] After publishing the plan for this society in the *Berlinische Monatsschrift*, Campe drafted his members, one of whom was Karl Friedrich Bahrdt. Since Bahrdt had printed, in that same year, his third edition of the New Testament translation, one might assume that like the second, this edition too would be aimed at pedagogical reform, perhaps even taken up by Campe's *Society* as a blueprint for its changes in religious education. But nothing was further from the truth, for although pedagogy was apparently alive and well in the public domain in the last two decades of the century, the pedagogical Bible—as a genre of translation—would show its face no more. We might read this disappearance as a sign of the successful repression of this polemical form, especially in the wake of Frederick II's death and the new emphasis on religious orthodoxy introduced by Frederick William. But that would be to miss the wider transformations in German cultural and intellectual life that made the pedagogical Bible obsolete, transformations that would nonetheless keep pedagogy a vital foundation for biblical authority.

Bahrdt's 1783 New Testament was marked by these wider changes. For Bahrdt personally, this Bible represented the complete repudiation of his own literary past. "All my work published before 1780—not excluding my *Confession*

[109] Flygt, *Notorious Dr. Bahrdt*, 106.

[110] [Karl Friedrich Bahrdt], *Briefe über die Bibel im Volkston: Eine Wochenschrift von einem Prediger auf dem Lande* (Frankfurt u. Leipzig, 1786), 1:142.

[111] Christa Kersting, *Die Genese der Pädagogik im 18. Jahrhundert* (Weinheim, 1992), 71.

of Faith," Bahrdt later wrote, was garbage.[112] The ideal of an open and accessible Bible; the ideal of Jesus as a universal moral exemplar; the ideal of his teachings as limpid and reasonable: all of these were tossed aside. If Jesus remained "the model of wisdom and virtue," this was only known to the few, the select disciples invited into the esoteric wisdom concealed in the New Testament. In place of openness, Bahrdt offered secrecy. His translation did the same, as in this infamous passage from 1 John:

> There are three witnesses in heaven: the father, the word, and the holy ghost: and these three are one. And there are three witnesses on earth: the spirit, the water, and the blood: and these are for one.[1088]

> [1088] . . . for my part I still believe both verses were inserted. . . . It was very natural, that a brother of the second level would want to point out [on the margin] the three symbols, water, blood and spirit . . . and then in later times, when the knowledge contained in the third level began to die out with the brothers [the margin entered the text].

Bahrdt's new history of Christianity was completely different from his old. In contrast to the lean New Testaments of the 1770s, here was a volume that displayed the full array of scholarly tools, among them hundreds of footnotes. And inside the Bible, Bahrdt had a new story to tell too. There he revealed a hierarchy of initiates, spreading out from Jesus into the rest of the world. "Christ," wrote Bahrdt, "must have planned—by creating a secret society—to preserve and spread among men the truths banished by priests."[113]

This emphasis on secrecy soon undermined the project of translation. The Bible simply could not reveal everything to everyone, if only because many of its secrets could not be revealed except after long preparation and elaborate ritual. Instead of a fourth edition of the translation, then, Bahrdt began in 1786 to publish his *Bible in the People's Voice*, a periodical that described in detail how Jesus was recruited by the Essenes, a sect of Jews with powerful connections across Babylonia and Egypt, how he himself collected his Apostles, initiated them into the true knowledge of God, and used them in ways both scrupulous and unscrupulous to spread the faith across the world. As one reviewer wrote, "[Jesus'] friends and helpers create a secret society. . . . they are known in the story of Jesus as the Angels of God . . . and Paul is later initiated into this society."[114] In this work and others, then, Bahrdt put esotericism at the heart of the Christian

[112] Bahrdt, *Das neue Testament oder die neuesten Belehrungen Gottes durch Jesum und seine Apostel* 3rd ed. (Berlin, 1783), unpaginated preface.

[113] Bahrdt, *Geschichte*, 4:124, 126.

[114] *Allgemeine deutsche Bibliothek* 56.1 (1783): 49. On this history of Jesus, see Schweitzer, *Leben-Jesu-Forschung*, 80. In Bahrdt's vision of this secret society, Jesus's goal—along with the Essenes—was actually to eradicate messianism and the dominance of priests: thus Jesus posed as a messiah in order to abolish messianism and folk superstition.

religion. Christ—"the hero of my life"—became, just as Bahrdt himself became, a freemason.[115]

The publication of this final edition was not a world-shaking event, but it revealed some of the changes that began to overwhelm German cultural life in the last decades of the eighteenth century, changes that would turn the enormous energies poured into biblical translation after 1750 in new directions. These changes will be examined in more detail in chapter 9, but here we can use Bahrdt to recover at least their outlines. First, in Susannah Heschel's terms, we can see in Bahrdt's turn to secrecy a piece of a wider effort to dissociate Christianity from Judaism, to deny, in effect, the "Jewish Jesus" that would take on new forms in the nineteenth century.[116] By making Christ into a freemason, Bahrdt repudiated any real connection between him and pharisaic Jewry, imagining him instead as a repository of wisdom inaccessible to Jews (or more broadly, the literal minded) and reserved for disciples like Paul. This was an idiosyncratic approach, but one which resonated more widely across the spectrum of German religious and cultural commentators in the late century. The simple faith that Christ could be a *universal* moral teacher disappeared, and was replaced by more nationally and racially circumscribed stories. Second, Bahrdt's turn away from pedagogical Bible translation resonated with the powerful tide of *Sturm und Drang* and German idealism, which would replace *Erziehung* (education) with a broader and flexible notion of *Bildung* (cultivation or culture). *Bildung*—with its focus on "self-formation" and organic principles of development—expressly denied the effectiveness of the standard pedagogical platforms evinced by Campe, Basedow, and others.[117] Within the pedagogical tradition itself, this shift was marked by the success of Johann Pestalozzi, who turned from institutional change to the interior life of the child. "I seek to psychologize human education," he wrote in 1800, and in doing so, left the Bible entirely out of his pedagogical schemes.[118] In the face of this shift, the pedagogical Bible as such was too mechanical a tool for cultivating the inner religious sensibilities of the child. External textual forms could neither substitute for, nor adequately prompt, inner personal transformation.

The disappearance of the pedagogical Bible was consistent, then, with these formidable transformations. But this disappearance should not be exaggerated, for, while vanishing as a genre, still the aims of the pedagogical Bible had

[115] Bahrdt, *Geschichte*, 4:124. On Bahrdt as freemason, see Agathen, *Geheimbund und Utopie;* Günter Mühlpfort, "Europarepublik in Duodezformat. Die internationale Geheimgesellschaft 'Union'—Ein radikalaufklärerischer Bund der Intelligenz (1786–96)," in *Freimaurer und Geheimbünde im 18. Jahrhundert in Mitteleuropa*, ed. Helmut Reinalter (Frankfurt a. M., 1983), 319–64.

[116] Susannah Heschel, *Abraham Geiger and the Jewish Jesus* (Chicago, 1998).

[117] Ernst Lichtenstein, "Die Entwicklung des Bildungbegriffs," in Ulrich Herrmann, ed., *Die Bildung des Bürgers* (Weinheim, 1982), 167.

[118] Johann Heinrich Pestalozzi, "Die Methode," in *Wie Gertrud ihre Kinder lehrt und Ausgewählte Schriften zur Methode*, ed. Fritz Pfeffer (Paderborn, 1961), 30.

permeated deeply into the religious landscape by the turn of the century. The intimate connection between the figure of Christ and individual morality became a commonplace in early nineteenth-century biblical scholarship and theology. For Romantics in Germany and England alike, the essence of Christianity rested not in the tensions of sin and salvation, but in the moral rejuvenation offered by Christ. If this theme did not need to written directly into the text of the Bible, this widely shared sentiment nonetheless crucially helped to create a fully cultural Bible by the first decades of the next century. But such a cultural Bible was not a product of pedagogy alone. Nor did it arise solely out of treatments of the New Testament. Indeed, the Old Testament too would have to be transformed for the cultural Bible to appear. One crucial tool for this was poetry.

Chapter Six

POETRY: NATIONAL LITERATURE, HISTORY, AND THE HEBREW BIBLE

In 1778 Robert Lowth—the greatest scholar of the Hebrew Bible that England ever produced—furnished the English republic of letters with a translation of *Isaiah*, the "single English commentary" of the eighteenth century, as the later critic Frederick Farrar claimed, to stake out wholly new territory in biblical studies.[1] Whether Farrar was correct or not, the translation was surely a major literary monument. Unlike the biblical paraphrases that dominated English letters at least since Addison began presenting them in the *Spectator* in the 1710s, Lowth offered his readers what was designed to be a perfect reproduction of the Hebrew originals. "It is incumbent on every Translator," Lowth commented in his *Preliminary Dissertation*: "to study the manner of his Author; to mark the peculiarities of his style, to imitate his features, his air, his gesture, and, as far as the difference of language will permit, even his voice; in a word, to give a just and expressive resemblance of the Original."[2] In sharp contrast to the paraphrastic tradition—alive and well in England since popularized by people like John Dryden and Isaac Watts—Lowth's translation strove for absolute integrity. "Words in one language elegantly used / will hardly in another be excused": Lowth discarded this fundamental assumption of the Augustan imitators in favor of a strict attention to the letter of the original.[3] But Lowth also wanted *Isaiah* to be a *poetic* translation, and this in an age when poetic translations of the Bible were rarely well received in England. "The sacred and sublime truths of our holy religion are very unfit subjects for poetry," commented the *Critical Review* in its 1763 review of Friedrich Klopstock's epic *Messiah*.[4] Johann Bodmer's 1767 *Noah* poems received equally short shrift, and this was not just a xenophobic reaction to German enthusiasms, for neither James Merrick nor Christopher Smart found favor for their respective 1760s versifications of the psalms. "A northern bard," the *Review* said shortly, "cannot easily add a sentiment which is equal to the grand conceptions of the oriental prophet."[5] "It may be questioned whether fiction is at all allowable when the Divine Being is the

[1] Frederick William Farrar (ca. 1885) quoted in William Neil, "The Criticism and Theological Use of the Bible, 1700–1950," in *CHB*, 3:271.

[2] Robert Lowth, *Isaiah: A New Translation* (London, 1995), xxxv.

[3] Earl of Roscommon, *Essay on Translated Verse* (London, 1684), 14.

[4] *Critical Review* 16 (1763): 417.

[5] *Critical Review* 23 (1767): 280–81; *Critical Review* 20 (1765): 210.

subject of it," commented the *Gentleman's Magazine* in 1765.[6] More bluntly put: "*Divine* poems . . . are, for the most part, very dull, unedifying, and even sometimes tedious and disgustful."[7]

If John Fellows's 1778 *History of the Holy Bible . . . Attempted in Easy Verse* afforded reviewers the starkest example of hopeless bathos, Lowth's 1778 *Isaiah*, by contrast, tendered something refreshing and crisp.[8] As far as the *Review* was concerned, Lowth's genius was to realize that a genuinely poetic translation was only possible without the encumbrance of verse and rhyme. If the eighteenth century saw "the emergence into gradual respectability of literal translation" within the classical tradition—signaled by the move away from the paraphrases of Dryden or Pope—then the same general tendency applied to the Hebrew Bible too.[9] To express its poetry, literal translation sufficed perfectly, for our ordinary language itself had "such a conformity with that of the original scriptures, that it can, upon occasion, assume the Hebrew character, without appearing altogether forced and uncertain."[10] This apparent paradox—where only abandoning poetic conventions enabled real poetry—was not an insight of the late 1770s. Instead, it was first grasped some forty years earlier, when Lowth himself struggled to reveal the specific graces of Old Testament verse in a series of lectures inaugurating his new professorship at Oxford. These 1741 lectures—what became the 1753 *Lectures on the Sacred Poetry of the Hebrews*—established him as a "biblical commentator and exegete of rare sensitivity and ability," one whose poetic theory captivated generations of biblical scholars across the Protestant world.[11] And Lowth's theory explicitly rejected the wisdom, common since Aristotle, that a "metrical form" was at least a necessary (if not sufficient) component of any poetry worthy of the name.[12] Not so, insisted Lowth. The key to Hebrew poetry lay not in meter, but rather in "parallelism," the repetitious echoing of phrases such as "I will bless the LORD at all times; his praise shall continually be in my mouth" (Ps. 34.1) or "Behold! He comes, leaping upon the mountains, bounding over the hills" (Song of Sol. 2.8). Literal translation of these echoes reproduced the poetic elements of the Old Testament.

So Lowth already had it figured out in 1741. But then he waited another thirty-seven years before he gave his theoretical skeleton the living flesh of a translation. This temporal gap between theory and practice represented *in nuce* the wider pattern of religious development in England, where the fruits of

[6] *Gentleman's Magazine* 35 (1765): 69.

[7] *Critical Review*, 51 (1781): 185.

[8] *Critical Review* 46 (1778): 296.

[9] Penelope Wilson, "Classical Poetry and the Eighteenth-Century Reader," in Isabel Rivers, ed., *Books and Their Readers in Eighteenth-Century England* (Leicester, 1982), 80. See also Dror Wahrman, "Gender in Translation: How the English Wrote Their Juvenal, 1644–1815," *Representations* 65 (Winter 1999): 1–41.

[10] *Critical Review* 46 (1778): 334.

[11] James Kugel, *The Idea of Biblical Poetry: Parallelism and Its History* (New Haven, 1981), 57.

[12] Aristotle, *Poetics*, 1447^{b} 17, in *The Complete Works of Aristotle*, ed. Jonathan Barnes (Princeton, 1984), 2:2316.

biblical scholarship only began to be reaped in the late 1770s and the 1780s. But if Lowth's theory was barren of immediate practical effects in English soil, in Germany Hebrew versification bloomed into full flower.[13] It was no accident, for example, that the *Lectures* were reviewed in the very first issue (1757) of Germany's new premiere literary magazine, the *Bibliothek der schönen Wissenschaften und freyen Künste*. Nor that they were republished with a set of extensive notes in Göttingen in 1758, and several times after that before the end of the century. Nor that, according to Johann Eichhorn, this edition sold twice as many copies in Germany as in England.[14] Nor, finally, that every edition of Lowth's other major works—including the *Isaiah* translation and even his *Short Introduction to English Grammar*—was quickly translated and republished in German. If the eighteenth century "was a period in which Germany assimilated the contemporary literature of England . . . with an intensity that has few parallels in the relations between the two national cultures," the veins of English poetics were among the most completely mined. That Robert Wood's *Essay on the Original Genius and Writings of Homer* was published in German *before* it even appeared in the English literary marketplace was testament to the depths of Germany's interest in this material.[15] As Stephen Prickett has commented, in Germany "the idea of the 'poetic' as the expression of the life of a people took hold and flourished as it never could in the less theoretical climate of England."[16]

But just as translation always, in the words of George Steiner, "invades, extracts, and brings home" in its aggressive shift from one language world to another, Germany would process, once again, these English raw materials into original tools.[17] It was exactly the quality, for example, that the *Critical Review* praised in Lowth's *Isaiah*—"its αρχαισμος, its air of antiquity"—that the German poetical Bible, as it developed over the course of the 1750s, strove tirelessly to overcome.[18] Indeed, in a wider sense, the desire to overcome archaism was the engine that powered this entire poetic translation tradition. The issue was not the age of the Bible, which everyone recognized as ancient. Rather, it was the sense or "air" of antiquity that was so problematic. Because the very notion of archaism suggested that the distance between past and present was

[13] See Rudolf Smend, "Lowth in Deutschland," in *Epochen der Bibelkritik* (Munich, 1991), 43–62.

[14] Eichhorn, "Robert Lowth: Lord Bischoff von London," *Allegemeine Bibliothek der biblischen Litteratur* 1 (1787): 718.

[15] Bernhard Fabian, "English Books and Their Eighteenth-Century Readers," in Paul Korshin, ed., *The Widening Circle: Essays in the Circulation of Literature in Eighteenth-Century Europe* ([Philadelphia], 1976), 119; on Wood, see 124. Also see W. Reginald Ward, "The Eighteenth-Century Church: A European View," in John Walsh et al., eds., *The Church of England, c. 1689–c. 1833* (Cambridge, 1993), 288.

[16] Stephen Prickett, *Words and* The Word: *Language, Poetics and Biblical Interpretation* (Cambridge, 1986), 50.

[17] George Steiner, *After Babel: Aspects of Language and Translation* (New York, 1975), 298.

[18] *Critical Review* 46 (1778): 419.

radical and unbridgeable, it forced translators to ask whether the Bible was anything more than a mere repository of antique customs and stories.[19] It thus bled quickly into anxieties about the possible role the Bible might play in modern life.

The "air of antiquity" was most stifling around the Old Testament, and for good reasons. It was no accident that, when scholars sought to reinvest the Bible with moral and pedagogical virtues, they turned to the New Testament, since it was the New Testament that offered the traces of Christianity "within the limits of reason alone." The usual connective tissue between Old and New Testaments—prophecy—had weakened since the beginning of the century, and as it did so, Christian theology confined its interests even more narrowly to the figure of Christ. In the words of Henning Graf Reventlow, "the attitude of almost the whole of the Enlightenment period" understood "the Old Testament as finished with, as far as being part of the Christian Bible."[20] Viewed more widely, the emergence of what Jacob Katz has called a "semineutral society"—in which Jews and Christians could at least theoretically coexist without mutual antagonism—signified on a broader social level the separation of spheres between Old and New Testament, Jew and Christian.[21] The eighteenth-century concept of religious toleration, after all, imagined a world divided into independent religious traditions. And at the very moment that toleration gave up the idea of the universal Christian community—that "great global communit[y] of the past" in Benedict Anderson's words—as the normative model for European society, it also gave up the universal and unitary Bible.[22] Just as Christians resigned themselves to the fact that Jews were unlikely to forswear the Torah, they also resigned themselves to the increasing disconnection between this Torah and Christian hopes for salvation.

All of these changes left the Old Testament in a precarious yet productive position in the Christian context. On the one hand, as the Old Testament fell in theological importance, Christian scholars were forced to address the question of archaism, to consider whether this collection of ancient Hebrew writings had *any* bearing on modern Christian life. On the other hand, however, this same devaluation of the Old Testament opened it up to more speculative interpretations and, more importantly, more speculative translations. With the loss of the unitary Bible, the Old Testament would be ramified into new forms, forms independent of the old Christian unities, and its meaning renovated with the aid of new generic, scholarly, and disciplinary practices.

[19] Debora Kuller Shuger, *The Renaissance Bible: Scholarship, Sacrifice, and Subjectivity* (Berkeley, 1994), 71–72.

[20] Reventlow, *Authority of the Bible*, 284–85.

[21] Jacob Katz, *Out of the Ghetto: The Social Background of Jewish Emancipation, 1770–1870* (Cambridge, MA, 1973), 42.

[22] Benedict Anderson, *Imagined Communities: Reflections on the Origin and Spread of Nationalism*, 2nd ed. (London, 1991), 14.

Indeed, as the Old Testament was freed from theological constraints in the 1740s and 1750s, it became the focus of increasingly vibrant inquiry. Far from being "in decline," as Peter Gay would have it, there was a virtual renaissance of the Old Testament in later eighteenth-century Germany.[23] This renaissance made the Old Testament into the gravitational center for the poetic Bible. This poetic Bible pushed beyond the "explicit literary awareness of the texts"—the awareness that the Bible in its original and translated forms had established literary qualities—that had been developing since the seventeenth century and gaining strength, as David Norton has shown, during the early eighteenth.[24] Instead, in Germany after 1750, literature (and poetry specifically) became a tool for reinventing the Old Testament by scholars committed to overcoming archaism, and to preserving a relationship between the increasingly distant biblical world and late eighteenth-century Germany. The effort to invent the poetic Bible was never merely a secularizing impulse, in other words, but one motivated by the religious concern to keep the Bible an active participant in modern life.

After Prophecy: The Poetic Bible and the Recuperation of the Old Testament

Two years after Robert Lowth first published his *Lectures on the Sacred Poetry of the Hebrews*, the poet Johann Andreas Cramer set before the German public a new vision of the Old Testament. In his 1755 *Poetic Translation of the Psalms*, he both acknowledged the peculiar place of the Hebrew Bible in the Christian canon and sought to reinstall it at the center of religious devotion. Its appearance was immediately applauded throughout Germany, not least by that scion of the Berlin Enlightenment, Friedrich Nicolai—editor and publisher of the *Bibliothek der schönen Wissenschaften und freyen Künste*—who blessed Cramer with pride of place at the head of the very first issue of the journal (some forty pages *before* the review of Robert Lowth!). "We could begin our library in no worthier a fashion," Nicolai wrote, "than with a book, whose author knows how perfectly to connect the sentiments of religion and virtue with the most stirring aspects of poetry."[25]

Cramer was, of course, not the first to admire the poetic qualities of Scripture. Since antiquity, the Church Fathers had justified the Bible to a classically trained and skeptical literary audience, arguing that the *eloquentia sacra* of the Bible equaled, indeed far outweighed, the merit of other merely secular

[23] Peter Gay, *The Enlightenment: An Intepretation, Vol. 1: The Rise of Modern Paganism* (New York, 1967), 87.

[24] David Norton, *Bible As Literature*, 229.

[25] *Bibliothek der schönen Wissenschaften und freyen Künste* 1.1 (1757): 69.

writers.[26] Thus Augustine wrote of the sacred writers that "for my part, no one seems either wiser than them, or more eloquent," while Isidore of Seville remarked that Moses had employed hexameter "long before . . . Homer." Not only were the sacred writers more beautiful than the secular ones—contended the ancient fathers—but they were also the very *fons et origo* of secular poetic conventions. These two virtues were praised well into the seventeenth century, when the Calvinist polymath Johann Alsted declared that "Homer, Hesiod, Sophocles, Ovid and innumerable others derive from Moses, the book of Judges, and the Psalms" and his contemporaries—the poets Martin Opitz and Georg Harsdörffer—looked to the Song of Songs, over Vergil and Theocritus, as the "most beautiful justification" for their pastoral poetry.[27] This praise for the poetic merits of the Bible was always marked, of course, by a whiff of apologetic anxiety. Biblical poetry certainly seemed coarse and primitive compared with the solemn rhythms of Greek and Latin verse. It conformed to few of the Aristotelian poetic unities and was structured by no obvious metrical scheme. Indeed, all of the tortured efforts to assign metrical quantities to the Bible only emphasized the distance that lay between it and the classical tradition. But for exegetes from antiquity through the Early Modern period, these criticisms never marred the core of biblical text. After all, even if defenders of Scripture granted that the Bible was not as eloquent as classical literature (which they did not), they still admitted nothing challenging to biblical authority. This authority did not, in the end, depend on stylistic quality. Style was an adiaphorous aspect of Scripture: nice to have, but in the end peripheral to the major issue of human salvation.

For this reason, even such an eager defender of Scriptural style as Robert Boyle—whose 1663 *Considerations Touching the Style of the Holy Scriptures* sought to exonerate Scripture from the charge that it was "obscure . . . immethodical . . . incoherent . . . unadorned . . . flat and unaffecting"—happily acknowledged the strangeness of Scripture to the modern ear. Scripture was so peculiar, Boyle contended, because "the *geniuses*, the capacities and the dispositions of men are so distinct." Otherwise put: "In those parts of the Scripture whose Eloquence is not Obvious to us *Europeans*, the Pretended Want of Eloquence may be but a Differing and Eastern kind of it." Boyle embraced scriptural oddity not because he was a historicist but because for him the qualities of the Bible that made it seem alien to the modern disposition were always overcome by its special nature. In particular, prophecy knit the Bible together, both internally and externally. Internally, prophecy guaranteed that Old and New Testaments were one book: the "Books of Scripture illustrate and expound

[26] On the general discussion of eighteenth-century poetics and the Bible, see Prickett, *Words and* The Word, and Joachim Dyck, *Athen und Jerusalem: Die Tradition der argumentativen Verknüpfung von Bibel und Poesie im 17. und 18. Jahrhundert* (Munich, 1977).

[27] Dyck, *Athen und Jerusalem*, 32–33, 82, 83. For the English scene, see Lewalski, *Protestant Poetics*, esp. chap. 3.

each other; *Genesis* and the *Apocalypse* are . . . reciprocal Commentaries," as Boyle put it. Externally, prophecy guaranteed that the Bible could be knit into the fabric of modern life. Just as the obscurities of the Old Testament were "abundantly Illustrated by the Rising of that Sun of Righteousness" that was Christianity, so too were the remaining obscurities simply prophecies as yet unfulfilled.[28] Prophecy, in short, was the sinew that tied Old and New Testaments, Jews and Christians, ancients and moderns together. It allowed the Bible to be both unitary and "omnitemporal," as Erich Auerbach has put it. When all the episodes of the Old Testament "are interpreted as figures or phenomenal prophecies of the events of the New Testament . . . the here and now is no longer a mere link in an earthly chain of events . . . in the eyes of God, it is something eternal."[29] No matter how much one historicized the events of the Old Testament, from antiquity until the Early Modern period, prophecy always guaranteed the integrity of the Scriptures writ large.

Beginning in the eighteenth century, though, this integrity began to crumble as prophecy lost its power over the biblical imagination. This was the precondition of the "eclipse of Biblical narrative" that Hans Frei has so carefully unpacked, that separation between the narrative form of the Bible and the "separable subject matter . . . now taken to be its true meaning."[30] We have already seen this crumbling in the Wertheimer Bible, which insisted with pedantic rectitude that every book of the Old Testament had to be alienated from the Bible as a whole. With this separation of form and meaning, with the decline of a prophetic interpretation, with the concomitant separation of Old and New Testaments, affirmations of the distance between Hebrew and modern became increasingly commonplace in the early eighteenth century. Nowhere were such affirmations so ubiquitous as in the study of Hebrew verse. "Each Nation, each Country, each Temper or Constitution, each Passion has its natural Rhetorick and Poetry," proclaimed the popular antiquarian scholar of biblical antiquities Augustin Calmet in the 1720s, and these sentiments echoed in the words of scriptural enthusiast John Husbands: "We have a very imperfect knowledge of the Antiquities of the *Hebrews*. Their Notions, their Taste, their Manners, their Phraseology, are but little understood by Us."[31]

But if indeed the Hebrews were so far from the moderns; if indeed the Bible was written by and for a people completely unlike us, how can we understand it, or, more relevantly, translate it into a modern idiom? This dilemma sprang fully formed out of the corpse of prophecy. Once the prophetic sinews were broken, what could bind Hebrew and modern? Fortunately, the poetic Bible

[28] Robert Boyle, *Some Considerations Touching the Style of the Holy Scriptures*, 4th ed. (London, 1675), 4, 28, 163, 72, 75, 37.

[29] Erich Auerbach, *Mimesis: The Representation of Reality in Western Literature* (New York: Doubleday, 1953), 64.

[30] Frei, *Eclipse of Biblical Narrative*, 51.

[31] Augustin Calmet, *Antiquities Sacred and Profane: or, A Collection of Critical Dissertations on the Old and New Testament*, trans. Nicholas Tindal (London, 1727), 30; Husbands, *Miscellany*, d4.

offered an answer to this too, a new set of sinews for tying the Old Testament to modern life. What was an adiaphorous quality of Scripture—its poetic style—became essential to its modern relevance. This shift was nowhere more obvious than in the 1755 *Poetic Translations of the Psalms* by Johann Cramer. The focus on the psalms was not accidental. Already in the sixteenth century, Luther had praised their language for its ability to speak directly to the human heart and "imagine for us the truly noble, living holy men."[32] Throughout the seventeenth century, these texts were versified and given such evocative titles as *The Holy Crown Harp Played with German Strings* (1680).[33] By the eighteenth century, the poetic imagination became key to the psalms. And so when Samuel Lange (son of the Halle Pietist theologian Joachim Lange) published his 1746 *Odes of David*, he dedicated them to that connoisseur of the poetic imagination, the Swiss poet Johann Breitinger—who advocated for what Johann Bodmer called "the miraculous in poetry"—and thus aligned the psalms with the "sublimity of spirit" that characterized John Milton.[34] Like Lange, Cramer believed that his odes were sufficient to convey these high-flying poetic qualities.[35] More specifically, Cramer followed in the footsteps of his mentor Friedrich Klopstock, the German poet who gave the ode the specifically religious task of "setting the entire soul in motion."[36] For Cramer, the scriptural odes would set the modern soul aflame with the passions of the Hebrews.

This optimism was apparent in the very first of Cramer's psalms, what Nicolai's *Bibliothek* called the "perfect example of simplicity and majesty together":

Heil, Heil dem Manne, der dem Rathe Der Frevler sich entzieht, Dem Manne, der den krummen Pfad Der Uebertreter flieht!	Hail, Hail to the man, who runs From the advice of the wicked To the man, who flees The crooked path of the sinner!	[RSV]: Blessed is the man who walks not in the counsel of the wicked, nor stands in the way of sinners,
Der, wo der Gottheit Spötter lacht, Die fromme Seel entfernt; Sich Gottes Recht zur Freude macht	Where the mocker laughs at the divine, Far from the pious soul, He takes God's law for his delight,	nor sits in the seat of scoffers; but his delight is in the law of the LORD, and on his law he

[32] Martin Luther, *Biblia*, 1:965 (preface to the Psalms).

[33] [Wolf H. von Hohlberg], *Die mit teutschen Saiten überzogene Heilige Kron-Harffe* (Nürnberg, 1680).

[34] Johann Bodmer, *Critische Abhandlung von dem Wunderbaren in der Poesie* (Zürich, 1740), 3.

[35] On the ode, see Johann Gottsched, *Versuch einer critischen Dichtkunst* 4th ed. (Leipzig, 1751), 419f. and, more generally, Karl Vietor, *Geschichte der deutschen Ode* (München, 1923).

[36] Vietor, *Geschichte der deutschen Ode*, 110, 111. For other odes, see Christian Furchtegott Gellert, *Geistliche Oden und Lieder* [1757] in *Gesammelte Schriften*, ed. Bernd Witte (Berlin, 1997), vol. 2.

Und Tag und Nacht es lernt. . . .	And learns it day and night. . . .	meditates day and night . . .
Das ist der Fromme! Was er macht	That is the pious man! What he does,	In all that [the pious] does, he prospers.
Geräth ihm und gedeiht,	Serves him well, and he prospers.	
Der Sünder ist, der seiner lacht,	The sinner who laughs,	The wicked are not so,
Spreu, die der Wind zerstreut. . . .	Is straw, scattered by the wind. . . .	but are like chaff which the wind drives away. . . .
Gott kennt und zeichnet selbst die Bahn,	God knows and shows the road	for the LORD knows the way of the righteous,
Die der Gerechte geht.	That to his justice leads,	but the way of the wicked will perish.
Er schaut im Zorn den Sünder an	He looks in anger at the sinner	
Des Sünders Weg vergeht![37]	Who goes the sinner's way!	

Cramer's ode traced a complex poetic pattern, one colored by the conventions of eighteenth-century verse. Unlike the RSV or Luther's Bible, the ode was composed of four verse stanzas, with alternate lines rhyming. Each line was metrically arranged in iambs. Sentences were short and the language was simple. That ubiquitous ingredient of eighteenth-century poetry, the exclamation point, was liberally sprinkled in the text (Psalm 24 had eight in the first stanza alone!). And the translation was punctuated with elements foreign to the original, elements added for rhythmic, metrical, and poetic effect.

The Psalms translation was designed to re-create texts whose thoughts were "uncommon, sublime . . . full, easy, and most harmonious . . . rapturous, somewhat abrupt, and immethodical to the vulgar eye," as the English poet Edward Young wrote in 1728.[38] Cramer's Psalms in effect gave the negative answer to Young's plaintive questions: "are passions, then, the pagans of the soul? Reason alone . . . ordain'd to touch things sacred?"[39] If, for Cramer, the odes of David had the power to "inspire wonder, to transform wonder to astonishment, to ignite love, to kindle hatred, to shake the soul through fear and horror," then the *Poetic Translation of the Psalms* was an effort to use the passions to re-create this Davidic spirit in the German tongue.[40] In an age where reason was venerated

[37] Cramer, *Poetische Uebersetzung der Psalmen mit Abhandlungen über dieselben*, vol. 1 (Leipzig Berhard Christoph Breitkopf, 1755), Psalm 1.

[38] Edward Young, "On Lyric Poetry," 58.

[39] Edward Young, *The Complaint, or, Night Thoughts* in *Poetical Works* (London, 1844), 1:71. *Night Thoughts* was translated into German first in 1751, and then printed three more times in the next five years. Klopstock's 1752 poem "To Young" ended with an ecstatic cry—"die, and become my genius!" ("An Young," in *Werke* [Leipzig, 1798], 1:117).

[40] [Klopstock], *Nordische Aufseher*, 1:534.

above all human faculties, Cramer's Psalms affirmed the passions as tools of Christian salvation, as instruments of the sacred. His essay *On the Essence of Divine Poetry*—appended to the psalms translations—made this explicit. Like Klopstock, whose introduction to his 1749 epic *The Messiah* (entitled "On Divine Poetry") echoed many of Cramer's sentiments, Cramer was "concerned less with actual events than with the mental and emotional effect" of the Bible on its readers.[41] But where Klopstock offered secular poetry at least faint praise, for Cramer, all poetry worthy of the name had to refer back to its own divine center. And at this divine center burned the fires of the passions. "Enthusiasm," Cramer wrote, "is the origin and the goal of poetry; that is its nature and the quality that distinguishes it from other arts; that is also the true essence of Biblical poetry."[42]

The barb that G. E. Lessing fired at Klopstock—that he replaced "thinking" with "feeling" in matters religious—would have stuck, in other words, even more firmly into Cramer.[43] For Cramer, religion itself had little to do with thought or reasoned analysis. Instead, at its heart was passionate poetry: verse was, in Cramer's aesthetic religion, promoted from an adiaphorous quality to the organizing principle of religion in general. This shift was a profound one. It is not just that the Bible became a "literary standard," as David Norton has it. Rather literature, or more precisely poetry, was injected into the very veins of religion.[44] The Bible was poetic because, in essence, religion was poetic. What the Halle theologian Sigmund Baumgarten, in his preface to Lange's *Odes*, confined to the domain of human eloquence—pretty packaging with some didactic, but little essential value—Cramer made into the essence of religion itself.[45] For Cramer, the Psalms were steeped in this essence. In them were concentrated all of those "divine passions that . . . truly animated the poets of God's people" and distinguished them from secular poets "simply agitated by a fiery imagination." In short, the Psalms surpassed the imagination: they contained "*nature itself*, and not a simple imitation of nature."[46] They were direct manifestations of divine passion.

And these very passions—this extreme fire buried in the belly of the Psalms—allowed poetry to bind together ancient and modern through the vehicle of vernacular translation. "To be moved by the odes and hymns of Pindar or Callimachus, one must transform oneself into a Greek," Cramer announced, "but to be animated with the noblest and most sublime feelings by the poetry of

[41] Katrin Kohl, *Rhetoric, the Bible, and the Origins of Free Verse: The Early "Hymns" of Friedrich Klopstock* (Berlin, 1990), 56.

[42] Cramer, "Wesen," 262.

[43] Lessing criticized Klopstock's anonymous essay "Von der best Art über Gott zu denken," which appeared in *Der Nordische Aufseher*; see Lessing, *Briefe, die neueste Literatur betreffend*, in *Werke*, 4:607.

[44] Norton, *Bible As Literature*, 241.

[45] Baumgarten, preface to Samuel Gotthold Lange, *Oden Davids, oder poetische Uebersetzung der Psalmen* 2nd ed. (Halle, 1760),)()()(6^{r}.

[46] Cramer, "Wesen," 263, 273.

Scriptures, one only has to be a man."[47] The chasm that dropped between ancient and modern was bridged by the fire of Hebrew passion. In this sentiment, Cramer was in good company. Already in the 1730s, John Husbands had declared that if even "the most noble of the Heathen Poets," Pindar, were "render'd word for word, 'twou'd seem as if one Madman had translated another." But how different in the case of Scripture: "how beautiful do the HOLY WRITINGS appear, under all the Disadvantages of an old Prose Translation? So beautiful, that, with a charming and elegant Simplicity, They ravish and transport the Learned Reader; so intelligible, that the most Unlearned are capable of understanding the greater Part of them."[48] Scripture, then, was the great exception to the radical heteronomy of different peoples and times. No matter how strange the content, still the Bible has the power to "ravish and transport" its readers, moving the ignorant with its "elegant and charming Simplicity." As Richard Blackmore had it in his 1700 *Paraphrase on the Book of Job*, "what an inimitable kind of Eloquence must be supposed in the Original" that it should spur "such an Admiration of its Beauty and its Morals" despite its age.[49] Translation, in other words, was the place where historical difference and relativity could be overcome.

This bridge across historical time was forged by the unique qualities of Hebrew poetry. More specifically, the bridge was built by the sublimity of the Old Testament, a quality attributed to Scripture at least since Longinus, whose text *Peri hupsous* was an early modern sourcebook on the sublime and who praised Gen. 1.3, "Let there be light, and there was light," as an exemplary sublime text.[50] Hebrew verse was "nothing else but figurative, sublime, and sententious," proclaimed Augustin Calmet, and when the critic Anthony Blackwall praised the style of the New Testament, he attributed its coarse Hebraisms to that "rich treasury of all the sublimity of thought," the Hebrew Old Testament.[51] Overall, this interest in the sublime was common enough in the eighteenth century. From texts like Edmund Burke's *Philosophical Inquiry into the Origins of our Ideas of the Sublime and Beautiful* to Kant's *Critique of Judgment*, this aesthetic category served a panoply of purposes in philosophical and aesthetic discourse.[52] Thankfully we do not have to rehearse this panoply here, but merely point out its implications for the translation of Hebrew poetry. John Dennis's hyperbolic

[47] Gutzen, *Poesie der Bibel*, 71.

[48] Husbands, *Miscellany*, d4^{r-v}.

[49] Richard Blackmore, *Paraphrase on the Book of Job* (London, 1700), e^{v}. For more discussion of this point, see Norton, *Bible As Literature*, 194ff.

[50] On Boileau, see Samuel H. Monk, *The Sublime: A Study of Critical Theories in XVIII-Century England* (Ann Arbor, 1960), 29ff.

[51] Calmet, *Antiquities Sacred and Profane*, 30–31; Anthony Blackwall, *Sacred Classics Defended and Illustrated* (London, 1725), 1.

[52] See, inter alia, Monk, *The Sublime*; David B. Morris, *The Religious Sublime: Christian Poetry and Critical Tradition in 18th-Century England* (Lexington, KY, 1972); Peter DeBolla, *The Discourse of the Sublime* (Oxford, 1989).

1704 pronouncement—that the sublime "commits a pleasing Rape upon the very Soul of the Reader . . . whenever it breaks out where it ought to do, like the Artillery of Jove, it thunders, blazes, and strikes at once, and shews all the united Force of a Writer"—gets us part of the way, as did Burke's claim to "know of nothing sublime which is not some modification of power."[53] What characterized the sublime was its power to move the passions in a way beauty never did. Imagination is stirred, even violated, by the sublime, a violation that produces passions ranging from awe to sheer terror.

Exactly this power of sublimity—what one might call the extratextual aspect of sublimity, its direct appeal to emotions—allowed the Bible to vault the distance between ancient and modern. For the sublime allowed monumental passions to transcend the stylistic conventions of texts. And in this transcendence, the pathos of the biblical language was free to puncture the barriers of linguistic and cultural difference. As Blackwall put it: "the sublime . . . appears beautiful in the plain or figurative style; it admits all the ornaments of language; yet needs none of 'em; but commands and triumphs in its own native majesty. The true sublime *will bear translation into all languages*, and will be great and surprising in all languages."[54] If sublime pathos guaranteed translatability, only the Bible achieved the true heights of sublimity—even such an "intoxicating" author as Pindar, who possessed an "*original*, unindebted energy," and burned with a "*vigor igneus* and *caelestis origo*," did not blaze with a fire hot enough to melt the barrier between languages.[55] This failure represented less the darkening hand of the translators than the comparatively feeble light of the original. For Cramer, like Blackwall, only Hebrew poetry burned bright enough to pierce the veil of time. And because of this glow, the Bible was assured of its easy expression in all tongues. We do not have to become David to be moved by his poetry. Nor do we need theology, history, or geography for his words to ignite our passionate response. Instead, Cramer's project declared, the gap between ancient and modern was bridgeable: the Hebrews and their antique poetry would be brought back into the fold of the contemporary Christian community without loss. And the tool for accomplishing this was the poetic Bible.

But, however optimistic Cramer's rhetoric, a hitch remained in his plan. Namely, all of these passions had to be translated—actually and physically—into textual form. Cramer's odes were, after all, *German* odes: they hewed rigorously to conventions of style characteristic of eighteenth-century verse. Despite Cramer's insistence that the sacred poems "lacked both the symmetry of meter and the harmony of true rhyme," the translation itself was both metrical and

[53] John Dennis, "The Grounds of Criticism," [1704] quoted in Monk, *The Sublime*, 53. Edmund Burke, *Philosophical Inquiry into the Origins of our Ideas of the Sublime and Beautiful*, ed. Adam Philips (Oxford, 1990), 59.

[54] Blackwall, *Sacred Classics*, 276–77 (my italics).

[55] Edward Young, "On Lyric Poetry" [1725] appendix to *Conjectures on Original Composition*, ed. Edith Morley (Manchester, 1918), 59, 17. See also Monk, *Sublime*, 102.

rhyming.[56] In the end, it seems, it was far easier to assert the perfect translatability of Scripture, than to show it in an actual translation. Cramer's optimistic desire to "sympathize with" David and translate "the affect with which he wrote," to offer not the "work of belabored imitation," but "the inspiration of feelings," was actually quite difficult to put into practice.[57] After all, should one follow the theory, the result would be, in essence, free verse. Would this work to re-create Hebrew affect for *Germans* accustomed to the conventions of rhyme and meter? One critic of the age, Johann Gottfried Herder, thought not. Cramer had "become so used to . . . repetitions and circuitousness," Herder commented, that he forgot "to note whether the German ear, which demands brevity, and the German mind, which loves emphasis, is thus satisfied."[58] In a sense, then, for Herder, Cramer's odes were not German enough to convey adequately the real essence of Hebrew sentiment. If poetry was at the center of the divine, then it had to be a poetry familiar to the German mind.

For Cramer, Klopstock, and other midcentury devotees of the sacred hymns, however, this familiarity was guaranteed by the nature of the Bible itself. In a sense, Cramer's recuperation of the Psalms by poetic means stood as a (final) compensatory effort to retain the "omnitemporal" quality of the Old Testament, to deny the sense of *archaismos* that threatened to veil the Old Testament. It represented a last effort to ensure that the imagined community of the Christian nation, paraphrasing Benedict Anderson, remained fully intact.[59] Never again, after him, would there be such extreme optimism about the power of poetry to single-handedly keep the Bible fresh. Although the poetic Bible was ceaselessly elaborated in the 1760s and 1770s, it was done with the conscious sense that the Bible was "separated from the present . . . by completely different conditions of life."[60] Even if poetry was put into the heart of religion, it was done with a profound sense of historical distance. To bridge this distance, translators relied, on the one hand, on antiquarian scholarship and, on the other, on the faculty of sympathy. No figure concentrated history and sympathy more than Job.

The Book of Job: History, Sympathy, and the Poetic Bible

If the story of Exodus was "a paradigm of revolutionary politics" during the English Revolution, as Michael Walzer has argued, the English and German Enlightenments alike venerated another considerably less optimistic Old

[56] Cramer, "Wesen," 257; "Untersuchung, ob die biblischen Gedichte in abgemessnen, oder gereimten Versen verfasst sind," appendix to *Psalmen*, 318.

[57] Cramer, preface to *Psalms*, *6r.

[58] Herder, "On Recent German Literature: First Collection of Fragments," 7th fragment [1767], in *Johann Gottfried Herder: Selected Early Works, 1764–1767* (University Park, PA, 1992), 116.

[59] Anderson, *Imagined Communities*, 24.

[60] Auerbach, *Mimesis*, 282.

Testament text, the Book of Job.[61] It is an ironic commentary on the psychological disposition of the age of progress that Job's story of patient suffering at the hands of a testing God—his lamentations over arbitrary evil and his quiescence in front of God's ultimate power—was retold dozens of times in the period. It was, after all, this story that prompted the publication of that epitome of eighteenth-century biblical scholarship, Lowth's *Lectures on the Sacred Poetry of the Hebrews.* "When I undertook the present investigation," as he wrote in one of the concluding lectures, "my *principal object* was to enable you to form some definite opinion concerning the poem of Job."[62] If Cramer sought to replace the scholarly investigation of the Old Testament with affective poetics, then Lowth provided the scholarly alternative, a synthetic analysis of Hebrew poetics from a philological perspective. Here as much as anywhere, Germany took from England the raw material of its own religious transformation, for this blend of poetics and scholarship would prove especially endearing to German scholars and translators of the Bible. Not only did Lowth clear a path out of the tangled discussion of Hebrew meter by making parallelism the key to its poetics, he also strove to relate the genius of Hebrew poetry to the conditions of its emergence.[63] As that paragon of Enlightenment philosophy, Moses Mendelssohn wrote, Lowth was the first to present "the rules of art by which the divine poets among the ancient Hebrews awaken the most sublime feelings inside of us."[64] "Lowth appeared and breathed a new spirit" into the Old Testament, wrote Johann Eichhorn.[65] By tracing the affiliations between poetic imagery and, variously, the natural world, common life, and sacred ritual, he wedded aesthetic considerations and scholarly concerns in a happy bond.

But Lowth was only one part of a Job revival in midcentury England, a revival epitomized in texts like John Garnett's *Dissertation on the Book of Job* (1749), Charles Peters's *Critical Dissertation on the Book of Job* (1752), and Leonard Chappelow's *Commentary on the Book of Job* (1752). It was a revival spurred by the insults offered in that monument of antiquarian research, William Warburton's *Divine Legation of Moses* (1738–1740) and, as Jonathan Lamb has carefully shown, a revival fueled by the potent mix of religion and politics.[66] In opposition to Warburton's insistence on the unprophetic nature of the Job text and the allegorical and dramatic genre of its composition, this Job revival insisted on both the unique virtues of Hebrew poetry and the prophetic nature of Job's

[61] Michael Walzer, *Exodus and Revolution* (New York, 1985), 7.

[62] Robert Lowth, *Lectures on the Sacred Poetry of the Hebrews* (London, 1787), 2:386 (my italics).

[63] For Lowth on parallelism, see ibid., lectures III and XIX. See Kugel, *Biblical Poetry*, 274ff.

[64] Mendelssohn, review of Lowth, *Bibliothek der schönen Wissenschaften und freyen Künste* 1.1 (1757): 122.

[65] Eichhorn, "Robert Lowth," 717.

[66] Jonathan Lamb, *The Rhetoric of Suffering: Reading the Book of Job in the Eighteenth Century* (Oxford, 1995), esp. chap. 6.

lamentations. That staple of Christian typological interpretation—Job's cry that "I know that my Redeemer liveth, and at last he will stand upon the earth; and after my skin has been thus destroyed, then from my flesh I shall see God" (19.25–26)—was rehabilitated by commentators who both emphasized its poetic originality and stoutly refused to abandon its Christological portent. No one did this more effectively than Robert Lowth, who insisted that poetry and prophecy were identical, with "one name, one common origin, one common author, the Holy Spirit," and, at the same time, praised the unparalleled "force of composition" in Oriental poetry that "strikes and overpowers the mind" with its "figurative style."[67] In this way, like Boyle and older Christian commentators, Lowth used prophecy to compensate for historical distance.

Aesthetics slipped quickly into politics in the English Job revival. The Tory Lowth's confrontation with the Whig Warburton involved pressing political stakes in light of the 1745 attacks of the Jacobites on the authority of the Hanoverian Kings. For Lowth, for example, Job's sublimity "flow[ed] from the futility of [his] self-vindication," the helpless cries of someone "finding his integrity weltering on the margins of the polity as the result of a power-play from which he has no legal exit." Where the Whig would seek to restore to Job "the efficacy of the laws and principles which the hero denies," and thereby maintain Job as tool of social order, the Tory would read in Job a lesson about terror, "the unregulated exercise of power," and the fate of the upright man with no legal recourse.[68] In a sense, then, what Warburton called the *Alliance between Church and State*—or more exactly, the disagreements about what such an alliance would look like—gave the poetic investigation of Job a political charge it would lack in Germany, where church-state relations were essentially uncontested in the eighteenth century.

Instead the German Job revival was powered by the electricity of religion. In accordance with the broader pattern of this period, this loss of political charge opened a zone of freedom in Germany, where the Job obsession was manifested not in English-style paraphrases and commentaries, but in translation. More specifically, the book of Job offered translators what seemed the best chance of bridging the chasm between Hebrew and modern. And so, by the late 1760s, the poetic Bible coalesced around Job, as translation of the book took on a frenzied tone, with at least seven new versions before 1780, more than any other single Old Testament book. From Simon Grynäus to Johann Cube to Johann Eckermann, these translations styled themselves—like Cramer's translation before—as "poetic" translations. Where Cramer had divorced Hebrew verse from scholarly and antiquarian concerns in the 1750s, these later translators were fascinated by the historical origins of Job's poetic form. Through scholarship, these translations affirmed, that far-off landscape of the Old Testament might

[67] Lowth, 2:18, 1:307, 306.

[68] Lamb, *Rhetoric of Suffering*, 119, 121, 112, 119.

be brought home, mapped, and enjoyed by German explorers. And through poetry, they affirmed, this landscape might be felt by modern readers.

The turn to scholarship can be neatly (if somewhat arbitrarily) dated to 1768, a year bracketed by two major Job translations, those of Simon Grynäus (1767) and Johann David Cube (1769). When Simon Grynäus, a classicist in Basel, presented readers with a new Job in 1767, he happily gilded it with quotations from Lucretius, Horace, and Cicero, implicitly comparing it with the dramatic forms of classical antiquity.[69] Precisely this comparison, of course, was scorned by a researcher like Lowth: Job cannot "possibly be classed with them, unless the whole nature and form of either the Greek or Hebrew poem be changed."[70] A year after Grynäus published his Job, Robert Lowth's *Lectures* and the attached notes of the foremost scholar of oriental antiquities in Enlightenment Germany, Johann David Michaelis, appeared in a second edition in Germany. The next year introduced Michaelis's own monumental Bible translation (see chapter 7), a project that itself commenced with the Book of Job. And it was to Michaelis and his "linguistic knowledge, fine taste, [and] poetic feeling" that the translator Johann Cube appealed when seeking the ideal judge for a translation that veered hard from both classical prototypes and what Cube called Cramer's paraphrases.[71] It is hard, of course, to know whether these differences represented more than idiosyncratic preferences (Grynäus, after all, staged the Song of Solomon as a modern drama, complete with a cast of characters, in his 1776 translation of the entire Bible).[72] But 1768 works as well as any date to mark the shift away from classical norms and toward oriental scholarship.

But it was not the external forms of scholarship that distinguished Cube from Cramer. Like his poetic predecessor, Cube foreswore the paratextual annotations that swelled Michaelis's work to gigantic proportions. Rather, what set Cube apart was his refusal to read Job, or the Bible for that matter, as a "rule [*Theticum*] for the eighteenth century." Job could not function—as the Psalms did for Cramer—as key to unlocking the inner mystery of religion. Instead, Job was a historical text, but one that "even if it were not given by God, would still always be the oldest masterpiece of sublime, human eloquence and would—given its worthy content, its thoughtful simplicity, its fiery affect . . . and its strong expression—leave Homer and Pindar far behind."[73] The human eloquence of the text, not its divine secrets, preoccupied Cube, just as they did Johann Eckermann, who seized on the humanity of the Hebrews in his 1778 Job translation: "only in the ancient poets does one find . . . the still untainted

[69] See Simon Grynäus, *Das Buch Hiob: in einer poetischen Übersetzung nach Schultens' Erklärung* (Basel, 1767).

[70] Lowth, *Lectures*, 403.

[71] Johann David Cube, *Poetische und prosaische Uebersetzung des Buches Hiob* (Berlin, 1769), 1:xxxii.

[72] *Die Heilige Schrift*, 3 vols. (Basel, 1776).

[73] Cube, *Hiob*, xvi.

innocence of the childlike age of man. . . . whoever does not sense this, whoever does not sympathize with this, does not read them as they . . . must be read."[74] The childhood of man as a mythic origin for poetry—a notion that spread from the French and German debates about the origins of language into wider cultural circulation—was important for these poetic Bible translators first and foremost because it put human beings at the origin of the biblical text, not just formally but also with regard to its affective content. Thus Cube and Eckermann produced a kind of historical metaphorology (to borrow the phrase of Hans Blumenberg), in which the poetic peculiarities of Oriental imagery were attributed to the conditions of their genesis.[75] Social factors, economic conditions, farming and hunting practices, features of the natural world: in short, the humanity of the Hebrews, not the divinity of their text, was the key to translating oriental poetics.

This humanity allowed the Old Testament to resonate with modern ears, a resonance otherwise designated by that term beloved by eighteenth-century moral psychology, "sympathy." "Whoever can sympathize with a part of the high, enthusiastic feelings" of the ancient poets, Eckermann cried, "he rips himself from time, from daily life." Sympathy casts mankind like a spear from the quotidian into the very heart of the antique world:

> Whoever can imagine their imaginings, can repaint with the greatest fidelity the fantasies sketched by the magical hands of nature itself. . . . he forgets the decade, the city, society, customs, and men; forgets relations, lifestyles, ways of thinking, and prejudices . . . and flings his free spirit back into the ancient world, three-thousand years old.[76]

Sympathy was, in this view, the very foundation of aesthetic response. It was, in essence, a time machine: it gave the reader a tool to "rip himself from time" and hurl himself back into the world inhabited by ancient Hebrews. As the necessary condition of both historical representation and poetic response, sympathy would be that very faculty that made translation from ancient to modern possible.

This interest in sympathy as a span across distance was, of course, widespread in the midcentury, especially in Britain, where, for example, David Hume in his 1739 *Treatise of Human Nature* made sympathy into the yarn that knit together human society. "No quality of human nature is more remarkable" than sympathy, which allows feeling to communicate itself to others.[77] Sympathy not only

[74] J.C.R. Eckermann, "Vorerinnerungen über das Buch Hiob," in *Versuch einer neuen poetischen Uebersetzung des Buches Hiob* (Leipzig and Lübeck, 1778), 28.

[75] Hans Blumenberg, "Paradigmen zu einer Metaphorologie," *Archiv für Begriffsgeschichte* 6 (1960): 7–142.

[76] Eckermann, "Vorerrinerungen," 8.

[77] David Hume, *A Treatise of Human Nature*, ed. L. A. Selby-Bigge (Oxford, 1967), 316. My thanks to Dror Wahrman for his excellent tutoring on sympathy and for sharing his analysis of it from his book, *The Making of the Modern Self: Identity and Culture in Eighteenth Century England* (forthcoming, New Haven, 2004).

bridges distance in the present, but also allows us to feel "the pains and pleasures of others, which are not in being, and which we only anticipate by the force of imagination."[78] The "changing places in fancy with the sufferer" that Adam Smith's 1759 *Theory of the Moral Sentiments* made the source of sympathetic feeling applied, in other words, to the distant, the dead, even the merely imaginary.[79] In Germany, no one described the working of sympathy better than Lessing, who, in his 1766 *Laocöon*, wrote of the "pity" or *Mitleid*—one of a number of synonyms for "sympathy" or "compassion" in the eighteenth century—aroused by the torments of the Trojan Laocöon and his sons. Later, in the *Hamburgische Dramaturgie* of the late 1760s, Lessing would find the origin of this pity in that "love of our fellow men . . . that we can never fully lose under any circumstances."[80] If common affection linked humanity, one way of revealing this affection, in the German Job revival, was to recapitulate how one's *own* suffering inspired translation. Thus Johann Cube's *Job* was, by his account, inspired by the deaths of his father, mother, and brother, among others, and Christian Kessler's 1784 *Job* was ostensibly a product of the death of his only child.[81] Even the incredibly graphic and revolting description—in Johann David Michaelis's 1769 *Job*—of a modern patient dying from leprosy (in which the rotting of the penis played no small role) can be seen as a personalization of the genre of complaint in order to sympathetically re-create the real suffering of Job.[82]

But in moral psychology and aesthetics alike, sympathy was never merely an affirmation of proximity (between man and man, Hebrew and modern). Sympathy was always a double-edged sword, inserting distance between sympathizer and victim even while assuming that feeling could spin a web across the space. In Lessing's example, the genius of *Laocöon* was its ability to ride the line between distance and proximity: if the sculptor had actually portrayed Laocöon's torment realistically, he would only have aroused "disgust" and forced the viewer's gaze elsewhere in an effort to avoid exact identification with the victim of pain. To achieve this, the sculptor "soften[ed] screams to sighs," so that the viewer was aroused to sympathetic compassion—that Aristotlian tragic effect—rather than repulsion at the corporeality of agony.[83] Put in the modern terms offered by Dror Wahrman, sympathy allowed us "both to remain ourselves and to experience a transference of identity."[84] Or in David Wellbery's terms, "the precondition of pity is *distance*: the impending catastrophe cannot

[78] Hume, *Human Nature*, 385.

[79] Adam Smith, *Theory of the Moral Sentiments*, ed. Knut Haakonssen (Cambridge, 2002), 12.

[80] Lessing (22 January 1768), *Hamburgische Dramaturgie* in *Werke*, 6:565.

[81] Cube, *Hiob*, xxiii. Christian David Kessler, *Hiob aus dem hebräischen Original neu übersetzt* (Tübingen, 1784), *4^{v}.

[82] Johann David Michaelis, *Deutsche Uebersetzung des Alten Testaments mit Anmerkungen für Ungelehrte. Der erste Theil welcher das Buch Hiobs enthält.* (Göttingen und Gotha, 1769), 6–7.

[83] Lessing, *Laocöon*, in *Werke*, 5.2:29.

[84] Wahrman, *Modern Self*, 188.

be our own; we cannot be existentially implicated in the tragic event."[85] If "distancing . . . [was] a necessary condition for deriving pleasure from pain," then sympathy was the reagent that enabled this particular piece of psychological alchemy.[86] It acknowledged both the distance that lay between people (or historical times) and the elements of commonality that bound them together. And Job was the very personification of this sympathetic paradox. He stood at the intersection of personalized suffering and the distance implied in every act of representation. Job wanted sympathy and yet, as Leonard Chappelow paraphrased him, insisted that the "miseries which I undergo . . . are too heavy to admit of any comparison."[87] He combined, in other words, "personal anguish with a poetic effect" in the sense that his own individual suffering tensely coexisted with the "genre of complaint" in which his text was written.[88]

The double nature of sympathy helps to account for the attraction of Job within this particular aesthetic regime. Job's immense suffering aligned him and his translators in relationships of exchange and identification. If *Job* could not become an object of sympathy, after all, who could? In this way, suffering overcame the distance imposed by the irrevocable passage of time. But at the same time, this distance was endlessly asserted. One sympathizes with Job but one does not in fact become Job. "What we would call rashness of speech, the Syrians and Arabs call a happy and beautiful idea," Johann Wilhelmi wrote in his 1764 *Attempt at a Poetic Translation of the Song of Songs*.[89] The authors of the Hebrew verses, as Johann Griesbach declared in 1780, "lived in an entirely different world than we do. . . . born under a different sky, surrounded with a different nature, accustomed to entirely different mores, they perceived differently, thought differently, and expressed themselves differently than we do."[90] This compulsive insistence on difference was no less common among Job translators. So, for instance, in nearly the same breath that Eckermann praised translation as a time machine, he declared just as emphatically that "men with such strong . . . passions speak necessarily an entirely different language [than us]. . . . they act and exist completely differently from us." And the differences extended beyond languages to the very bodies that Hebrews occupied: moderns cannot entirely grasp the genius of Hebrew poetry because of our "overworked, pampered brains and irritated nerves."[91]

[85] David Wellbery, *Lessing's Laocoon: Semiotics and Aesthetics in the Age of Reason* (Cambridge, 1984), 165 (my italics).

[86] G. J. Barker-Benfield, *The Culture of Sensibility: Sex and Society in Eighteenth-Century Britain* (Chicago, 1992), 63.

[87] Leonard Chappelow, *A Commentary on the Book of Job* (Cambridge, 1752), 2:153.

[88] Lamb, *Rhetoric of Suffering*, 121.

[89] Johann Gottlob Wilhelmi, *Versuch einer poetischen Uebersetzung des Hohenlieds Salomo* (Leipzig, 1764), 6–7.

[90] Johann Griesbach, "Ueber die verschiedenen Arten deutscher Bibelübersetzungen," *Repertorium für Biblische und Morgenländische Litteratur* 6 (1780): 270.

[91] Eckermann, *Hiob*, 13, 33.

Translation of the Old Testament, in the German Job revival of the 1760s and 1770s, was thus caught between affirmations of both distance and proximity. These dual affirmations were manifested in dual commitments—on the one hand, to scholarship (which declared the past a foreign country) and on the other, to poetry (which handed out sympathetic visas to interested travelers). These two commitments help, I believe, to account for the uncertain practices of translators confronting the actual text of Job. Compare, for example, Cube's 1767 with Eckerman's 1778 version:

CUBE:		RSV:
Mein Ehrweib blickt mich an; und ihre Gleider beben: Sie schleichet schaudern weg; für mein zu langes Leben: Ich seh ihr jammern nach; und mein bethränter Blick, mein unterbrochnes Wort ruft kläglich sie zurück	My wife looks at me; and her legs quake; She slides away shuddering; for my too long life: Moaning I watch her off; and my tearful gaze, My broken word calls her plaintively back	I am repulsive to my wife. . . . my bones cleave to my skin and to my flesh and I have escaped by the skin of my teeth.
Noch hangen, an der Haut, am Fleische, meine Knochen: Kaum kam ich, da mir Gott die Backen durchgebrochen, mit meiner Zahnhaut weg. (Cube, *Job*, 19.17, 20)	Still my bones hang in my skin, my flesh; I had barely come, when God pierced my cheeks, Taking off the skin of my teeth.	

ECKERMANN:

Ekelhaft ist schon Mein Odem meiner Frau. . . .	Already my breath Is disgusting to my wife. . . .
Bedeckt mit Haut und Fleisch fault mein Gebein, Und glänzend wird die Haut auf meinen Zähnen. (Eckermann, *Job*, 19.17)	Clothed with skin and flesh, my bones do rot. And bright becomes the skin atop my teeth.

Both of these translations showed marks of the tensions between proximity and distance, scholarship and poetry, that the faculty of sympathy was supposed to overcome. Despite his professed fidelity to the scholarly model, for example, Cube's poetic translation was distinguished from the "literal" version that he had printed alongside it mostly by its slavish conformance to the conventions of proper eighteenth-century verse. Like Cramer some fifteen years earlier, rhyme and meter helped Cube to reproduce the affective power of the original by transferring its unique idiom into distinctively German poetic form. Cube thus transformed the brutal simplicity of "I am repulsive to my wife" into a poetic drama of separation, complete with groans and parting tears. The tension between distance and familiarity was no less prominent in Eckermann's 1778 version. On the one hand, its version of a revolting Job—"My breath is disgusting to my wife"—conveyed those corporeal peculiarities that set Hebrew poetry into its historical landscape. On the other hand, however, this implied historical distance coexisted tensely with Eckermann's supreme concession to proximity, his refusal to give up metrical translation. Iambic pentameter might have evoked the scenes of Greek tragedy familiar to German readers, but it had little do with the poetry of the Hebrews.

The failure of these translations to live up to their own standards testified, I think, less to the deficiencies in the translators than to the paradoxes of the poetic Bible in the 1760s and 1770s. The sympathetic translator essentially assumed that good history and good poetry would unite to replace the religious drives that had long kept the Old Testament a living part of the Christian patrimony. But good history and good poetry were not practically compatible. On the one hand, the German Job revival wished to mark sharply the historical distance between the Hebrew past and modern present; on the other, it wished to affirm their mutual translatability through the power of poetry. These two goals intersected on the theoretical plane—through the strange workings of sympathy—but diverged in practice. Neither pure history nor pure aesthetics, in other words, could by themselves articulate how the Old Testament ought to stand in relationship to modern readers because, as Johann Gottfried Herder was the first to clearly see, this normative "ought" could not entirely be supplied from within history or aesthetics alone. It was an "ought" that had always been supplied by religion, in particular, by the typological reading that subsumed Job to New Testament theology. But in the absence of theology, it was an "ought" that needed a different source of legitimacy. Herder and the generation of poetic translators that extended well into the nineteenth century found this "ought" in the politics of national literatures.

The Poetic Bible and the Politics of National Literature

"Bible translation!" exclaimed Herder in the opening words of his 1774 *Most Ancient Documents of the Human Race*, "—see here the newest study of the day. . . . We've already nearly created . . . ourselves a new religion, why not also a new Bible . . . ?"[92] Though cantankerous about the fad for Bible translation that swept later eighteenth-century Germany, Herder was not opposed to a new Bible per se. On the contrary, Herder himself long planned a new version, one that would be "perfected not as the Bible, but as a collection of ancient writings."[93] And in 1778 Herder in fact published a comprehensive translation of the Song of Songs, a work he wanted to maintain in its "ancient Hebrew simplicity."[94] But the most intriguing and important series of translations were offered in Herder's monumental work on Hebrew poetics, the 1782 *On the Spirit of Hebrew Poetry*, a book that, as Christoph Bultmann has commented, marked his stature as "a leading figure of the break in Biblical studies . . . through which the Bible changed from a book of revelation to a book of antiquity."[95] These translations of the most aesthetically significant portions of the Bible were, Herder reported, the "point of his book . . . the stars of this otherwise barren space; they are the fruit and my book only the peel."[96] And the most succulent fruit for Herder was the Book of Job, not least the most theologically—and poetically—significant chapter, Job 19. This was his translation of verse 20:

An meiner Haut, an meinem Fleisch hängt mein Gebein; die Haut hab' ich in meinen Zähnen kaum als Raub davon getragen.*	To my skin, to my flesh cleaveth my bone; barely my skin in my teeth have I taken away as spoil.*

*The image is taken from the spoils that beasts carry away in their teeth; his skin is his poor suffering body, which alone he had escaped with (not the skin upon his teeth). His friends are represented as carnivorous beasts that gnaw upon his skin.

From "shabby . . . useless documents of the dissipated Orient" like this text of Job, Herder would strive consistently from the 1780s until his death in 1803 to make a monument whose centrality to the story of humanity was as incontrovertible as it was essential.[97] Job 19 was particularly attractive to Herder for it provided a stunning exemplar of the naturalistic system of Hebrew poetry. From a passage that had always served translators to exemplify odd turns of Hebrew phrase (how do teeth have skin?), Herder made naturalistic hay, reinterpreting the expression "skin of my teeth" to mean "skin in my teeth," and linking it to primitive hunting life. This sense of the historical *place* of the Hebrews would

[92] Herder, *Älteste Urkunde des Menschengeschlechts* in *Werke in zehn Bänden*, ed. Martin Bollacher (Frankfurt a.M., 1985–2000), 5:183.

[93] Rudolph Smend, "Herder und die Bibel," in Herder, *Werke*, 5:1318.

[94] Herder, *Lieder der Liebe: Die ältesten und schönsten aus Morgenlande* [1778] in *Werke*, 5:483.

[95] Christoph Bultmann, *Die biblische Urgeschichte in der Aufklärung: Johann Gottfried Herders Interpretation der Genesis* (Tübingen, 1999), 6.

[96] Herder, *Vom Geist der ebräischen Poesie* in *Werke*, 5:667.

[97] Ibid., 5:897–98, 185.

run like a red thread through Herder's work. As Frank Manuel has noted, "in every line of the Old Testament Herder recognized the poetry of a pristine simplicity and the piety of nomads."[98] How, one might ask, can we honor a people who "even from their origin, cherished narrow, exclusive, and arrogant views" and who made heroes of a weak Abraham, a duplicitous Jacob, and a drunken Noah? Herder did not defend the Jews, but rather found in their herding economy the origins of the distinction between Hebrew poetry and the "fables . . . and monstrous exaggerations" of a Homer or an Ossian.[99] When, for example, Abraham prostituted his wife Sarah to King Abimelech (Gen. 20), it was doubtless a mistake, but one of "a shepherd, who knew not how to conduct himself at court." Observed in his "uprightness, dignity, benevolence, and simplicity," such a mistake was a mark of Abraham's primitive humanity, and in turn a mark of the primitive origins of Hebrew poetry.[100] "One must read the Bible in a human way, for it is a book written by men for men," declared Herder in his 1780 *Letters on the Study of Theology*, and it was the very human details of Scripture that made Hebrew poetry unique; where a Homer might sing of heroes, gods, and monsters in all of their wondrous and supernatural detail, Hebrew poetry was low, and an expression of common life.[101]

Herder's Job vaulted out of the narrow politics that had imagined Job as either a victim of temporal injustice or a prototype of political obedience. Even the theophany, when God cowed Job into submission, Herder did not treat as a model of political terror, but as an archetypal version of "natural poetry."[102] And yet, politics was still never far from Herder's mind. For if earlier translators had shown anything, it was that a purely poetical reading of the Old Testament brought out utterly perplexing problems concerning the Bible's place in the modern world. "The Bible is no longer the Bible when it [becomes] a decorated aesthetic book of art," declared Herder.[103] As Karl Barth has seen, it was not "Herder's project . . . to arrive at an aesthetic appraisal of the Bible, in so far at least as 'aesthetic' . . . would be taken to mean the same as 'artistic.' "[104] It was only when Herder pushed beyond artistry and pure aesthetics into the politics of national literatures that the poetic Bible truly found the footing that would make it such an important part of the Enlightenment Bible more generally.

[98] Frank E. Manuel, *The Broken Staff: Judaism Through Christian Eyes* (Cambridge, MA, 1992), 271.

[99] Herder, *Vom Geist der ebräischen Poesie*, 5:889. The Alciphron and Euthyphron characters are references to George Berkeley's 1732 *Alciphron, or the Minute Philosopher* (German translation, 1737).

[100] Herder, *Vom Geist der ebräischen Poesie*, 5:881.

[101] Herder, *Briefe, das Studium der Theologie betreffend* in *Werke*, 9.1:145.

[102] Lamb, *Rhetoric of Suffering*, 119, 123.

[103] Dieter Gutzen, "Ästhetik und Kritik bei Johann Gottfried Herder," in *Historische Kritik und biblischer Kanon in der deutschen Aufklärung*, ed. Henning Graf Reventlow (Wiesbaden, 1988), 278.

[104] Karl Barth, *Protestant Thought: From Rousseau to Ritschl* (New York, 1959), 219.

Already this push can be found in Herder's first major publication, his supplements or fragments to Lessing's *Briefe, die neueste Literatur betreffend* (1767). The second of these, *On the German-Oriental Poets*, spoke hopefully of some future "Poetic translation of the poems of the Morn in which they are explicated on the basis of the land, the history . . . of their nation, and transplanted into the genius of our day, our mentality, and our language." Were such a work ever written, Herder declared, it would "set apart the frontiers of foreign peoples from our own, no matter how convolutedly they may run." It would define, in other words, the boundaries between nations, determining their distinctive beauties and graces. But such a translation would also make us "more familiar with the beauty and the genius of a nation that we had viewed quite askance," bringing home those foreign graces for *our own* understanding and appreciation. And, finally, through this process, the translation would proclaim to all readers: "Behold here your own nature and history, your idols and world, your mentality and language: model yourself after them to become the emulator of yourself."[105] The perfect translation, in short, would establish the borders and frontiers between nations and peoples, just as it would inaugurate controlled diplomatic exchange across that frontier. As such, then, translations were political events that helped to produce the historical entities that we call nations and peoples, by establishing what is the same, and what is different. This process of national definition was never abstractly historical. Instead translations produced a moment of self-confrontation and self-definition. They were that "sphere of mirroring" that Herder talked about in his *Essay on the Origins of Language*, a tool that allowed man to "mirror himself to himself."[106] In short, translations converted the Delphic γνωθι σεαυτον, "know thyself," into Herder's clumsier but perhaps more appropriate apothegm: "model yourself after them to become an emulator of yourself."

Put into a more prosaic form, translations establish national literatures: they confirm national literatures in others, and establish national literatures for us. Translation was not simply, as Andreas Kelletat has argued, a means of establishing "world literature" as an object of appreciation.[107] It was always an act of appropriation as well. As Herder said of Homer, only "when I translate him for myself . . . am I able to give a living . . . account of Homer to myself and others, and feel him with my entire spirit."[108] More than any other ancient peoples,

[105] Herder, "On the German-Oriental Poets," in *Selected Early Works*, 187.

[106] Herder's "Abhandlung über den Ursprung der Sprache," [1769] quoted in Dorthea von Mücke, *Virtue and the Veil of Illusion: Generic Innovation and the Pedagogical Project in Eighteenth-Century Literature* (Stanford, 1991), 165.

[107] Andreas Kelletat, *Herder und die Weltliteratur: Zur Geschichte des Übersetzens im 18. Jahrhundert* (Frankfurt a.M., 1984).

[108] Ernest A. Menze, "On Herder As a Translator and on Translating Herder," in *Johann Gottfried Herder: Language, History, and Enlightenment*, ed. Wulf Koepke (Columbia, SC, 1990), 158.

the Hebrews functioned as a model for Herder to understand the relationship between nations and their literatures. In part, the Hebrews were so important simply because they were not Greek: we will enrich our literature most when we "capture the treasury of thoughts of a people who were neither slaves nor a colony of the Greeks."[109] But the Hebrews were particularly interesting because they showed, more clearly than any other people, the extraordinary durability of a nation across time and space. And so the number of "national-" compounds in *The Spirit of Hebrew Poetry* is simply staggering: "national-belief," "national prejudice," "national worship," "national-idiom," "national-poetry," "national-god," "national-spirit," among others.[110] If the literature of the Hebrews was a national one, then translation would be the secret to resurrecting the Bible within a German national canon. "If only we could first fully *explain* their poetry on the basis of their national history; and thereupon begin to translate and emulate!" exclaimed Herder, stressing at one and the same time the uniqueness of the Hebrew people and the means of recuperating this uniqueness for modern readers.[111] These two elements of differentiation and similarity were encapsulated in the translations of Michaelis (see chapter 7) and Cramer: "Were *Michaelis* given *Cramer's* versification, or *Cramer Michaelis's* feeling for the East, we would only then be able to preserve the poetry of the Morn *as a German treasure*, in keeping with the genius of our language."[112] Through differentiation and emulation, Hebrew poetry would be transfigured into an exemplar of German national literature.

That such reflections stemmed from Herder's interest in translation of the Old Testament was unsurprising. To a generation confronted by the waning theological relevance of the Old Testament, a generation that sought to prevent the Bible from becoming what Viscount Bolingbroke called "nothing more than compilations of old traditions, and abridgments of old records," Herder's new approach—of transposing Hebrew poetry from the domain of dogmatics to that of national literature—must have been attractive.[113] By doing so, Herder did what no other poetic Bible translator succeeded in doing: he detached the poetry of the Bible from theology without demoting the Bible to irrelevance. National literatures—the idea of the Old Testament as a *German* book—supplied the "ought" that was missing to earlier generations of translators. Through this normative intervention, the collapse of a universal Christian community was both confirmed and transcended. This was, in Benedict Anderson's words, a nodal point in that "larger process in which the sacred communities integrated

[109] Kelletat, *Weltliteratur*, 69.

[110] For a longer list, see Wulf Koepke, "*Kulturnation* and Its Authorization through Herder," in *Johann Gottfried Herder: Academic Disciplines and the Pursuit of Knowledge* (Columbia, SC, 1996), 197.

[111] Herder, "German-Oriental Poets," 178.

[112] Herder, "Fragment 8: Concerning the aesthetic language tinkerers who promote translations," in *Selected Early Works*, 117.

[113] Lord Bolinbroke, *Letters on History*, 2:204.

by old sacred languages were gradually fragmented, pluralized, and territorialized."[114] The fragmentation of the sacred Christian community that welded together Old and New Testaments was here embraced, and the fragments collected within entities called nations. In this way, the Bible (and especially the Old Testament) was made once more relevant to modern life, in the form of a programmatic and politicized national literature.

In practice, this shift can be confirmed by the utter abandonment of the prophetic reading of that famous "I know my redeemer liveth" passage in Job (19.25) long used in Christianity as the cornerstone of its understanding of the Hebrew texts. Herder's translation read:

Ich weiss, dass mein Blutracher lebt!	I know that my avenger lives!
Zuletzt wird Er noch auf dem Kampfplatz treten.*	In the end He will walk onto the battlefield.

*[Job] has One Friend, One Relative who will be his—avenger . . . and this is . . . God. He would stand in the dust and draw his sword for me, the sword of the avenger and the judge.

What was, in Christian tradition, a clear reference to the afterlife, and the vindication of every just man in heaven, Herder transformed into a parable of this-worldly vindication. God the avenger (rather than Christ the redeemer) perfectly matched what Herder saw as the "national God" of the Hebrews. This abandonment of prophecy in the face of "national religion" would become absolutely standard in the years that followed Herder's work on the Old Testament. Translations of Job 19.25 followed suit. Here are a few examples:[115]

Wilhelm Hufnagel (1781)

Dass ich weis, mir lebt ein Retter.*	That I know, a saviour will live for me,
Besiegen wird er der Feinde Rott.	He will conquer the enemy tribe.

*Here Job predicts the coming of Immanuel, who was supposed to come in his time.

Johann Eichhorn (1800)

Denn ich weiss es, dass mein Ehrenretter lebt,	Because I know that my avenger lives,
und zuletzt noch auf den Kampfplatz treten wird.	And will walk at last on the battlefield.

[114] Anderson, *Imagined Communities*, 19.

[115] Wilhelm Friedrich Hufnagel, *Hiob neu übersetzt* (Erlangen, 1781), 109; Eichhorn, "Hiob," *Allgemeine Bibliothek der biblischen Litteratur* 10 (1800): 663; Matthias Heinrich Stuhlmann, *Hiob: Ein religiöses Gedicht* (Hamburg, 1804), 128; Friedrich Umbreit, *Das Buch Hiob: Uebersetzung und Auslegung* (Heidelberg, 1824), 149.

Matthias Stuhlmann (1804)

Zwar weiss ich, dass mein Ehrenretter lebet,*	Yes I know that my avenger lives,
Zuletzt auf meinem Grabe stehen wird.	At last will stand on my grave.

*The poet prepares here for the appearance of God at the end of the poem.

Friedrich Umbreit (1824)

Doch ich weiss, mein Unschuldsrächer* lebt	Yet I know that my avenger lives,
und hintennach wird er auf dem Staube sich erheben.	And later he will stand on the dust.

*the nearest kin of a murdered man has the duty to avenge it.

Although the translations differed in details, all agreed that the Christological reading of "avenger" was insupportable, and offered instead translations rooted in the traditions of what Eichhorn called the "holy national writings," what Umbreit called the "national literature," and what Karl Justi, in his 1803 translation of the Psalms, called the "national-songs" of the Hebrews.[116] In all of these cases, then, Hebrew national literature was both affirmed and, through translation into the German domain, transfigured. It was both defined in relation to the nation of Jews that produced it and, in the act of translation, was wrenched out of the hands of this nation, "captured" in Herder's words, for the German nation. It was here that the German poetic Bible moved decisively away from the poetic models invented and expounded by Robert Lowth and his followers in midcentury England. The great Oriental scholar Johann Eichhorn marked this divergence clearly in his 1787 obituary for Lowth. Speaking specifically of the 1778 *Isaiah* translation, Eichhorn commented that it "did not make the impression . . . in Germany that one . . . might have predicted," for it showed only too clearly "the steps that Germany has made beyond the English in the interpretation and criticism of the Old Testament." Lowth was not able to make the final step away from the prophetic reading of the Hebrew texts and toward understanding "the modes of representation of the Hebrew poets after their origin, their propagation, transformation and cultivation."[117] The English had not, in short, understood the Old Testament as a national literature.

[116] Eichhorn, *Allgemeine Bibliothek der biblischen Litteratur* 3 (1790): 86; Umbreit, *Hiob*, xxxviii; Karl Wilhelm Justi, *National-Gesänge der Hebräer* (Marburg, 1803–1818).

[117] Eichhorn, "Lowth," 722, 719.

But despite this German confidence, a peculiarity remained. How, after all, was the *Hebrew* Bible supposed to become a piece of *German* national literature? In his more optimistic early days, Herder imagined a new translator, one able to effect this piece of nationalist alchemy. But in the face of the repetitive efforts of Germans to create this philosopher's stone through new translation, Herder, along with his contemporaries, would look much closer to home for a solution, discovering it in a text that was so intimately familiar to German readers that it would look very much like the word of God itself: Luther's translation.

This was the final twist in the history of the poetic Bible as it developed in the second half of the eighteenth century. For centuries, the Luther Bible had existed as the theologically canonized text for German Lutherans. It was cheaply and widely published, easily accessible, and despite what critics called the archaic feel of its language, still deeply legible to legions of German Protestants. It was also a text that remained fundamentally unaltered from 1700 to 1800, indeed, has remained largely unaltered until this century. As such, as I argued in the introduction, the Luther Bible itself did not register what happened to the Bible in the period. Its very stability desensitized it to the changes happening around it. But viewed from the outside, the Luther Bible *was* a barometer of a changing religious climate. Although the fuller story of the Luther text will unfold in chapter 8, it was here, in the 1780s, that the Luther Bible began to serve the purpose of reconstituting the Old Testament as a piece of German national literature. It was, for example, no accident that when Herder began to revise his 1774 translation of the Song of Songs, as Robert Clark has noted, "every change [was] in the direction of Luther. . . . Luther's language was, or had become, folk language."[118] As Herder put it in *On National Religions*, "every German, if he wants to be read by the better part of the nation, writes an *evangelical, protestant, Lutheran*" German.[119] For Herder, the Luther Bible was the literary monument that served to define and produce the quintessentially German mode of expression. Indeed it was Luther's Bible that stood, alongside his hymns, "as model examples of meaningful national poetry" and it was through this Bible that Luther "awoke and liberated the German language, a sleeping giant."[120] And these sentiments would reverberate in the words of Johann Goethe—"We have sent no prophet to the people, except in his language! And thus the German first became a people through Luther"—and those of Heinrich Heine—Luther "gave words to thought. He created the German language. This happened, because he translated the Bible."[121]

As a microcosm of this shift—where the Luther Bible could function to convert the Hebrew national literary treasury into German notes—we can look to Friedrich Klopstock, familiar to us for his once optimistic sense that

[118] Robert T. Clark, *Herder: His Life and Thought* (Berkeley, 1955), 257.

[119] Herder, "Ueber National-Religionen" in *Adrastea* in *Werke*, 10:613.

[120] Michael Embach, *Das Lutherbild Johann Gottfried Herders* (Frankfurt a.M., 1987), 23, 36.

[121] Embach, *Lutherbild*, 57. Heine, "Zur Geschichte der Religion und Philosophie in Deutschland," *Sämmtliche Werke* (Hamburg, 1884), 7:34.

poetry could re-create the spirit of the Hebrews for modern readers. His 1782 ode "The German Bible" signaled a shift away from this ex nihilo creation, and toward a reinvestment of energy in the already monumental Lutheran edifice. "Holy Luther, pray for the poor," Klopstock's poem began, and soared into ecstatic heights about the transformational effects of this Bible:

> Always dark to them was each summit,
> That you boldly climbed, and there the speech
> Of the fatherland made into the speech of angels,
> And of men.
>
> Times flow by: only the regenerated
> Remain; and this design will never change!

What began, for Klopstock and for his disciple Cramer, as a project to recapture Hebrew passions in the German tongue metamorphosed in the 1780s when it was discovered that the passions had, in effect, already been captured in the words of Luther. It was not so much that the intelligentsia "were catching up with the people" in their appreciation of this standard text, but rather that the "folk" aspects of the Luther Bible were valorized by a generation of poets and scholars questing for an authentic biblical treasury of the nation.[122] If the Luther Bible was indeed already infused with the "speech of angels and of men," what need was there to look any further?

The Jews and the Consequences of the Poetic Bible

This transformation of Hebrew literature into a German cultural monument was not without consequences, either for Germans, who discovered that the Hebrew texts could be made modern by absorbing them into the German cultural canon, or for those people who had with some justice regarded the Old Testament as their own patrimony for over three thousand years, namely the Jews. Nobody sensed the peculiarity of the relationship between modern Jews, modern Germans, and ancient Hebrews more poignantly than Moses Mendelssohn, who grappled with all of these in his 1783 Psalms translation.[123]

[122] Norton, *Bible As Literature*, 242.

[123] The full translation was presaged by his "Versuch einer Übersetzung einiger Psalmen Davids vom Herrn Moses Mendelssohn," *Berliner Neuesten Mannigfaltigkeiten: Eine gemeinnützige Wochenschrift mit Kupfern* 4 (1781). On Mendelssohn's Pentateuch translation, see the conflicting readings of Edward Breuer, *The Limits of Enlightenment: Jews, Germans, and the Eighteenth-Century Study of Scripture* (Cambridge, MA, 1996) and Alexander Altmann, *Moses Mendelssohn: A Biographical Study* (University, AL, 1973).

Already in 1770, Mendelssohn expressed some dislike for the new Christian enthusiasm for the Psalms. Writing to Johann Michaelis, Mendelssohn complained that Johann Cramer in particular had produced an unsatisfying version, one written "as if the Psalms were composed in a cloister, by some penitent monk."[124] To remedy this, Mendelssohn sent along a copy of his own translation of Ps.91. This psalm was of particular interest to Mendelssohn because of its curious person changes in the ninth and fourteenth verses. Here is his version:[125]

9. Hast du zu meiner Zuversicht zu Gott, dem Ewigen, Vertrauen.	You have entrusted in my care, in God the eternal.
13. Du magst auf Löw und Otter gehen, zertreten Löwenbrut und Drachen.	You tread on the lion and the adder, trample the young lion and the serpent underfoot.
14. "Denn er begehrt mein, Darum errett' ich ihn. Er kennet meinen Namen, Drum heb ich ihn empor."	"Because he desires me, thus I save him. He knows my name, thus I elevate him."

Unlike the standard translation that would treat this psalm in a Christological vein, Mendelssohn presented it as one long and personal speech, perhaps of a priest, to a believer. Thus what Lowth and others read as signs of this psalm's mystical design, namely the interruption of the personal voice ("my care") in the ninth verse and the final person change, Mendelssohn read as a literary prosopopoeia, or projection, by the priest of God's own voice. Such a strategy produced a halting translation but it also excluded the Christian typological reading of the final passage as the address of God to his only Son. In a sense, then, Mendelssohn was, from the Jewish side, trying just as hard as people like Herder to move beyond the Old Testament as prophecy.

But unlike Christian advocates of the poetic Bible, Mendelssohn wanted his psalm translation to express something specific about the relationship between Germans and *modern* Jews. Even in his dedication, to Karl Ramler, the Horatian odist, it was clear that he, like Cramer and Psalms translator Georg Knapp, saw the Psalms as the exemplary "lyric poetry of [his] nation."[126] To explain this poetry, Mendelssohn looked—like his Christian contemporaries—to the nexus between Hebrew poetry and the history of the Jews. As he commented in his 1763 observations on Lessing's *Laokóon*: "Oriental poetry distinguishes

[124] Letter dated 17 November 1770, in *Literarischer Briefwechsel von Johann David Michaelis*, ed. Joh. Gottlieb Buhle (Leipzig, 1795), 546.

[125] *Literarischer Briefwechsel*, 547.

[126] Mendelssohn, dedication to Ramler, *Die Psalmen* in *Gesammelte Schriften: Jubiläumsausgabe*, (Stuttgart, 1971), 10.1:5. Georg Knapp published a well-reviewed translation of the Psalms in 1778 (*Die Psalmen* [Halle, 1778]).

itself principally . . . through the following signs: 1) it is irregular in its entirety, and 2) daring, yet unpainterly [*unmalerisch*] in its design. It is similar in quality to the works of all great geniuses that lived in uneducated and uninspired times." The irregular form of Hebrew verse was determined, in particular, by internal socioreligious factors, namely the prohibition against graven images. Because of this, "the Hebrews could not . . . have either painting or sculpture," the arts through which "the rules governing the beauty of the whole" are easily discovered.[127] But if in these sentiments, Mendelssohn did not stray far from the poetic Bible as we have seen it, he did have a completely different vision of the function that his psalms should perform. His Psalms translation, after all, sought in large part to convince the Germans of the "level of enlightenment (*Aufklärung*) . . . that the age of the kingly singer [David] had already achieved."[128] As his biographer Alexander Altmann puts it, Mendelssohn "wanted to show to his age the ancient Jewish Enlightenment," implying in this parallel of Davidic and modern times that the eighteenth-century Germans could look back at the ancient Jews as a repository of wisdom and affirm the status of modern Jews as preservers of this ancient Enlightenment.[129]

And for this reason, Mendelssohn felt compelled to defend the Jews against the charge of poetic deficit. Of course, by the time he published his Psalms translations, this deficit had long been replenished in the wider Enlightenment discourse by the positive surplus of the sublime. But the sublime was a double-edged sword: it may have helped to regenerate interest in *Hebrew* poetry, but it did nothing to recuperate the *Jews*. If, as David Sorkin has argued, Mendelssohn "thought the Psalms eminently suitable for [the] task of edifying readers of all faiths because . . . he considered this book a model of the 'sublime,'" then he was a less perceptive reader of his age than generally thought.[130] For the two qualities—universal edification and sublimity—had little to do with each other in the wider context of Christian biblical commentary, as the story of the poetic Bible clearly shows. Indeed, the story of the Enlightenment Bible was *in nuce* a story of the *separation* of these qualities, as moral-pedagogical virtues were invested in the New Testament, and the Old was given affective power by its sublime style. The New got truth, the Old beauty. The repeated insistence on the distance between ancient Jew and modern German was thus legitimated by a system in which the Hebrew sublime served to mark the alterity and thus irrelevance of the Hebrews to modern moral reform. It was, after all, a bit difficult, as Rolf Lessenich has pointed

[127] Mendelssohn, "Zu einem Laokoon-Entwurf Lessings," in *Gesammelte Schriften*, 2:254.

[128] Thus David Friedländer, who sat with Mendelssohn as he made the translation, in "Etwas über die Mendelssohnische Psalmenübersetzung," *Berlinische Monatsschrift* (Berlin, 1786), 525.

[129] Altmann, introduction to the Psalm translation in *Gesammelte Schriften*, 10.1:xi.

[130] David Sorkin, *Moses Mendelssohn and the Religious Enlightenment* (Berkeley, 1996), 47.

out, to find much uplifting in the Psalm's cheerful cry: "Happy shall he be who takes your little ones / and dashes them against the rock!" (137.9)[131] Certainly the shift to national literature did little to make the Jew familiar to the German; as Matthias Stuhlmann put it in 1804, "our literature has shown far more excellence in imitating the Greek . . . classics than it has the oriental, and especially the Hebrew poets."[132] And so Herder, however he cherished the Old Testament, happily admitted that the Hebrews "had a narrow, exclusive, and arrogant point of view" and "were not certainly chosen for their own worthiness," even while praising their poetic endeavors.[133] Herder had no need, in other words, to justify modern Jews through their Hebrew forebears. Indeed I think we can safely say that at least in part his "praise of Hebrew, biblical poetry . . . [was] a criticism of contemporary Jews," who did not live up to the mighty example of their ancestors.[134] His recommendation that the Jews, as Frederick Barnard has put it, "return to their ancient homeland . . . to regain their national respect" was not precisely anti-Semitic, but was surely cavalier in its posture toward contemporary Jews.[135]

Sublimity was thus a sticky category, and it is not surprising to see that Mendelssohn's disciple David Friedländer sharply turned away from it.[136] Instead he described the Psalms translation in the near neoclassical language of beauty. The great translator always needs "a sense of the ideal of beauty" and must "carefully avoid the ugly, the distorted, [and] the troublesome." Without careful appreciation of the "originality, spirituality, and beauty of the original," no adequate translation would be possible.[137] The psalms were called many things at the end of the German eighteenth century, but they were rarely called "beautiful" nor were they seen as emblems of any enlightened sensibility.[138] As one reviewer of Mendelssohn's Psalms made clear: "If this was the most brilliant period of the Jewish people, if this was the highest level of enlightenment they achieved, then it is truly clear how imperfect their religious and moral outlook was."[139] The reviewer's separation of the German from the Jewish Enlightenment was clearly intended as a negative commentary on the moral worth not just of

[131] Lessenich, *Dichtungsgeschmack*, 201.

[132] Stuhlmann, *Hiob*, v.

[133] Herder, *Vom Geist der ebräischen Poesie*, 5:876–77.

[134] Liliane Weissberg, "Juden oder Hebräer? Religiöse und politische Bekehrung bei Herder," *Johann Gottfried Herder: Geschichte und Kultur* (Würzburg, 1994), 205.

[135] Frederick M. Barnard, "Particularity, Universality, and the Hebraic Spirit: Heine and Herder" *Jewish Social Studies* 43 (Spring 1981): 128.

[136] On Friedländer, see Altmann, *Mendelssohn*, 350f.

[137] Friedländer, "Psalmübersetzung," 538, 540.

[138] Lowth was one crucial exception, praising the "beauty, solemnity, and elevation" of Hebrew verse in his 1778 Isaiah translation (Lowth, *Isaiah*, xxxvi). In Germany, however, the early enthusiasm for Lowth was waning.

[139] [Anonymous], "Ueber den Werth der Mendelssohnschen Psalmen-Uebersetzung," in *Deutsches Museum* 1 (February 1788): 449.

the Hebrews but also of Jews in general. Mendelssohn's Psalms translation—written in the context of the bruising battles between Mendelssohn and Lavater over the worth of contemporary Judaism—thus had to justify both the Hebrew and the Jew. Hence his clear possessiveness about the Psalms as the literary treasure of "his nation" and his insistence, late in life, that the Psalms "must be sung with true edification by the most enlightened people."[140]

For Mendelssohn, in other words, the national literature of the Hebrews had to be both justified and reconstituted as the national literature and legacy of the Ashkenazim. As beautiful, rather than sublime texts, the Psalms could establish a continuum between a specifically Jewish Enlightenment and the contemporary German version. This peculiar goal seems also to have generated some of the ambiguities in Mendelssohn's Pentateuch translation, a translation that was, in a complex and contradictory way, supposed to give largely Yiddish-speaking Jewish children a subtly rendered German text in order that they might have access to the Hebrew original. One cannot help but sympathize with the rabbi who complained that such a work "induces the young to spend their time reading Gentile books in order to become sufficiently familiar with refined German to be able to understand this translation!"[141] Indeed the task was incredibly complex. Mendelssohn sought, at one and the same time, to train the Jews in German culture, to produce a German-Jewish literary monument, and to persuade Germans that the wisdom of the ancient Hebrews lived on in meaningful poetic and philosophical terms.[142]

But for Christians, of course, the task was much simpler. To someone like Herder, the Jews were irrelevant to the ultimate goal of recasting Hebrew literature as a form of German national literature. And his embrace of the distance between ancient Jew and modern Christian was of a piece with the wider move in Protestant theology of the day to distinguish Christianity and Judaism, a tendency that manifested itself in someone like Semler in the assumption that (despite his own historicist insights) Jesus was fundamentally "Jew and non-Jew . . . a spiritual revolutionary," in the words of Peter Reill.[143] This fits also into what Susannah Heschel has nicely termed the "Protestant flight from the historical Jesus," the urge to discover a "sui generis" Christianity, one "immune from the influences of the surrounding Jewish culture."[144] Herder's response to the Hebrew Bible was more interesting than Semler's, but he too finally had little concern for the impact his national appropriation might have for those who regarded the Old Testament as their natural patrimony. We can see the

[140] Letter to Sophie Becker, 27 December 1787, in Altmann, *Mendelssohn*, 719. On the Lavater affair, see Altmann, *Mendelssohn*, 194–263.

[141] Ibid., 383.

[142] Nothing evidences this latter better than his translation of Gen. 3.14: *"ich bin das Wesen, welches ewig ist."*

[143] Peter Hanns Reill, *The German Enlightenment and the Rise of Historicism* (Berkeley, 1975), 170.

[144] Heschel, *Abraham Geiger*, 129.

emergence of the poetic Bible, then, as a moment of national consolidation, one that allowed the Christian Bible to survive the decay of prophecy and the diminution of theology, but one that also set the stage for the nationalist interpretations of Judaism and Christianity that would soak the nineteenth century. We can also see the poetic Bible as a necessary antithesis to the historical Bible produced by scholars like Johann David Michaelis: if the poetic Bible sought evermore to keep the Old Testament safe from αρχαισμος, the historical Bible would embrace the archaism of the Hebrew world. Estrangement would be its purpose.

Chapter Seven

HISTORY: THE ARCHIVAL AND ALIEN OLD TESTAMENT

BETWEEN 1740 and 1780, the landscape of English religious scholarship was largely arid and infertile. One exception was the strange oasis of Hutchinsonianism, a "delightful fantastic system," Horace Walpole mocked, but one that he admitted was unexpectedly successful in convincing eighteenth-century Britons.[1] Founded on the principle that the very letters of the Old Testament revealed "God's divine plan . . . untainted by the machinations of the Jews," this Hebraic fundamentalism declared loudly its faith that the language of Moses was "a monument of Brass or Rock of Adamant . . . [that can] not be destroy'd by all the Efforts of Men."[2] In an age when the Hebrew and Greek Bibles were parting ways, Hutchinsonianism energetically tried to keep the Old Testament in the center of the story of Christian salvation. Perhaps unsurprisingly, given what we have seen in Germany, this effort included translation:

> At first the Aleim* created the heavens and the earth. And the earth was unformed and hollow; and darkness *was* upon the face of the deep: and the spirit of the Aleim brooded upon the face of the waters.
>
> *A Title of the ever-blessed Trinity. It means the Persons under the oath or binding curse of a covenant.[3]

Behind the veil of the odd language, Gen. 1.1 gleamed. Its features were distorted in many ways, but most of all by the *Aleim*, a name for God produced by a typically elaborate etymological punning on the familiar word *Elohim*. If *Elohim* conveyed the sense of God's plurality, the *Aleim* expressly asserted "the co-equality of all three persons of the Trinity" and the existence of this Trinity from the very beginning of the Old Testament.[4] For the author of the translation,

[1] Walpole, *Correspondence*, 35:156; David Katz, "The Hutchinsonians and Hebraic Fundamentalism in Eighteenth-Century England," in *Sceptics, Millenarians, and Jews*, eds. David Katz and Jonathan Israel (Leiden, 1990), 237–55; C.D.A Leighton, "Hutchinsonianism: A Counter-Enlightenment Reform Movement," *Journal of Religious History* 23 (June 1999): 168–84.

[2] Katz, "Hutchinsonians," 245; Leighton, "Hutchinsonianism," 174.

[3] Julius Bate, *A New and Literal Translation from the Original Hebrew of the Pentateuch of Moses* (London, 1773), Gen. 1.1.

[4] David Ruderman, *Jewish Enlightenment in an English Key: Anglo-Jewry's Construction of Modern Jewish Thought* (Princeton, 2000), 68. On Hutchinsonians, see Mandelbrote, "The Bible and Its

Julius Bate, "the true Genius of the Tongue" of the Hebrews had to be recovered by wrenching the Old Testament from the fierce grip of "those Wretches called *Rabbies*."[5] Translation would reforge the bonds between Old and New Testament, reconfirming the ancient presumption that both books alike were infused with the sanctifying spirit of Christ.

The Jews were not the only enemy the Hutchinsonians faced. Among the many threats to Scripture, few were as disconcerting as Benjamin Kennicott, whose project of collating all of the Old Testament manuscripts made him into the public face of Hebrew Bible textual scholarship in England between the 1750s and the 1770s. His *State of the Printed Hebrew Text of the Old Testament* (1753) was the overture in his effort to "carefully collat[e] the most ancient Copies and their best Versions."[6] It would culminate in a massive subscription drive over the course of the 1760s, which raised over £9,000 to finance research into approximately six hundred Old Testament manuscripts. This effort, "one of the noblest and most extensive schemes of a literary and religious nature that hath ever been undertaken by a single person" as the *Gentleman's Magazine* commented in 1768, tried to accomplish for the Old Testament what Mill, Bengel, and Griesbach did for the New, namely to produce a text free of the "*very many* and *very material* MISTAKES . . . first *introduc'd* by the Jews . . . in concurrence with the unaccountable Authority of an imperfect, contradictory and corrupted *Masora*."[7] Freeing the Bible of its Jewish trappings—not least the vowel points added by the ancient Jewish Masoretes—was one of Kennicott's goals. Another was protecting the Bible against the excesses of the Hutchinsonians, who "despising Reason and Learning . . . make *Words* signify what they please, turn *the plainest History* into *sublime Prophecy*."[8] To Julius Bate's insistence that the Old Testament was "a Record . . . not to be tampered with, altered, or *amended*," Kennicott answered that only such amendments revealed the genuine "*Treasures of Wisdom and Knowledge*" obscured by the fanciful conjectures of the Hutchinsonians.[9]

If Kennicott stood at the apex of English biblical scholarship at midcentury, he was—like most English scholars of the period—inhibited by a timidity that endlessly annoyed German observers in the 1770s and 1780s. Although he was

Readers," 41–43; also Derya Gurses, "The Hutchinsonian Defence of an Old Testament Trinitarian Christianity: The Controversy over Elahim, 1735–1773," *History of European Ideas* 29 (2003): 393–409.

[5] Julius Bate, *The Examiner Examin'd* (London, 1749), iv; Julius Bate, *A Defence of Mr. Hutchinson's Plan* (London: James Hodges, 1748), 23.

[6] Benjamin Kennicott, *The State of the Printed Hebrew Text of the Old Testament Considered* (Oxford, 1753), 10; on Kennicott, see William McKane, "Benjamin Kennicott: An Eighteenth-Century Researcher," *Journal of Theological Studies* 28 (October 1977): 445–64.

[7] *Gentleman's Magazine* 38 (1768): 114; Kennicott, *State*, 247.

[8] Kennicott, *A Word to the Hutchinsonians* (London, 1756), 42.

[9] Julius Bate, *The Integrity of the Hebrew Text* (London, 1754), v; Kennicott, *State*, 564–65.

happy to declare the need for a "New Translation . . . prudently undertaken and religiously exercised," for example, he was far too narrowly focused on textual criticism to actually produce one.[10] Neither Kennicott's enormous labors nor its costs were justified by their fruits, in German eyes, fruits that still left the Old Testament in far poorer shape than the New. And so when the Orientalist scholar Johann Eichhorn looked back at this period, he noticed how "everyone looked with eager hopes to England. . . . no name was spoken more often than that of Kennicott," and yet "the result did not match the great expectations."[11] Lacking was any trace of that "great idea, a *critical edition of the Bible*."[12] And none felt this lack more sharply than Johann David Michaelis, whose scholarly bona fides endowed him with vast authority among late-century scholars. His uncle, Johann Heinrich Michaelis, was one of the foremost Hebraists of the early eighteenth century and worked closely with August Hermann Francke at the University of Halle in its earliest days, editing the *Biblia Hebraica* (1720) and heading Halle's *Collegium orientale theologicum* for many years. Young Michaelis's father, Christian Benedikt, showed his dedication to the Orient with extensive Old Testament commentaries, numerous works on Hebrew antiquities, and a full edition of the Bible in its original languages. After Johann David's studies at Halle, he traveled to Leiden, where he met Albrecht Schultens, the Dutch scholar who first claimed that Hebrew was no divine tongue but rather a branch of the Arabic language family. Later, too, Michaelis sat at the 1741 Oxford lectures of Robert Lowth, the lectures that became the *Lectures on the Sacred Poetry of the Hebrews*, and in turn was the material and spiritual conduit between Lowth and his German audiences, annotating the 1758 and 1770 editions of Lowth's *Lectures*. On his return to Germany, Michaelis began a career as a scholar of biblical languages and antiquities that would last nearly fifty years. Called in 1745 to Göttingen by its founder, the Baron Gerlach Freiherr von Münchhausen, he was appointed professor *ordinarius* of philosophy in 1750 and, until his death in 1791, helped to shape that institution into the center of philological research in Enlightenment Europe.

Michaelis's disappointment with the Kennicott Old Testament was thus the disappointment of someone fully committed to the philological study of the Hebrew Bible. Kennicott's failures were glaring: on the one hand, he had failed to organize his manuscripts in a coherent way; on the other, he had focused his attention too narrowly on extant Hebrew manuscripts without understanding that the correct readings might not be preserved in these relatively recent texts but instead in those texts translated by "the Seventy, the Chaldeans, the Syrians, Aquila, Symmachus, Theodotian, and Jerome."[13] Kennicott had simply cast his net too narrowly, substituting "purely mechanical collation" for a more nuanced

[10] Ibid., 565.

[11] Eichhorn, "Johann David Michaelis," 872, 873.

[12] Eichhorn, *Jenaische Zeitungen von Gelehrten Sachen* 12 (1776): 827.

[13] *Orientalische und Exegetische Bibliothek* 11 (1776): 91.

sense of the history of the Bible.[14] For Michaelis, indeed, modern biblical scholarship simply could no longer confine itself to pure text criticism. If philological scholarship had been a theme running throughout the translations of the eighteenth century, here it truly came into its own: in more familiar terms, the lower criticism of texts was turned into the higher criticism of things. In Michaelis's polymathic world, no matter was too large or too trifling to escape the clutches of his historical analysis. As the *Critical Review* put it in 1769, to understand the Bible:

> it is not barely sufficient to know the mere sense of the words and phrases of the original, but . . . it is likewise necessary to be acquainted with the circumstances of the world at the time of our Saviour's coming; to have a knowledge of the government, Sanhedrim, sects, customs, traditions, and opinions of the Jews; a knowledge of ancient history, chronology, geography, and the general system of pagan mythology, which is not to be acquired by turning over a Lexicon.[15]

Michaelis would take these sentiments to heart, and in his hands, make historical philology into a comprehensive science, not only of the very small—those inexplicable details of ancient Hebrew life—but also of the very big: the movements of peoples in the historical past. No longer was this historical philology confined to the textual canons elaborated over long centuries of theological consolidation. Instead, his "cool philology" devoured all of the materials that today find homes in disciplines as various as anthropology, archaeology, and ethnography, and regurgitated them into a monumental Bible translation.[16]

This translation—the product of over twenty years of dedicated labor—was the ultimate manifestation of the historical Bible and as such completed the Enlightenment Bible. Just as philology shed its theological chrysalis in Michaelis's hands, so too did the Bible itself here find its theological foundation finally swept away. In consonance with the other Bibles that haunted late eighteenth-century Germany, Michaelis's historical project was not principally destructive in either intent or effect. Instead, history would inject the Bible with the rejuvenating juice of authority, the authority of human languages and the human past. Its centerpiece was the Old Testament, the text closest to Michaelis's own heart, and, as we have seen, the most difficult portion of the Bible for the eighteenth century to digest. If the poetic Bible was obsessed with making the Old Testament familiar to its modern readers, though, the historical Bible had the opposite goal. National literature was not, after all, the only way to recuperate

[14] William McKane, "Benjamin Kennicott: An Eighteenth-Century Researcher," *Journal of Theological Studies* 28 (October 1977): 452.

[15] *Critical Review* 28 (1769): 91.

[16] *Orientalische und Exegetische Bibliothek* 22 (1783): 57.

the Old Testament. Rather, as Michaelis showed, the Hebrew Bible could be made relevant just as much by alienation as by incorporation. In his hands, the strangeness of the Old Testament would shine from every word, no longer comforting in its familiarity, but disorienting in its alien splendor. The path to this strange Bible lay through the heart of a foreign landscape, the landscape of far-off Arabia.

Finding a Philology of Things in Arabia

"When Moses stretched his hand out toward the sea, God drove away the waters with strong wind that blew through the entire night, so that the ground became dry and the water was divided in the middle. And the Israelites went through the middle of the sea on the strip denuded of water, and what water remained on either side, served them as a wall."[17] This was Johann David Michaelis's 1771 translation of Exod. 14.21, just part of what became—from 1769 to 1790—the largest and the most detailed translation produced by the Enlightenment, a translation that synthesized the universe of information that scholars had about biblical languages, customs, people, landscape, and natural history. This was an enormous task, and a task that depended on the outlay of enormous resources, intellectual and financial. As it would turn out, it was easier for the Israelites to cross the Red Sea than for the biblical scholar to learn all that was to be known about its environs. The Israelites, after all, did have a powerful backer.

It was with the help of another powerful backer, though, that Michaelis helped to organize his own expedition to uncover those mysteries hidden on the shores of the Red Sea, an expedition that departed in early January 1761. Funded by the ample coffers of Frederick V, the king of Denmark, a group of explorers set out from Copenhagen aboard the Danish war ship *Greenland* with their sights on the antiquities of the Red Sea, hoping to uncover the secrets of *Arabia Felix* and bring them back to European scholars hungry for information about the biblical world. None was hungrier than Michaelis, who longed for the kind of concrete data absent from biblical scholarship until the late eighteenth century. It was his brainstorm to send a group of scholars to investigate the shadowy world of present-day Yemen and it was his reputation that convinced Danish Foreign Minister J. H. von Bernstorff in 1756 that such a trip would crown the Danish king with the glory of discovery. Three months after proposing the trip, Bernstorff and Michaelis were already in negotiations about the duration, route, and costs of the venture. From the earliest visions of the trip—where a single explorer was expected to master mathematics, botany,

[17] Johann David Michaelis, *Deutsche Uebersetzung des Alten Testaments, mit Anmerkungen für Ungelehrte . . . welche das zweite und dritte Buch Mose enthält* (Göttingen und Gotha, 1771), 37.

and fossils, Arabic languages, oriental and biblical philology, not to mention all the relevant travel literature and geographies—the trip grew steadily in scope and expense.[18] In the end, the ideal polymathic explorer was broken into six different roles, played by the Danish philologian Friedrich von Haven, the Swedish botanist Peter Forsskål, the German engineer and mathematician Carsten Niebuhr, the Danish doctor Christian Cramer, the German illustrator Georg Baurenfeind, and their Swedish servant Berggren. The group was a truly international one and although the expedition was intended to aggrandize the Danish crown (that "true father not only of his country but also of the entire empire of learning"), this lack of national chauvinism was remarkable, and stemmed at least in part from the "republic of letters" sensibility that characterized its beginnings.[19]

When it set out from Copenhagen in January 1761, the expedition was buoyed by the optimism of those who see themselves on the cutting edge of history. After a stormy start, the expedition sailed through the Strait of Gibraltar in April. By May they were in Marseilles, from which they traveled to Malta, Smyrna, Rhodes, Constantinople, and arrived in Egypt in late September. There they would remain for nearly a year, exploring Alexandria and the outlying regions and peoples of Cairo, before they finally crossed onto the Arabian Peninsula. In this early phase, Forsskål was particularly industrious, collecting samples of the local flora and fauna and recording his observations of the natural world first in Egypt and later in Djidda, Loheia, and Mocha. These materials were periodically sent back to Denmark, some to Forsskål's teacher in Sweden, Carl Linnaeus. Of particular interest to Linnaeus was the Mecca balsam tree (*commiphora gileadensis, amyris gileadensis*), the source of the biblical "balm of Gilead" (Gen. 37.25, Jer. 8.22), which Forsskål—much to his delight—discovered in 1763.[20] Botanical successes compensated for philological failures, the most dramatic of which was on the Sinai peninsula in September 1762. There von Haven was unable to get access to the Monastery of St. Catherine, a monastery that housed a priceless collection of Hebrew and Arabic manuscripts, including the most important extant manuscript of the Greek Bible, the

[18] Michaelis's letter to Bernstorff, 30 August 1756, already indicated some doubts as to whether this could be undertaken by one person (*Literarischer Briefwechsel von Johann David Michaelis*, ed. Johann Gottlieb Bühle [Leipzig, 1794], 1:299ff.). See also Thorkild Hansen, *Arabia Felix: The Danish Expedition of 1761–1767*, trans. James and Kathleen McFarlane (London, 1964); Stig Rasmussen, ed., *Carsten Niebuhr und die Arabische Reise 1761–67* (Heide, 1986); Jonathan Hess, "Johann David Michaelis and the Colonial Imaginary: Orientalism and the Emergence of Racial Antisemitism in Eighteenth-Century Germany," *Jewish Social Studies* 6 (Winter 2000): 56–101, and *Germans, Jews, and the Claims of Modernity* (New Haven, 2002), chap. 2.

[19] *Göttingische Anzeigen von gelehrten Sachen* (5 February 1760): 129.

[20] Forsskål, *Flora Aegyptiaco-Arabica, sive descriptiones plantarum quas per aegyptum inferiorem et arabiam felicem detexit* (Copenhagen, 1775), 79. Also see Niebuhr, *Entdeckungen im Orient: Reise nach Arabien und anderen Ländern 1761–1767*, ed. Robert and Evamaria Grün (Tübingen, 1975), 79.

Codex Sinaiticus, stolen and brought to Europe by Constantin von Tischendorf in the mid–nineteenth century.[21] Stung by the Sinai debacle, the expedition left Egypt on a merchant ship, and arrived in Djiddah in October 1762. There they remained for six weeks, waiting further transportation to Yemen proper. They arrived in the city of Loheia shortly before the New Year and spent the next six months exploring and measuring the coast and inland regions of southern Arabia. In these happy months, it seemed that the expedition had drilled a well into the very heart of the biblical world, and its secrets were set to flood Europe.

But this well soon ran dry. Within short months of their departure, in the first place, relations inside the group began to resemble those between the nations of Europe in the late 1750s. The battles over position and power that marred the trip had their darkly amusing aspects (as when Forsskål and Niebuhr discovered to their dismay that von Haven had brought enough arsenic to kill an elephant), but they also hampered an already difficult journey. Far more significant to the ultimate fate of the trip than these squabbles was the death, by September 1763, of five-sixths of the expedition. The lone exception was Carsten Niebuhr, who tottered back into Copenhagen in 1767 after a perambulation through Constantinople, Cairo, Djiddah, Beit el-Faikh, Mocha, Bombay, Basra, and Baghdad. All of the other explorers perished in the service of science, as it were, leaving Niebuhr to publish their papers and organize the reams of scholarly materials the expedition brought back.

But even if it ultimately ended in disaster, the Niebuhr expedition would reverberate long in the study of the Old Testament. Not least, it became a model of how exploration could be corralled and utilized by philological and historical researchers. This exemplary quality was created by the design of the expedition, a design unique, as Michaelis saw it, because organized from the outset along purely scholarly principles. This was an expedition designed to answer specific questions: if, for example, as August Rösel von Rosenhof declared in 1749, a locust is "disgusting" no matter how prepared, what was it that John the Baptist ate in the desert?[22] "His food was locusts and wild honey," the Apostle Matthew told his readers (3.4), but if locusts were inedible, then what did the word ακριδεζ mean? This was the kind of information that the Arabian travelers could provide. To facilitate their efforts, Michaelis collated his 1762 *Questions for a Society of Learned Men*, whose thirty-second question noted that: "The Bible speaks of eating locusts, and I do not know what to call what John the Baptist was supposed to have eaten . . . besides locusts. . . . Since Arabia is the homeland

[21] The most vitriolic account of von Haven's incompetence comes in Barthold Niebuhr (the son of Carsten and the great Roman scholar), *The Life of Carsten Niebuhr* (Edinburgh, 1836), 18ff. On the trip to Sinai, see Carsten Niebuhr, *Entdeckungen*, 39ff. On Tischendorf and the Codex Sinaiticus, see Metzger, *Text of the New Testament*, 42ff.

[22] August Rösel von Rosenhof, "Die . . . Sammlung derer Heuschrecken und Grillen," in *Der monatliche-herausgekommenen Insecten-Belustigung* (Nuremberg, 1749), 2:39.

of locusts, I have no doubt that, even without my question, Professor Forsskal will bring back an accurate description of them."[23] This was only one of the many queries whose contents were compiled out of replies to Michaelis's description of the trip and his request for scholarly inquiries in the February 1760 issue of the *Göttingische Anzeigen von gelehrten Sachen*.[24] Responses came from scholars across Europe, from the French *Académie des Inscriptions* and from researchers in Denmark, Sweden, Germany, the Low Countries, and England. These questions were organized along both philological and ethnographical principles and were oriented specifically toward Michaelis's specialty, the Bible. This orientation, he remarked, might strike some as too "theological" but, he maintained, the Old Testament was a unique book, one that "forces us to delve into both the whole of natural history and the mores of Orientals": "nearly three hundred plant names, I don't know how many animal names, appear . . . in this remarkable fragment of Oriental antiquity."[25] As a fragment of oriental antiquity, the Old Testament uniquely captured a history, a geography, and a complex of social customs found nowhere else in ancient literature. Only such a fragment could found a comprehensive review of the ancient history of the East.

Taking off from the Old Testament, Michaelis's questions focused on far-flung topics. Besides the locusts, he asked about the tides at the outmost reaches of the Red Sea; he inquired into diseases like leprosy and elephantiasis, the relative tastiness of southern versus northern barley, the tree in Exod. 15.25 that made bitter water sweet, the ubiquity of Arabian gold, the nature of the Agallochus tree, the Arabic name for the oxlike animal found in Job 39.9, the purity of various animals and birds, and the precious stones common to the region. Often directed at specific Old Testament textual problems—unknown words, seemingly nonsensical passages, odd customs, and so on—the questions spanned the full range of scholarly concerns. From anthropology to ethnography, from cuisine to geography, Michaelis hoped that his appointed scholars could provide a virtual survey of the culture of Arabia, and thereby a survey of the culture of the ancient Hebrews.

This immense collection of problems—some given to the explorers before they departed from Copenhagen, others enclosed in letters sent to them en route, and still others delayed until after most of the expedition already lay in their graves—were prefaced and organized by a detailed set of instructions worked out by Bernstorff and Michaelis. The instructions were a tool of organization: they divided up the labor of scholarship and apportioned it among the explorers. All of the explorers, the instructions commanded, were to investigate "not simply the coast, but the land" itself. All were to keep a written

[23] Michaelis, *Fragen an eine Gesellschaft gelehrter Männer, die auf Befehl Ihro Majestät des Königes von Dännemark nach Arabien reisen* (Frankfurt a.M., 1762), 81.

[24] *Göttingische Anzeigen von gelehrten Sachen* (5 February 1760): 131.

[25] Michaelis, *Fragen*, b7r.

diary, which was to be excerpted periodically and sent directly to Copenhagen. All were to look for manuscripts, not beautiful or costly ones, but ones important for their "utility and above all their age."[26] Each explorer was also given specific tasks according to their scholarly expertise: Forsskål was to observe the protocols established by Linnaeus in his *Instructiones Peregrinatoris*, collect naturalia, carefully record their Arabic names, and particularly take note of evidence related to the "philological explanation of the Bible." Niebuhr's task was the investigation of geography, the preparation of a map of Yemen and the Red Sea, the careful notation of Arabic place names, as well as the observation of polygamous customs and their impact on population. And finally von Haven was to attend to the "customs and mores of the country, especially those that illuminate Scripture and the Mosaic law," to seek out ancient manuscripts, to note particular language uses, especially where they bore on biblical matters, to record important *varias lectiones* for the Bible (countersigned by the other members of the group) and to copy carefully all inscriptions encountered.[27]

The Niebuhr expedition to Arabia, in other words, was to be organized and scientific. Despite the protestations of Halle Orientalist Johann Callenberg, the expedition would not give the "unhappy souls" of Arabia the "divine knowledge of Christ."[28] On the contrary, the royal instructions specifically forbade all religious disputation, forbade anything that might "even implicitly" impugn Muslim beliefs.[29] While scholars might look to missionaries for revealing materials, they had no missionary mandate whatsoever. Instead, the expedition was supposed to be something new in the history of European travel, a voyage of purely scholarly discovery. The questions and the instructions were the cornerstone of this voyage. "If the European scholar lends his efforts to give the traveler complete and elaborated questions," Michaelis declared in his *Questions*, "he will be in the position to provide what other travelers have not been able to provide. . . . How many travel descriptions do we have from Palestine and Egypt? . . . how many useless things about fabulous holy places?"[30] As Forsskål wrote to Michaelis in September 1759, "travel descriptions . . . have almost nothing but the voyage itself, the mores of the people, and a bit of history."[31] To surpass the traditional Oriental voyage—long content to sup on Eastern ambience and to spin elaborate biblical fantasies for

[26] "Die königliche Instruktion für die Teilnehmer der Expedition," §5, 8, 11 in Rasmussen, *Niebuhr*, 61–65. A shorter version of this was published in Michaelis's *Fragen*, but this longer version comes from von Haven's diary, where he copied out the entire document.

[27] "Instruktion," §16–17 (Forsskål); §27, 29, 33 (Niebuhr); §35, 37, 41, 42 (von Haven) in Rasmussen, *Niebuhr*, 67–77.

[28] Letter from Callenberg to Michaelis, 24 July 1758, in *Briefwechsel*, 1:369.

[29] "Instruktion," §10 in Rasmussen, *Niebuhr*, 64.

[30] Michaelis, *Fragen*, a5^r.

[31] Forsskål letter to Michaelis, 25 September 1759, in *Briefwechsel*, 1:410.

naive readers—all had to change. Voyages had to be directed by definite goals laid out by the scholarly community at large. Expeditions in other words had to rely on scholars, not scholars on the vagaries of idle travelers. This would, in Michaelis's mind, revolutionize travel, philology, and the study of the world of the Old Testament.

The Alienated Traveler and the Bible

Travel to the Orient in search of knowledge was hardly an earth-shaking novelty, of course. As an expedition, Niebuhr's Arabian voyage shared with countless earlier travels—to the New World, to Africa, to the Far and Near East—the interest in local customs, flora, fauna, and geography that had burgeoned in the post-discovery period, when such travelers as Jean de Léry brought back from the New World detailed accounts of peoples and places.[32] The Spanish exploration of the New World brought back detailed ecological and cultural information organized principally to display the usefulness of these resources to mainland medicine and food. Exchange with the East was similarly common during the Early Modern period: travelers like Felix Faber (ca. 1483) went to Jerusalem, Egypt, and Arabia on pilgrimage, while diplomatic relations, especially during the period of Ottoman expansion in the later sixteenth century, brought back to Europe reports on the customs, religion, and politics of the Turks. Scholarship was not out of the question either, even in the most political of these ventures: Ogier Ghislain de Busbecq, a Flemand in the service of Charles V, for example, paused on the way to Suliman's court in Constantinople to collect old coins and inscriptions subsequently sent back to Justus Lipsius and Joseph Scaliger.[33]

Even the organization of travel became, by the late sixteenth century, an object of considerable scholarly attention. The general use of instructions—published advice on the correct methods of observing foreign cultures—were common from Peter Ramus right into the eighteenth century. There were any number of publications written for the hordes of students who poured out of European universities on their educational peregrinations and indeed the first volume of the Royal Society's *Philosophical Transactions* (1665) gave travelers a set of *General Heads for a Natural History of a Countrey*. Robert Hooke—secretary of the

[32] Michel de Certeau, "Ethno-Graphy: Speech, or the Space of the Other: Jean de Léry," in *The Writing of History* (New York, 1988), 209–43. In general, see Anthony Pagden, *The Fall of Natural Man: The American Indian and the Origins of Comparative Ethnology* (Cambridge, 1982) and Margaret Hodgen, *Early Anthropology in the Sixteenth and Seventeenth Centuries* (Philadelphia, 1964).

[33] Pierre Bayle, *Dictionary Historical and Critical* (London: Knapton, 1735), s.v. "Busbequius." Also Busbecq, *Augerii Gislenii Busbeqvii D. legationis turcicae epistolae quatuor* (Frankfurt a. M., 1595) and in English: *The Four Epistles of A. G. Busbequius* (London, 1694).

Society—recommended that all travelers be given instructions "how to make their observations and keep registers or records of them."[34] Formally speaking, both the royal instructions to the Arabian voyagers and Michaelis's preparatory questions were part of this larger tradition. They were attempts to prepare the eyes of the travelers and discipline their inquiries, to mitigate the "wonder" that, as Stephen Greenblatt has shown us, was such the common experience of cultural and social novelty.[35]

So what was new about Niebuhr? Two aspects stood out. First, the Arabian expedition had a research program unrivaled by any other expedition. This research program was not driven by questions privately distributed to the explorers or secret directions opened only when the voyage was well begun, but by questions widely known across the eighteenth-century republic of letters. Indeed, the questions became a minor best-seller, circulating in German markets as well as French (two editions!) and Dutch. That a set of questions might be published is, superficially, curious, but it reflected the sense of collaboration that inspired the voyage. Also unique were the questions themselves. The Royal Society instructions, for example, were vague enough to provoke highly eclectic responses: the 1667 *Observations Made by a Curious and Learned Person, Sailing from England to the Caribe Islands*, for example, included observations of rotting sails, preserving ale, the color of the ocean, and blood transfusions, among other things.[36] In contrast, the Arabian voyagers were given precise topics organized around key problems in biblical history. Their investigations were structured by a carefully focused research program that suggested problems and fruitful avenues for their resolution.

Second, and more startling, was the new ethos of the Niebuhr expedition, an ethos I would term that of estrangement. Exploration for these travelers was a way of "making things strange," in Bertold Brecht or Carlo Ginzburg's terms, of dissolving the shell of recognition that prevented real encounters with the exotic.[37] This estrangement manifested itself most clearly in the literary products that the Niebuhr expedition generated. As the questions already made clear, the aim of the Arabian voyage was not to produce a "travel description" in the classical sense. When Forsskål praised Thomas Shaw's *Travels, or Observations Relating . . . to the Levant* (1738), he did so grudgingly. Although Shaw recorded Latin inscriptions, copied Arabic nomenclature, and

[34] Hooke quoted in Joan-Pau Rubiés, "Instructions for Travellers: Teaching the Eye to See," *History and Anthropology* 9 (1996): 139. See also Justin Stagl, "Der wohl unterwiesene Passagier: Reisekunst und Gesellschaftbeschreibung vom 16. bis zum 18. Jahrhundert," in B. I. Krasnobaev et al., eds., *Reisen und Reisebeschreibungen im 18. und 19. Jahrhundert als Quellen der Kulturbeziehungsforschung* (Berlin, 1980), 372.

[35] Stephen Greenblatt, *Marvelous Possessions: The Wonder of the New World* (Chicago, 1991), esp. 73–85.

[36] *Philosophical Transactions* 11 (2 April 1666): 186–89; 27 (23 September 1667), 494ff.

[37] Carlo Ginzburg, "Making Things Strange: The Prehistory of a Literary Device," *Representations* 56 (Fall 1996): 8–28.

included beautiful engravings of Levantine plant life, his descriptions were largely organized by the happenstance chronology of his journey.[38] In contrast, Forsskål's reports were purged of chronology; his posthumously compiled *Flora Aegyptiaco-Arabica* bore no resemblance at all to a "travel description." The narration of discovery that held together all earlier descriptions vanished, replaced by a list of plant names arranged in Linnaean orders and produced with greatest textual economy (fig. 10). What was merely an appendix in Shaw became the whole story. Even Niebuhr's first publication, the 1772 *Beschreibung von Arabien* was not a travel narrative per se, but rather a synthetic treatment of the geography, customs, and natural history of the region. The difference in approach between this and, for example, the voyages of Jean de Thévenot (ca. 1620s) was striking. Even the images told vastly different stories. Instead of Thévenot's striking and dramatically narrative renditions of Oriental scenes (mummies, fakirs, and ritual wife burning), Niebuhr gave us sober collections of coffee pots, inscriptions, and farming instruments (figures 11 and 12).[39] Niebuhr substituted, in other words, a fragmented systematicity for the coherence and narrative power of personal experience. Instead of mapping the voyage along the temporal axis of experience—a narrative gambit peculiar to travel writers from Montaigne to Lady Mary Wortley Montagu—he fractured experience. The traveler, along with the reader, was estranged from its flow. We can read this new ethos as a preparation for the total erasure of experience that we find in the later comments of Alexander von Humboldt:

> I left Europe firmly resolved not to write what is customarily called the historical narrative of a voyage but rather to publish the fruits of my research in works of pure physical description. I have ordered the facts, not in the order in which they successively presented themselves, but according to the relationships they bear to one another.[40]

And nothing would epitomize this erasure of experience more than the enormous volumes of description that emerged from Napoleon's scholarly invasion of Egypt, volumes that offered only a synthetic and monumental topography of institutionalized science.

This ethos of estrangement was the brainchild of Michaelis, who proclaimed that "no probabilities, no systems, only simple facts will be enough"

[38] Thomas Shaw, *Travels, or Observations Relating to Several Parts of Barbary and the Levant* (Oxford, 1738); Forsskål to Michaelis, 25 September 1759, *Briefwechsel*, 1:410.

[39] Niebuhr, *Beschreibung von Arabien* (Kopenhagen, 1772), tables I and XV. See, for comparison, *Voyages de Mr. de Thevenot, tant en Europe qu'en Asie & en Afrique* (Paris, 1689), 1:431, 3:202, 255.

[40] Humboldt quoted in Michael Dettelbach, "Global Physics and Aesthetic Empire: Humboldt's Physical Portrait of the Tropics," in David Miller and Peter Reill, eds., *Visions of Empire: Voyages, Botany, and Representations of Nature* (Cambridge, 1996), 261.

FLORA
ARABIÆ FELICIS.

MONANDRIA.

1. (*)	BOERHAVIA *a) scandens.*		Ph. *Örkos.* Môr.
2. (*)	*b) diandra.*	- -	Ph. Ps. *Vuddjef.* Môr. *Rokâma.* Surdûd. *Chaddîr.* خضار vel خضير Brf. Uhf.
3. (*)	- *c) diffusa.*	- -	Ps. - - Dahhi.
4.	AMOMUM *zingiber.*	- -	CP. *Zenjebîl.* Mochrat.
5.	CURCUMA *rotunda.*	- -	CM. *Kurkum.* Hæs.
6. (*)	SALICORNIA *a) europæa.*		Pm. - - Mochha.
7. (*)	- *b) perfoliata.*	-	Pm. - - Ghomfudæ.
8. (*)	CINNA.	- -	Mm. - - Barah.

DIANDRIA.

9.	NYCTANTHES *sambac.*	-	CP. CM. *Full* vel *Fyll.* فل
10.	JASMINUM *officin.*	-	Mm. *Kæjan.* قين *Ses.* سيس Blg.
11.	VERONICA *anagall.*	-	Ma. - Uhf.
12. (*)	JUSTICIA *a) lanceata.*	-	Mm. *Sokæjt.* سقية Srd.
13. (*)	Spinosæ. *b) trispinosa.*	-	Ph. Mi. *Schechar.* شخر Hadîe. *Uuzal.* Srd. *Kulliba* Uhf. *Uusar.* Mlh.
14. - -	Spinosæ. *c) bispinosa.*	-	Mi. *Schechadd.* شخض Hadîe. *Kulibe.* كلبه
15. (*)	Spinosæ. *d) appressa.*	-	Mm. Id. nom. Taæs.
16. (*)	Spinosæ. *e) viridis.*	-	Mi. *Kossæjf.* Srd. *Chasser.* خسير
17. - -	Inermes. *f) sexangularis.*	-	Mm. *Sovudvud.* Blg.
18. (*)	Inermes. *g) triflora.*	-	Mm. *Chodie.* خوضيه Blg.
19. (*)	Inermes. *h) fœtida.*	- -	Mm. Mi. *Tuna.* طونه Hadîe.
20. (*)	Inermes. *i) paniculata.*	-	Ph. *Uusar.* وزر Srd. Mlh.
21. (*)	Inermes. *k) cærulea.*	-	Ph. Id. nom. Mlh.
22. - -	Inermes. *l) resupinata.*	-	Ph. Id. nom. ib. Corolla alba, parva, resupinata.
23. - -	Inermes. *m) dubia.*	-	Mm. Spicis terminalibus; bracteis linearibus; foliorum ciliis nullis. Mlh.

24.

Figure 10. Peter Forsskål's lists of plants from Yemen from the *Flora Aegyptiaco-Arabica* (Hauniae, 1775), cii.

for him. Only simple fact would cut through the fabulous accounts of the Holy Land: by plucking them from the familiar systems that had long given meaning to the place, these facts would reveal a new, and foreign, land of the Jews. A rhetoric of "simple facts" did not, of course, free the expedition from ideological baggage, as Jonathan Hess has shown. Whether casting the Arabs "as a stagnant people . . . impervious to the historical process" or attempting "to establish intellectual hegemony over the Orient," the expedition maps

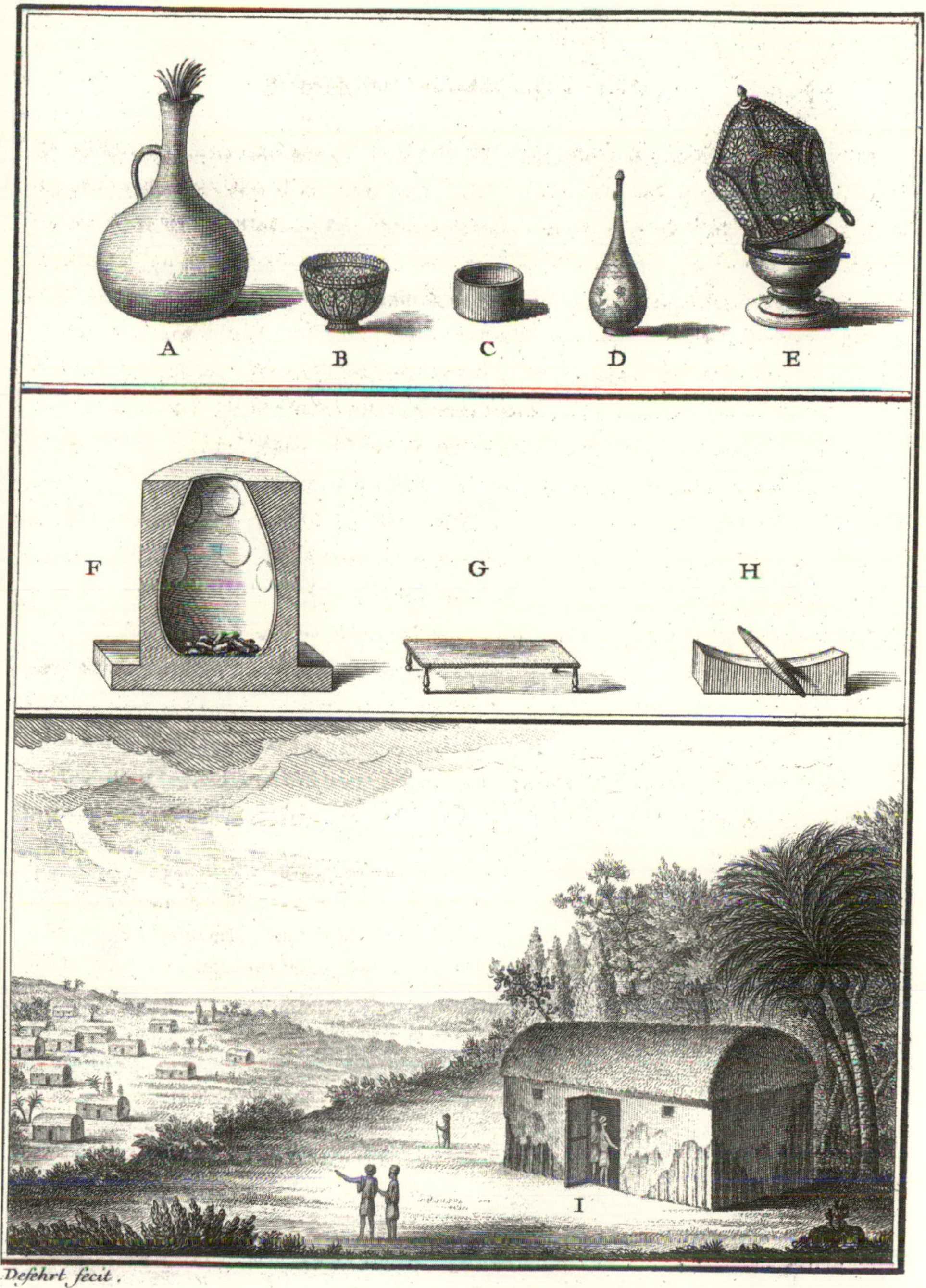

Figure 11. The coffee pots of Yemen from Carsten Niebuhr's *Description of Arabia*. Courtesy of the Bancroft Library, University of California, Berkeley.

Figure 12. The farming implements of Yemen. Courtesy of the Bancroft Library, University of California, Berkeley.

nicely onto what Mary Louise Pratt has called the "anti-conquest."[41] In other words, despite the fact that Germany—in the eighteenth century—was not yet an imperial power, we might read (along with Hess) this expedition as an ideological exercise in domination, one that avoided the overblown rhetorics of disgust and enchantment that so irritated Edward Said, but one that, nonetheless, exerted a subtle power over its object of study.[42] If "the Orient proposes and the West disposes," then scholarship was surely an effective disposal mechanism.[43]

But there was a substantive difference between this voyage and those of, say, English explorers in India or South Africa, a difference that highlights a significant use of estrangement in the Arabian voyage. For the Niebuhr expedition did not simply exemplify the abstract principle of domination, but was also a historically specific event. It did not, for example, explore the periphery of European settlement, did not push the boundaries of the known, did not attempt to beard the savage in his den, so to speak. Rather, this was a voyage inward, to the most familiar place in European consciousness, to the homeland of Christianity, Judaism, and everything European scholars called their own. With the coming of peace after centuries of war between the Ottoman Empire and European states, and the (partial) pacification of the Barbary pirates in the middle of the century, suddenly the inner domains of Europe's own virtual heartland were ripe for investigation. The childhood, not of an abstract, primitive, Rousseauian "man," but of a very concrete European and Christian man, was to be laid bare in the investigation of the familiar terrain of Arabia and the Levant.

Or at least, it *should* have been the most familiar: centuries of pilgrimages had provided Europeans with plentiful narratives of the landscape and peoples of the Holy Land, narratives that brought the Holy Land into the comforting circle of familiarity. Early modern accounts of the place made the obvious theological connection between God's (particular) favored land and Christ's (universal) redemption of mankind; they invented analogies between the travels of Noah, Abraham, and the modern pilgrim; or, more dramatically and personally, they claimed the place afforded "a mirror and table of an entire human life."[44] But, as Michaelis made clear in his questions, all of these were "useless," "fabulous" tales that coddled and surrounded a place "rich

[41] Michaelis, *Fragen*, b6r. Hess, "Colonial Imaginary," 69, 71. Mary Louise Pratt, *Imperial Eyes: Travel Writing and Transculturation* (London, 1992), esp. chap. 3.

[42] On Germany's fantastic relationship to colonization, see Suzanne Zantop, *Colonial Fantasies: Conquest, Family and Nation in Precolonial Germany, 1770–1870* (Durham, NC, 1997).

[43] Edward Said, *Orientalism* (New York, 1979), 137.

[44] For analogies of wandering and travel, see the preface to Salomon Schweigger, *Eine newe Reyssbeschreibung auss Teuschland nach Constantinopel und Jerusalem* (Nuremberg, 1608), aiivff.; for the "mirror" analogy, see Anne Simon, *Sigmund Feyerabend's* Das Reyssbuch dess heyligen Lands: *A Study in Printing and Literary History* (Wiesbaden, 1998), 120.

with the unknown gifts of nature" with a halo of blurry and illusory homeliness.[45] Instead, the goal of the Arabian explorers was to defamiliarize the region and thus make the oddness of the place stand out in sharp definition. To use the language of Viktor Shklovsky, the Russian formalist literary critic, this travel was supposed to "make forms difficult" and increase the "difficulty and length of perception," both for the travelers themselves and for those back home.[46]

We find a clear statement of this estrangement from Forsskål's teacher Linnaeus, who prefaced his edition of Fredrik Hasselquist's Near Eastern voyages (ca. 1751) with the declaration that:

> with [Palestine] we were less acquainted than with the remotest parts of India; and though the natural history of this remarkable country was the most necessary for Divines and writers on the Scriptures, who had used their greatest endeavours to know the animals therein mentioned, yet they could not, with any degree of certainty, determine which they were, before someone had been there, and informed himself of the Natural History of the place.[47]

When the "remotest parts of India" become more familiar than Palestine, we should pay attention, especially since, in a short fifty years, Indologists ranging from Friedrich Schlegel to William Jones would claim exactly the opposite. But at this moment, Palestine and Arabia were truly alien lands. As Niebuhr put it, "Arabia has been hitherto but very little known. . . . Prejudices relative to the inconveniencies and dangers of traveling in Arabia, have hitherto kept the moderns in equal ignorance. . . ."[48] It is in this context that we should read Michaelis's requirement that "no missionary or spiritual man" be sent on the expedition.[49] Spiritual vision, in this case, would become a kind of blindness: the missionary could not help but substitute comforting theological familiarity for the reality of the alien landscape of Palestine and the Near East. In a secular inversion of the mythical Teiresias, only those blind to spirit might see the truth of the place, its rarity and its peculiarity. This principle of knowledge through alienation would become a leitmotif in both Michaelis's scholarship and his translation. If the Arabian expedition was an effort to make the familiar Holy Land foreign, then Michaelis attempted to put this

[45] Michaelis, *Fragen*, a5^{v}-a6^{r}.

[46] Victor Shklovsky, "Art As Technique" in *Russian Formalist Criticism: Four Essays*, trans. Lee T. Lemon and Marion J. Reis (Lincoln, NE., 1965), 13, 22, 23.

[47] Linnaeus, introduction to Fredrik Hasselquist, *Voyages and Travels in the Levant, in the Years 1749, 50, 51, 52* (London, 1766), ii.

[48] Hess, *Germans, Jews*, 76.

[49] Michaelis, "Selbstbiographie von J. D. Michaelis, nach Febr. 1790," Niedersächsische Staats- und Universitätsbibliothek, *Cod.MS.Michael.98c-e*, Bl. 67.

expedition—and the weight of scholarly inquiry—to work in making that comforting object, the Bible, odd and foreign to his readers. And he did this not just in theory—by imagining the Bible in new ways—but also in practice, by making the experience of reading the Bible itself disorienting. He did this by building on top of the Niebuhr expedition a monumental translation of the Old Testament, whose notes—part philology, part geography, part natural history—integrated the range of materials available to this polymathic scholar and presented for the first time a compendium of biblical antiquities to the lay audience.

Bible Translation and the Experience of Disorientation

A bit of apocrypha provides a telling introduction to Michaelis's translation. It was said, at the end of the eighteenth century, that the inspiration for Michaelis's translation was no less than Gotthold Ephraim Lessing, who supposedly took him aside and directed him to turn his scholarly skills to the art of translation. Annotation, Lessing reportedly stressed, was essential, for "*Christians* are rarely able to use and apply those things that *scholars* discover in their studies, proclaim in their lectures, and publish in their scholarly, usually Latin writings."[50] The bridge across the abyss between these two ideals, between the Christian and the scholar, was to be built, by Michaelis, in a truly monumental Bible translation. As Michaelis's biographer and student, the philologian Johann Christian Eichhorn later noted, this translation marked "a new period in Biblical exegesis." "With [Michaelis], Germans once again began to be interpreters; to develop the meaning of Scripture, as was common during the Reformation, through grammatical interpretation and then historically [analyze it] from the spirit of ancient times, from history, antiquities, mores, customs, and archaic beliefs."[51] For Eichhorn and others, Michaelis represented a renewed Reformation, a return to the spirit of the Protestant fathers and their rejuvenation of the Bible. Just as the Reformation had its holy monument—the Luther Bible—so too would the Enlightenment have its own monument, now less a theological one, than a scholarly one.

Even Eichhorn, however, recognized that Michaelis's strong suit was not literature, or aesthetic translation. Unlike Herder or Cramer, he did not have the feeling for the German language that could have made the translation appealing to connoisseurs of German literature. We do not have to look far to see his problematic style:

[50] Johann Schulz, *Anmerkungen, Erinnerungen und Zweifel über des Herrn geheimen Justizrath Joh. David Michaelis Anmkerkungen* (Halle, 1790–94), 205.

[51] Eichhorn, "Johann David Michaelis," 885–86.

Wer hat den Wolkenbrüchen ihren Canal bereitet?	Who gave the cloudbursts their canals?
Und dem donnernden Blitze den Weg?	and prepared the way to the thundering lightning?
So dass es über Länder ohne Einwohner regnet,	That it might rain on lands without residents,
Ueber die Wüste, in der kein Sterblicher ist,	on deserts, where no mortal is,
Um die tiefste Einöde zu sättigen,	that the deepest waste might be satisfied,
Und Gras und Kräuter aus ihr hervorwachsen zu Lassen?	And grass and weeds grow out of it?[52]
	Job 38.25–27

Or, even more tellingly, here are Job's opening words:

Der Tag gehe unter, da ich gebohren bin,	Might the day perish when I was born
Und die Nacht, die sprach, es ist ein Sohn empfangen!	and the night, which said, a son is conceived!
Der Tag müsse Finsterniss seyn!	Let the day be dark!
Gott habe von oben kein Aufsehen auf ihn gehabt!	Might God from on high have no sense of it!
Und kein Licht ihn bestrahlt!	and no light touch it!
Finsterniss und alte Nacht müssen ihn zurück Fodern!	Let darkness and ancient night take it back!
	Job 3.3–5

Michaelis clearly wanted his book to be read as a poetic text. That he chose Job as the first installment of his translation was testament both to his belief that the book represented the most ancient part of the biblical corpus and to that culture-wide interest in Job's poetry we have already noted. But his translation was stilted and awkward. Rather than translate, as Luther did, in an idiomatic and flowing style, Michaelis kept to the original, and his attempts at poetic license often fall flat. For "darkness and ancient night," for example, Luther happily retained the echoing "darkness and shadow"; for Michaelis's awkward "That it might rain . . . where no mortal is," Luther provided a powerfully simple "Let it rain in a land where no one is / in the wastes where no man is." Like many in his period, too, Michaelis had an overly optimistic view of the exclamation point and its ability to convey poetic sublimity. Even an admirer like Johann Schulz admitted that his translation was "too slavishly literal, too ungerman, often entirely meaningless and tasteless." Even less sympathetic was

[52] Michaelis, *Das Buch Hiobs* (2nd ed., 1773), 81. Contrast with the RSV: "Who has cleft a channel for the torrents of rain, / and a way for the thunderbolt, / to bring rain on a land where no man is / on the desert in which there is no man; / to satisfy the waste and desolate land, / and to make the ground put forth grass?"

the reviewer in the *Allgemeine deutsche Bibliothek*, who commented that "under the hands of Mr. M. the historical and poetic style of the Hebrews is . . . nearly entirely lost."[53] The pedagogue Karl Bahrdt—hardly a shining example of a Bible translator—was particularly incensed, writing that Michaelis had fallen into the old trap of regarding the Bible as a book that "has nothing in common with other human books other than its external design." Accusing him of "*Wörterbuchsdunkelheiten*" (lit. dictionary-obscurities), Bahrdt asked "what help does the entire philological project offer, if it always leaves us with the old barbarism, and never brings light and clarity to religion?" The task of philology, for Bahrdt, was merely to teach the correct meaning of the words: the "unexpected glimpse of antiquity," the "striking usage of history, geography, or chronology" were disposable erudition that blocked rather than revealed biblical truths.[54]

But precisely this erudition was indispensable both to Michaelis and to many of his readers. For Michaelis, Eichhorn rightly noted, "the translation was nothing more than a side show, the notes an inestimably rich centerpiece."[55] The bridge between Christian and scholar would be founded, in other words, upon annotations, annotations that presented the unexpected history, geography, and chronology of the Bible. Bridging the gap between these two ideal types would prove, however, a disorienting experience. Indeed, from all appearances, and to nearly all of Michaelis's commentators, vertigo rather than connection was the predominant emotion, and for good reason. Just as the Arabian voyagers traveled to the familiar only to make it strange, Michaelis too made estrangement—and the dialectical cycling between the comforting object that was the Bible and the alien world of the ancient Hebrews—the primary tool of his translation enterprise. Annotations were the key to these vertiginous effects.

On a superficial level, these effects were achieved through mere accumulation of more stuff. Even the physical appearance of this Bible was daunting. In the Old Testament translation, Michaelis appended notes to each book, notes that often ran to twice the length of the translation itself. The notes were paginated separately and given full attention of their own. The final product was an impressive thirteen-volume edition, whose pages totaled well over three thousand. When he decided, in 1790, to publish a New Testament translation, he published the notes in four separate volumes, making it possible either to buy just the translation, or, more likely, to buy just the notes. The thud of these notes as they landed on the literary market was echoed by Johann Schulz's six-volume *Notes . . . concerning the Notes of . . . Michaelis* (1790–94), testament to the cornucopia effects of scholarship.

[53] Schulz, *Anmerkungen*, 204. Anonymous reviewer, *Allgemeine deutsche Bibliothek* (Berlin, 1773), 19:345.

[54] [Karl Bahrdt], *Kritiken über die Michaelische Bibelübersetzung* (Frankfurt a. M., 1773), 5, 59, 10, 23, 24.

[55] Eichhorn, "Johann David Michaelis," 886.

Inside the Bibles, stuff piled up in great and confusing density. Take the opening passage of Job, usually translated "There was a man in the land of Uz." *Uz*, our scholar rendered as "in the graceful valley around Damascus" and said this about it:

> Damascus sits in a very pleasant valley, which is watered by two small streams and made most lovely by the neighboring mountains. Thus the Orientals not only count it among the so-called four earthly paradises, but also think it the most beautiful of them. Even European travelers, though they are used to more beautiful locations, agree that this valley is outstanding. Arabians call it *Gutta*, and the Hebrews *Gutz*. Around here the poet puts Job, that he might lack nothing of earthly blessings.[56]

The translation was nothing special. Indeed, by substituting "the lovely valley around Damascus," for the simple word "Uz," Michaelis might be accused of unjustified poetic liberality. But the note explained the odd translation at the same time as it provided a wealth of minor details about Uz (its beauty, its water, the neighboring mountains), some ethnography of the Orientals (their myths of the four paradises), and some confirmatory evidence given by the unnamed travelers. But it is not clear that our unlearned reader would leave this note feeling satisfied: after all, the familiar Uz is not even present in the commentary. Where is Uz? Is it just a misspelling of Gutz? And who cares, the reader might ask, what the Arabians call this place? This kind of disorientation, where the originally familiar tale is made suddenly even more obscure than ever, is a characteristic effect of his accumulative work. We can look almost anywhere to see this in action. Thus in Job 38, God thundered to Job: "Can you bind the chains of the Pleiades, or loose the cords of Orion? Can you lead forth the Mazzaroth in their season, or can you guide the Bear with its children?" Michaelis commented:

> It is impossible to translate this passage without taking the freedom to forge some new words where the names of single stars are lacking. The fact is that, in the region where Job lived, in Babylon (the ancient source of astrology), the great Bear, or, as we call it in real German, the Wagon, divided nature itself into two markedly different parts. The northern star, that is, the outermost one on the tail of the Bear . . . remains visible and above the horizon for the entire night. . . . [This one] the Hebrews called the Mother, and the rest her sons, wherein perhaps lies an Oriental fable yet unknown to me.[57]

His explanation was curious but typical. It provided an attentive reader with a great deal of information, about astrology and Oriental fables, but the

[56] Michaelis, "Anmerckungen zu Hiob," 1.

[57] Ibid., 168.

information was puzzling. Some terms were translated (Bear, Pleiades), some not (Mezzaroth); there is an apparent tale behind the astronomical names (and indeed Michaelis imaginatively reconstructed it) but no conclusive story; some "new words" have been forged, but Michaelis did not indicate which. It is hard not to agree, in this case, with Johann Schulz's comment that "the annotations would have better been titled for *the learned*, than for the unlearned."[58] At least the learned would have been better equipped to organize these prodigious materials.

But estrangement was not just an unintended consequence of Michaelis's method of accumulation. Rather, his was a deliberate program, one that had no intention of depriving "the Hebrew authors, especially the poets, of their own peculiarities."[59] Keeping the Bible peculiar was a program that depended on the kinds of materials he used and the purposes to which he put them. To see this program in action, it is useful to compare Michaelis's biblical polymathy with that of his seventeenth-century predecessors. It was not an accident, for example, that Michaelis began publishing his *Spicilegium geographiae Hebraeorum exterae post Bochartum* in the same year he began his translation.[60] This catalog—based in part on the researches accomplished by Niebuhr and the others—extended in new directions the researches of Samuel Bochart, the Huguenot polymath whose *Geographia sacra* (1646) and zoological treatise, *Hierozoicon sive bipertitum opus de animalibus S. Scripturae* (1663), represented a compendium of Baroque knowledge about the Holy Land.[61] In encyclopedic fashion, Bochart collated ancient accounts of the Sabaeans—the descendents of Noah's son Shem—their cities, local flora and fauna, and so on. Data was provided by ancient testimony (Pliny, Ibn-Ezra, Dioscorides, Josephus, and Eusebius among others), and etymology was his analytical tool of choice. Thus Bochart discussed the Sabaean capital Mariaba not in terms of its locale but as a word meaning, according to Pliny, "the masters of everyone," and thus derived from the Hebrew word *rabba*, "which means to rule."[62] And in this recourse to ancient testimony and etymology, Bochart was in good company. His contemporary Edward Pocock, for example—the recipient of the first chair of Arabic at Oxford (1636), and later collaborator with Brian Walton on the famous English Polyglot Bible (1657)—was similarly inclined to fetishize texts over things. Pocock's own stay in Arabia was thus marked not by any interest in local *realia* but rather by his efforts to buy rare Arabic manuscripts. He brought these textual concerns to his commentary as well, as in the note to Mic. 1.8, "I will make a wailing like the dragons, &c.," where Pocock noted that "almost all

[58] Schulz, *Anmerkungen*, 1:204.

[59] Michaelis, *Das Buch Hiobs*, xx. My italics.

[60] Michaelis, *Spicilegium geographiae Hebraeorum exterae post Bochartum* (Göttingen, 1769–80).

[61] On Bochart, see François Laplanche, *L'Ecriture*, 250–54; also Johann Fück, *Die arabischen Studien in Europa bis in den Anfang des 20. Jahrhunderts* (Leipzig, 1955), 84–85.

[62] Bochart, *Geographia sacra*, in *Opera omnia*, 4th ed. (Leiden, 1712), 130.

the Interpreters render the word mynt *Tannim, Dragons*, only the ancient Syriack translations renders it by . . . *yororo*, which in that language signifies . . . *Jakales*." This made sense, he went on, since, although jackals could indeed be said to wail, there was no question that dragons hissed.[63]

But for Michaelis etymology was only one source of information about the geography and customs of Arabia. In his annotations to Bochart, for example, Michaelis frequently turned to Niebuhr and other writers to add concrete longitudinal, natural historical, and geographical information to the Baroque author's collection of ancient testimonies.[64] New kinds of materials, then, were the basis of his startling effects, which put things on equal footing to texts. Michaelis would have found inspiration for this approach in the work of Job Ludolf, the German linguist who, in his day, was the foremost European scholar of Amharic (the principal language of Ethiopia). Ludolf was well known. Indeed, Michaelis's uncle prepared Ludolf 's Ethiopian psalter for European publication, and his younger brother, August Benedict, edited the correspondence between Ludolf and Leibniz.[65] Ludolf 's best known work, however, was his *Historia Aethiopica* (1681), a tome divided between firsthand source reports from an Ethiopian—the Catholic Abba Gregorius, who was converted by the Jesuits and later met Ludolf in Rome—and more traditional humanistic methods.[66] On the one hand, his book began in a classically etymological vein by looking at the name for the Ethiopians, who "are now generally called *Habessines*, by others *Abessines*, or *Abassenes*; the Name being given to them by the *Arabians*, in whose language [*Habesh*] signifies a confusion."[67] On the other hand, however, Ludolf showed an atypical ability to integrate firsthand reports of the Ethiopian landscape into his text. Speaking of grains, for instance, Ludolf reported: "Rye they have none: Yet when Gregory smelt a Rye Loaf, he said, It was the true *Tef*, and that it had the true smell of *Tef*. He look'd upon Oats as not worth sowing, saying, It was no better esteemed than Cockle in their country."[68] This dual usage of firsthand accounts and lowly physical artifacts was remarkable in Ludolf 's work, in particular in those sections treating flora, fauna, and geography.

[63] Edward Pocock, *Commentary on the Prophecy of Micah* (London, 1677), 5. On Pocock, see the biography by Leonard Twells that prefaces the *Theological Works of the Learned Dr. Pocock* (London, 1740), here 7ff.; Fück, *Die arabischen Studien*, 85–90; and Bernard Lewis, *Islam and the West* (Oxford, 1993), 86f.

[64] See e.g., Michaelis, *Spicilegium*, 1:205; 2:153, 158, 164, 173, 182, 191, and so on.

[65] Ludolf, *Psalterium Davidis Aethiopice et Latine* (Frankfurt a. M., 1701); August Benedict Michaelis, *Iobi Ludolfi et Godofredi Guiliemi Leibnitii Commercium epistolicum* (Göttingen, 1755).

[66] Job Ludolf, *A New History of Ethiopia, Being a Full and Accurate Description of the Kingdom of Abessinia*, trans. J. P. Gent (London, 1682); on Gregorius, see Siegbert Uhlig, ed., *Hiob Ludolfs "Theologia Aethiopica"* (Wiesbaden, 1983), 32.

[67] Ludolf, *New History*, 7–8. On Aethiops as a name for all dark skinned races, see V. K. Mudimbe, *The Idea of Africa* (Bloomington, IN, 1994), 26.

[68] Ludolf, *New History*, 48.

One of the priceless bits of information Ludolf reported to European scholars had to do with our old friend the locust: the Ethiopians "may support themselves by feeding upon the locusts themselves, which they greedily eat, as well to satisfie their hunger as in Revenge; for it is a very sweet and wholesom Dyet."[69] The ambiguity in the report, the taste of apocryphal fabulousness, undoubtedly gave it a tainted flavor to Michaelis, whose love of physical *realia* exceeded even that of Ludolf. And so he encouraged Niebuhr to bring back all available data about this bothersome insect. With pleasure, then, Michaelis read the report in Niebuhr's *Beschreibung von Arabien* that:

> It is just as incomprehensible to the European that the Arabs enjoy eating locusts, as it is unbelievable to the Arabs . . . when they find out that Christians like to eat oysters, crabs, crustaceans, and so forth. . . . In all Arabian cities, from *Bab el mandeb* to *Basra*, locusts are brought to market on strings. . . . When Arabs have a bunch of locusts, they roast them, or dry them in an oven, or boil and eat them with salt.[70]

This description of Arabian eating habits, along with oral reports Niebuhr gave to Michaelis on his way back to Copenhagen, underwrote the notes to Leviticus and John:

> it is certain that they eat locusts. . . . they dry them to preserve them for later consumption. In Basra they eagerly await them, so they can have them for food.[71]
>
> Not only from ancient testimony, but also from the most credible modern travel descriptions it is certain that locusts are eaten in Africa, Syria, Arabia, and on the Euphrates, and are so much the food of the poor that they usually look forward to their arrival. They collect them, preserve them for the future, and dry them. Even as I am writing this, I notice that, in the reports of the Herrnhuters from North America . . . even the savages in North America, taught by nature, eat locusts.[72]

The excitement about locusts—which flitted across Michaelis's letters, his *Fragen*, his annotations, his reviews, and so on—represented only one element of Michaelis's zoologico-ethnographic imagination, which hungered for real data revealed by unpredjudiced minds.

And so Niebuhr and his travelers became cornerstones in Michaelis's annotations. In reference to Num. 11.31 ("the wind . . . brought quails from the

[69] Ibid., 67.

[70] Niebuhr, *Beschreibung*, 171.

[71] Michaelis, "Anmerkungen zum zweiten Buch Mose," 137.

[72] Johann David Michaelis, *Anmerkungen für Ungelehrte zu seiner Uebersetzung des Neuen Testaments. Erster Theil, Anmerkungen zu Matthäus, Marcus und Lucas* (Göttingen, 1790), 29.

sea"), he sent his reader to Forsskål, who apparently noted how "quails, when they fly over the sea, really do collapse from exhaustion as soon as they reach land." Or in Deut. 11.11, he reported, this time relying on Niebuhr, that "Arabian geographers . . . carefully note whether a place is irrigated by an overflowing or channeled stream, or by rain: the latter they call *healthy land*. . . . I see from Niebuhr's notices that grain is much sturdier in a land watered by rain." More oblique was the note to Jer. 8.22, "Is there no balm in Gilead?" Indeed, Michaelis asserted, there was balm in Gilead, as well as in Mecca and "happy Arabia," as Forsskål had discovered.[73] And more dramatic was the zoological illustration—the only one I know of in *any* eighteenth-century translation—that accompanied Numb. 21.6, "the Lord sent fiery serpents among the people" (fig. 13). And, finally, the longest of such notes appended to his naturalistic translation of Exod. 14.21: "when Moses stretched his hand out to the water, God let the sea be driven away by a strong wind that blew through the night, so that the ground dried and the water was parted in the middle." His commentary—prefigured in his preface to the 1758 *Essai physique sur l'heure des marées dans la mer rouge*—hinged on the tides in the Red Sea: whether in fact there were tides in this minor body of water, their extent, their timing, and so on. Niebuhr's own observations of the place, on 3 October 1762, confirmed that on that day the tidal variation amounted to 3.5 feet. Michaelis used Niebuhr's estimations of the schedule of the tides at full moon to "calculate" what time the tide must have been when the Israelites crossed the sea. The pharaoh caught the Israelites at dead low tide, he argued. When Moses raised his arm, a strong storm came from the north-northwest, keeping back the tide long enough for the Israelites to cross. "The drying," Michaelis concluded, "was itself natural, and no miracle, but a work of providence."[74]

Niebuhr and the Arabian expedition provided Michaelis and his translation with the data to extend its zoological, geographical, natural-historical, and meteorological claims. But more significantly, it also provided him with the tools to flush out the odd features of the Bible. The locust, the parting of the Red Sea, the fainting quails: all were "obscure" places, where the Bible "deals with oriental matters . . . or foreign and, to us, alien images," places that demanded all the attention of the biblical scholar and the biblical translator.[75] For the scholar, the task was a great one: to recover those legacies of the biblical world that had endured the ravages of time, the loss of memory, and the

[73] Michaelis, *Deutsche Uebersetzung . . . welche das vierte Buch Mose enthält* (Göttingen, 1772), 16; Michaelis, *Deutsche Uebersetzung . . . welche das fünfte Buch Mose enthält* (Göttingen, 1773), 34; Michaelis, *Deutsche Uebersetzung . . . welche die Weissagungen und Klagelieder Jeremiä enthält* (Göttingen, 1778), 32;

[74] Michaelis, "Anmerckungen zum zweiten Buch Mose," 50.

[75] Michaelis, *Das Buch Hiobs*, xxxiii.

Zu S. 42. der Anmerk. 4 b. Mos. 21. CERAST. nach J. Ellis Zeichnung.

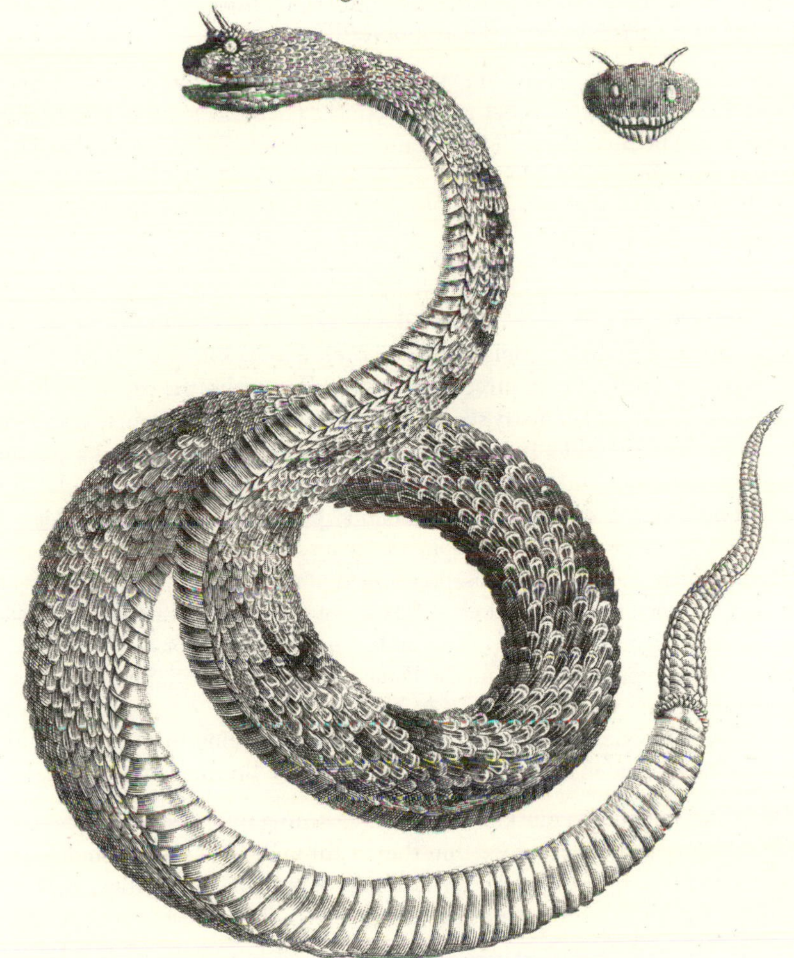

Figure 13. A desert snake, illustrating Num. 21.6. Johann David Michaelis, *Deutsche Uebersetzung des Alten Testaments . . . welche das vierte Buch Mose enthält* (Göttingen, 1772), 41. Courtesy of the Center for Advanced Judaic Studies Library, University of Pennsylvania.

depravation of texts, legacies odd to the modern mind but utterly characteristic of the ancient one. For the translator, the task was even greater, namely bringing this passage of time home to the reader, by disorienting him from a text long familiarized. Every trace of the alien past helped in this mission, for it reminded readers of the Old Testament just how distant its contours were from the present.

For Michaelis, then, nothing was more cherished than those immutable marks of historical time. We sense, then, his disappointment when he reported, in a note to Jer. 51, Niebuhr's description of Babylon:

> The ruins of this great city are much less handsome, and much more rotten, than one finds in other similiar cities (Thebes, Palmyra, Baalbeck, Persepolis) because the walls were built not out of stone but out of bricks. From the ruins of the other cities . . . one can take splendid materials for building palaces, and indeed they have been taken, much to the distress of the lovers of antiquity.[76]

Babylon—Michaelis learned from Niebuhr—was built on a marshy plain. Its walls were built not of stone, but of baked clay; and as a result, its traces were largely vanished. Babylon could not be recovered in its foreign beauty.

But against this failure in preservation stood Persepolis, the site of Niebuhr's greatest personal and scholarly successes, where the entire structure was carved into the sturdiest marble. In the ruins of Persepolis, Niebuhr found a treasure trove of inscriptions and art, all of which he had reproduced in loving detail in the second volume of his *Reisebeschreibung*, published in the same year as Michaelis's *Jeremiah* (1778). His copies of the inscriptions, and of the figures inscribed into the walls of the ruins, occasioned not only antiquarian attempts to decipher the ancient scripts but also efforts to understand the nature of Persian art. "I find," Niebuhr wrote in response to one commentator, "little similarity between the Egyptian sphinx and the Persian quadrupeds with human heads."[77] The commentator was Herder who, in his 1787 *Persepolis: Eine Muthmaassung*, waxed elegiac about the remnants of ancient Persia, seeing in them traces of a "fully asian" art, evidence of a "higher level of culture" in the plains of Persia:

> We make so much in our knowledge and learning unnecessarily difficult! We block our own vision, we thin the air through fantastic chronologies and histories, and afterwards wheezingly complain about inexplicable things. Let the Hebrews and the Greek testify about whatever they can testify, but we will never cover our eyes in order not to see what is right there.[78]

If Herder's advice—"just open your eyes and look"—seems simple enough, that is because it had already become a standard, and by the late eighteenth century, nauseatingly repetitious piece of advice. But more lurked beneath this comment. Where Herder looked for remnants of Persia in Persepolis, it was the most cherished aim of Michaelis's scholarship to see those Hebrews that Herder

[76] Michaelis, "Anmerckungen" in *Deutsche Uebersetzung . . . welche die Weissagungen und Klagelieder Jeremiä enthält* (Göttingen, 1778), 164.

[77] Niebuhr, *Reisebeschreibung nach Arabien und andern umligenden Ländern* [1778] (rpt., Graz, 1968), 2:288; "Persepolis" in *Deutschen Museum* (March 1788), reprinted in ibid., 3:126.

[78] Herder, *Werke*, 15:598.

dismissed. Von Haven—as poor a scholar as he was—had his eyes wide open to these enigmatic Hebrews. After collecting several Hebrew manuscripts and assigning them improbably ancient pedigrees, von Haven cried "what are these compared to the monuments of stone, if these monuments were indeed inscribed by Moses and the Israelites? What inscriptions, what amazing manuscripts!"[79] The stoniness, the sheer endurance and implacability of granite and marble, was a guarantee—for von Haven, for Michaelis, and for many of his contemporaries—of the implacability of the materials inscribed there. There is "no country in the world less capable of variation," the classical scholar Robert Wood later commented, "than the extensive deserts of Arabia."[80] Edward Gibbon, who had read his Niebuhr, declared that only two adjectives pertained to Arabia, "the *stony* and the *sandy*." In this "vacant space between Persia, Syria, Egypt and Aethiopia," people worship and embrace the black stone at Mecca and hew rocks into altars and idols.[81] Surrounded by the swirling sands of time, Arabia was itself a stone, its rough face inscribed with the words of Moses and the Israelites, preserving the oddness of the Hebrew past for a near eternity.

And this is why—on the surface a curious idea—Michaelis wanted to send a trip to Arabia, the homeland of Islam, to find out about the Old Testament. This was by no means an obvious move. In its review of Thomas Harmer's *Observations on Divers Passages of Scripture* (1764), the *Critical Review* had already expressed some doubt about the utility of such exercises:

> There has been a total alteration in the religion, laws, and manners of the natives, since the days of Moses. A traveler sees the ground which the patriarchs trod: he observes the same temperature of the air, the same aspect of the heavens, and the like; but customs and modes of living are circumstances of a transitory kind; few reliques of these things have subsisted through the revolutions of three thousand years.[82]

But Michaelis completely disagreed. Where are the "remnants . . . of a once ruling Jewish religion" still preserved, he asked? Only in Yemen, where Arabs will not marry two sisters, or, in an "exaggeration of Mosaic law," eat meat already gnawed by dogs.[83] Foreign and alien customs, foreign and alien images, were etched into the stony fastness of Yemen, the only place on earth where one could literally touch ancient Judaism. As Niebuhr put it, "Arabia has scarcely known any changes."[84] The anthropological motivations and strivings that underlay both the Arabian trip and the monumental Bible translation

[79] Von Haven, letter to de Gäbler, Danish envoy in Constantinople, 26 August 1762, in Michaelis, *Briefwechsel*, 2:74.

[80] Robert Wood, *An Essay on the Original Genius and Writings of Homer* (London, 1775), 146.

[81] Edward Gibbon, *Decline and Fall of the Roman Empire* (London, 1954), 5:205, 225.

[82] *Critical Review* 19 (1765): 109.

[83] Michaelis, *Bibliothek*, 4:92, 114.

[84] Hess, *Germans, Jews*, 76.

were, in other words, forensic. They were forensic because their subject was already dead. They were forensic because the problem was now not so much the resuscitation of the body as its reconstitution into a recognizable form. In this reconstitution, all the encrustations of time would be sloughed away, and the "foreign" and the "alien" would stand out in gleaming and shining new skins.

For this reason, Islam held little interest for Michaelis, as Jonathan Hess rightly points out. Anthropological study of the customs and habits of the present day Arabians was only a means to an end. Michaelis's forensic mission was less to understand a living culture systematically, than to use this living culture as an archive of materials preserved since the most ancient of times. Just as Herder read Hebrew and archaic Eastern literature as "the oldest archive of the human race," so too did Michaelis treat living people as archival repositories of ancient languages, customs, and landscapes.[85] Yemen, he later wrote,

> is still rich in gifts of nature that are unknown to us; its history extends back to the most ancient times; its dialect is as yet quite different from the familiar western Arabic, and because this familiar form of Arabic has proven until now the surest aid for explaining the Hebrew language, could we not reasonably expect to shed much light on the most important book of antiquity, the Bible, if we knew the eastern Arabian dialect as well as we do the west? That which has disappeared in the one dialect, will perhaps remain in the other.[86]

Into the Arabic dialects was engraved—with just as much fixity and durability as the inscriptions preserved at Persepolis—the history of the Hebrews and the history of the Bible. But this history was broken into pieces, and distributed across the languages of the Arabian peninsula. Full reconstruction required collecting fragments embedded in a multiplicity of dialects. In contrast to the common, familiar Arabic language—weak and rotten, like bricks of Babylon—the interior of Arabia represented, in Michaelis's view, a veritable Persepolis of preservation. Yemeni languages and customs were "a kind of Archive, where human discoveries are safe from the worst accidents; Archives which fire cannot destroy, and which can never perish but with the total ruin of a people."[87] In these archives, all of the biblical customs made dusty and dilapidated by the passing of time would be found, shining in their original alien splendor. The job of scholarship was to open the archives; the job of translation to put those archives to work, to make the reader feel the disorienting difference between the familiar words of the Bible and the unfamiliar landscapes buried beneath them.

[85] On the archival ideal, see Maurice Olender, *The Languages of Paradise: Race, Religion, and Philology in the Nineteenth Century*, trans. Arthur Goldhammer (Cambridge, MA, 1992).

[86] Michaelis, *Fragen*, a5r.

[87] Michaelis, *De l'influence des opinions sur le langage, et du langage sur les opinions* (Bremen, 1762), 29.

For Karl Bahrdt, this was reason enough for his furious indictment of Michaelis's book. According to Michaelis, reported Bahrdt scornfully, "Orientalism must, in a good translation, always shine through." But what a hideous mistake! "I keep Orientalisms only when they make a language elegant," he continued. And the retention of Orientalisms was not just a matter of personal preference. Instead it was a grave offence against good taste and against the afterlife of religion more generally. Bahrdt was so vexed by this issue of Orientalisms that he, the author of a book on press freedoms, imagined with some delight a total suppression of the translation: "Truly if I ruled a country, I would have this translation confiscated: because the great reputation of the author so authorizes and confirms horrible errors . . . that now we will have to wait another 50 years longer for the dissemination of a healthy Bible translation and a dogmatics freed of obscurely oriental expressions!"[88] Rather than "de-Orientalizing" the Bible, in Bahrdt's eyes, Michaelis was guilty of a far greater crime: making the Bible seem foreign and alien to the German ear. Just as orthodox theologians criticized the early religious radicals for their ungerman and odd turns of phrase, Bahrdt took Michaelis to task for making the Bible strange. This transformation of the Bible could only be accomplished in fact (not just theory) through translation. Only a translation could put this theory into effect, could create an *experience* of alienation in readers. In Michaelis's hands, Bible translation was a practical tool of estrangement, a way of removing a literary object "from the automatism of perception."[89]

Greeks, the New Bible, and the Old Judaism

What did it mean to translate the Bible into an archive of an alien civilization? The answer helps to complete our picture of the Enlightenment Bible. It was not unique to Michaelis, after all, to embrace the historical distance between modern humans and ancient texts. In the classical domain, for example, the immense eighteenth-century interest in Homer produced an extensive set of reflections on the nature of antiquity and the extent to which it should govern the spiritual productions of modernity. With the simultaneous decline of allegorical and strict neoclassical readings of Homer—which read Homer either as a veiled exemplar of Christian wisdom or as heuristic model for all aesthetic endeavor—early eighteenth-century critics ranging from Alexander Pope to Thomas Blackwell began pushing the Homeric epics off their literary pedestals and into the murkier realms of "our dark past."[90] By midcentury, the Italian Giambattista Vico characterized the customs of the Homeric era as "crude,

[88] Bahrdt, *Kritiken*, 30, 54, 59.

[89] Shklovsky, "Art As Technique," 13.

[90] Michael Murrin, *The Allegorical Epic: Essays in Its Rise and Decline* (Chicago, 1980), 188.

coarse, wild, savage, volatile, unreasonably obstinate, frivolous and foolish" and raised questions about that paragon of divine genius, Homer, and his authorship of the *Iliad* and *Odyssey*.[91] Later, Robert Wood's *Essay on the Original Genius and Writings of Homer*—translated and published in German before being widely available in English—directly compared Homer's ancient Greece with the Jewish patriarchs and Arabian Bedouins: all three would shock the modern reader with their "cruelty, violence, and injustice." The ancient East, which included Greece, was a "continued narrative of bloodshed and treachery" and it was as a reflection of this brutal time that Homer had to be read. This new Homer was as tied to the experience of travel as Michaelis's Old Testament. "It is as a Traveller only," Wood concluded, that he was able to restore to Homer his "time, place, persons, and things."[92] Like other members of the Society of Dilettanti—an active group of English Grecophiles who put their considerable private fortunes into the study of Greek antiquities—Wood toured the Mediterranean in 1750–51 with an eye to discovering the physical texture of Homeric life.[93] This enterprise was duly followed in Germany: Michaelis, in fact, received one of the seven copies of the *Original Genius* that Wood published in 1769, and the two men corresponded for a time in 1770. "What many travelers did for the explanation of sacred scripture, others performed for Homer," commented Goethe, and in a sense, he was right: in both cases, travel was key to establishing the distance between the antique texts and their modern readers.[94]

But this story is only partial. It is one half of a paradox: for if the classics lost normative status under the pressure of travel and historicism, this loss was recuperated by the juggernaut of philhellenism that followed in the wake of Johann Joachim Winckelmann. Winckelmann's 1755 *Gedanken über die Nachahmung der Griechischen Werke* began with a simple claim: "good taste . . . first began to develop under the Greek skies," and between this early work and his monumental *Geschichte der Kunst des Altertums* (1764), he developed a strongly normative ideal of Greek aesthetics. "The only way for us to become great, even, if it is possible, inimitable, is to imitate the ancients," Winckelmann declared.[95] For him, Greece was, in Suzanne Marchand's words, "the symbol and embodiment of humankind's true, free, and uncorrupted nature" and under his

[91] Kirsti Simonsuuri, *Homer's Original Genius: Eighteenth-Century Notions of the Early Greek Epic* (Cambridge, 1979), 95.

[92] Robert Wood, *Original Genius*, 160–61, 302.

[93] Simonsuuri, *Homer's Original Genius*, 135. See also Bruce Redford, "The Measure of Ruins: Dilettanti in the Levant, 1750–1770," *Harvard Library Bulletin* 13 (Spring 2002): 5–36, and Hans Hecht, *T. Percy, R. Wood, und J. D. Michaelis: Ein Beitrag zur Literaturgeschichte der Genieperiode* (Stuttgart, 1933), 55–70.

[94] Hecht, *Wood und Michaelis*, 23–26, 19.

[95] Johann Joachim Winckelmann, *Gedanken über die Nachahmung der Griechischen Werke in der Malerei und Bildhauerkunst* [1755] (rpt., Nendeln, 1968), 7, 8.

tutelage, subsequent generations of Germans embraced not an alienated, but an ideal antiquity.[96]

As is proper to a paradox, Winckelmann's Graecomania was never fully victorious. The philological seminar at Göttingen under Christian Heyne and the later classical scholarship of Friedrich August Wolf (see chapter 8) were at times disinclined to embrace antiquity as a moral exemplar, preferring what Ulrich von Wilamowitz-Moellendorff later called "the conquest of the ancient world by scholarship" to the pure aesthetic experience of Greek genius.[97] And in the world of speculative philology, critics like Friedrich Schlegel too were reticent to embrace the fully normative aspects of Greek art. The "relation of antique poetry to modern" should not be one of dominance, but rather distinction.[98] After all, even for Winckelmann, the goal of modern art was to become "inimitable" itself, to make the "experience of freedom" into the foundation of a modern aesthetic.[99] If Greece offered the art of freedom, wouldn't the slavish imitation of freedom merely confirm modernity's essential inadequacy? And yet, once more cycling through the paradox, even these doubters never imagined a modernity fully alienated from the spiritual baggage of antiquity. Antiquity was foreign, but never so much that its difference could not "ultimately be resolved in some commonality."[100]

Michaelis's Old Testament was subject to the same paradoxes of distance and proximity that attended the classical corpus, if rendered all the more difficult because of the religious stakes. On the side of proximity, Michaelis aimed, like many of his contemporaries, at the recuperation of a text whose authenticity and authority could no longer be guaranteed by the comfortable cradle of theology. His historical Bible—as a facet of that larger entity I have called the Enlightenment Bible—can be read as the final nail in the coffin of the Bible as it had long existed within Christianity generally, and Protestantism more specifically. It was, Michaelis declared, for everyone: "for Lutherans, Calvinists, Catholics . . . for Socinians, even for enemies of religion." It would be a Bible for a new, post-theological age: "my intention is to introduce into the Bible *no religious system at all*," for any such introduction would deny the Bible its rights as the "communal well of knowledge" for Christians.[101] Instead, what Eichhorn later called Michaelis's second Reformation would be a historical one, one that recaptured the spirit of antiquity

[96] Marchand, *Down from Olympus: Archaeology and Philhellenism in Germany, 1750–1970* (Princeton, 1996), 15–16. Also see Robert S. Leventhal, *The Disciplines of Interpretation: Lessing, Herder, Schlegel, and Hermeneutics in Germany 1750–1800* (Berlin, 1994), 262.

[97] Marchand, *Down from Olympus*, 17.

[98] Leventhal, *Disciplines of Interpretation*, 264.

[99] On Schegel, see Leventhal, *Disciplines of Interpretation*, 263–65;

[100] Leventhal, *Disciplines of Interpretation*, 302.

[101] Michaelis, *Das Buch Hiobs*, xxiv–xxv, xxiv. My italics.

through its history, geography, ecology, and cultural practices. Just as the decline of Christian allegory made it possible for the Greeks to stand as a pure spiritual resource for a liberated modern age, so too did the decline of theology make possible a purely nonpartisan translation, a well of knowledge for German readers of *all* religious persuasions.

And yet digging this common well also entailed digging a trench between ancient and modern, such that neither Greek nor Jew might enslave the modern reader with their alien nature. In the Homeric context, Germans (and Europeans more broadly) were assured of the primitive and coarse mentality of the ancient Greeks. They were assured that Homer was an illiterate bard, that both the *Iliad* and the *Odyssey* were the products of a land distant in time and space from European modernity. In the biblical context, Germans were estranged from their familiar texts and made to see the Bible as a bewildering archive of ancient humanity. They were given a new Bible filled with the foreign and peculiar expressions of an ancient Semitic tribe.

But precisely here, of course, lay a set of crucial distinctions between the classical and biblical contexts. First, while Greeks could serve as (distant) exemplars of human freedom, rare was the German who would look to the ancient Jew as a model of cultural development. Philosemitism did not occupy a large space in the intellectual landscape of the period, to put it mildly. Second, while Greeks were comfortably remote—confined either to an ancient past or to a land long months' travel away—the people who inhabited the archives of the Bible were still dwelling among the scholars and citizens of modern Europe. So it is with interest we discover the resonance of this archival ideal: Michaelis's student, Johann Eichhorn, extolled the Bible as "simply an archive of revelation" and the biblical canon, less enthusiastically, as "the national library" of the Hebrews, for example, while the theologian and physiognomist Johann Lavater advised people to "read the Bible for once not as a divine book, but just as the oldest archive of the human race; just as you read any other ancient historian."[102] It is not just that the Bible became a work of ancient history; not just that we can see here that "rise of historicism" that Peter Reill has located in the second half of the eighteenth century.[103] Rather, the refashioning of the Bible into an archive had extra-theoretical implications, especially for that one group excluded from the "everyone" that Michaelis had in mind as an audience for his new translation, namely the Jews, the people whose primordial ancestors provided the raw and foreign data to his biblical project. Although the classics and the Bible were enmeshed in a similar grid of cultural responses, in other words, these responses produced different effects. In the case of the Scriptures, the historical Bible excluded the Jews from their religious patrimony by

[102] Eichhorn, "Briefe, die biblische Exegese betreffend," *Allgemeine Bibliothek der biblischen Literatur* 5 (1793): 206; ibid., 4 (1792): 254; Johann Caspar Lavater, *Antworten auf wichtige und würdige Fragen und Briefe* (Berlin, 1790), 1:128–29.

[103] Reill, *Rise of Historicism.*

transforming the Bible into an archive of an alien people, just as the poetic Bible had done in the name of a German national literature.

This aspect of his scholarship has not gone unnoticed. Frank Manuel, for example, argues that, like many Christian Hebraists of the Enlightenment, Michaelis's interest in Mosaic Law and the Old Testament went hand in hand with his distaste for the "sordid reality of Jewish communities divided between court Jews . . . and Jews living in squalor." The distinction maps onto one we have already seen, in chapter 6, between Jews and Hebrews, where the former are in general "depraved and corrupt"—as Michaelis wrote—and the latter noble and inventive.[104] It also maps neatly onto the distinction between rabbinics—the study of which Michaelis consistently repudiated and scorned as "distortions of Mosaic laws"—and the study of, on the one hand, Scripture itself and, on the other, the landscape and customs of the peoples of the Near East.[105] Michaelis's "politics of national self-sufficiency, [which left] no place in Europe for the integration of contemporary Jews," clearly stood behind part of this bifurcated interpretive landscape, as Jonathan Hess and others have noted.[106] Just as Michaelis (and Eichhorn for that matter) set themselves in opposition to the efforts by people like Christian Dohm to work toward "the civil improvement of the Jews," too their scholarship can be read against the efforts—first in England with the Jew Bill (1753–54), later in Austria with Joseph II's *Toleranz Patent* (1781)—to incorporate the Jews into the civil and political architecture of the emerging European states.

For Michaelis, Judiasm—the concatenation of ancient and modern Jews—was definitely old and, as such, excluded from the project to make the Bible a new communal well of historical knowledge. But we should be cautious here not to ascribe too much to his work. The "primary goal" of Michaelis's scholarship was not "to intervene in contemporary politics," in Hess's terms.[107] Instead, his limited interventions in contemporary politics grew out of his immense struggles to understand and rewrite the religious heritage of Christianity. Obviously, this does not "excuse" Michaelis's vitriol toward the Jews, but it does help to explain some of his idiosyncracies. Seen in light of the enormous effort to create the Enlightenment Bible, for example, Michaelis's separation of the Jews from their patrimony looks far more like the product of *religious* rather than political (let alone racial) concern.[108] For if the Jews, in Michaelis's scheme,

[104] Frank Manuel, *The Broken Staff: Judaism through Christian Eyes* (Cambridge, MA, 1992), 286; Michaelis's review of Christian Dohm, reprinted in the latter's *Ueber die bürgerliche Verbesserung der Juden* (Berlin: Friedrich Nicolai, 1783), 2:33.

[105] Michaelis quoted in Breuer, *Limits of Enlightenment*, 102.

[106] Hess, "Colonial Imaginary," 75; see also Anna-Ruth Löwenbrück, *Judenfeindschaft im Zeitalter der Aufklärung: eine Studie zur Vorgeschichte des modernen Antisemitismus* (Frankfurt a.M., 1995).

[107] Hess, "Colonial Imaginary," 65; Hess, *Germans, Jews*, 60.

[108] By seeing Michaelis in this larger tradition we can reconcile some problems in Hess's argument. First of all, we notice that the argument for the Egyptian origins of Jewish ceremonial law was a standard move in OT scholarship since the end of the seventeenth century (see Jan Assmann,

were threatened with historicist obsolescence, another object, one even more troubling to eighteenth-century Germans, was threatened as well, namely the Bible itself. For if indeed the Bible is made alien, is it thereby divorced from modern life, as religiously irrelevant as the tales of Hesiod? Or has it just become, as Lessing wryly commented, a storybook, with "no more and no less value than Aesop's fables"?[109]

Michaelis's answer to these questions was undoubtedly "no." And so, he embraced our paradox and reconstructed an ancient biblical world both continuous with, and discontinuous from, the modern. The very first paragraphs of his *Mosaic Law* are a monument to this apparent contradiction. Study of Moses' laws was necessary so that they would: "*not remain as foreign and Asiatic* to theologians, jurists, and those who philosophize about the wisdom of the law. [The Laws] are already worthy of our attention, if *one sees them laws of a very distant land*, and remnants of the most ancient law giving wisdom."[110] On the one hand, Michaelis wanted to ensure that the Law not be alien to theologians and jurists; on the other, he wanted to ensure that it be seen as *entirely* alien, distant from the present in time and space. In his translation, similarly, the notes were to display the "foreign" and "alien" elements of the Old Testament. It is less clear whether they are to explain these elements, and make them familiar, or to let them stand out in their alien garb. This ambivalence leads his two most recent commentators—Manuel and Hess—to absolutely divergent interpretations of his attitude toward Moses and the Mosaic dispensation: where Hess characterizes Michaelis's reading of Mosaic Law as an attempt to "de-Orientalize" contemporary jurisprudence, Manuel paints a picture of him "idealiz[ing] the jurisprudence of the ancient Hebrews."[111]

In fact, he did both. We have seen this ambivalence not just in the classical arena, but throughout the German Enlightenment and its efforts to come to terms with the nature and future of Christianity. Michaelis, like Herder and the host of apologetes who inhabited this period, walked a very fine line: neither could he relinquish Christianity to the hands of the "enemies of religion,"

Moses the Egyptian [Cambridge, MA, 1997]). Granted, old rhetoric can be applied to new situations, but even so it is not clear that Michaelis really wants to legitimate "the intellectual hegemony of Egypt over Israel" (71): in fact, in the *Mosaic Law*, Egypt is not the unambigious home of "legislative wisdom" (Hess, 70) but also the home of "false religion," "superstition," "priestly lies," and "idolatry" (*Mosaisches Recht* [Reutlingen, 1785], 1:36, 159). Here, as throughout the *Mosaic Law*, Michaelis played a high-stakes game, trying not just to purge contemporary law of Mosaic custom, but also to preserve the relevance of the OT. Second, this new context clears up some chronological issues in Hess's article: Michaelis's arguments on the nature of the OT and the Jews were, after all, in place long before either the Dohm or the Lavater-Mendelssohn controversies, and so related only contingently to these particular conflagrations.

[109] Lessing, "Bibliolatrie," in *Samtliche Schriften*, 16:472.

[110] Michaelis, *Mosaisches Recht*, 1:1–2.

[111] Hess, "Colonial Imaginary," 65; Manuel, *Broken Staff*, 258.

nor could he embrace it—as it currently stood—as a normative and regulative system of religious, political, and moral governance. For this reason, we see his *Mosaic Law* describe Moses as "true prophet" of religion and, at the same time, read his message in the simplest possible terms as "you should honor only one God." Scorn for Jewish custom should be framed, then, not just within a culture-wide pervasive discriminatory attitude against the Jews, but also within the long-standing conflict among Christians about the normativity of all doctrinal proclamations and of the Bible more generally. The problem of the Jews was a by-product—though certainly one that harmonized nicely with the rationalist anti-Judaism that plagued people like Michaelis—not the central focus of this larger, and longer-standing conflict.

The Enlightenment Bible emerged as a set of solutions to this conflict. Translation and scholarship worked together to produce not a single authoritative text, but rather a panoply of Bibles. It was an Enlightenment Bible precisely because it no longer was singular in form, but rather disseminated across a wide spectrum of what I have called media, across a variety of scholarly, generic, and disciplinary domains whose expansion in the eighteenth century compensated for the loss of definite centers of meaning, political or religious. In the (textual) philological Bible, the Bible was made into a document whose study would perfect the practice of criticism. In the poetic Bible, it was given authority insofar as it participated in man's literary heritage, and more specifically as a piece of Germany's literary heritage. In the pedagogical Bible, it became significant for its moral content. And the historical Bible was designed to make it significant as an archive, as an infinitely variegated library of human customs and origins. And in this historical Bible, the ideal of a familiar text was abandoned for one perpetually in translation. Its difference, its peculiarity, its estrangement from the present, became instead key elements to this Bible. If the word of God "console[s] fallen man and help[s] the human race again and again to find the correct path of divine knowledge," the Bible errs and is "disfigured" by time.[112] But it was these disfigurements, and the peculiarities of the text that was the basis of a new biblical authority. For the difference and alienness of the Bible would bind together Christians in a community of scholarship and perpetual labor over the text of the Bible. Christians will indeed become scholars in this vision and together they will look into the Bible for traces of the "common well of knowledge" not just about their own Christian tradition, but also about humanity more generally. The most ancient archive of the human race has found its textual expression, in the endlessly annotated and infinitely belabored books of the Bible.

[112] Tobler, *Anmerkungen zur Ehre der Bibel*, 4.

PART III
The Cultural Bible

WHEN THE ORIENTALIST Johann Eichhorn fondly gazed back over the life of Michaelis, he regretted only that the older scholar had not gone far enough in making the Hebrews strange. Because he had seen "the ancient times in a condition of higher spiritual development," Michaelis had lacked the key insight of the late century, the insight that "spirit and customs are always in step and when the latter is still simple, then the former remains in its primitive simplicity; high scholarly *culture* is foreign to it."[1] In essence, Michaelis had not adequately studied his Herder, who, more than anyone in his time, defined what he and future generations would call "culture." Culture named exactly the particularity—that "entire living picture of the ways of life, customs, needs" of a nation—that set the Hebrews apart from the modern age.[2] As a student of religion, Michaelis's omission was particularly grievous, for culture was defined from the beginning expressly in relation to religious history. "The real living culture of a people, where does it start?" asked Herder, and his answer was simple: "with the awakening and cultivation of their language—and this depends on religion."[3] "Religion alone introduced the first elements of culture and science to all peoples; more precisely, culture and science were originally nothing more than a kind of religious tradition," he emphatically declared, and none served more clearly as a "primary model for a *Nationalkultur*" than the Jews, whose national religion was the self-contained source of its cultural development.[4] This new sense of culture was the doorway, for Eichhorn, to a new kind of biblical study:

> What a different spirit blows through our most recent writings on Hebrew antiquities than in those of the past decades! It is as if the Hebrews have become an entirely different nation, so changed is the view that we now have of their habits of thought, their customs and morals, their laws

[1] Eichhorn, "Michaelis," 889–90, my italics.

[2] Herder, "Auch eine Philosophie der Geschichte zur Bildung der Menschheit," in *Werke*, 4:33.

[3] Herder, "Ueber National-Religionen" in *Adrastea* in *Werke*, 10:612.

[4] Herder, *Against Pure Reason: Writings on Religion, Language, and History*, trans. Marcia Bunge (Minneapolis, 1993), 88; Wulf Koepke, *"Kulturnation,"* 184.

> and rights. The antiquarian study of the Hebrews is . . . now what it must be, if it is to interest philosophical minds and to suit the current state of literature—the history of the culture of the Hebrews.[5]

Where Michaelis had walked right up to this doorway, Eichhorn and his contemporaries strode confidently through, making the Hebrews into "an entirely different nation" and, for better or worse, making the Bible into what Germans came to call culture.

By the 1780s, in short, the Enlightenment Bible was complete in Germany. The philologians, pedagogues, poets, and historians had invented a distributed, ramified, diverse Bible, but one independent of theology, one that could survive embedded within the matrix of "culture." As such, the concept of culture took over all of these aspects of the Enlightenment Bible—its literary quality, its pedagogical virtues, its philological exemplarity, and its historical depth—and unified them beneath a single enormous banner, collapsing the diverse Bibles of Enlightenment into a singular cultural Bible. And at this moment, that endless project of Bible translation—such a ubiquitous interest earlier—collapsed, losing its force as older orthodoxies themselves dissipated. What had been, for Germans, *the* problem of scholarly work, was resolved as the Bible was transformed from a work of theology to a work of culture. Secularization does not adequately describe this transformation, a transformation that took place not against the Biblical tradition, but *within* it, as scholars, pedagogues, and poets preserved that text that we know as the Bible for a modern age. They did so, ultimately, by inserting the Bible into the heart of culture.

And so this final transformation enshrined the Enlightenment Bible within the broader literary, aesthetic, and scholarly world of the nineteenth and twentieth centuries. Indeed, the very familiarity of the cultural Bible—the familiar sense that the Bible is part of "our" Western culture, a cornerstone of the literary, poetic, moral, and pedagogical values of Western civilization—betrays the expansiveness of this change. When a modern critic like Northrop Frye, for example, wonders "why . . . this huge, sprawling, tactless book sit[s] there inscrutably in the middle of our cultural heritage," he is not only asking a question answerable by a set of empirical investigations (into how, for example, the Bible has influenced literature, love, law, or lampshades).[6] He is also making a substantial claim, that in fact the Bible has something to do with what we understand to be "our" culture and heritage. This sense had its origins, on the one hand, in the Enlightenment Bible developed in the eighteenth century, and, on the other, in the cultural Bible invented in Germany and exported to the English-speaking world over the course of the nineteenth. After 1800, England would no longer be the model for a liberal biblical humanism. That honor would pass

[5] Eichhorn, review of Johann Babor, *Alterthümer der Hebräer* in *Allgemeine Bibliothek der biblischen Literatur* 6.3 (1795): 528–29.

[6] Northrop Frye, *The Great Code: The Bible and Literature* (New York, 1982), xviii.

to Germany and the flow of scholarly commerce that had dominated the eighteenth century would reverse, haltingly in the 1790s and then fully in the 1830s, when the cultural Bible became an inextricable part of the Protestant English scholarly world. These final two chapters trace the broad contours of this change, ranging more widely than previous ones to show how this Bible was infused into German and English theology, scholarship, and pedagogy, until it became the familiar figure we know today as our biblical heritage.

Chapter Eight

CULTURE, RELIGION, AND THE BIBLE IN GERMANY, 1790–1830

NOTHING SIGNIFIED MORE clearly the German sense that by the 1780s and 1790s the Gordian knot of the Bible had unraveled than the decline in fortune of Bible translation. In dramatic terms, the Bible had become, in the words of Johann Griesbach in 1780, "untranslatable."[1] More prosaically, it was clear to someone like Eichhorn that it would be "more useful and profitable for the expansion of true knowledge of the Bible" if the project of Bible translation were stopped.[2] As a consequence, he refused to review new translations in his *General Library of Biblical Literature*. But if the translators' day was done, it was because their labor over the Enlightenment Bible had prepared the ground for a cultural Bible, indeed opened the door more generally to a synthetic notion of culture. Precisely at this time, as Norbert Elias has argued, the concept of culture, as the name for that "self-consciousness of a nation which had constantly to seek out and constitute its boundaries anew, in a political as well as a spiritual sense," colonized the German imagination.[3] From Kant to Mendelssohn, Johann Adelung to Johann Eichhorn, culture became a powerful tool in the rhetorical arsenal of German savants and would come to subsume man's entire spiritual, political, artistic, historical, and scholarly heritage.[4] The largest and most potentially indigestible part of this spiritual heritage was the Old and New Testaments. Without a cultural Bible, in other words, "culture" would have remained in opposition to religion, spiritual "heritage" dispersed across different social, literary, and intellectual domains. But culture was never opposed to religion, at least not directly. Not only was the concept itself invented in the

[1] Griesbach, "Bibelübersetzungen," 267.

[2] Eichhorn, *Allgemeine Bibliothek der biblischen Literatur* 3 (1790): 82.

[3] Norbert Elias, *The Civilizing Process: The History of Manners* (New York, 1978), 1: 5–6.

[4] The vocabulary of "culture" was complicated, not least because of the strange rhetoric of *Bildung* that so dominated the era: most of my usages of "culture" below are translations of *Kultur*, but at times *Bildung* can mean virtually the same thing. In general, see W. H. Bruford, *The German Tradition of Self-Cultivation: "Bildung" from Humboldt to Thomas Mann* (Cambridge, 1975); Joseph Niedermann, *Kultur: Werden und Wandlungen des Begriffs* (Firenze, 1941); on Mendelssohn's idea of culture, see Alexander Altmann, "Aufklärung und Kultur bei Moses Mendelssohn," in Norbert Hinske, ed., *Ich handle mit Vernunft* . . . (Hamburg, 1981) and Carola Hilfrich, "'Cultur ist ein Fremdling in der Sprache': Zu Moses Mendelssohn's Kulturbegriff," *Zeitschrift für Ästhetik und Allgemeine Kunstwissenschaften* (forthcoming)—my thanks to Prof. Hilfrich for sharing this essay in manuscript.

language of religious analysis, but it also consistently described a sacralized space of communal heritage. The forging of a cultural Bible was thus one key move in the broader development of "culture" per se. The cultural Bible allowed scholars to imagine an unbroken and universal spiritual heritage, one unaffected by particular religious commitments, unaffected by belief or unbelief. It enabled the culture-religion axis to articulate freely. And it allowed religion itself to become a cultural phenomenon par excellence.

Luther and the Forging of the Cultural Bible

If the Enlightenment Bible had taken shape around the conviction that only through a distributed set of translations could the Bible be invested with a new post-theological authority, the cultural Bible discovered that more translations were not necessary after all. It discovered that the single most exquisite exemplar of a cultural text was already present in the homes of every good Lutheran. The Luther Bible, in other words, came back into fashion with a vigor that testified to the power and pleasure of the cultural Bible. Where Frederick the Great advocated the pragmatic use of the Luther Bible—as an antidote to the "instructional manuals, especially explanations of catechisms and so-called orders of grace" that "flood" the nation—the late eighteenth and early nineteenth centuries made the Luther Bible an integral part of their cultural patrimony. For Goethe, the Luther Bible was the epitome of this patrimony, a translation that far surpassed those "critical translations" of the eighteenth century that served only "for discussion between scholars." Luther's "poetic, historical, devout, educating tone" in his translation did "more for religion than if he had wanted to reproduce in detail the characteristics of the original."[5] Goethe's exclamation—that "we have sent no prophet to the people, except in his language! And thus the German first became a people through Luther"—was only one expression of this new cultural reading of Luther and his translation. Heinrich Heine went even further: "[Luther] gave words to thought. He created the German language. This happened, because he translated the Bible. In fact, the divine author of this work . . . himself chose his translator and gave him the miraculous power of translating from a dead language, one nearly buried, into a language not yet alive."[6] What were speculations on the part of Goethe and Heine were put into practice in the new *Deutsches Wörterbuch* created by the brothers Jakob and Wilhelm Grimm. Already in his letter to the famous philologian Karl Lachmann, Jakob Grimm gave Luther pride of place in the planning of the new dictionary. Luther marked the beginning of "new high German," and his Bible was the particular treasure trove, filled with the "noblest and most sensible" language. "Only

[5] Goethe, *Dichtung und Wahrheit* in *Werke*, 16:527, 526.

[6] Embach, *Lutherbild*, 57. Heine, "Religion und Philosophie in Deutschland," 7:34.

since Luther has the full and free treatment of literature arisen" and his Bible "sits among all sources as the most accessible."[7] Luther's Bible was not just theoretically, but also practically, at the foundation of German linguistic patrimony.

We can read these sentiments as elaborations of Herder, who, as we already saw, explicitly linked Luther to a German national literature. "We mutilate the language," he wrote. "[T]he pure and true German that our forefathers wrote . . . has virtually disappeared in modern times. It will find itself once more. . . . wait and practice quietly. Accept Luther's translation into your hand and make corrections in your version."[8] Indeed it was Luther's Bible that stood, alongside his hymns, "as model examples of meaningful national poetry," and it was through this Bible that Luther "awoke and liberated the German language, a sleeping giant."[9] If the text of the Luther Bible had remained essentially static in the eighteenth century—and the most vibrant areas of experimentation on the vernacular text were concentrated in the new translations—these new translations ironically set the stage for their own dissolution. For though they never actually replaced the Luther Bible, still they were able to transform it, from a book about theology to one embedded in cultural heritage. The Luther Bible was a fundamentally different animal in 1700 than it was in 1800, and it was the generations of eighteenth-century scholars who renovated it by remaking the Bible into an image of what would be called culture. All that was left, for the enthusiasts of the nineteenth century, was to reap what the Enlightenment had sown. A new cultural Luther Bible was the greatest harvest on offer.

This harvest was liberally appreciated across the spectrum of post-Enlightenment commentators. Most exuberant were the celebratory writings that attended the 300-year anniversary of the Reformation, the 1817 Reformation Jubilee. Two years after the Congress of Vienna had dashed the hopes of liberal-nationalists for a greater Germany, these same forces used the Reformation Jubilee as an occasion to show their displeasure. The festivals at the Wartburg (the site of Luther's own translation) in particular dramatized the German hero and his Reformation as the opening scenes in the staging of Germany's "national independence."[10] It was in conjunction with these festivals that a group of German theologians produced the *Reformation Almanac*, a collection of essays and reflections on the heritage of the Reformation. Common to these essays was an expansive sense of the meaning of the Reformation: "Protestantism is a manner of thinking . . . [and thus it] is as old as truth has

[7] Jacob Grimm, letter of 24 August 1838 to Lachmann, in *Briefwechsel der Brüder Jacob und Wilhelm Grimm mit Karl Lachmann*, ed. Albert Leitzmann (Jena, 1927), 2:688–89; Grimm, preface to *Deutsches Wörterbuch* (Leipzig, 1854), 1:xviii, xxxv.

[8] Klopstock, "Sprache der Poesie," 204; Herder, *Briefe, das Studium der Theologie betreffend*, in *Werke*, 9.1:599.

[9] Michael Embach, *Das Lutherbild Johann Gottfried Herders* (Frankfurt a.M., 1987), 23, 36.

[10] Heinz-Hermann Brandhorst, *Lutherrezeption und bürgerliche Emanzipation* (Göttingen, 1981), 38. See also Thomas A. Howard, *Religion and the Rise of Historicism* (Cambridge, 2000), 71f.

been known. . . . the Reformation was a birthing process that is not yet complete" or "the Reformation must progress, otherwise there never was one.[11] The conservative theologian Claus Harms famously attacked these sentiments—declaring that "with the idea of a progressive Reformation . . . you will reform Lutheranism into paganism, and Christianity out of the world."[12] But still national theologians succeeded in re-creating the Reformation as a grandly philosophical and world-historical event significant "not just for the German fatherland, but also for the culture [*Bildung*] of the entire inhabited earth," which profited by its effects on the "arts and sciences, on business and trade, on spiritual commerce and human culture [*Bildung*]."[13] Luther's Bible, however, translated this cosmopolitan spirit into German particularity. A "German hero and a martyr of the faith," Luther allowed the German to "become truly German" by giving him the textual means to "transform his Germanness with the light of the Gospels." And so, as the theologian Wilhelm de Wette wrote, "the most powerful lever of the Reformation was Luther's German Bible translation. Through it, teachings that were formerly tinged with foreignness were brought to the German people . . . in their own living language." The "living spirit" of Christianity was made German, in other words, by the Luther Bible, and it was Luther who "created a new language" for the German religion.[14]

For the first generations of the nineteenth century, then, the Luther Bible became, quite literally, a monument. "One might call our age, the age of monuments," wrote Christian Berger, superintendent in Eisleben, in 1817: "how could such an age . . . forget one for Luther?" The answer was that in fact it had not. In 1803, as Berger himself recalled, the Mannsfeld literary society had proposed a collection to erect such a monument, and its cornerstone was laid by Fredrick Wilhelm III himself in the market in Wittenberg on the second day of the Reformation Jubilee. Berger was pleased with this stony monument, but insisted that Luther already had a monument after all, a "living monument" written on the pages of his Bible for all Germans to read. This living monument was better than any stone one, for it had become "the national property of the Germans." "I would call him the German Shakespeare," Berger contended, for Luther "created, in a dead language, new words and expressions; his strong spirit overcame the language, and he made from it what *he* wanted." When Germans read the Luther Bible, then, they came to realize that they are reading not "a translation from an ancient Oriental language, but rather an originally German book."[15]

[11] Jonathan Schuderoff, "Über Protestantismus und Kirchen-Reformation," in *Reformations Almanach für Luthers Verehrer* (Erfurt, 1817), 249–50, 265. De Wette, "Über den Verfall," in ibid., 308.

[12] Claus Harms, "Das sind die 95 theses oder Streitsätze Dr Luthers," in *Ausgewählte Schriften und Predigten* (Flensburg, 1955), 1:211.

[13] Schuderoff, "Kirchen-Reformation," 260–61.

[14] De Wette, "Über den Verfall," 370, 302, 304, 305, 319.

[15] Christian Berger, *Kurze Beschreibung der Merkwürdigkeiten die sich in Eisleben, und in Luthers Hause daselbst besonders, auf die Reformation und auf D. Martin Luthers beziehen*, 2nd ed. (Merseburg, 1827), 1, 9, 124, 113, 117.

Luther made the Bible fully German, in other words, wresting it from its Oriental trappings and giving it to the German people as the cornerstone of their cultural heritage. The philologian Franz Passow was only restating this remarkable claim when he decried the original language texts of the Bible: "The writings of the New Testament terrify me with their horrible Greek, [but] LUTHERS translation I find infinitely more noble and beautiful."[16] The contention was implicit but clear: the German Bible simultaneously created a German religion, a German culture, and a German nation. As the nineteenth century progressed, this view became a commonplace, from Tübingen school theologian David Strauss—who described Luther's reformation as "the first vital expression of a culture" that had finally "acquired strength and independence sufficient to create a reaction against the soil of its birth"—to late-century liberal Protestant Adolph von Harnack, who proclaimed that with Luther, Germans were "freed from the chains of spiritual narrow-mindedness and as a consequence of our developing culture, readied to . . . grasp Christianity in its purity."[17] The Luther Bible, in short, became the cultural Bible, a Bible relevant and authoritative even separated from its original theological roots.

FROM THE CULTURAL BIBLE TO THE RELIGION OF CULTURE

Forging the cultural Bible was a key step in the broader development of "culture" per se. In an abstract sense, the cultural Bible became exemplary for the incorporation of diverse literatures into nationally circumscribed cultural canons. When the philosopher Franz Rosenzweig wrote in 1926 that "every great work of a language can in a certain sense be translated into another language only once," his model was the translation of the Luther Bible.[18] He was not arguing for a ban on translations—as a Bible translator himself this would have been an odd position—but rather insisting that literary canons are constituted in acts of translation. The appearance of a great translation fixes the face of a foreign literature into place, ripping it from its original soil and planting it firmly in the soil of its new possessor. If, as John Guillory has argued, translation is a "technique of deracination" that has traditionally provided "a powerful institutional buttress of imaginary cultural continuities" in the construction of modern literary canons, this particular tool was honed upon the text of the Bible.[19] It is not accidental, I think, that the concept of a literary or cultural canon—a "transhistorical textual community," in Robert Alter's words—shadows the biblical

[16] Paulsen, *Geschichte*, 234.

[17] David Friedrich Strauss, *The Life of Jesus, Critically Examined*, trans. Marian Evans (New York, 1860), 18; Adolph von Harnack, "Martin Luther in seiner Bedeutung für die Geschichte der Wissenschaft und der Bildung (1883)" in *Ausgewählte Reden und Aufsätze*, ed. Agnes von Zahn-Harnack (Berlin, 1951), 60.

[18] Franz Rosenzweig, *Die Schrift und Luther* (Berlin, 1926), 17.

[19] John Guillory, *Cultural Capital: The Problem of Literary Canon Formation* (Chicago, 1993), 43.

canon.[20] Nor that nearly every major theorist of translation—from the Romantics to Jacques Derrida—refers back to the Bible as the primal scene of translation. The translation of the Bible has become this primal scene not just because it was the earliest translation, but because it is seen as offering "the basic categories in the history of translation."[21] Other literatures (one thinks of Shakespeare and Homer here) have certainly received their own "cultural" translations, but the sense of the "original text . . . as *property*"—and in particular, as cultural property—originated in the Bible and, in Germany, in the Luther Bible.[22] On a less abstract level, however, the making of the cultural Bible was also an important step in the invention of a cultural religion, a religion arranged under the heading of culture. Culture colonized spiritual heritage, in other words, only when Christianity and its texts became cultural too. This integration of religion and culture was key to the larger renewal of religion that preoccupied so many German figures in the late eighteenth and early nineteenth centuries.

When the generation who lived through the French Revolution and the Napoleonic Wars looked back on the eighteenth century, they saw only the ruins of rationalism, the dry-as-dust remnants of a religion in decline. For them—and it is above all from them that we have our sense of the irreligiosity of the eighteenth century—the Enlightenment saw the "flame of religious enthusiasm" quail under the cold "influence of doubt."[23] In contrast to this chilly age, the new generation felt themselves on the verge of a Christian religious revival unequaled since the Reformation, felt themselves in the midst of a grand desecularization. The lyricism of Novalis, in his 1799 *Christianity or Europe*, offered a panegyric vision of this new religious landscape.

> Shouldn't Protestantism finally come to an end and make way for a new, sturdy Church? The other parts of the world await Europe's reconciliation and resurrection, that they might join her and become together citizens of Heaven. . . . Christianity must come alive again and become real; it must make itself once more into a visible church, without regard for borders. . . . From the divine womb of a venerable European council, Christianity will rise from the dead and the enterprise of a religious awakening . . . will be undertaken.[24]

Novalis's pan-European, post-Protestant vision of a newly awakened Christianity, one that would overcome the divisions between European nations and European sects, was distinctively apocalyptic in its tone. But it was not untypical

[20] Alter, *Canon and Creativity*, 5.

[21] André Lefevere, "Translation: Its Genealogy in the West," in Susan Bassnett and André Lefevere, *Translation, History, and Culture* (London, 1990), 15.

[22] Susan Bassnett-McGuire, *Translation Studies* (London, 1988), 69.

[23] de Wette, "Über den Verfall," 312, 329.

[24] Novalis, "Die Christenheit oder Europa," in *Schriften*, ed. Richard Samuel (Stuttgart, 1983), 3:524.

for an age that saw itself as inaugurating what Adolph von Harnack called "the great spiritual revolution" of the nineteenth century.[25] Central to this revolution was the figure of Friedrich Schleiermacher, the most important theologian of the period, and the figure on whose shoulders the hopes of this revolution rested. The year 1799 was crucial for him as well. In that year, his *On Religion: Speeches to Its Cultured Despisers* outlined *in nuce* an enormous project of theological renovation that would span nearly thirty years. Nothing less than the redefinition of religion was at stake here, and with it the renovation of Christian theology. If, as we have seen, the Enlightenment Bible was predicated on the separation of the Bible and theology, Schleiermacher installed this separation into the heart of what would become known later as *Kulturprotestantismus*.

In its simplest form, Schleiermacher's theology was, as Karl Barth later wrote, a "theology of feeling, of awareness," one that took the intuition of God to be its highest aspiration.[26] At the beginning of all religion stood "religious consciousness," which recognized an absolute dependence on God. From this consciousness in the individual—a product of his or her human nature as much as any aspect of conscious life—stemmed religious community, a body of people who recognized in each other similarities in religious emotion, and in doing so began a communion and a church. This anthropological drama formed the bedrock of Schleiermacher's understanding of what he called "*religion in general*," which was simply the "tendency of the human mind in general to give rise to religious emotions."[27] Despite this originality of religious emotion, religion per se was never "found among human beings . . . undisguised," never appeared in a "pure state." Instead, religion was always shrouded by human contrivances, contrivances that Schleiermacher protested were mistaken, by the "cultured despisers," for the essence of religion.

> You are right to despise the paltry imitators who derive their religion wholly from someone else, or cling to a dead document by which they swear and from which they draw proof. *Every holy writing is merely a mausoleum of religion*, a monument that a great spirit was there that no longer exists. . . . It is not the person who believes in a holy writing who has religion, but only the one who needs none and probably could make one for himself.

Never before had the distinction between religion and the Scriptures been made so clearly, and with such dramatic impact. Religion was the "diamond" encrusted by the base books of the Bible, buried in them but essentially independent of them. Re-creating, even understanding, this religion meant destroying this crust, what Schleiermacher called the "caved-in walls of their Jewish Zion and its

[25] Adolph von Harnack, *History of Dogma*, trans. Neil Buchanan (New York, 1961), 1:32.

[26] Karl Barth, *Protestant Theology in the Nineteenth Century: Its Background and History* (London, 1972), 457–58.

[27] Friedrich Schleiermacher, *The Christian Faith* (New York, 1963), 1:26–30.

Gothic pillars."[28] No more was the Bible a part of this thing Schleiermacher called "religion" or "theology." In this sense, Barth was certainly right when he wrote that "in the very places where the theology of the Reformation had said 'the Gospel' or the 'Word of God' . . . Schleiermacher, three hundred years after the Reformation, now says, religion or piety."[29] Religion had given up the Bible, now safely preserved in the realm of culture.

Schleiermacher's vision contained an ecumenical promise that appealed to many in his generation, a promise incarnated when—in a renunciation of the Westphalian division of churches—the Prussian king Frederick Wilhelm III announced his *Kirchen Agende*, formally dissolving the distinction between the Lutheran and Calvinist faiths and collapsing them into a new "evangelical" union. The dream here was to set aside confessional differences and build a "newly animated, evangelical-Christian Church in the spirit of its holy founder," Christ.[30] Religion, one might say, should be more than just its particular incarnations, more than Judaism, Christianity, or Islam. Inside the "dead slag" that characterized those religions "long since degenerated into a code of empty customs . . . was once the glowing outpouring of the inner fire that is contained in all religions, and is more or less of the true essence of religion."[31] An ecumenical Christianity promised to rediscover that inner fire by discarding all of the external and formal slag that concealed it.

In short, in Schleiermacher's hands, Christianity stood poised for a rebirth. On the plane of theology, this rebirth would free Christianity from the Bible. It would free Christianity of those biblical apologetics that were such a part of the Enlightenment analysis and defense of religion. Where the cultural Bible assured any concerned that Scriptures would remain a part of the national heritage, Christian theology was allowed to range away from its foundational text and seek its grounds in a more stable medium. It was no accident, then, that at this moment the discipline of "Biblical theology"—defined by its founder J. P. Gabler in 1787 as "conveying what the holy writers felt about divine matters"—was born, spawned from the sense that the heterogeneous (and historically determined) theologies of the biblical authors had to be distinguished from proscriptive Christian dogma.[32] It was necessary, wrote this student of Semler and

[28] Schleiermacher, *On Religion: Speeches to Its Cultured Despisers*, trans. Richard Crouter (Cambridge, 1988), 97, 100, 134 (my italics), 101, 78–79.

[29] Barth, *Protestant Theology*, 458.

[30] On the union, see Gerhard Fischer, "Die Altpreussische Union (1817–1834)," in *Kirche und Staat im 19. und 20. Jahrhundert* (Neustadt, 1968), 106ff., 107.

[31] Schleiermacher, *On Religion*, 194.

[32] John Sandys-Wunsch and Laurence Eldredge, "J. P. Gabler and the Distinction Between Biblical and Dogmatic Theology: Translation, Commentary, and Discussion of His Originality," *Scottish Journal of Theology* 33 (1980): 137. On Gabler, see Loren Stuckenbruck, "Johann Philip Gabler and the Deliniation of Biblical Theology," *Scottish Journal of Theology* 52 (1999): 139–57; R. E. Clements, "The Study of the Old Testament," in Ninian Smart et al., ed., *Nineteenth Century Religious Thought in the West* (Cambridge, 1985), 3:111. More generally, see James Barr, *The Concept of Biblical Theology* (Minneapolis, 1999).

Eichhorn, to "distinguish among each of the periods of the Old and New Testaments, each of the authors, and each of the manners of speaking."[33] Biblical theology would tell readers what the biblical authors believed. Dogmatic theology in turn would be liberated from these historical particularities, freed to leave the Bible behind.

At the same time as the Bible became cultural, however, so too was this reborn theology invented under the sign of culture. Schleiermacher himself was forged by later generations into a potent sign of this cultural rebirth, a corporeal manifestation of the great renovation in religion marked by the nineteenth century: The modern period, one devotee claimed in 1860, "had to befriend Religion again . . . that it might be shown as an essential part of spiritual life. . . . This was done first by Schleiermacher."[34] From Schleiermacher, taught another, "a new period in the history of the Church will one day take its origin." Schleiermacher "did not found a school, but an era"; he was "priest and prophet in one person and a king in the realm of the mind."[35] He was the hero who at the "high point of our spiritual culture" managed to unite "culture and religion."[36] But if Schleiermacher was one center of this whirlwind of associations, the "new era" for the culture of Christianity extended beyond him. Across the political and religious spectrums, Germans seized on this new, cultural religion. Even the radical philosopher Johann Fichte—no friend of religion—commented that "religion is as old as the world," and that early on in human history, it grew and "spread across the empire of culture." "You will not be amazed, after hearing this, that we must return here back to Christianity as the principle of all morals in the modern era," Fichte commented in his *Grundzüge des gegenwärtigen Zeitalters*, a sentiment uncannily similar to those of French conservative critic Joseph de Maistre, who insisted that scholars must "examine our European institutions one by one and . . . show how they are all *Christianized*, how religion mingles in everything, animates and sustains everything."[37] For Germans, in particular, this mingling of religion and institutions was proof of the inextricability of religion from culture.

This entanglement of religion and culture had two sides. First, it had an anthropological aspect, one rooted in a definition of culture as *any* set of human social, intellectual, and religious practices. In this aspect, culture had only a descriptive and historical function. Religion was—as in Herder—conceptually crucial to this anthropological culture because it represented the most coherent, distinctive, and universal set of practices known to mankind. Next to Schleiermacher's "anthropological" theology, for example, were Friedrich Schlegel's

[33] Wunch and Eldredge, "Gabler," 139.

[34] Ferdinand Christian Baur, *Kirchengeschichte des neunzehnten Jahrhunderts* (Tübingen, 1862), 89.

[35] Barth, *Protestant Theology*, 425–26.

[36] Wilhelm Dilthey, *Leben Schleiermachers* (Berlin: Georg Reimer, 1870), 378, 420.

[37] Johann Fichte, "Die Grundzüge des gegenwärtigen Zeitalters," in *Gesamtausgabe* (Stuttgart, 1991), 8:325–26, 365; Joseph de Maistre, *Considerations on France*, trans. and ed. Richard A. Lebrun (Cambridge, 1994), 42.

ruminations on the nature of *Urreligion.* At the beginning of time, "there was one, original religion. . . . the degeneration and the depravation of [this] is . . . the primary generative cause of the religion of revealed law."[38] Religion, in other words, preceded all of its formal incarnations; in Friedrich Schelling's words, "Christianity existed before [paganism]."[39] For all three—opposed in nearly all else—there was a consensus that religion was a primordial and essential feature of human development. In parallel to this general anthropological bent were investigations that assigned more specific anthropological principles to religion. David Strauss's mythical account of the life of Jesus, for example, was couched in a precise language of cultural development: "The religion and sacred literature of the Greeks and Hebrews had been gradually developed with the development of the nation, and it was not until the intellectual culture of the people had outgrown the religion of their fathers, and the latter was in consequence verging towards decay, that . . . varying interpretations became [possible]."[40] Although Strauss and Schleiermacher began in radically different places—the latter with "the ideal of the dogmatic Christ" and the former with "the historical Jesus of Nazareth"—each was able to launch anthropological approaches to religion that took it as a fundamental expression and cornerstone of every human culture.[41] Even outside this particular circle, this became a commonplace. Ludwig Feuerbach, whose 1841 *Essence of Christianity* was only one of many similarly titled investigations from the period, spoke of religion as "man's earliest and also indirect form of self-knowledge. Hence religion everywhere precedes philosophy; as in the history of the race, so also in that of the individual."[42] Then, when Karl Marx inverted Feuerbach—instead of "descend[ing] from heaven to earth, here we ascend from earth to heaven"—and made religion a product of social and material conditions, he was only adding to the various nineteenth-century ways of accounting for religion as a *cultural* phenomenon.[43]

But the union of religion and culture had another aspect, a normative and ultimately political one rooted in the sense that "culture" describes not just man as he is, but also as he ought to be. In this sense, culture offered a set of aspirations, a body of human knowledge that represented the best humanity had to offer. The Luther Bible was made into a piece of culture because it offered a vision of a normative German heritage steeped with both history and spirituality. Similarly,

[38] Friedrich Schlegel, review of J. G. Rohde, *Über den Anfang unserer Geschichte*, in *Kritische Friedrich-Schlegel-Ausgabe* (Munich, 1975), 8:496.

[39] Friedrich Schelling, "Ueber das Studium der Theologie," in *Die Idee der deutschen Universität*, ed. Ernst Anrich (Darmstadt, 1964), 75.

[40] Strauss, *Jesus*, 17.

[41] David Strauss, *The Christ of Faith and the Jesus of History: A Critique of Schleiermacher's* Life of Jesus, trans. Leander Keck (Philadelphia, 1977), 169.

[42] Ludwig Feuerbach, from *Das Wesen des Christenthum* in *Religious Thought in the Nineteenth Century*, ed. Bernard Reardon (Cambridge, 1966), 95.

[43] Karl Marx and Friedrich Engels, *The German Ideology* (New York, 1947), 14.

for Novalis and others, religious culture was bound to normative judgments. It was no accident that, for them, authentic religious culture could only be found in Germany. In building the new religious rebirth, it was the Germans who "first took the slow but sure way" by forging a "higher epoch of culture." In this epoch, Germans would find "a new history, a new humanity, the sweetest embrace of a youthful and surprised church and a living God, and the inner conception of a new Messiah."[44] Schleiermacher himself—a workhorse of German nationalism in the period following the Napoleonic wars—was already convinced in 1799 that only his German audience would understand his true revolution:

> To whom shall I turn with this matter other than you? . . . you are the only ones capable, and thus also worthy, of having the sense for holy and divine things aroused in you. . . . Here in my ancestral land is the fortunate climate that denies no fruit completely. . . . Here, therefore, [religion] must find a refuge from the coarse barbarism and the cold earthly sense of the age.[45]

Religious man was not only Christian man but, culturally, also German man. In a sense, this move to a national rhetoric is not shocking, especially if we believe Benedict Anderson's claim that the loss of "the idea that a particular script-language offered privileged access to ontological truth" was an essential precondition to modern nationalism.[46] As the Bible was separated from universal theological truth—and reconfigured as a particular cultural document—and as theology itself conformed to an ideal of religious culture, the nation in effect stepped in to guarantee the cohesiveness of (religious) community. Luther's Bible was one key plank in this nationalist rhetoric of culture: the Luther Bible in effect guaranteed the integrity of culture. It allowed German culture to free itself from bondage to Oriental and foreign texts, to become autonomous. German Christianity followed the model of the Bible as, over the course of the nineteenth century, the idea of a religious culture became the banner for generations anxious to rejuvenate a specifically German religion. As Friedrich Graf put it, culture and its composites—moral culture, political culture, Christian culture—became the "leading concepts of theological reflection" in Germany.[47] More bitter were the late-century comments of the Jesuit Robert von Nostitz-Reineck, that "always the talk is of culture. . . . the cultural life of the culture-man, the cultural mission of the cultural peoples, the cultural progress of our age is all the time celebrated and praised . . . everywhere culture and no end of it."[48]

[44] Novalis, "Christenheit," 519.

[45] Schleiermacher, *On Religion*, 85–86.

[46] Anderson, *Imagined Communities*, 36.

[47] Friedrich Wilhelm Graf, "'Christliche Kultur'? Über die konfessionellen Kulturen im Europa des 19. Jahrhunderts," in *Gott im Selbstbewusstsein der Moderne* (Gütersloh, 1993), 184.

[48] Robert von Nostitz-Rieneck, *Das Problem der Cultur* [1888], quoted in ibid.

Jesuits were not the only ones with cause for concern about this new cultural religion. For the German effort to weld together culture and religion was performed on the back of the religious group who, it was thought, evidenced an anthropologically cohesive culture that consistently failed to live up to the normative expectations of culture more generally. Just as the cultural Bible implied that the Hebrew Bible had become what Schleiermacher called a "mausoleum"—a monument for a dead people—so too was it already clear to Christian scholars that no community was more rigorously excluded from this new cultural ideal of religion than those most slavishly dedicated to this monument, the Jews. Judaism, Schleiermacher insisted, "is long since a dead religion, and those who at present still bear its colors are actually sitting and mourning beside the undecaying mummy . . . [it] has long persevered, as a single fruit, after all the life force has vanished from the branch, often remains hanging until the bleakest season on a withered stem and dries up on it."[49] Because of its dependency on an immutable Bible, Judaism was condemned to contemporary irrelevance, absolutely distinct from this entity that Schleiermacher called Christianity. In contrast to Germans freed from the originals by the work of Luther, Judaism remained imprisoned by its original texts, enslaved because it could never translate the Bible for a modern world. It was no accident that Schleiermacher virtually never preached on the Old Testament, or that, in his *Brief Outline of the Study of Theology*, he excluded all Jewish custom and the entire Old Testament from the purview of Christian theology. Knowledge of "primitive Christianity . . . can only be obtained from the Christian documents originating in this age of the Christian Church," and even these documents are only useful "insofar as they are held capable of contributing to the original, and therefore for all times normative, representation of Christianity."[50] As the Jewish scholar Abraham Geiger rightly noted, Schleiermacher completely destroyed "the old link between the Hebrew Bible and the so-called New Testament."[51] For Schleiermacher, the latter alone was the sole document worthy of attention by the Christian theologian and the Christian exegete. The first edition of the *Outline* (1811) said it clearly: "to include the Jewish codex within the canon means to view Christianity as a development of Judaism and contradicts the whole idea of the canon."[52] Over the course of the nineteenth century, this "flight from the . . . historical Jesus" came to define German biblical scholarship, which, as Susannah Heschel has so beautifully shown, consistently rejected the Jewish origins of Christianity in favor of a religion in which (to paraphrase Kant) Judaism was euthanized.[53]

[49] Schleiermacher, *On Religion*, 211, 213.

[50] Schleiermacher, *Brief Outline of the Study of Theology*, trans. Terrence N. Tice (Richmond, VA, 1966), 46, 50.

[51] Abraham Geiger, "Die Schleiermacher-Feier und die Juden," *Jüdische Zeitschrift für Wissenschaft und Leben* 7 (1869): 213.

[52] Schleiermacher, *Brief Outline*, 53.

[53] Heschel, *Geiger*, 144. On Kant's language (from the *Conflict of the Faculties*), see Hess, *Germans,*

At the root of this exclusion was, once again, this peculiar new thing called culture. If Christianity was an expression of German culture, Judaism expressed the culture of the Jews. Such a culture was, by definition, intransigent. And so religion—usually understood in the modern era as an expression of personal choice—settled into firm immobility. The ultimate theoretical and (sometimes) practical guarantee of Jewish religious parity, namely conversion, suffered a fall in reputation in some quarters, given up as a missionary ideal by some Christians and, in some circles, proclaimed a sheer impossibility. The 1791 dissolution of the *Institutum Judaicum* in Halle can be read as a symbol of the former, while Schleiermacher's heated disagreement with David Friedländer (over the latter's scheme to convert nominally the Berlin Jews in order to achieve political and civil rights) marked a new sense of the permanence of religious conditions.[54] Jews should not have to convert to gain political rights, argued Schleiermacher: their political rights should be independent of their religious status. In any case, "Judaism and its spirit sits so deeply" in these Jews that they will "remain always a Jew" no matter if they are baptized. "It is impossible for someone who has truly embraced a religion to accept another one": in this statement burned an anthropology of religion, one that saw religion as so deeply embedded in the structure of humans that its alteration is, in all true senses, utterly impossible.[55] For this reason Schleiermacher rejected the model proposed in the anonymous *Political-Theological Task* that with adequate "acculturation" of the "heart, disposition, [and] way of thinking" of the Jews, they could be awarded civil rights and freedoms.[56] Religion was not a matter of "schooling or instruction." Instead it was inscribed with indelible firmness into the heart of men.[57]

Schleiermacher was hardly alone in seeing the Jews as a symbol of intractable resistance to real religion. Olof Tychsen's sentiment, that "a Jew baptised did not cease to be a Jew," was only one expression of this.[58] A more virulent form came from Schleiermacher's colleague at the new Prussian university in Berlin, William de Wette, who proposed not merely a discontinuity between Judaism and Christianity but their absolute opposition: "neither one tolerates the other;

Jews, 157. More generally, see Amy Newman, "The Death of Judaism in German Protestant Thought from Luther to Hegel," *Journal of the American Academy of Religion* 61 (Fall 1993): 455–84.

[54] On conversion in this period, see Jacob Katz, *Out of the Ghetto* (Cambridge, MA, 1973), 105ff. Conversion of the Jews was never completely outside the Germany imagination—in 1822, after all, Frederick Wilhelm III approved the new "Society for the Propagation of Christianity among the Jews" (Michael Meyer, "The Religious Reform Controversy in the Berlin Jewish Community, 1814–1823," *Leo Baeck Institute Year Book* 24 [1979]: 147.)

[55] Schleiermacher, *Briefe bei Gelegenheit der politisch-theologischer Aufgabe und des Sendschreibens jüdischer Hausväter*, in *Kritische Gesamtausgabe* (Berlin, 1984), 2.1:345–47 (hereafter cited KGA).

[56] Anonymous, "Politisch-theologische Aufgabe über die Behandlung der jüdische Täuflinge" (1799), in Schleiermacher, *KGA*, 2.1:378.

[57] Schleiermacher, *On Religion*, 207.

[58] Katz, *Out of the Ghetto*, 112.

their basic ideas, their innermost essences are different from each other; and yet, incredibly, a great number of Christians strive to give Jews German civil rights."[59] De Wette's extremism was not necessarily the norm (if the 1812 Prussian Act of Emancipation was any indication), but even those who advocated Jewish political freedom (as Schleiermacher did) and saw the Jews as educable (as Schleiermacher did not) were adamant that what would be called "religious culture" was an ingrained feature of a people. In 1807, for example, at the moment of the founding of the Berlin university, the head of the reformed Prussian *Kultus und Unterrichtsministerium*—the ministry for religion and education—Karl von Altenstein advocated for a total renewal of German religious education, education that would start with the Jews. The goal was not to make Christians of them, but merely to make them into citizens "less dangerous to the state": "the only way to effect reform is to found educational institutes for them, in which they will be kept so busy that they cannot be spoiled by the Talmud."[60] But as Altenstein's sentiments indicated, even such an education would not remove the Jewish character of the student. Indeed, as the century waned, the sense that Judaism was utterly distinct from Christianity grew only more ubiquitous among Protestant scholars. If racialized anti-Semitism was still in its very earliest forms in German life, still nearly all agreed that the *culture* of Judaism was the central dilemma.

It is important not to be seized by the lunatic ravings that will come later, however, and to see *why* the Jews were sucked into this particular vortex here. The answer, I believe, returns us back to the amalgamation of religion and culture in the early nineteenth century. If, as Wilhelm Dilthey later wrote, Schleiermacher "gave himself . . . the task of reconciling religion and culture," he did so as part of this "great spiritual revolution" that shook the period.[61] For the politician Altenstein, the discussion of the Jews was only part of a larger discussion of how religion might be profitably integrated into a new Prussian state and, more specifically, into a new theory of religious instruction. The "high priest" of religious instruction should see religion not as a "simple morality or . . . formulas" but must be able to honor "all religious sects" and distinguish between "merely human works" and the "interiority and spirituality" that is the essence of religion.[62] But this effort to define the essence of religion as "interiority" was *not* religiously neutral. Indeed, it was prejudicial against the Jews, seen by Christians as the most fanatical connoisseurs of external trappings. Even that paragon of the new Prussian humanism, Wilhelm von Humboldt, was caught by this language. As someone who argued vigorously in 1809 for the immediate emancipation of the Jews and someone who

[59] De Wette, "Über den Verfall," 332.

[60] Altenstein's "Erzeihungs- oder Unterrichtspolizei," 11 September 1807, in Ernst Müsebeck, *Das Preussische Kultusministerium vor hundert Jahren* (Stuttgart, 1918), 246.

[61] Dilthey, *Leben Schleiermachers*, 420.

[62] Altenstein's "Erzeihungs- oder Unterrichtspolizei," 252–53.

insisted that, from the legal perspective of the state, the "word *Jew* [should] not be pronounced with any other meaning than the religious," nonetheless Humboldt could not but ascribe an essential (and alien) culture to the Jews. It was this culture that the Jews would, in his view, overcome over the course of generations, when

> [i]ndividuals will see that they have *no real religion* and only a ceremonial law and, driven by an innate human need for a higher faith, will turn to Christianity by themselves. Their conversion, which now—when they leave behind their oppressed brethren and cast back upon them the burden they used to share, in order to be given the name *baptized Jew* among fully franchised Christians—is only justifiable under special circumstances, will then become desirable, joyful, and salutary.[63]

And so, like Schleiermacher, Novalis, de Wette, and many others, Humboldt revealed the double-edged sword of this new cultural religion. On the one hand, religion was redefined, and made abstract, deracinated from the particularisms of Protestantism, Catholicism, Judaism, and so forth. On the other, religious culture was invented as a mark of permanent distinction. Only for Germans—as Novalis said it—did a particular religious culture and a universally true religion combine in perfect harmony.

Given this increased ambivalence about the Jews, then, it was not terribly surprising that professional philological scholarship would be marked by a significant shift away from Hebrew antiquities and toward classical ones. Where, for Eichhorn, the Old Testament still contained the "history of the entire human race," this sentiment seemed absurd to the new rising star of the philological sciences, Friedrich August Wolf.[64] Just as Luther freed the Germans from Jewish culture on the level of religion, Wolf "unquestionably" excluded "*Asians* and *Africans* . . . as literarily uncultivated, and merely civilized peoples . . . from [the] boundaries" of the study of ancient antiquities. Hebrews might be a holy people, but their literary remains testify to a character "heterogeneous" to that of Europe, Rome, and Greece.[65] Greek philologists, as August Boeckh insisted, were best poised to teach the German nation, "since they had before their eyes the example of a people who preserved a *Bildung* independent of 'foreign' influence."[66] And this *Bildung* was particularly suited to the German temperament. Only in Greece (and occasionally Rome), could be found what Wolf called the roots and foundation of true "spiritual culture," "higher culture," "better culture,"

[63] Humboldt's "Über den Entwurf zu einer neuen Konstitution für die Juden," 17 July 1809 in *Gesammelte Schriften* (Berlin, 1968), 10:101, 102, 105.

[64] Eichhorn, *Einleitung*, 15.

[65] Friedrich August Wolf, "Darstellung der Altherthums-Wissenschaft" [1807] in *Kleine Schriften*, ed. G. Bernhardy (Halle, 1869), 818–19.

[66] Brian Vick, "Greek Origins and Organic Metaphors: Ideals of Cultural Autonomy in Neohumanist Germany," *Journal of the History of Ideas* 63 (July 2002): 495.

"national culture," "scholarly culture," "common culture," in short "European culture."[67] Although Wolf 's disdain for Hebrew antiquities was hardly a universal sentiment, still his sense that the distance between Athens and Jerusalem had suddenly increased was not. What the early twentieth-century neohumanist Werner Jaeger (himself a product of this new separation) called the "emancipation" of philology from "theology and jurisprudence" depended on this shift—one of the "hallmarks of the professional (particularly Prussian) classicist"—away from Hebrew antiquities to the nearly exclusive study of Greece.[68]

More surprising perhaps was the embrace by Jews themselves of this religion and culture synthesis. Since the days of Mendelssohn and the *Haskalah*, German Jews had striven long to distinguish themselves from the "state inside a state" notion of Judaism that had long stymied the progress of civil emancipation. This notion would insist that the Jews constituted a distinctive legal and social polity that could not help but compete with the state for the affections of its adherents. Because Jews were unable to fulfill the demands of the state, went this argument, the state was under no obligation to confer citizenship. The so-called *Maskilim*—the advocates of reformed Judaism in the generation following Mendelssohn's death—worked hard to erode this and reconstitute Judaism as "a religion, not a nationality."[69] As David Fränkel said in 1807, "We no longer constitute a distinct entity but . . . are merely members of the state."[70] "The Jews are absolutely not a *people*. . . . They are to be regarded only as a *confession*," was another formulation of the same idea, and was part of a program to develop Judaism into a religion founded less on ceremonial tradition than on firm dogmatic tenets.[71] Of course the parallels with Schleiermacher's own efforts to distinguish "religion" per se from the mausoleum of historical traditions that surrounded it were clear: both were concerned (for different reasons, of course) to differentiate the core of religion from its extraneous trappings.

But in tandem with this insistence on Jewish "religion" came the seemingly contradictory insistence that Judaism was indeed a "distinct entity," the manifestation of a "people." As Michael Meyer has argued, these two trends went hand in hand in someone like Salomon Steinheim, who used the doctrinal essence of Judaism as the mark of what "set Judaism once and for all sharply apart from its pagan surroundings." For Steinheim, like Schleiermacher, Judaism and Christianity were utterly distinct, both doctrinally and in the communities and cultures

[67] Wolf, "Darstellung," 817, 818, 821, 822, 857, 875, 882.

[68] Werner Jaeger, "Philologie und Historie," in *Humanistische Reden und Vorträge* (Berlin, 1960), 4; Marchand, *Down from Olympus*, 24; see also Anthony Grafton, "Juden und Griechen bei Friedrich August Wolf," in *Friedrich August Wolf: Studien, Dokumente, Bibliographie*, ed. Reinhard Markner and Giuseppe Veltri (Stuttgart, 1999).

[69] Michael Meyer, *The Origins of the Modern Jew* (Detroit, 1967), 121.

[70] David Sorkin, *The Transformation of German Jewry, 1780–1840* (Oxford, 1987), 101.

[71] Meyer, *Modern Jew*, 141.

that developed around them.[72] And this turn to a cultural reading of Judaism was nowhere more pronounced than in the movement that began with the 1819 Society for the Culture and Scholarship of the Jews and blossomed into what is now known as the *Wissenschaft des Judentums*. The first (and only) issue of the Society's journal—the *Journal for the Scholarship of Judaism*—opened its pages with an extravagant elegy to the particularity of the Jews:

> From its first formation until our own time, i.e. for a period of at least three millennia, Judaism has preserved itself as a characteristic and independent whole. . . . all that has come forth from Judaism everywhere bears the imprint of [the same] basic idea and reveals it in every form. . . . Judaism, as a result of its own inner characteristics, has always remained strange and isolated.[73]

The embrace of the cultural integrity of Judaism—along with the affirmation of its strangeness and isolation—was in turn the systematic assumption of the most sophisticated member of this circle, Leopold Zunz, who ranged far and wide in his search for the full panoply of Jewish historical texts. "Our scholarship should . . . emancipate itself from the theologians," this student of Friedrich August Wolf declared in his 1845 *On History and Literature*, and treat the Jewish textual corpus as cultural patrimony.[74] Rabbinic texts like the *halakhah* were, for him, "national texts . . . the property of everyone—the results of a thousand-year development, monuments of the life of the nation, the achievements of its best minds."[75] The Society thus embraced the identification of Jews as a culture and determined that their scholarly task was to "discover the cultural content of Judaism."[76]

This affirmation of a culture of Judaism may have been a purely scholarly task. Or it may have reflected the social reality of "an independent social world reinforced by a separate cultural identity" that, as David Sorkin has shown, was characteristic of the emancipationist Jews of the early nineteenth century.[77] Whatever the case may be, Heine's self-identification as the "Jew that can never be washed off" was symptomatic of a larger sensibility—driven by the huge intellectual shifts in ideals of religion and culture—that would permeate

[72] Michael Meyer, "Judaism and Christianity," in *German-Jewish History in Modern Times* (New York, 1996), 2:186.

[73] Immanuel Wolf, "On the Concept of a Science of Judaism," (1822) trans. Lionel Kochan, *Leo Baeck Institute Year Book* 2 (1957): 194.

[74] Leopold Zunz, *Zur Geschichte und Literatur* (Berlin, 1845), 1:20. On Zunz and Wolf, see Meyer, *Modern Jew*, 159.

[75] Ismar Schorsch, "Scholarship in the Service of Reform," *Leo Baeck Institute Year Book* 35 (1990): 81

[76] Meyer, *Modern Jew*, 167.

[77] Sorkin, *Transformation*, 134.

the period.[78] By the middle of the nineteenth century, the sense of the Bible as a cultural text—and the concomitant sense that religion itself had an essential cultural core—became a commonplace in Germany, among theologians, literati, and pedagogues. Of course, the Bible was never *only* culture: plenty of theologians would speak with reverence of the Bible's divine authority. But the cultural core of the Bible became a fundamental assumption. On the one hand, the Hebrew and Greek Bibles were read and studied as expressions of the underlying cultural tendencies of the Jewish and ancient Christian communities, a basic assumption that drove the efforts (among Christians) to distinguish between the Old and New Testaments and (among Jews) to rediscover their essential affinities. On the other hand, the Luther Bible was itself enshrined as a cultural text, a foundational script for the establishment of the German language, literature, politics, and culture. A real German religion and thus a distinctive German spiritual heritage was possible only because the Luther Bible had freed Germany from the enslavement of the originals. And so the Luther Bible was transformed into the founding event of the German nation and Luther himself made into the man

> who more than any other hit the sincere, exact, rough, powerful, healthy expression and tone of the people. No academic lexicon should be the canon of language, but rather [this canon should be] a book in which a new humanity schools and cultivates itself, and that happened in Germany, like nowhere else, through a people's book, [the Luther Bible].[79]

Invested with the power of nation building, the vernacular Bible—the originally canonical work—was put thus into the heart of the new cultural canon that developed in the nineteenth century, its authority guaranteed and its influence ensured for generations to come. And with it was enshrined the "idea of *Kultur* with a capital K," whose history, as Thomas Mann sadly commented, would shape and misshape generations of Germans well into the inferno of the twentieth century.[80]

[78] Michael Meyer, "Becoming German, Remaining Jewish," in *German-Jewish History,* 2:209.

[79] Georg Gervinus, *Geschichte der poetischen National-Literatur der Deutschen* (Leipzig, 1835), 2:454. On Gervinus and others, see Michael A. Batts, *A History of Histories of German Literature, 1835–1914* (Montreal, 1993).

[80] Thomas Mann, "Kultur und Socialismus" (1928), in *Gesammelte Werke* (Oldenburg, 1960), 12:644.

Chapter Nine

"REGENERATION FROM GERMANY": CULTURE AND THE BIBLE IN ENGLAND, 1780–1870

IF THE CULTURAL Bible stormed across Germany in the early nineteenth century, in England, it was a more hesitant process. It began with great promise in the 1780s, as English scholars began to recognize that their biblical scholarship had fallen far behind their continental neighbors. In contrast to "Dutch and German philologists of the eighteenth century [who] . . . vigorously carried forwards their disquisitions" on the Bible, complained one critic, the English had not "sufficiently adverted to the necessity of *Critical Philology*."[1] In the last twenty years of the eighteenth century, scholars from across the religious spectrum tried to make up this deficit. From Unitarians like Gilbert Wakefield and William Hopkins, to Catholics like Alexander Geddes, to Jews like Isaac Delgado, these decades saw a virtual explosion in sacred translation in the British Isles, an explosion that compressed together a variety of themes familiar from the German scene: the sense that the older translations were in need of revision, the sense that the Bible could only be protected from skeptics by transfiguring its vernacular face, the sense that scholarship was the key to this transfiguration. It was crucial, believed many in the period, to offer the nation "a New Translation, or a Revision of the present Translation, of the Holy Scriptures" in order to destroy the "foundations on which free-principled men have built their cavils against the truth and purity of our religion."[2] This exuberance for biblical renovation would be short-lived, however. Above all, this exuberance was broken by the resurgent religious orthodoxies that dominated England during and after the Napoleonic Wars. The cultural Bible would only find its home in English letters long after the turbulence of the 1790s, on the wings of a "regeneration coming from Germany."[3]

[1] *Eclectic Review* 5 (1809): 29, 24.

[2] Lowth, *Isaiah*, lxix.; *Eclectic Review* 5 (1809): 9. This shift has also been noted, in different form, in Mandelbrote, "The Bible and Its Readers," 60–61.

[3] Ieuan Ellis, *Seven against Christ: A Study of "Essays and Reviews"* (Leiden, 1980), 1.

The Birth and Death of the Enlightenment Bible in England, 1780–1800

Ten years before the French Revolution, England's scholars discovered that—like their colleagues in Germany—their Bible was crying out for rehabilitation. Some complained about its shortfalls: Isaac Delgado's *New English Translation of the Pentateuch* "lamented, that, in a Christian country, which abounds with men eminent for their abilities and learning, a correction of the present translation of the Bible . . . hath been hitherto neglected."[4] Similarly, John Mead Ray—whose 1799 *Revised Translation and Interpretation of the Sacred Scriptures after the Eastern Manner* was one of only two new translations of the entire Bible generated in the eighteenth century—mourned those "ridiculous or barbarous absurdities which furnished hardened sinners and hypocrites with excuses, libertines and Atheists with matter of jesting."[5] But others were optimistic that they could effect this rehabilitation. The Unitarian Hopkins's 1784 *Exodus: A Corrected Translation* was to be the first step toward "a new translation of the Bible" that he hoped might be "undertaken by public authority, formed upon a corrected Hebrew Bible."[6] For his part, the Presbyterian George Campbell thought 1789 a particularly auspicious time to revise the Bible, a time when "learning is in more hands," "critics are multiplied," and "the press is open." Forcing people to read a faulty King James Bible is "exceedingly incongruous to the spirit of [our] religion," he declared, and this sentiment rang true for many in the period.[7]

Across the board (with one exception) all of these translators agreed that only scholarship could recuperate a Bible threatened by libertinism. Benjamin Kennicott's compilation of the Old Testament manuscripts, for example, was much admired. His *Exodus*, Hopkins declared, was inspired "by the late learned Dr. Kennicott's edition of the Hebrew Bible," and William Green's 1781 *Poetical Parts of the Old Testament*, though not entirely satisfied with Kennicott's collations, praised its effect of "deliver[ing] us from the shackles of the Hebrew Verity."[8] Campbell's twelve prefaces—on the "Language and Idiom of the New Testament," the "Origin of the Changes produced on . . . the Idiom of the Jews," the "Style of Scripture History," and so on—were testament enough to the sense that good translation was a product of philological scholarship. Even evangelicals like Josiah Pratt embraced "the business of sacred criticism" as a

[4] Isaac Delgado, *A New English Translation of the Pentateuch* (London, 1789), v.

[5] John Mead Ray [aka David Macrae], *A Revised Translation and Interpretation of the Sacred Scriptures after the Eastern Manner* (London, 1799), a2^{r}.

[6] William Hopkins, *Exodus: A Corrected Translation* (London, 1784), vii.

[7] George Campbell, *The Four Gospels* [1789] (Boston, 1811), 1:li. On Campbell, see Jeffrey M. Suderman, *Orthodoxy and Enlightenment: George Campbell in the Eighteenth Century* (Montreal, 2001).

[8] Hopkins, *Exodus*, v; William Green, *Poetical Parts of the Old Testament* (Cambridge, 1781), viii.

tool for studying Scripture, and his proposed *New Polyglott Bible* would have included Kennicott's Hebrew text, the "Chaldee paraphrases," and the Samaritan Pentateuch, among other texts.[9] And the exception to this general veneration of philological scholarship itself furnished more proof of the rule. Isaac Delgado felt the pressure of a philological scholarship threatening to colonize the Hebrew and English Bibles alike and thus, like other Jewish scholars in late-century England, tried to "justify the traditional Hebrew text of the Bible as authentic."[10]

This philological interest was not confined solely to that manuscript fetishism that had so characterized earlier eighteenth-century English scholarship. Although Kennicott was certainly appreciated, the translators of the 1780s tried to follow the footsteps of Lowth, reaching out to what Campbell called "the rites, customs, and incidents, well known to the natives of the writer's country." Thus Campbell's annotation, for example, to Luke 2.2 ("all the world should be enrolled") presented readers with a minor treatise on ancient Roman taxation and the census while Matt. 13.25 occasioned a minor botanical excursus on the "weeds" sown with the "good seed" in the field.[11] The perfect translator, as Alexander Geddes remarked, was a polymath: "Poets, philosophers, historians, philologists, geographers, naturalists–all ought to enter into his plan of reading; because from all he may, occasionally, derive advantage. Nor should modern travels, voyages and topographical descriptions escape his notice. In short he must be as much as possible a universal scholar."[12] James Macknight's 1790 *Literal Translation . . . of all the Apostolical Epistles* made sure to offer "those allusions to ancient manners and historical facts, implied in the phraseology, by which the age and nation of the authors of these writers are known."[13] Similarly, when the *Critical Review* examined Wakefield's 1783 *New Translation of the Gospel of Matthew*, it praised his attention to "oriental idioms," "context and connection," and "the peculiar circumstances and customs" of the Bible.[14] And one of the peculiar customs that Wakefield highlighted concerned our old friend the locust: "*Locusts* were *animals* permitted to the *Jews*. . . . [They] are commonly eaten in the *East*. . . . *Dampier*, in his *Voyage*, mentions a *locust* that the *Tonquinese*, I think, commonly eat."[15]

Given such newfound interest in biblical translation and scholarship, it would hardly be surprising if these translators and scholars turned to the Germans for inspiration. And in certain cases, they did, none more dramatically than

[9] Josiah Pratt, *Prospectus with Specimens of a New Polyglott Bible* (Oxford, 1797), 13, 8.

[10] Delgado, *Pentateuch*, vii; Ruderman, *Jewish Enlightenment*, 21, 226.

[11] Campbell, *Four Gospels*, xvi, 4:269f., 103f.

[12] Alexander Geddes, *Prospectus of a New Translation of the Holy Bible* (Glasgow, 1786), 140.

[13] James Macknight, *New Literal Translation from the Original Greek, of All the Apostolical Epistles* [1790] (Boston, 1810), 30.

[14] *Critical Review* 55 (1783): 131.

[15] Wakefield, *A New Translation of the Gospel of Matthew* (Warrington, 1782), 41.

Alexander Geddes, who offered a prodigious list of German (and Dutch) exemplars in his *Prospectus*—including "Koppe, Schnurrer, Eichorn, Cramer, Teller, Scheidius, Biel, Knappe, Doederleim [*sic*], Dathe, Rare, Griesbach, Velthusen, Woide, Maldenhover, Adler," and more—who together had "dispelled more clouds . . . than perhaps the writers of any other nation."[16] In Germany, Geddes applauded, "almost every man of learning is an Orientalist. In short, Sacred Criticism is everywhere the predominant study of the learned of all communions. . . ."[17] None was more inspiring to Geddes than Johann David Michaelis: "His erudition, taste and judgment are well known in the literary world by his numerous and varied productions; and his version of the Old Testament, which is now happily concluded, must appear to those, who can relish all its beauties, one of the best that ever was made."[18] Taking leave from the Germans, Geddes resolved over the course of fifteen years to produce an entirely renovated Bible. It would contain an Old Testament free of dependence of the Masoretic text and a New Testament founded on the best work of scholars like Mill, Bengel, Wettstein, and Griesbach. Like the Germans, Geddes proposed to exert the most "severe rational critique" to produce a text on the same footing as those secular works of "Homer, Virgil, Milton, Shakspeare [*sic*]."[19] The creation of an authoritative and authentic vernacular Bible required not the separation of sacred and secular literatures but their equivalence. The Bible must be held to the same standard as any literature, in short; and that "straining" (in Campbell's words) after dogmatic purity that marred the criticism of Scripture—straining never found in classical criticism—must vanish.[20] "The BIBLE! the BIBLE! Is the original text of the Bible to be corrected" like any text? "With a proper deference and due distinction, I answer, undoubtedly it is," concluded Geddes.[21]

But Geddes's enthusiasm for things German—indeed the enthusiasm of scholars from across the religious spectrum for a rehabilitated Bible—was destined to die a quick and painful death. As scholars noticed some years ago, "in the 1780s and the first years of the 1790s there was considerable interest in, and knowledge of, the German Biblical criticism," but this interest was strenuously opposed as the "political climate darkened" in the years following the French Revolution.[22] Few attracted such opposition as Geddes, whose work on the Bible

[16] Geddes, *Prospectus*, 122, 121.

[17] Reginald Fuller, *Alexander Geddes, 1737–1802: A Pioneer of Biblical Criticism* (Sheffield, 1984), 29.

[18] Geddes, *Prospectus*, 83.

[19] Geddes, *Dr. Geddes Address to the Public on the Publication of the First Volume of his New Translation of the Bible* (London, 1793), 5.

[20] Campbell, *Four Gospels*, 2:404.

[21] Geddes, *Prospectus*, 57.

[22] E. S. Schaffer, *"Kubla Khan" and The Fall of Jerusalem: The Mythological School in Biblical Criticism and Secular Literature, 1770–1880* (Cambridge, 1975), 22. See also Prickett, *Words and* the Word.

brought down a storm of invective on his head. He was denounced (in his own words) as "an Oppositionist, a Republican, a Democrate, a Reformist, a Liberty of the Press-man, a Painist, a Leveller, an Antaristocrate, and, to sum up all, a violent FOXITE, disaffected to Government and hostile to the British Constitution."[23] The spearhead of the anti-Geddes campaign was the fiercely partisan *Anti-Jacobin Review*, which branded Geddes with the unenviable titles of "desperate renegado . . . audacious leveler . . . a mere pygmy." Like Tom Paine, Geddes was the kind of critic that "effected the revolution in France" and his "attack[s] upon . . . Scripture" were, in the reviewer's eyes, "civil crime[s]" fully deserving prosecution by an offended state.[24] And Geddes's offenses were minor, the *Anti-Jacobin Review* laboriously showed, compared to that "exotic poison from the envenomed crucibles of . . . the new German school" that threatened to corrupt the very soul of English life.[25] The "passion for German Literature . . . making rapid strides among my countrymen" was a lamentable but "systematic plan for corrupting the public taste and national morality of Englishmen."[26] The "violent love of paradox, of novelty, and of extravagant positions" that so characterized German intellectual production was the illness causing that German disdain for religion epitomized by "the principles of Eichhorn."[27]

This distaste for things German was not simply a symptom of the English aversion to continental novelties (although it was that also). In the sphere of religion, rather, it also originated in a wholesale shift in attitudes toward the Bible in the mainstream of the Anglican Church in the last decades of the eighteenth century. Anglicans—who had pioneered many of the general themes of the Enlightenment Bible in the early part of the century—turned away from the liberal assumptions of historical biblical scholarship and instead moved decisively toward a more traditional view of the Bible as a work of divine inspiration. As the Unitarian Joseph Priestley put it, by 1790, "the body of the clergy seem[ed] to be more orthodox than they were in the last reign, and more bigotted."[28] "The people of England liked old things" after the French Revolution, John Stuart Mill later wrote, and chief among the venerable icons of stability was the Bible.[29] This reverence for the traditional was spread across England's two great religious revivals at the turn of the century: the reinvigorated High Church movement that would culminate with the Tractarians in the 1830s and the Evangelical explosion that took place under the auspices of such

[23] Geddes, *Address*, 12–13.

[24] *Anti-Jacobin Review* 1 (1798): 695, 436.

[25] *Anti-Jacobin Review* 4 (1799): vii.

[26] *Anti-Jacobin Review* 5 (1800): 568.

[27] *Anti-Jacobin Review* 6 (1800): 563, 571.

[28] Peter B. Nockles, *The Oxford Movement in Context: Anglican High Churchmanship, 1760–1857* (Cambridge, 1994), 290.

[29] John Mill, "Coleridge," [1852] in *Utilitarianism and Other Essays*, ed. Alan Ryan (London, 1987), 203.

luminaries as William Wilberforce. Whatever their theological differences, Wilberforce's sentiment—that the Bible was nothing more or less than humanity's "blessed repository of heavenly truth and consolation"—was precisely matched by those of High Church bishops like William van Mildert, who declared unequivocally that "a right interpretation of [the Bible] depends principally upon a due reverence for Scripture itself, as the work of Divine Inspiration."[30] For Mildert, this meant that "the purity of the Bible" could not be "safely lodged in the hands of Sectarists of all denominations" but had to be firmly guaranteed by "persons of tried and approved orthodoxy."[31] It is with little surprise, then, that we find Hannah More, the princess of the evangelical Clapham sect, lamenting the Germanic influence: "ladies who take the lead in society" ought to "oppose with the whole weight . . . those swarms of publications now daily issuing from the banks of the Danube."[32] German literature, politics, and scholarship all together threatened the integrity of this newly invigorated scriptural piety.

In the face of these new enthusiasms, Priestley's sense—that the Bible was certainly not an "*inspired*" text and indeed was "strange" for modern readers—quickly lost its grip on the English imagination.[33] By 1800 the English were looking for familiarity, not strangeness. In particular, they sought a familiar Bible. The destruction of the materials for Priestley's new Unitarian Bible translation in the Birmingham riots of 1791 offered an apt symbol of this change, as did the ill fortunes of the translation projects of the 1780s and 1790s, which failed decisively in the face of the general English affection—what David Norton has called "A Volatry"—for the King James Version after 1800.[34] "If ever an almost superstitious veneration for our excellent version of the Bible" is required, George Burgos declared in 1796, it was now, when "the spirit of revolution, driving rapidly through the world, assimilates in one discordant and heterogeneous mass the sentiments of the philosopher, the Christian, and the infidel." That appreciation of the literary quality of this version—that sense that it was a "standard of our tongue," as Joseph White put in 1779—which had paralleled the literary veneration of the Luther Bible, took on a new and more polemic edge.[35] Where the literary reading of the Luther Bible was paired with an essentially liberal theological and scriptural agenda, in England this same literary affection was embraced by a conservative and traditional scriptural piety. "A Volatry" took such a firm grasp in England because it accorded so well with the sense that the

[30] William Wilberforce, *A Practical View of the Prevailing Religious System of Professed Christians* [1797] (London, 1829), 14; Nigel Cameron, *Biblical Higher Criticism and the Defense of Infallibilism in 19th Century Britain* (Lewiston, NY, 1987), 27.

[31] E. A. Varley, *The Last of the Prince Bishops: William Van Mildert and the High Church Movement of the Early Nineteenth Century* (Cambridge, 1992), 67.

[32] Walter Roloff, *German Literature in British Magazines, 1750–1860* (Madison, 1949), 46.

[33] Joseph Priestley, *Letters to a Philosophical Unbeliever* (Birmingham, 1787), 2:xiii, xii.

[34] See Shaffer, *"Kubla Khan,"* 24.; Norton, *Bible As Literature*, 299.

[35] Norton, *Bible As Literature*, 262, 245.

traditional Bible should be left essentially untouched. It was in step with this new veneration of the King James Bible that the British and Foreign Bible Society declared in 1804 that "the translation of the Scripture established by Public Authority" would be the only one used by the Society. In a conscious disavowal of scholarship, these cheap Bibles would only be distributed "without note or comment."[36] By the first decade of the nineteenth century, even those who did call for scholarship stopped demanding a new translation: "We do not wish to see our common version, now become venerable by age and prescription, superseded by another entirely *new*; every desirable purpose would be satisfactorily attained by a *faithful* and *well-conducted Revision*."[37] By 1800, then, the fragile bloom of the Enlightenment Bible had withered. Biblical scholarship and translation was painted with the threatening colors of infidels like Tom Paine. To keep the Bible whole, the English devout insisted with ever-greater vehemence on the inspiration, divinity, and theological authority of the biblical text.

The Regeneration: Culture and the Bible in England, circa 1830–1870

If the Enlightenment Bible never flourished in England, the cultural Bible, in contrast, found fertile soil later in the age of Victoria. This cultural Bible—as in Germany—was built out of eighteenth-century stock, built out of a conviction that a post-theological Bible would be authenticated through the practices of poetry, scholarship, history, and pedagogy. And it was built, above all, upon the German practices and ideals of biblical scholarship that developed in the early nineteenth century as the flow of scholarly innovation reversed and Germany became the model for English scholars eager to reinvent a Bible strong enough to survive the climate of modernity.

This reversal has traditionally been associated in English scholarship with Samuel Coleridge, the hero of what John Stuart Mill in 1852 called the "Germano-Coleridgian school" of biblical studies.[38] This school replaced "*bibliolatry*" and "slavery to the letter" with the insight that "every form of polity, every condition of society, whatever else it had done, had formed its type of national character," in short, had its own "culture."[39] The Bible was the Word of God, in this context, only because it represented what Coleridge famously called "the living *educts* of the imagination."[40] It was divine because of its human qualities, in other words. Coleridge's interest in biblical critics like Eichhorn and Herder,

[36] Leslie Howsam, *Cheap Bibles: Nineteenth-Century Publishing and the British and Foreign Bible Society* (Cambridge, 1991), 6.

[37] *Eclectic Review* 5 (1809): 31.

[38] John Mill, "Coleridge," 201; see also Raymond Williams, *Culture and Society, 1780–1950* (New York, 1958), 60.

[39] Mill, "Coleridge," 205, 201.

[40] Prickett, *Words and the Word*, 43.

his sense that the Bible was a "'cycle' . . . held in common by the members of the primitive community," his embrace of the mythological aspects of Scripture, his insistence that it be compared "coolly with the sacred and secular writings of other nations": all of these factors aligned him with those German inventors of the Enlightenment Bible that this book has studied.[41]

But in fact, Coleridge effected no revolution in the early nineteenth century, at least among biblical scholars, who roundly rejected what Hugh James Rose called, in 1825, the "wild hypotheses" and the "rash and innovating spirit in religion" that characterized German religious letters.[42] Despite E. S. Shaffer's insistence that Coleridge could not have been alone in his Germanophilia, Rose, far more than Coleridge, represented the mainstream of English religious letters. If "the . . . reinterpretation of the major religious text of the West is a communal event," this communal reinterpretation did not happen in England in the first third of the nineteenth century.[43] Indeed it was telling that while Rose's *State of Protestantism in Germany Described* offered English readers its most sustained dosage of German theology ever, this dosage was hidden in a *diatribe* against a Germany seen as the new seedbed of irreligion, revolution, and moral corruption. Rose's disgust for his continental kin was ecumenical—practically every page of German theology supplied "fresh instances of the defiance of every law of thought, of sense, of language and of truth"—but his particular ire was directed against the German treatment of Scripture, for it was here, he thought, that the root of the evil lay. By subordinating Scripture to human authority, German theology had paved a path to spiritual sickness. Only if we "recur to the fountain head for pure and unsullied water," only if divine and inspired Scripture were reestablished as the rock of authority for Christians, could this plague be dispelled.[44]

Rose's hysteria might indicate that the German disease had already spread. In 1825, after all, Connop Thirlwall published the first English translation of Schleiermacher—the *Critical Essay on the Gospel of St. Luke*—in which he spoke of a "regeneration coming from Germany" for the Christian world.[45] Immediately after Rose's work was published, too, the future Tractarian Edward Pusey—who had traveled to Göttingen in the late 1820s—leaped to an (admittedly restrained) defense of the Germans, arguing that their rationalist character was merely a stepping-stone in the progress of the human spirit. In Germany, he insisted, "there is a rich promise, that the already commenced blending of belief and science . . . will be perfected beyond even the degree to which it was realized in . . . the earlier Reformation."[46] But these were the

[41] Shaffer, "*Kubla Khan,*" 79, 62.

[42] Hugh Paul Rose, *The State of Protestantism in Germany Described* 2nd ed. (London, 1829), 87.

[43] Shaffer, "*Kubla Khan,*" 6.

[44] Rose, *State of Protestantism*, 129, 33.

[45] Ellis, *Seven against Christ*, 1.

[46] Edward Pusey, *An Historical Enquiry into the Probable Causes of the Rationalist Character Lately Predominant in the Theology of Germany* (London, 1828), 176.

exceptions in that decade. Instead, English theologians and critics abandoned the thorny paths of historical criticism for the smooth highways of orthodoxy. Certainly this was true among the evangelicals, whose influence was still on the rise even at Oxford until the 1830s.[47] But their opposite number—the so-called Oxford Noetics, a group of liberal theologians in Oriel College whose number included Edward Hawkins, Richard Whateley, and Renn Dickson Hampden—were also indisposed to either critical or cultural readings of Scripture, insisting (along with the evangelicals) that only a "return to Scriptures" could rejuvenate theology. Although their most radical member, Thomas Arnold, did insist that, because "inspiration does not raise a man above his own time," a fully divinized scriptural text was impossible, he too had little interest in the developments in Germany.[48] In general, the names of Germany's theologians provoked fear rather than interest. "I trust, sir, that you don't understand German?" the Bishop Blomfield was supposed to have asked one aspiring divine and so-called "Schleiermacherei" was deeply frowned on.[49] English scholars, the *Gentleman's Magazine* declared in 1834, were

> too alive to the real worth of Old England, to be carried away by the fine-spun theories of German Literati, who, in divinity, philosophy, and even in philology, have winged their flight so far into the higher, or rather into the lower regions, as not only to enter into palpable darkness themselves, but by their mysticism have decoyed a few inexperienced followers.[50]

Finally, to close the circle, was the case of Edward Pusey, who in later years formally recanted the Germanophilia of his 1828 *Historical Enquiry* and even grew so grumpy as to ascribe "all of the troubles of the Church since the Reformation . . . to German professors."[51]

But by the 1840s, the intemperate insistence on the inspiration of Scripture and the enormous anxiety about German biblical study both began to ease. There are likely many explanations for this shift, but among the more significant would have to be the simultaneous decline of evangelicalism—as its various factions began to squabble and splinter—and the rise of Tractarianism. The 1833 *Tracts for the Times* announced the need for a church revival, a revival not of the "spirit" of individual religion, but of the heritage of the English Church, its liturgies, its doctrines, and its traditions. This call for a revival of church heritage involved a reconstruction of the apostolic succession of the Church, its roots in the ancient Fathers, and its claim on an unbroken chain of authentic teachings. None of this looked, of course, very auspicious for the production of

[47] J. S. Reynolds, *The Evangelicals at Oxford, 1735–1871* (Oxford, 1975); Grayson Carter, *Anglican Evangelicals: Protestant Secessions from the* Via Media, *c. 1800–1850* (Oxford, 2001).

[48] Bernard M. G. Reardon, *Religious Thought in the Victorian Age* 2nd ed. (London, 1995), 33, 37.

[49] Ellis, *Seven Against Christ*, 7.

[50] Hans Aarsleff, *The Study of Language in England, 1780–1860* (Princeton, 1967), 197.

[51] Ellis, *Seven Against Christ*, 23.

a cultural Bible, especially since the Tractarians looked at the "presumptuous turn of mind, the reliance on intellectual ability" that characterized historical criticism as its chief nemesis.[52] But if the Tractarians were no friends of either Germany or criticism more generally, neither were they friends of the inspired Scriptures. In his 1840 preface of Augustine's *Confessions*, for example, Pusey very carefully threaded his way around this evangelical assumption, arguing that if "the Old and New Testaments are the fountain, the Catholic Fathers [are] the channel, through which [doctrine] has flowed down to us."[53] More dramatic was John Newman's bald-faced assertion in the *Tracts* that Scripture

> is a great number of writings, of various persons, living at different times, put together into one, and assuming its existing form as if casually and by accident. It is as if you were to seize the papers or correspondence of leading men in any school of philosophy or science, which were never designed for publication, and bring them out in one volume.[54]

In this sentiment, Newman and the Tractarians approached the Catholicism that the former would formally embrace in 1845. Although Newman's enthusiasm for Rome was not the rule among the Tractarians, still the Tractarians overall broke from that widespread consensus about scriptural authority that had dominated England at least since 1800. Richard Hurrell Froude's antagonism for "*Bible*-Christians" and his sense that the Reformation was "a limb badly set" that "must be broken again" were only more dramatic instances of the same rupture.[55]

The Tractarians could not have imagined a cultural Bible, of course. But the decade that followed their scandalous publications opened itself up to such a notion. If we use our marker of German letters, we can see this clearly. Thomas Carlyle's 1827 *State of German Literature* declared that these continental borrowings had already "taken . . . firm root" in England, but was two decades premature.[56] Rather, it was Carlyle's friend George Eliot who more accurately reflected this change: her translations of David Strauss's *Life of Jesus* (1846) and Ludwig Feuerbach's *Essence of Christianity* (1853) were both completed exactly in the middle of that spike of translations of German works that Walter Rohloff and others have detected in their bibliographical surveys of the period.[57] Despite her complaint that people in England were "as slow to be set on fire as a *stomach*" by these new works, and despite her parody of German scholarship in the figure of Mr. Casaubon, it was Eliot who brought this material into the public

[52] Nockles, *Oxford Movement*, 202.

[53] Edward Pusey, "Preface to the Confessions of St. Augustine," in *Library of the Fathers* (Oxford, 1840), 1:iii.

[54] *Tracts for the Times* (London, 1840), §85, 5:30.

[55] Richard Hurrell Froude, *Remains* (London, 1838), 1:412, 433.

[56] Thomas Carlyle, "State of German Literature," *Works* (New York, 1885), 7:35.

[57] Rohloff, *German Literature*, 127.

eye.[58] But she was not alone in this endeavor. If "English universities were very slow to welcome the new philology" in the early part of the century, they made up for it with a "rapid absorption of Continental scholarship . . . after 1830."[59] John Mill's favorable 1852 review of Coleridge and the Germans was part of the same absorption, as was Frederick Farrar's 1850 translation of Schleiermacher's *Brief Outline of the Study of Theology*. At this time too English theologians began to look and even travel to Germany for inspiration. Arthur Stanley, Benjamin Jowett, Henry Alford, Mark Pattison, and many others made scholarly pilgrimages to Bonn, Göttingen, Berlin, and Tübingen, among other places. Germans offered "the theological movement of the present," declared one scholar. "Nobody else in the last hundred years," declared Stanley in 1861, has exerted such "a power influence on the rest of Europe . . . as the speculative and critical theologians of the German universities." Beginning at the middle of the century, Klaus Dockhorn has argued, "English theology was . . . almost fully under German influence."[60] Even the translation of German conservative theologians—begun in earnest in 1846 with T. and T. Clark's *Foreign Theological Library*—went some way in introducing German critical coin to the English realm. It showed, argued John Colenso in 1862, "how feebly they reply to some of the more striking objections" of the German critics.[61] Perhaps the most telling sign of the times was the drastic shift in the fate of German theology in the *Encyclopedia Britannica*. The "Bible" articles in the seventh (1830–42) and eighth (1852–60) editions were virtually devoid of contemporary German works. But in the 1878 edition, *all* the literature cited, save three volumes, stemmed from German divines.[62]

Among the many markers of the new higher criticism in England, the 1860 *Essays and Reviews*—compiled by the "greatest names in the Germanizing party"—distilled most purely the various forces transforming the nineteenth-century Bible. At the very least, its 22,000 copies and thirteen editions (in two years!) widely publicized the questions, as did the four hundred published responses before 1865.[63] Its signature article—Benjamin Jowett's "On the Interpretation of Scripture"—showed just how far the pendulum had swung in England. "The diffusion of a critical spirit in history and literature," Jowett announced, "is affecting the criticism of the Bible . . . in a manner not unlike

[58] George Eliot, letter to Sara Hennell 18 January 1854, in *The George Eliot Letters*, ed. Gordon Haight (New Haven, 1954), 2:136; also see Gisela Argyle, *Germany As Model and Monster: Allusions in English Fiction, 1830s–1930s* (Montreal, 2002), chaps. 5 and 6.

[59] Aarsleff, *Study of Language*, 166, 165.

[60] Klaus Dockhorn, *Der deutsche Historismus in England* (Göttingen, 1950), 88, 89, 79.

[61] Cameron, *Higher Criticism*, 66.

[62] *Encyclopedia Britannica* 9th ed. (New York, 1878), s.v. "Bible."

[63] Ellis, *Seven Against Christ*, 13, 124, 117. One response was tellingly titled: *"Essays and Reviews" Anticipated: Extracts from a Work Published in 1825* (London, 1861), which republished parts of Thirlwall's translation of Schleiermacher.

the burst of intellectual life in the fifteenth and sixteenth centuries." The inspiration of the Bible was a farce for him. Indeed, no doctrine had done more to harm the Bible, to make it "the most uncertain of all books," than that of inspiration, which put the Bible into the hands of partisan theologians rather than independent scholars. As a result, the "unchangeable word of God . . . is changed by each age and each generation in accordance with its passing fancy." To put interpretation back on a scholarly basis, and accomplish Jowett's double renaissance and reformation of biblical criticism, only one fundamental rule was necessary: "*Interpret the Scripture like any other book.*"[64] As Nigel Cameron has shown, Jowett was one of many commentators and critics in the 1850s and 1860s looking to Germany for theological guidance, rejecting the inspired vision of Scripture, distinguishing between the text of the Bible and the Word of God, and imagining Scripture on a continuum with secular literature.[65] Author Thomas de Quincey's 1847 disdain for the "superstitious allegiance . . . to the words, to the syllables, and to the very punctuation of the Bible" was only an early symptom of this larger trend.[66] And alongside these other profound shifts, the English would also begin to read the Bible through the lens of culture.

Even within the *Essays and Reviews*, the language of culture crept in as a device for underwriting the authenticity and authority of the Bible. Thus Frederick Temple's essay "The Education of the World" echoed Lessing's sentiments, in his *Education of the Human Race*, and presented a vision of man in its "earliest ages"—read *Jews* here—and its distinct "cultivation" as a necessary step in the history of mankind: belief in the unity of God was a "habit of the nation" among the Jews, making them "proper instruments" for its promulgation.[67] The Jews, S. R. Driver later wrote, "were a nation like other nations of antiquity. . . . they passed through similar phases of mental growth and similar stages of culture."[68] But this development of the national habitus extended over millennia: at any given moment, its contours were fixed in place and immutable. The Bible and its religions were products of the "mind of a nation"—Jowett later wrote—and therefore "prior to the thoughts of individuals; no one is responsible for them."[69]

The integration of the Bible (and religion) into the rhetorical complex of "culture" was, like in Germany, a wide-ranging affair. In Raymond Williams's seminal analysis of this topic, the language of "culture" in the 1850s meant "that an idea had been formulated which expressed value in terms independent of 'civilization,' and, hence, in a period of radical change, in terms independent of the progress of society." Culture emerged "as an abstraction and an absolute,"

[64] *Essays and Reviews* (Boston, 1862), 374, 409, 416.

[65] Cameron, *Higher Criticism*, see chap. 3.

[66] Norton, *Bible As Literature*, 299.

[67] Temple, "The Education of the World," in *Essays and Reviews*, 5, 13.

[68] Cameron, *Higher Criticism*, 82.

[69] Benjamin Jowett, "Essay on Natural Religion," in *Theological Essays* (London, 1906), 103.

Williams argued, in the face of social changes that seemed to separate the progress of civilization from the progress of the human spirit.[70] The language of culture, in short, was a response to what Thomas Carlyle called "the Mechanical Age," an age in which cold and heartless utility stood like a menacing Goliath over a spiritual David.[71] It named that essential core of a nation unaffected by material and mechanical progress. And it comprehended all of the virtues that were hidden inside the national mind and thus free from the corruptions of technical progress.

As in Germany, these qualities were expressly connected to the Bible and to religion more generally. Indeed, inspired by their German counterparts, English theologians and literati would begin in the 1850s to build a chain that would bind the Bible and Christianity tightly to the idea of culture, Western civilization, and heritage. For this we might look to one of the most eloquent (and to this day, influential) affirmations of the cultural ideal, John Henry Newman's 1854 *Idea of a University*. Newman was, of course, highly resistant to the idea that either Bible or Christianity was *merely* cultural. But nevertheless, his "Christianity and Letters" address articulated clearly the analogous relationship between Scripture and those texts called "classics" in the Greco-Roman canon:

> Christianity is built upon definite ideas, principles, doctrines, and writings, which were given at the time of its first introduction. . . . Civilization too has its common principles, and views, and teaching, and especially its books. . . . In a word, the Classics . . . have ever, on the whole, been the instruments of education which the civilized *orbis terrarum* has adopted; just as inspired works . . . have ever been the instrument of education in the case of Christianity.[72]

Newman carefully distinguished between the literary and what he called the scientific aspects of the Scriptures, but nonetheless his insistence on the parallels between Scripture and the secular canon was symptomatic of a time when the Bible increasingly found itself authorized by the agency of culture. Education of the mind into its "perfect state" was precisely what Newman called "culture": the Bible and the classics were two sides of the same coin.[73] It was probably not an accident that it was in these decades that indeed the King James Bible became the "first English classic," the "first classic of our literature," and "one of the greatest classics in the language."[74] When Homer became the first "Apostle of Civilization," then a chain of equivalences was established that would prove durable enough to last until the current day.[75]

[70] Williams, *Culture and Society*, 63, xviii.

[71] Thomas Carlyle, "Signs of the Times," *Critical and Miscellaneous Essays* (New York, 1969), 2:59.

[72] John Newman, *The Idea of a University* (Oxford, 1976), 216.

[73] Williams, *Culture and Society*, 111.

[74] Norton, *Bible As Literature*, 305.

[75] Newman, *Idea*, 217.

As in Germany, the move toward culture had an anthropological dimension already intimated by Mill's argument that "even barbarians" and "unmitigated savages . . . all had their own education, their own culture. . . . Every form of polity, every condition of society . . . formed its type of national character."[76] The anthropology of religion was seized upon with great gusto, of course, by English researchers in the second half of the nineteenth century, from the displaced German Max Müller to William Robertson Smith to James Frazer. The "bible of British cultural anthropology" for the period became Edward Tylor's *Primitive Culture* (1871), which opened its magisterial treatment of human mythology and animism with a famously ecumenical definition of culture: "that complex whole which includes knowledge, belief, art, morals, law, custom, and any other capabilities and habits acquired by man as a member of society."[77] "Nowhere," insisted Tylor, "are broad views of historical development more needed than in the study of religion," and his followers believed him, making religion into the primary site of cultural anthropology for generations to come.[78] Paralleling these anthropological investigations were blanket declarations that at the heart of every major religious culture was a "Bible," that in fact all major religions were built atop a canonical set of books analogous to the Christian Bible. Philip Almond, for example, has shown how Buddhism took shape "as an entity that 'exist[ed]' over against the various cultures which can now be perceived as instancing it" by the end of the 1830s, and how by mid-century, this "object" (or "culture") was reconstructed as a set of canonical texts produced in the West.[79] A similar transformation took place in researches on Hinduism: "to know and understand Indian culture is to study their texts," as S. N. Balangangadhara has argued.[80] In the language of a premier Sanskritist: "our own Holy Bible is the only true Bible of God," but there are "five Bibles of non-Christian systems" as well, including the Hindus, Parsis, Chinese Confucians, Buddhists, and Muslims.[81]

Semantic equivalence did not, however, imply equality. The "gulf" between the Bible and the "so-called sacred books of the East" was enormous, the Sanskritist insisted, separating one from the other "utterly, hopelessly, and for ever."[82] And so the English idea of culture, like the German, was never merely an anthropological descriptor. It also had a strong normative dimension—it was fundamentally better to have culture than mere technology and better to

[76] Williams, *Culture and Society*, 60.

[77] Sir Edmund Leach, "The Anthropology of Religion: British and French Schools," in *Nineteenth-Century Religious Thought*, 221. Edward Tylor, *Primitive Culture*, 3rd ed. (New York, 1889), 1.

[78] Tylor, *Primitive Culture*, 22.

[79] Philip Almond, *The British Discovery of Buddhism* (Cambridge, 1988), 12–13.

[80] S. N. Balangangadhara, *"The Heathen in His Blindness": Asia, the West, and the Dynamics of Religion* (Leiden, 1994), 147. Thanks to Gyan Prakash for this reference.

[81] M. Monier Williams, *The Holy Bible and the Sacred Books of the East* (London, 1900), 30.

[82] Ibid., 18.

have Christian culture than any other—which was what made it so attractive to a generation worried about moral decline. Culture represented that "heritage of an accumulated ineluctable racial memory" that undergirded the essential qualities of "western civilization."[83] Like literature more generally, it was "called in to redress the balance of the present," to supplement a deficient present with the virtues contained in Western heritage.[84] When the hugely popular theologian Frederick Maurice declared in 1850 that the Bible was "the ground of civilization and the cause of civilization," he was affirming both the preeminence of the Bible as a source of "cultural heritage" and the "religious value of literature" more generally.[85] It was in this light that Christian missionaries in India imagined what Gauri Viswanathan has called a "structural congruence . . . between Christianity and English literature," in which the teaching of English literary culture could not *but* teach the Bible. "Let the books . . . giving the highest products of the European mind, be pruned as they may of Christian references," still the "Christian element will . . . tinge the information imparted."[86] And it was in this light too that the King James Bible was reconfigured not just as a work of literature, but as an expression of a culture. As F. W. Faber wrote in 1853, the King James Bible was "part of the national mind and the anchor of the national seriousness. . . . The memory of the dead passes into it. . . . It is the representative of his best moments, and all that there has been about him of soft, and gentle, and pure, and penitent, and good, speaks to him forever out of his English Bible."[87] As in Germany, then, "culture" was sotto voce *Christian* culture. And so we find, at the same time, an effort to develop a Christianity free of alien traces. Baden Powell's 1856 *Christianity without Judaism*, for example, insisted that "*Gentile Christianity* stands on its own ground, entirely independent of the obligations of the Old Testament dispensation" while Benjamin Jowett more prosaically asserted that the "Old Testament is not to be identified with the New."[88] As in Germany, then, a cultural Bible was tied to the effort to create a religion and a culture free from alien influences.

All of these tendencies—toward a normative ideal of culture, toward a cultural Bible, toward a cultural religion, toward a sanitized Christianity—converged in one person, the literary critic, poet, and maverick Matthew Arnold. More than another single writer in the second half of the English nineteenth century, it was Arnold who made culture, and the appreciation of the ideals of culture,

[83] Franklin E. Court, *Institutionalizing English Literature: The Culture and Politics of Literary Study, 1750–1900* (Stanford, 1992), 78.

[84] D. J. Palmer, *The Rise of English Studies* (Oxford, 1965), 39.

[85] F. D. Maurice "On Christian Civilization" [1850], *The Friendship of Books and Other Lectures* (London, 1893), 98; Court, *English Literature*, 94.

[86] Gauri Viswanathan, *Masks of Conquest: Literary Study and British Rule in India* (New York, 1989), 80–81.

[87] Norton, *Bible As Literature*, 303–304.

[88] Baden Powell, *Christianity without Judaism* (London, 1856), 41; Jowett, "Interpretation," 421.

into the commonplaces they are today. Culture was nothing more, in Arnold's mind, than the "study of perfection, and of harmonious perfection, general perfection." Culture was the quest for a perfection that "consists in becoming something rather than having something, in an inward condition of the mind and spirit, not in an outward set of circumstances." In an age dominated by "Philistines," by the ceaseless pursuit of wealth, by the ideals of a mechanized society, culture represented the only force that could reclaim the human spirit from within. By rejecting "middle-class liberalism," "middle-class Parliaments," "middle-class industrialists," and "middle-class Protestantism," culture sought to "awaken the 'best self' . . . [through] education, poetry, and criticism."[89] In this quest for inward perfection, Arnold's cultural ideal shared much with Christianity, so much that it is virtually impossible to imagine without reference to Christianity and its Scriptures.

And so Arnold immediately recognized that nothing mirrored culture more than religion: "religion comes to a conclusion identical with that which culture . . . likewise reaches. Religion says: *The kingdom of God is within you*; and culture, in like manner, places human perfection in an *internal* condition. . . . the expansion of our humanity, to suit the idea of perfection which culture forms, must be a *general* expansion." If religion were the model on which culture was built, not just any religion would do of course. The German insistence on "interiority" as a basic definition of religion was not, after all, religiously neutral, and neither was the English. Arnold's famous distinction between the Hellenic and Hebraic ideals made this crystalline. If Hellenism was the avatar of "sweetness and light" and so the apotheosis of "culture," Hebraism denoted those slavish obsessions about "conduct and obedience," that addiction to the "network of prescriptions" that "govern every moment . . . every impulse, every action."[90] The "empire of the world" was divided between these two principles, one of which offered the low road to Jacobinism, sectarianism, and violence, the other which lead to virtue, harmony, and perfection. Hebraism was, in other words, the "root of anarchy," and Hellenism—and its Christian manifestations—the fundament of culture.[91] "Hellenism is of Indo-European growth, Hebraism is of Semitic growth," declared Arnold, and even though some Christians, like the Puritans, could embrace the Hebraic model, in doing so they stepped away from the real cultural roots of Christianity.[92] Of course, Arnold identified at times with the Hebraic spirit—especially after the deaths of his sons—and in a dialectical fashion, saw this "eternal possession" of the human race as a necessary component in the development of human potential. And yet if its presence was necessary, only the "subordination

[89] Matthew Arnold, *Culture and Anarchy* [1869], in *The Complete Prose Works of Matthew Arnold* (Ann Arbor, 1965), 5:94, 107. Williams, *Culture and Society*, 121.

[90] Arnold, *Culture*, 5:93–94, 178, 165.

[91] Lionel Trilling, *Matthew Arnold*, 2nd ed. (New York, 1949), 258.

[92] Arnold, *Culture*, 5:173.

of the Hebrew temper," in Joseph Carroll's words, to Hellenic ideals guaranteed the full flowering of the human spirit.[93] It made some sense then that Arnold would, in 1865, praise his father's efforts "to get rid of all that was purely Semitic in Christianity, and to make it Indo-Germanic" and affirm, "with Schleiermacher," that "in the Christianity of us Western nations there was really much more of Plato and Socrates than of Joshua and David."[94] Culture and Christianity were, in other words, coextensive, which would account for the sense, among Arnold's critics, that culture was a "rival power" to religion.[95] Both performed the same kind of spiritual and educational work; both occupied the same spiritual and educational space; and both offered the same spiritual and educational critiques of the modern mechanical age.

At the very center of this ideal of culture—and of the cultural religion Arnold envisioned—lay the cultural Bible. We must, Arnold demanded in his 1873 *Literature and Dogma*, "put some other construction on the Bible than this theology puts . . . find some other basis for the Bible than this theology finds . . . if we would have the Bible reach the people." This new face on the Bible could not be accomplished without "culture," without "acquainting ourselves with the best that has been known and said in the world. . . . One cannot go far in the attempt to bring in, for the Bible, a right construction, without seeing how necessary is something of culture to its being admitted and used."[96] Without culture we can only echo the Hebrew—"*he knows*, says Hebraism, *his Bible!*" But with culture, we can answer: "No man, who knows nothing else, knows even his Bible."[97] "Only true culture can give us" a true Bible; it is "indispensably necessary" even integral to the very text of the Bible.[98] The Bible, Arnold declared in an 1875 letter to Walter Cassels, is "only means by which our people . . . gets any exercise of its soul and imagination."[99] This cultural influence must therefore be capitalized upon. Once the Bible becomes the people's source of "poetry, philosophy, and eloquence," it will not only exert a "beneficent wonder-working power" on them, it will also itself be transformed from theological text to cultural icon.[100] Only through such a transformation, only through culture, could we move beyond the talismanic fetishism for the Scriptures, a fetishism that characterized Jews and Muslims alike. Only through culture would we find in the Bible the condensed heritage of the West, a heritage conserved in tradition, passed down through time, and left for us as an emetic against the evils of

[93] Joseph Carroll, *The Cultural Theory of Matthew Arnold* (Berkeley, 1982), 93, 73, 83.

[94] Matthew Arnold, *Literature and Dogma* [1873], in *Works*, 6:465.

[95] J. C. Shairp, *Culture and Religion*, 2nd ed. (New York, 1872), 28.

[96] Arnold, *Literature*, 151.

[97] Arnold, *Culture*, 5:184.

[98] Arnold, *Literature*, 162.

[99] Cecil Y. Lang, *The Letters of Matthew Arnold* (Charlottesville, VA, 1996), 4:258.

[100] David J. DeLaura, *Hebrew and Hellene in Victorian England: Newman, Arnold, and Pater* (Austin, 1969), 98.

modernity. Only the cultural Bible, in short, could preserve the essential core of Christianity and inject it into the veins of modern society.

With Arnold, then, the implications of culture and the cultural Bible found their clearest expression. Along with dozens of scholars on religion, theologians, anthropologists, and literary critics, Arnold helped to forge a cultural Bible for England. If its full expression would remain always a contested matter, the model itself would not go away. Like the Germans, English scholars and literati held in their hands a new Bible, one reconstructed for a post-theological age. Beyond inspiration, beyond the Word of God, this Bible would stand its own as a modern classic.

AFTERWORD

At the end of any study that pretends to cover as much ground as this one, there are bound to be a host of partially or wholly unresolved questions. Rather than trying fully to anticipate these (an impossible and ultimately tedious task) I want to end on two related notes. First, we might ask whether this nineteenth-century cultural Bible is still "our" model in the contemporary United States or Europe. In one sense, it is certainly not precisely the model embraced in the early twenty-first century: at the very least, when we speak of the Bible as culture, relatively few of us are thinking specifically about the King James Bible or the Luther Bible. Nor is the specificity of its Jewish and ancient Christian origins, as far as I can tell, material to our contemporary language of culture, a fact that would have struck nineteenth- and eighteenth-century commentators as strange or shortsighted. Nonetheless, the Bible remains a cultural text—in a world at the very least self-conscious about its own nationalisms—in much broader ways. Although culture has been increasingly purged of its normative dimensions in the past fifty years, the culture of the "Culture Wars" is still far from dead. It still operates as a sometimes loose, sometimes rigid set of norms that organizes a canon of texts that guides how our students learn, what research projects get funded, what scholars unravel, what historians see as influential, and so on (in fact, this study itself is one example!). When advocates like Harold Bloom and William Bennett praise the virtues of Western culture; when detractors attack its hegemony, intolerance, or imperialism: they all very happily agree that this normative culture still plays a crucial role in our mutual spiritual, literary, artistic, and political lives. The more recent anxieties about the "clash of civilizations," in Samuel Huntington's words, are soaked with the language of a normative culture, one of whose central pillars is the Bible. The Bible is seen, in this normative language, as the fountain of the literary, artistic, spiritual, jurisprudential, and moral virtues that infuse what we call Western civilization. Indeed, the near universal acceptance of the cultural relevance of the Bible—not just among academics, but also among jurists, not just among doubters, but also among the devout—suggests indeed that the Bible, more than practically any other single text, continues to be *the* repository of Western heritage. In this way, then, we are inheritors of the Enlightenment Bible and its conventions.

Second, we might ask whether this reforging of biblical authority constitutes "secularization." Certainly there is good reason to think that it was, not least the reactions to this change by the various fundamentalisms that have shadowed the Enlightenment and the cultural Bible since their inceptions. Indeed, in some sense, modern fundamentalism was an antithetical creation of the cultural

Bible, at least in so far as it attempted to reclaim the biblical text not just from institutionalized religions (as in Early Modern fundamentalisms like Puritanism or Pietism) but also from secular society at large. But the language of secularization does not, I believe, do justice to the transformations that this book has investigated. At the very least the language of secularization supposes that like a swamp religion is "drained . . . emptied out, in order to provide modern culture with sufficient . . . capital to start up its own economy," in Debora Shuger's apt description.[1] In this vision, religion plays the role of the hapless onion, whose layers are constantly peeled away to make a secular soup. But what this book has shown, I believe, is not a stripping process, but a process of reconstruction, of productive transformation. If secularization assumes that religion is essentially and formidably stable, I have tried to show its malleability in the face of new challenges. To speak with Robert Alter, the invention of the Enlightenment and cultural Bibles was "an attempt to recover the religious truth of the Bible through means of investigation compatible with secular categories."[2] It was an effort not to discard, but to remake religion. And the continued life of the Bible—in colleges, curricula, and cultural canons—is testament enough to its success.

[1] Shuger, *Renaissance Bible*, 3.

[2] Robert Alter, *The World of Biblical Literature* (New York, 1992), 194–95.

INDEX